D1569495

Introduction to
Network Security

CHAPMAN & HALL/CRC
COMPUTER and INFORMATION SCIENCE SERIES

Series Editor: Sartaj Sahni

PUBLISHED TITLES

ADVERSARIAL REASONING: COMPUTATIONAL APPROACHES TO READING THE OPPONENT'S MIND
Alexander Kott and William M. McEneaney

DISTRIBUTED SENSOR NETWORKS
S. Sitharama Iyengar and Richard R. Brooks

DISTRIBUTED SYSTEMS: AN ALGORITHMIC APPROACH
Sukumar Ghosh

FUNDEMENTALS OF NATURAL COMPUTING: BASIC CONCEPTS, ALGORITHMS, AND APPLICATIONS
Leandro Nunes de Castro

HANDBOOK OF ALGORITHMS FOR WIRELESS NETWORKING AND MOBILE COMPUTING
Azzedine Boukerche

HANDBOOK OF APPROXIMATION ALGORITHMS AND METAHEURISTICS
Teofilo F. Gonzalez

HANDBOOK OF BIOINSPIRED ALGORITHMS AND APPLICATIONS
Stephan Olariu and Albert Y. Zomaya

HANDBOOK OF COMPUTATIONAL MOLECULAR BIOLOGY
Srinivas Aluru

HANDBOOK OF DATA STRUCTURES AND APPLICATIONS
Dinesh P. Mehta and Sartaj Sahni

HANDBOOK OF DYNAMIC SYSTEM MODELING
Paul A. Fishwick

HANDBOOK OF PARALLEL COMPUTING: MODELS, ALGORITHMS AND APPLICATIONS
Sanguthevar Rajasekaran and John Reif

HANDBOOK OF REAL-TIME AND EMBEDDED SYSTEMS
Insup Lee, Joseph Y.-T. Leung, and Sang H. Son

HANDBOOK OF SCHEDULING: ALGORITHMS, MODELS, AND PERFORMANCE ANALYSIS
Joseph Y.-T. Leung

HIGH PERFORMANCE COMPUTING IN REMOTE SENSING
Antonio J. Plaza and Chein-I Chang

INTRODUCTION TO NETWORK SECURITY
Douglas Jacobson

PERFORMANCE ANALYSIS OF QUEUING AND COMPUTER NETWORKS
G. R. Dattatreya

THE PRACTICAL HANDBOOK OF INTERNET COMPUTING
Munindar P. Singh

SCALABLE AND SECURE INTERNET SERVICES AND ARCHITECTURE
Cheng-Zhong Xu

SPECULATIVE EXECUTION IN HIGH PERFORMANCE COMPUTER ARCHITECTURES
David Kaeli and Pen-Chung Yew

Introduction to Network Security

Douglas Jacobson

Iowa State University
Ames, Iowa, U.S.A.

CRC Press
Taylor & Francis Group
Boca Raton   London   New York

CRC Press is an imprint of the
Taylor & Francis Group, an **informa** business

A CHAPMAN & HALL BOOK

Chapman & Hall/CRC
Taylor & Francis Group
6000 Broken Sound Parkway NW, Suite 300
Boca Raton, FL 33487-2742

Library of Congress Cataloging-in-Publication Data

Jacobson, Douglas.
    Introduction to network security / Douglas Jacobson.
        p. cm. -- (Chapman and Hall/CRC computer and information science
        series)
    Includes bibliographical references and index.
    ISBN 978-1-58488-543-6 (hbk. : alk. paper)
        1. Computer networks--Security measures. 2. Computer security. I. Title. II.
    Series.

    TK5105.59.J33 2008
    005.8--dc22   2008040768

Visit the Taylor & Francis Web site at
http://www.taylorandfrancis.com

and the CRC Press Web site at
http://www.crcpress.com

Contents

Preface

Approach

This book focuses on network security from the viewpoint of a network's vulnerabilities, protocols, and security solutions. Unlike other books that focus on security and security paradigms where networks are viewed as a mechanism for communication, this book focuses on the network as a source of both insecurity and security. The book will examine various network protocols looking at vulnerabilities, exploits, attacks, and methods to mitigate an attack.

Networks as communication systems have been around since the dawn of human history and rely on trust between communicating parties in order to function. Early communications systems relied on visual verification of the communicating parties involved and often used simple codes to protect the data. For example, couriers were known by both parties and messages were sealed with wax to help ensure privacy. As technology improved, methods used to transmit data also improved, and so did the methods to steal and protect data. However, even as late as the end of the twentieth century, data was still being transmitted directly between two parties with no concept of a network. These parties relied on additional knowledge to verify the authenticity of the data. The issues we face today are more complex than those of the past. Today we have interconnected computers using a network not controlled by any one entity or organization. Unlike data communications of the past, today's networks consist of numerous devices that handle the data as it passes from the sender to the receiver. These networks are designed to facilitate communication and are intended for a small group of trusted and knowledgeable individuals. Security is not part of the design process.

Organization

Part I of this book is a brief discussion of network architectures and the functions of layers in a typical network, along with a taxonomy of network-based vulnerabilities and attacks. This taxonomy is the framework for presenting the vulnerabilities and attacks at each layer of interest. The taxonomy divides the vulnerabilities and attack space into four categories:

Header-based vulnerabilities and attacks: The protocol headers have been modified or are not valid.

Protocol-based vulnerabilities and attacks: The packets are valid but are not used correctly.

Authentication-based vulnerabilities and attacks: The identity of the sender or receiver is modified.

Traffic-based vulnerabilities and attacks: The volume of traffic creates the attack.

The remainder of the book is divided into three parts. Part II covers the different layers of the network (physical, network, and transport), looking at the security for each. Using a bottom-up approach to network security allows the reader to understand the vulnerabilities and the security mechanisms provided by each layer of the network. For example, by understanding which vulnerabilities are introduced by the physical layer and what level of security can be provided, the reader can understand which vulnerabilities may exist in the network layer and which security mechanisms could be used to overcome the vulnerabilities. Part III looks at the security of several common network applications. On the Internet, applications treat the lower layers of the network as a simple pipe that sends data to another application, and it arrives without error. This book views vulnerabilities as network functions provided by the layer below, thus giving the reader insight into understanding the security needed to overcome the vulnerabilities. Part IV provides an overview of several network-based security solutions that are often deployed and relates them back to the taxonomy.

This book describes a define–attack–defend methodology for network security. The relevant protocols are briefly introduced, followed by detailed descriptions of known vulnerabilities and possible attack methods. The book then focuses on the attack methodology rather than on particular tools, though tools are introduced as possible homework problems and lab experiments. Once the reader understands the threats against the protocol, possible solutions will be presented. Each chapter has homework problems that are based on the concepts introduced in the chapter and will have lab experiments that will allow the reader to try some of the attacks and look at the effectiveness of the solutions. An appendix provides details to develop and deploy a low-cost lab environment that can be used to support the classroom or used as a small corporate test bed. Another appendix provides an overview to cryptology.

Target Audience

This book is targeted at two compatible audiences. The primary focus of the book is as a text for a senior or first-year graduate course in network security for students in computer science or computer engineering. The book can be used for a network security course that is part of a security curriculum or for a course that is part of a networking curriculum. The book is also intended as a reference for network and security professionals.

Differences between this book and other books include:

Network focused: This book looks at network security by exploring network protocols, their weaknesses, and countermeasures. Several books also have a network focus but primarily deal with a few application-level protocols (Kerberos, secure email, secure web, etc.) and are not concerned about the lower layers (physical, network, transport). Many of the difficult problems arise from the vulnerabilities in these layers.

Network view of security: This book looks at network security using the approaches found in most network books, by looking at the layers and what services and functions are provided. We will look at vulnerabilities and security as services and functions provided by the layer. By using a network view, the book could be used in either a networking curriculum to add security or in a security curriculum to add network security.

Lab experiments: This book contains lab experiments to support the material. The experiments will look at both attacks and defenses. The book also provides a low-cost lab configuration that can be used as a model.

Web site: A web site is provided to support the book (http://www.dougj.net/textbook/). The web site contains lecture materials, tutorials on UNIX, C, and socket programming, and detailed information to establish and maintain the test laboratory.

Practical view of network security: This book has a practical view of network security. We will look at actual protocols and provide readers with the details and information they need to understand the vulnerabilities and to develop appropriate countermeasures. This is reinforced through the lab experiments.

Attack-and-defend approach: This book looks at network security from an attack-and-defend approach. The book looks at the vulnerabilities in the current protocols and then looks at defense systems that could mitigate the attacks. While the book will not focus on attack tools, it will look at attack methods, and through the lab experiments, students will be able to study the effects of certain attacks on the network and the effectiveness of the security system.

Terms defined: So much of networking and security involves the use of terms, many of which are specific to the field. Thus, I feel that it is important after each section of a chapter to enumerate with a short definition any new terms that were defined in that section. Before we begin the text, there are a few terms that should be defined so readers have a common frame of reference.

Definitions

Application.
A computer program that allows a user to connect to the network and perform a task.

Attacker.
A person or persons that use the network to attack computer systems, networks, or other devices connected to the Internet.

Hacker.
Same as an attacker.

Host.
A term used to describe a computer connected to the Internet.

Internet.
A global collection of networks of interconnected network devices.

Network.
A group of interconnected devices that can communicate with each other.

Network device.
A device connected to the network. This is more generic than a host or computer in that it can be any network-enabled device.

Target.

The device, host, user, or object that the hacker is trying to attack.

User.

The individual using a computer application that utilizes the network, or a general computer user.

Acknowledgments

I thank my wife, Gwenna, and my children (Sarah, Jordan, and Jessica) for all of their support and patience. I also thank Sharon Sparks for her editing help.

The Author

Doug Jacobson is a university professor in the Department of Electrical and Computer Engineering at Iowa State University. He is currently director of the Iowa State University Information Assurance Center, which has been recognized by the National Security Agency as a charter Center of Academic Excellence for Information Assurance Education. Dr. Jacobson teaches network security and information warfare. He also works with local law enforcement and is a computer forensics analyst for the Iowa State University Police Department. Dr. Jacobson is the founder of Palisade Systems, Inc., an Ames-based company marketing Internet management and security devices. He has received two R&D 100 awards for his security technology and has two patents in the area of computer security.

Part I

Introduction to Network Concepts and Threats

This part provides an introduction to basic network concepts and the taxonomy for network-based vulnerabilities and attacks. Readers that have studied networking could skip the first three chapters of this part. Chapter 1 discusses the concepts behind the layered approach to networking and how the common network architecture provides insight into security. Chapter 2 provides an overview into network protocols and several key aspects of network protocols that relate to security. Chapter 3 focuses on key aspects of the Internet, such as routing and addressing, and how they relate to security. Chapter 4 introduces the taxonomy for network-based vulnerabilities and attacks and introduces a network threat model that is the basis for analyzing vulnerabilities, attacks, and countermeasures in the remaining chapters of this book.

Chapter 1

Network Architecture

Before discussing network concepts and security it would be helpful to review a brief history of networking [1–9], since we often discover that what was done in the past has an effect on the security of today. Figure 1.1 shows a timeline of the history of networking.

As can be seen from the figure, a lot has changed in the past 30 years. Both the size and complexity of networks have increased. The networks were designed to provide connectivity and not to support security. The first networks in the 1970s were between a small number of research organizations and universities [8, 9]. Everyone that was connected was trusted and security was not an issue. In 1988, the first major attack [10] against computers connected to the Internet was released, and to this day some of the same underlying methods used by that attack still work. What has driven innovation and growth in the network is ease of use and interconnection, not security. We will see this throughout the remainder of the book.

1.1 Layered Network Architecture

This section provides an overview into how networks are implemented and describes the functions provided by a network. A network is divided into different functional components called layers [11, 12]. Each of these layers has a different responsibility for providing the overall functionality of a modern network. The layers can be implemented in software or hardware, and not every layer is needed for every device on the network. For example, routers do not need to implement every layer since they are not responsible for the end-to-end transport of the data; they are only concerned with getting data to the next point on the network. This section starts with a description of the network's layered architecture and then describes the services and functions provided by the layers in the Internet.

The first examples of computer communication consisted of point-to-point connections between the two devices wishing to communicate. In this case, the

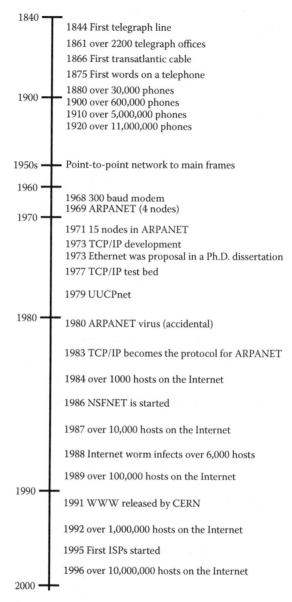

Figure 1.1: History of networking.

software required to communicate was completely self-contained and often was proprietary to the vendor. The physical connection was either direct using wires or over the telephone using a modem. The data rates were low compared to those of today's networks, and the applications often used simple text-based communications. These early applications were typically used for either simple file transfer or remote access. With these applications there was no need to have data relayed between computers. One of the first applications that used relaying of data between computers was email. Early email systems were designed to transport text messages between computers of like types. As with the early file transfer systems, they used proprietary software to enable communications, which made emailing between dissimilar computer systems difficult.

In the 1970s there was an effort started to develop standards [13] to allow different devices to communicate with each other over a network. The architects of the early standards decided that the problem should be divided into functional modules to enable the development of different methods for different computers to communicate with each other. Each of these modules, or layers, would perform a set of functions and provide a set of services to the layer above it using the services provided by the layer below. Figure 1.2 shows a diagram of the black box approach to defining a layer. Figure 1.2a shows that as with any black box design, the inputs and outputs are specified as a set of services along with the functions that need to be carried out. The services provided by a layer are called service access points (SAPs). Each layer carries out a set of functions specified in the standard. These functions are used to support the services and often involve communication between the corresponding layers on the two devices wishing to exchange data. This interlayer communication is called the protocol. The actual method to implement the layer is not specified as part of the standard. As we will see later, this can lead to some interesting security problems. This black box approach to defining each layer allowed different vendors to implement the same functions and services.

As we see in Figure 1.2b, layer A provides services to the layer above it and layer B provides services to layer A. These services are often specified as subroutine calls like we see in a program. For example, there might a service called send_data(destination, source, data, options, length) provided by layer A, which defines a service that is used to send a block of data to the corresponding layer A on another device specified by the destination address. The service has several parameters that can be used to instruct the layer on how to handle the service request, or may include information that is meant to be passed to the other peer layer. The parameter data in this example would contain the data that is to be passed from layer A to the corresponding layer A on the destination device. Each layer will use services provided by the layer below it to carry out the functions it provides. So as shown in Figure 1.2b, layer B might provide a service called send_packet(destination, source, data, options).

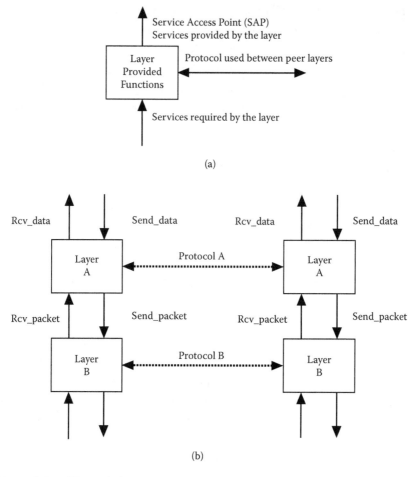

Figure 1.2:   Network layers.

Notice that in this example layer B provides a send_packet routine that sends
a fixed amount of data, but the upper layer A provided a service that could send
a larger amount of data. This is where the functions provided by a layer come
into play. In this example, layer A will need to provide a function that splits the
data it receives from the upper layer into smaller packets and sends them into
the lower layer. The corresponding layer A that receives the data will need to
provide a function that puts the packets back together and presents a block of
data to the upper layer. For a layer to communicate with its corresponding layer,
it must send data to the layer below. For a layer to carry out its functions, it
must also be able to communicate control information to the corresponding layer.
Based on our example shown in Figure 1.2b, layer A will need to send control

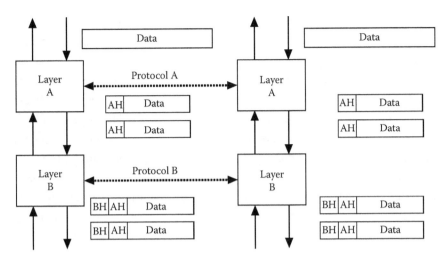

Figure 1.3: Control information encapsulation.

information that can be used by the receiving layer A to reassemble the packets. There are also rules that dictate the interaction between two corresponding layers, such as maximum packet size, format of the control information and data, timing and sequence of control messages, etc. These rules are called a protocol, and the control information is used to carry out the protocol. Every layer is defined as a combination of services, functions, and protocols. Figure 1.3 shows how the control information might be added (encapsulated) to the data as each of the layers processes the requests from the layer above it.

As we see in Figure 1.3, the data presented to layer A is divided into two packets by layer A. Each packet has control information added, which would include information on how to put the two packets back together when they are received by layer A on the destination device. The control information section of the packet is called the header. Layer A passes the two packets to layer B using the services provided by layer B. Layer B adds its own control information (header) to each packet it handles to enable it to communicate with layer B on the destination device. This continues as the packets flow down the network layers until the packets reach the physical transmission media. When the packets are received at the destination, each layer on the receiving device will use the control information to determine how to handle the packet. The layer will strip off the control information that is relevant to it and pass the rest of the packet up to the next-higher layer.

Figures 1.2 and 1.3 showed the interaction between layers as data was passed down the protocol stack and back up the receiving side. Another part of the layer specification is the protocol used between the corresponding layers. For example, in Figure 1.3, layer A on each device needs to understand how to handle packets of data. It needs to know the format of the control information. The protocol is used to provide the functions. For example, another function that could be provided by a layer would be to ask for packets to be resent if there is an error in a packet or a packet is missing. In order to implement this function, the layer would need to determine when a packet is corrupt or missing. This will require coordination between the layers using a protocol. A protocol defines how control information and data are exchanged between layers, and also defines the format of the information exchanged between the layers. The protocol is needed to implement the functions and services. Functions provided by a layer can be exploited by an attacker and will be detailed in subsequent chapters of this book. However, there are several basic functions provided by layers that are highlighted below:

1. **Segmentation and reassembly:** There are cases when a layer has a restriction on the amount of data it will allow from the layer above. This may be because of limits in the amount of buffer space, the protocol headers, or because of limits of the physical connection. For example, many physical local area networks (e.g., Ethernet) limit the packet size to a couple thousand bytes to ensure fair access to the physical network. As shown in Figure 1.3, if a layer receives more data from the upper layer than the layer below it can handle, the data must be divided into smaller packets (segmentation) and eventually put back together by the receiving layer (reassembly). The layer that does the segmentation is responsible for putting the reassembly instructions in its header, which is typically some type of packet number and data offset.

2. **Encapsulation:** Encapsulation is the addition of control information to the packet in the form of a header. This was shown in Figure 1.3. The headers typically contain the following information:

   Address: The address of the sender or receiver.

   Error detection code: Some sort of code is often included for error detection.

   Protocol control: Additional information needed to implement the protocol.

3. **Connection control:** A layer may use connectionless data transfer or connection-oriented data transfer. In connection-oriented data transfer, a logical association, or **connection**, is established between entities before any data is transferred. This is similar to the phone system, where a person dials the number and waits for the other side to pick up the phone before

the two sides can talk. In connection-oriented data transfer both sides have to be ready to talk at the same time. The connection is established using information in the headers of the packets, and in many cases the packets used to establish the connection contain no data. The three phases of **connection control** are the request/connect phase, the data transfer phase, and the termination phase. Many network-based attacks focus on the connection control exchanges. In a network that uses connectionless data transfer, each packet is independent of every other packet and can be delivered out of order and may not be delivered at all. This is analogous to the postal mail system. The sender can send a letter and it will arrive at some time, and each letter is independent of every other letter.

4. **Ordered delivery:** In some cases the service provided by the layer requires the packets to be delivered in order, but the packets may be delivered out of order by the layer below. This is true in the Internet, where the packets are transferred using a connectionless protocol, but the applications require the packets to be delivered in the same order they were transmitted. In order for a layer to provide this service, it will need to add control information to the header to be able to number the packets so they can be put back together by the receiving layer.

5. **Flow control:** Flow control is a technique for ensuring that the transmitting layer does not overwhelm a receiving layer. Flow control is typically implemented in several layers and is found in most connection-oriented protocols.

6. **Error control:** Errors can occur in the transmission of packets. Whether the packet is lost or corrupted, the layer may be responsible for detecting missing or damaged packets and retransmitting these packets. Not every layer is responsible for retransmission of packets, but most layers have some type of error detection (generally using a checksum) in the header. Attackers can sometimes use the error control protocols in an attack by sending corrupt packets to a device and causing the layer to react.

7. **Multiplexing:** Multiplexing is when packets from multiple upper layers share a lower layer. The best example of this is to consider a computer connected to a single physical network. If you think of all of the applications that are using the network at the same time (web, email, IM, etc.), each of them would send packets on the physical network. It makes sense to only have one layer that controls access to the physical network. Therefore, somewhere within the computer's multiple network layers there needs to

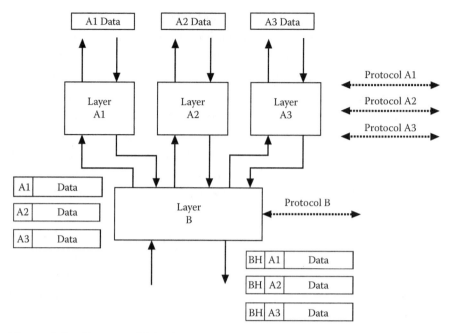

Figure 1.4:   Layer multiplexing.

be one or more layers that can support multiple upper layers. Figure 1.4 shows an example of multiplexing. Notice in the example that several layers use the services provided by layer B. In order for the receiving layer B to know which layer A is to get the packets, the layer B header will need to include an address in the packet header to indicate the identity of each of the upper layers.

Definitions

Connectionless.

No connection is needed to transfer data.

Connection oriented.

Before data can be transferred, the two communicating parties must agree to communicate by establishing a connection.

Encapsulation.

Adding layer headers to the data to create a new packet.

Error control.

A function provided by a layer that will detect and try to correct packet loss and packet corruption.

Flow control.

A function provided by a layer that will slow the sender's packet transmission rate when the receiver starts to get behind.

Layered network functions.

A set of operations provided by a layer in coordination with its peer layer on another device in the network designed to provide network services. Functions enable the services provided by a layer to work and rely on the services provided by the lower layer.

Multiplexing.

When a layer provides service access points to multiple upper layers and in turn only uses service access points from one lower layer to send and receive the packets for the multiple upper layers.

Network layer.

A functional component of a network architecture that has a defined set of inputs and outputs and provides a set of functions that aid in the operation of the network.

Packet.

A block of data that is passed between layers.

Packet header.

The part of the packet that is added by a layer to enable the protocol to function.

Protocol.

A set of rules that govern the interaction between two peer layers in the network architecture. The protocol is used to carry out the functions of the layer.

Reassembly.

A function provided by a layer that combines packets that were segmented by a peer layer back into the original data element.

Router.

A network device that is responsible for moving data from one network to another network. A router understands the route the data needs to take to get from the sender to the receiver.

Segmentation.

A function provided by a layer that divides the data received from an upper layer into multiple smaller data elements.

Service access point.

The set of services provided by a network layer. SAPs are often defined as a series of subroutine calls.

1.2   Overview of a Protocol

Protocols are in use every day. For example, the telephone system can be viewed as having multiple layers, each with a protocol. There is a protocol used between the two people talking. Think of this as the upper layer in a network. The phone system is the lower layer that provides basic services and functions to the layer above. Figure 1.5a shows the protocol exchange between the devices in the phone system, and Figure 1.5b shows the protocol exchange between two users of the telephone system. The protocol exchange is often expressed as a protocol diagram, as shown in Figure 1.5, where the vertical lines represent the communicating layers and the horizontal lines indicate information exchange. The diagram also can show a temporal element since time progresses down the diagram. The slanted horizontal lines represent the time it takes for the information to flow from one side to the other. The gaps between the lines represent wait or processing time by the layer.

So, as we can see in Figure 1.5a, the caller on the left side of the diagram starts by picking up the receiver. The caller listens for a dial tone, which is part of the protocol, after hearing the dial tone the caller dials the number. If the called party's phone is not busy, then the caller gets a ring tone and the called party's phone rings. We can also see that the diagram shows error conditions like a busy signal. Not all possible error conditions may have been specified as part of the standard, and therefore would not be covered in the protocol definition. As we will see later, this can cause security problems. Once the called party picks up the phone, the connection between the lower layers is completed and the two people start a protocol, as shown in Figure 1.5b.

First, the person answering the telephone starts the interaction by saying something and the other person responds. The figure shows a possible protocol and also shows an attempt at authenticating the called party. The two people will continue to talk (send data) in a back-and-forth manner until one of them terminates the communication. This is often done by saying goodbye; however, the call can be terminated by just hanging up. This abrupt termination is often used when something has gone wrong between the two parties. The protocol between the two parties is not well defined, and therefore the protocol may fail. One part of the protocol is often identification of one or more parties. This is done through many different methods. We do have a method that is part of the phone system to identify the calling device (caller id). However, caller id identifies the phone number of the caller and not the person using the phone. There is no method to identify the actual calling or called party. We can imagine that this could lead to problems if a

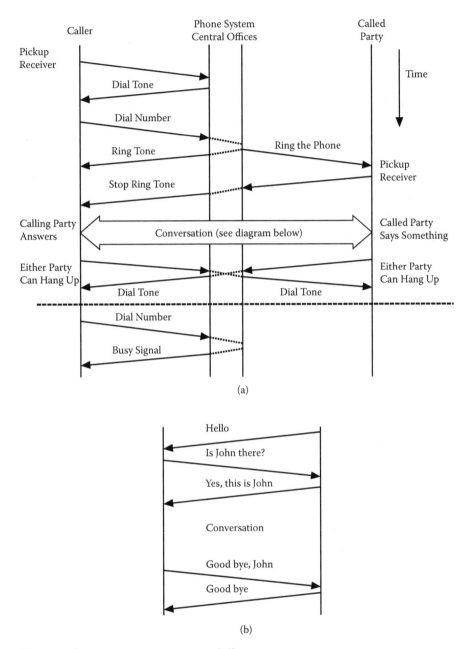

Figure 1.5: Phone system protocol diagram.

person wanted to use the phone for dishonest purposes. Even with caller id, only the phone is identified, even though it was primarily added to provide screening of incoming calls. The phone system was not originally designed to handle what we now consider to be a security problem. Throughout the book we will see many examples of protocols that were not designed with security in mind.

The phone system provides an example of what is called connection-oriented communications. This is where a protocol exchange is used to establish a connection between the two parties (dialing the phone, picking up the phone). Once the connection has been established, the data flows between the two parties and is received in the same order it is sent. There is another method that is used to transfer data between two parties referred to as connectionless. In connectionless communications the information is broken up into packets and each packet is handled separately as it is sent from one party to another. An example of a connectionless system is the post office. Each letter we send is handled independently and could follow a different route to get to the same destination. Each letter is self-contained and has its own address information. If we send multiple letters from the same place to the same destination, there is no guarantee they will all arrive at the same time and in the same order. While the connectionless method may seem to be less reliable than the connection-oriented method, that may not be the case. Let us look at the phone (FAX system) versus the postal mail system and compare sending a ten-page document. (For this analogy we will ignore the difference in data transfer times.) If we use the phone system, the connection must stay up the entire time we are sending the document. The phone system is very reliable; however, if the system were to fail during the transfer, it would need to start over again. If we took the document and divided it up into ten letters and mailed each one, the odds are that most, if not all, would make it. If one is lost, then we would only need to send the lost page again. Now we need a method to put the pages back together again, which can add overhead. This would be part of the protocol used by the sender and receiver of the letters. This would create a connection-oriented system on top of a connectionless service. Later in the book we will see some protocols within the Internet that are connectionless and others that are connection oriented.

Definition

Protocol diagram.

A diagram used to show the interaction between two entities using a protocol. The diagram shows the information flow and the timing between information exchanges.

1.3   Layered Network Model

As we discussed in the previous section, the network functions have been divided into multiple layers. As with many technologies, the standards often follow the first implementation and we can have competing standards. This is also true of networking. The first networks did not follow the layered architecture. In the early 1970s, the concept of packet switching [3, 7, 9] was proposed, and that gave way to the Transmission Control Protocol/Internet Protocol (TCP/IP). In 1984 the International Standards Organization (ISO) proposed a seven-layer network, the Open Systems Interconnection (OSI) model [14], and started to develop standards for each of the layers. The OSI model was heavily influenced by the telecommunications industry and its focus on circuit-switched (connection-oriented) technologies. So with two competing standards there were two competing forces at work trying to push their own agenda. At one point the federal government pushed for the adoption of the OSI standards, while at the same time the TCP/IP standards were being implemented at universities and research labs. As we know, the TCP/IP standards are used by the Internet, and with a few exceptions, the OSI standards have been abandoned. What has remained is the OSI model for describing network layers. Even though the standards are not used, any current standard is always mapped to the OSI model.

Figure 1.6 shows the layers of the TCP/IP model compared to the OSI model. A brief description of the functions provided by each layer in the OSI model is listed next, along with a description of the TCP/IP layers. As we see in Figure 1.6, some of the layers are implemented in hardware and some in software. We also see that in a typical implementation the lower layers are part of the operating system and the upper layers are part of the user space and often contained within the application. In addition, Figure 1.6 shows that not all devices need every layer, and how some protocols are between the end systems and some protocols are between intermediate devices like routers.

The following list highlights the functions [12] provided by each layer of the OSI and TCP/IP models.

1. Physical layer: The physical layer is responsible for the transparent transmission of bit streams across the physical interconnection of systems. The physical layer must provide the data link layer with a means to identify the endpoint (typically using source and destination addresses). The physical layer must deliver the bits in the same order in which they were offered for transmission by the data link layer.

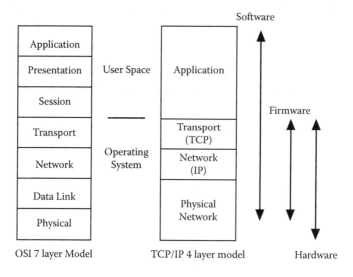

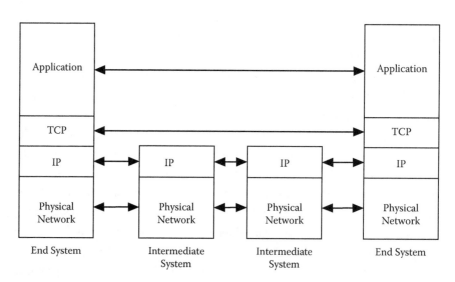

Figure 1.6: OSI and TCP/IP models.

2. Data link layer: The main task of the data link layer is to shield higher layers from the characteristics of the physical transmission medium. The data link layer should provide the higher layers with a reliable transmission that is basically **error-free**, although errors may occur in the transmission on the physical connection. Each data unit from the network layer is mapped to the data link protocol data unit along with the data link protocol information,

and is called a **frame**. The data link layer must provide a method of recognizing the start and end of the frame. Frames must be presented to the physical layer in the same order they are received. The data link layer can also implement **flow control** to prevent data overrun.

3. Network layer: The primary responsibility of the network layer is to provide the transparent transfer of all data submitted by the transport layer to any transport layer anywhere in the network. The network layer must handle the routing of data packets. The network layer can be the highest layer in a device, such as a gateway or router. In the OSI model the network layer was first designed to be connection oriented, and therefore the protocol was complex.

4. Transport layer: The transport layer is responsible for the **reliable** transparent data transfer between two session layer entities. The transport layer is only concerned with the transfer of data between session layers. It is not aware of the structure of the underlying layers or the topology. The transport layer will use the network layer to get data from one transport entity to another. Depending on the quality of the service provided by the network layer, the transport layer may have to perform additional functions, like ordered delivery, to offer the service. The transport layer provides flow and error control.

5. Session layer: The session layer is not concerned with the network. The session layer's goal is to coordinate the dialog between presentation layers. The session layer must provide the establishment of a session connection and the management of the dialog on that connection. The session layer in the OSI model was one of the last layers to be standardized and can be optional in that it can provide no functions and just pass data from the presentation layer to the transport layer. An example of a session layer would be an ATM, which maintains a constant connection with a bank (transport service). A session would start when the user starts a transaction.

6. Presentation layer: The presentation layer provides the application layer with services related to the presentation of information in a form that is meaningful to the application entities. The presentation layer provides the mechanism for the application layer to translate its data into a common format that can be translated by the peer application layer.

7. Application layer: The highest layer provides a means for application processes to access the OSI stack. The application layer provides the protocol
to carry out the functions of the application. The application layer typically
does not define the user interface or even the user-level commands to carry
out the functions. A good example is the web; the application protocol
(Hypertext Transfer Protocol [HTTP]) defines the functions and services
needed to access web pages and transfer information to the web browsers,
but does not specify how the browser will interact with the user.

Most of the functions provided in the OSI model are also provided in the TCP/IP
[15] model. The biggest difference is that the application layer in the TCP/IP
model encompasses the upper three layers in the OSI model. Many applications
do not require all of the functions provided by the session and presentation layers,
and even in the OSI model these functions were implemented as part of the
application. The descriptions below set the stage for the remainder of the book.
The service, functions, and security weaknesses of each of the TCP/IP layers will
be discussed in subsequent chapters.

1. TCP/IP physical network layer: The TCP/IP physical network layer combines the functions of the OSI physical and data link layers. The services
provided are simple and consist of sending and receiving packets. The
TCP/IP protocols are designed to operate on any type of network, and
therefore assume a minimal level of service.

2. Network (IP) layer: The network (IP) layer provides the routing of packets
across the Internet and also is concerned with the global address space. The
IP layer is connectionless, and the services provided consist of sending and
receiving packets.

3. Transport (TCP) layer: The transport (TCP) layer, just like the OSI transport layer, is responsible for the reliable end-to-end transfer of data across
the network. The TCP layer will use the send and receive packet functions provided by the network layer to communicate with its peer transport
layer. The TCP layer will need to compensate for the IP layer's unreliable
connectionless service.

4. TCP/IP application layer: The application layer provides the same types of
services as the upper three layers in the OSI protocol model. Depending on
the application, the functions of the session and presentation layer might
be minimal or nonexistent.

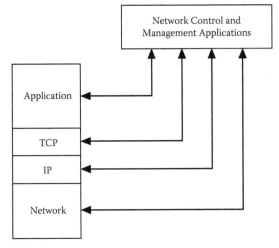

TCP/IP 4 layer model

Figure 1.7: Nonlayered services.

When the layered architecture was designed, little thought was given to network management, network security, or network monitoring. These services were not considered important when networks were small and primarily controlled by a few organizations. As networks have grown in size and complexity, the need for these services has also grown. As we look at the requirements for these services, it quickly becomes obvious that the layered model does not map into the requirements of these services. These services need access to the inner workings of each layer, and often need to read or modify internal parameters within the layer. Network management, for example, often requires direct control over each layer. This led to a modified network architecture where several nonlayered services are introduced, as shown in Figure 1.7. This also has an impact on security since programs are given access to each layer. For example, a rogue program might be able to interject packets at a lower layer that violates the header format of the layer above.

Definitions

Frame.
The name used to describe the packet used by the data link layer in the OSI networking model.

Nonlayered services.
Used to describe network services that need access to one or more layers directly, without using other layers. Often used in network management.

OSI model.

A seven-layer model that describes the high-level functions that should be pro-vided by each of the layers that make up a complete network implementation.

TCP/IP model.

A four-layer model that describes the high-level functions that are implemented to support the Internet.

User space.

Programs that run in user space have the same access rights as the user that is running them, which can limit the access the program has to system files.

Homework Problems and Lab Experiments

Homework Problems

1. From a design standpoint, provide three reasons why the layered network architecture is better than a nonlayered architecture?

2. Why would the network designers include fragmentation as a function in-stead of just requiring all packets to be a certain size?

3. Assume each layer adds 20 bytes of header information. Plot a curve that shows the percentage overhead versus the user payload size for both the seven-layer OSI model and the four-layer TCP/IP model. (Use data sizes from 1 to 1,400 bytes.)

4. Assume the four-layer TCP/IP network model, with each layer adding 20 bytes of header information and a maximum physical layer packet size of 1,500 bytes (the maximum size of the packets transmitted on the physical network). Create a table showing the number of packets and the total number of bytes transmitted given each of the following sizes for the user data.

   a. 1,000 bytes

   b. 10,000 bytes

   c. 100,000 bytes

   d. 1 million bytes

5. Compute the percentage overhead for each of the user data sizes in prob-lem 4.

6. Describe a common action (like using an elevator) in the form of a protocol diagram.

7. Research the history of the OSI networking model versus the TCP/IP model showing a timeline of the two models and their adoption. Comment on the government's efforts to standardize on the OSI model and why that did not work.

Lab Experiments

1. Using resources found on the Internet, plot the growth of the following over the past 20 years:

   a. Estimated number of hosts on the Internet

   b. Estimated number of web sites on the Internet

   c. Estimated total web traffic volume

   d. Estimated total FTP traffic volume

   e. Estimated total Internet traffic volume

2. Using resources found on the Internet, look up the history of the Internet and reference it to other world events.

3. Using resources found on the Internet, research the history of network speed and compare it to the history of the Internet developed in lab experiment 2. Comment on what you discover. Do you think the growth of the Internet was driven by the growth of network speed, or that the growth of the Internet drives the need to faster networks?

References

[1] Casson, H. N. 1910. *The history of the telephone*. Manchester, NH: Ayer Company Publishers.

[2] Winston, B. 1998. *Media technology and society: A history: From the telegraph to the Internet*. London: Routledge.

[3] Poole, H., et al. 1999. *History of the Internet: A chronology, 1843 to the present*. Santa Barbara, CA: ABC-CLIO, INC.

[4] Cerf, V. G. 2004. On the evolution of Internet technologies. *Proceedings of the IEEE* 92:1360–70.

[5] Leiner, B., et al. 1985. The DARPA Internet protocol suite. *IEEE Communications Magazine* 23:29–34.

[6] Baran, P. 1964. On distributed communications networks. *IEEE Transactions on Communications* 12:1–9.

[7] Cerf, V., and R. Kahn. 1974. A protocol for packet network intercommunication. *IEEE Transactions on Communications* 22:637–48.

[8] Abbate, J. 1994. *From ARPAnet to Internet: A history of ARPA-sponsored computer networks, 1966–1988*. Philadelphia: University of Pennsylvania.

[9] Hauben, M. 1994. *History of Arpanet*, 2000. New York: Columbia University.

[10] Spafford, E. H. 1989. The Internet worm program: An analysis. *ACM SIGCOMM Computer Communication Review* 19:17–57.

[11] Zimmermann, H. 1980. OSI reference model—The ISO model of architecture for open systems interconnection. *IEEE Transactions on Communications* 28:425–32.

[12] Halsall, F. 1995. *Data communications, computer networks and open systems*. Redwood City, CA: Addison Wesley Longman Publishing Co.

[13] Russell, A. L. 2006. Rough consensus and running code and the Internet—OSI standards war. *IEEE Annals of the History of Computing* 28:48–61.

[14] Day, J. D., and H. Zimmermann. 1983. The OSI reference model. *Proceedings of the IEEE* 71:1334–40.

[15] Forouzan, B. A., and S. C. Fegan. 1999. *TCP/IP protocol suite*. New York: McGraw-Hill Higher Education.

Chapter 2

Network Protocols

As discussed in Chapter 1, network layers use protocols to coordinate their interaction. These protocols are often designed to solve a particular problem or to address a need. Protocols are designed to provide a set of functions and are defined by a standard. Protocol standards are created and maintained by many different groups, ranging from international organizations to professional societies to ad hoc groups. Standards are often written as English narratives that are open to interpretation. Standards are also meant to be a functional description of how the protocol behaves and interacts with the other layers (above and below). Throughout the remaining chapters we will look in detail at several different standards and how their design and implementation impact security. There are several overarching protocol design concepts that have an impact on network security. These include protocol specifications, protocol addresses, and protocol headers.

2.1 Protocol Specifications

There is an ongoing debate about which is more secure: open-source or proprietary implementations. This discussion can also be applied to network protocols. Most network protocol standards are open and are subject to many rounds of review. This should lead to robust protocols with minimal design flaws; however, the requirements of most protocols are to implement a particular set of functions, and security is not a requirement. One side effect of an open protocol is that it is easier to discover security flaws in the protocol. Even though the protocol design is flawless from a functional standpoint, it might contain security flaws in the design.

It is often impractical to use a proprietary protocol since multiple vendors need to interoperate. The application layer is the most common place for proprietary protocols since there is not always a requirement for interoperability between vendors. With a proprietary protocol it is more difficult to discover the security flaws. This applies to both the attackers and the users. With an open protocol many people (both good and bad) will review the protocol, which might lead to the discovery of more security flaws. However, most proprietary protocols are reverse engineered within a short period of time and do not deter attackers.

One of the biggest security issues with protocol specifications is the methods used to express the specification. The specifications are written in English and are often tens of pages long. This can lead to different interpretations of the same specification by different vendors. The differences can occur when something is left out of the specification (often how to handle an error condition), is not well specified (using words like *must*, *should*, etc.), or there is an error in the specification. Even if the specification is clear, mistakes can be introduced during the implementation of the protocol. As we will see in later chapters of the book, hackers will try to take advantage of the protocol and its implementation.

There are several parts that constitute a standard. A standard starts out with a general description of the goals and uses of the standard and the relationship between the standard and any other standards. The standard will specify:

The service access points (SAPs) provided and the service access points required from the lower layer

The functions provided

The protocol, including the format of the packets and the meaning of each field with the packet (the headers)

The timing and sequence of the packets as they are used to implement the functions specified

In the Internet the most common method for a standard to gain widespread use is through the creation of a Request for Comment (RFC). The RFCs are maintained by the Internet Engineering Task Force (IETF) (http://www.ietf.org). This group consists of members from various organizations and is open to any person that has an interest. The mission statement for the organization is found in RFC 3935 [1]. A request for comment goes through several levels of review and oversight before becoming a standard. It is beyond the scope of this book to examine the details of the RFC process and is left to readers as a homework assignment. In addition to IETF, there are numerous standards groups that have released standards used in the Internet. A list of common standards groups is provided at the end of this section. One organization of interest is the Institute of Electrical and Electronics Engineers (IEEE). The IEEE standards group (http://standards.ieee.org) is responsible for many standards, including the Ethernet standard that is used by most computers today.

The text at the end of this section contains several excerpts from the RFC that describes the main protocol used by the Internet to get packets from end host to end host: the Internet Protocol (IP). This text is extracted directly from RFC 791 [2], and the entire text can be found on the IETF web site. The excerpts were chosen to show a couple of the sections found in most standards. Notice that the standard has a section on motivation (why have the standard) and scope (what the standard does not do). Another section is called "Interfaces," which describes the service access points, and the "Functional Description" section describes the basic function of the standard. The next section of the standard describes the fragmentation function of the layer. The IP standard is over forty pages of text and has had many additions over the years via other RFCs. The standard does contain descriptions of the packet headers and each field in the packet header. It is left up to the reader to review the entire standard.

Definitions

Ethernet.

A standard maintained by the Institute of Electrical and Electronics Engineers (IEEE) that describes the common local area network used by most computers today.

Open-source protocol.

A protocol specification that is made public and is often reviewed and discussed by many people before adoption.

Proprietary protocol.

A protocol specification that is not public.

Protocol specification.

A document that describes the services, functions, packet formats, and other information needed to implement a protocol layer.

Request for Comment (RFC).

A protocol standard that is created by individuals or groups associated with the Internet Engineering Task Force (IETF).

Standard.

A protocol specification that has gone through a process of review and verification and then is published so multiple vendors can use it to interoperate.

Standards Organizations

American National Standards Institute (ANSI).

ANSI is a private organization whose membership is made up of professional societies, government groups, and other associations. It develops standards that help groups compete in the global market. (http://www.ansi.org)

Institute of Electrical and Electronics Engineers (IEEE).

IEEE is an international professional society that creates international standards in many different areas. (http://www.ieee.org)

International Standards Organization (ISO).

A group whose membership is standards committees from across the world. ANSI represents the United States on ISO. (http://www.iso.org)

International Telecommunications Union–Telecommunications Standards Sector (ITU-T).

A group created by the United Nations that creates standards primarily for the phone system. (http://www.itu.int)

Internet Engineering Task Force (IETF).

This group develops standards for the Internet and consists of members from various organizations and is open to any person that has an interest. (http://www.ietf.org)

EXCERPTS FROM THE **RFC 791** (INTERNET PROTOCOL)

1.1. MOTIVATION

The Internet Protocol is designed for use in interconnected systems of packet-switched computer communication networks. Such a system has been called a "catenet" [1]. The internet protocol provides for transmitting blocks of data called datagrams from sources to destinations, where sources and destinations are hosts identified by fixed length addresses. The internet protocol also provides for fragmentation and reassembly of long datagrams, if necessary, for transmission through "small packet" networks.

1.2. SCOPE

The internet protocol is specifically limited in scope to provide the functions necessary to deliver a package of bits (an internet datagram) from a source to a destination over an interconnected system of networks. There are no mechanisms to augment end-to-end data reliability, flow control, sequencing, or other services commonly found in host-to-host protocols. The internet protocol can capitalize on the services of its supporting networks to provide various types and qualities of service.

1.3. INTERFACES

This protocol is called on by host-to-host protocols in an internet environment. This protocol calls on local network protocols to carry the internet datagram to the next gateway or destination host.

For example, a TCP module would call on the internet module to take a TCP segment (including the TCP header and user data) as the data portion of an internet datagram. The TCP module would provide the addresses and other parameters in the internet header to the internet module as arguments of the call. The internet module would then create an internet datagram and call on the local network interface to transmit the internet datagram.

In the ARPANET case, for example, the internet module would call on a local net module which would add the 1822 leader [2] to the internet datagram creating an ARPANET message to transmit to the IMP. The ARPANET address would be derived from the internet address by the local network interface and would be the address of some host in the ARPANET, that host might be a gateway to other networks.

2.3. FUNCTION DESCRIPTION

The function or purpose of Internet Protocol is to move datagrams through an interconnected set of networks. This is done by passing the datagrams from one internet module to another until the destination is reached. The internet modules reside in hosts and gateways in the internet system. The datagrams are routed from one internet module to another through individual networks based on the interpretation of an internet address. Thus, one important mechanism of the internet protocol is the internet address.

In the routing of messages from one internet module to another, datagrams may need to traverse a network whose maximum packet size is smaller than the size of the datagram. To overcome this difficulty, a fragmentation mechanism is provided in the internet protocol.

FRAGMENTATION

Fragmentation of an internet datagram is necessary when it originates in a local net that allows a large packet size and must traverse a local net that limits packets to a smaller size to reach its destination.

An internet datagram can be marked "don't fragment." Any internet datagram so marked is not to be internet fragmented under any circumstances.

If internet datagram marked don't fragment cannot be delivered to its destination without fragmenting it, it is to be discarded instead.

Fragmentation, transmission and reassembly across a local network which is invisible to the internet protocol module is called internet fragmentation and may be used [6].

The internet fragmentation and reassembly procedure needs to be able to break a datagram into an almost arbitrary number of pieces that can be later reassembled. The receiver of the fragments uses the identification field to ensure that fragments of different datagrams are not mixed. The fragment offset field tells the receiver the position of a fragment in the original datagram. The fragment offset and length determine the portion of the original datagram covered by this fragment. The more-fragments flag indicates (by being reset) the last fragment. These fields provide sufficient information to reassemble datagrams.

The identification field is used to distinguish the fragments of one datagram from those of another. The originating protocol module of an internet datagram sets the identification field to a value that must be unique for that source-destination pair and protocol for the time the datagram will be active in the internet system. The originating protocol module of a complete datagram sets the more-fragments flag to zero and the fragment offset to zero.

To fragment a long internet datagram, an internet protocol module (for example, in a gateway), creates two new internet datagrams and copies the contents of the internet header fields from the long datagram into both new internet headers. The data of the long datagram is divided into two portions on a 8 octet (64 bit) boundary (the second portion might not be an integral multiple of 8 octets, but the first must be). Call the number of 8 octet blocks in the first portion NFB (for Number of Fragment Blocks). The first portion of the data is placed in the first new internet datagram, and the total length field is set to the length of the first datagram. The more-fragments flag is set to one. The second portion of the data is placed in the second new internet datagram, and the total length field is set to the length of the second datagram. The more-fragments flag carries the same value as the long datagram. The fragment offset field of the second new internet datagram is set to the value of that field in the long datagram plus NFB.

This procedure can be generalized for an n-way split, rather than the two-way split described.

To assemble the fragments of an internet datagram, an internet protocol module (for example at a destination host) combines internet datagrams that all have the same value for the four fields: identification, source, destination, and protocol. The combination is done by placing the data portion of each fragment in the relative position indicated by the fragment offset in that fragment's internet header. The first fragment will have the fragment offset zero, and the last fragment will have the more-fragments flag reset to zero.

2.2   Addresses

One of the key aspects of a protocol is the addressing method used to distinguish between different components within the network. For example, addresses are used to distinguish one computer from another in the network, one instance of an application from another, or one protocol from another. Before we discuss network layer addressing, it might be useful if we look at a nonnetwork example and see how many addresses are required. Figure 2.1 shows a diagram of two people using the postal system to communicate with letters.

As we see in Figure 2.1, the sender who lives in a building at a certain street address in Los Angeles is sending a letter to another person living in a building in Washington, D.C. The sender will put their address (return address) and the

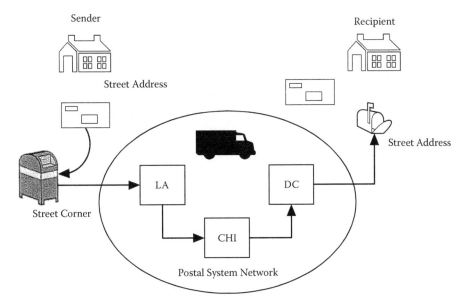

Figure 2.1:   Postal addressing.

recipient's address on the outside envelope. Both addresses contain several parts that are used to identify the person, building, city, and state. The envelope is like the header in a packet, and the data is contained inside the envelope. The sender will take the letter to a mailbox that has a physical address on a street corner. That physical address of the mailbox is not important to the recipient and is only important to the sender because he or she needs to know how to get the letter to the next place. The sender did not need to put the physical address of the mailbox on the envelope.

Once the letter is in the mailbox, the postal system will take over from there and route the letter to the recipient (the destination address). In the example the letter is taken from the physical mailbox to a sorting center in Los Angeles. The sorting center in Los Angeles will read the recipient address and determine where the letter should go next. (This is also called routing.) The letter is then placed in a truck and taken to the next sorting center, which in this example is Chicago. That sorting center has a physical address. That address is not important to either the sender or the recipient of the letter and only needs to be known by the truck taking the letter from Los Angeles to Chicago. Once the letter reaches Chicago, the recipient address is read and the letter is routed to the next sorting center, which in the example is Washington, D.C. Again, the physical address of the sorting center is not important to the sender or recipient.

When the letter arrives in Washington, D.C., the recipient address is examined to determine which local mail carrier will deliver the letter to the building where the recipient lives. The local mail carrier will deliver the letter to the physical mailbox at the building indicated by the recipient address. The physical location of the mailbox was not on the envelope; that information is known by the mail carrier. Once the mail carrier places the envelope in the recipient's mailbox, someone from the recipient's address can get the letter. Whoever picks up the letter will read the name on the recipient address to determine which person in the building should get the letter.

If we look at the same example, only this time look at two people using computers to communicate, we can see there are many similarities between the postal system addressing and how the addressing works in a network. Figure 2.2 shows two people using computers to send a message.

Figure 2.2 shows a sender at a computer who has a username, and is running an application like email. In the Internet every directly connected computer has a unique address that is used to identify the computer. Just like every postal address is unique. The computer application will take the message from the user and will read the destination (recipient) address from the header to determine where

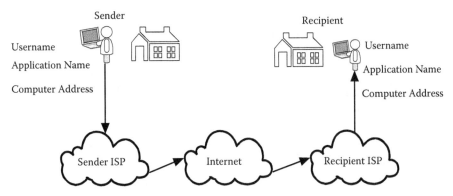

Figure 2.2: Network addressing.

to send the message next. The computer will send the message to the sender's Internet service provider (ISP). The computer knows the physical address of the ISP, and that information is not important to the computer user. The ISP will read the header to determine the next location to send (route) the message. The ISP will send the message into the Internet, where the message will be routed until it reaches the destination computer. Each step along the way the physical address of the intermediate devices will be used to help get the message to the correct place. When the message reaches the end computer as determined by the destination computer address in the message, the computer examines the message. The computer will look at the application address to determine which application should get the message. While there is not a one-to-one correlation between the postal system and the Internet, the reader should have an understanding about the need for multiple addresses.

If we refer back to the network protocol stack discussed in Chapter 1, several different addresses can be identified that are needed by the layers. As shown in Figure 2.3, each layer uses an address to help determine how the network traffic is handled. At the physical network layer there is an address used to identify the computer interface connected to the network. This address is often referred to as the machine, hardware, or physical address. The hardware address allows the network interface to filter out traffic that is not destined for that computer, which reduces the processing required. There is often another address contained within the packet that is used by the physical network layer to determine which network layer protocol should handle the packet.

The network (IP) layer needs an address to uniquely identify the computer within a larger network like the Internet [3]. The IP layer also contains an address

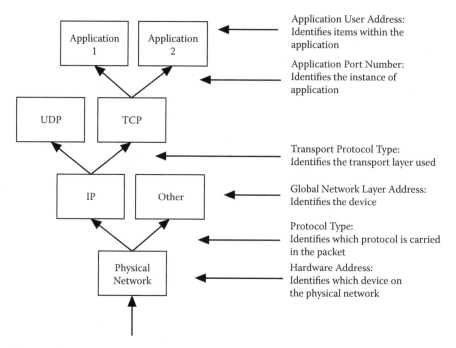

Figure 2.3: Layer addresses.

used to identify the transport layer protocol (Transmission Control Protocol [TCP], User Datagram Protocol [UDP], etc.). The TCP layer uses an address to identify the application that is using the network, called the port number. This allows multiple applications to share the network, and for multiple copies of the same application to share the network. Often, applications also have addresses that are typically supplied by the user and are used to access different items. For example, the URL on a web page is really an address that is used to identify the data element to be accessed. In addition, machines have names that are also used as an address.

From a network security standpoint we will see that each of these addresses can be used by an attacker to cause a security violation. Another issue to be discussed later is that addresses are often used not only as a way to identify the source and destination of the data, but also as a way to authenticate the source and destination. This can cause a large number of security problems.

One question that comes to mind is: How are the addresses assigned and by whom? Addresses can be assigned as either static addresses, which are often part of the system configuration, or as dynamic addresses, which are requested by the layer and assigned by an address server. This often depends on the layer and the type of address. In this chapter we will not look at the protocols that are used to obtain dynamic addresses. However, we will discuss each address type and how both static and dynamic address assignments can affect security. Once addresses are assigned, the next question is: How does a layer discover the address of the other layer?

The hardware address is typically assigned by the hardware vendor. In Ethernet [4], for example, each vendor is given a range of addresses [5] it can assign, and the vendor in turn configures each network controller with a unique address. This helps ensure that there are no address conflicts. The hardware controller then uses its address as a filter to only allow packets that are destined for that device to be read. The physical network layer uses an address discovery protocol to find the hardware address of the destination. This discovery protocol can be a source of attack, which will be discussed in Part II of the book. Also, Part II discusses methods that can be used to change the hardware address of a device or to ignore the address filter and read all packets on the network.

The network (IP) layer address can be assigned either dynamically or statically, and it often depends on who is providing access to the Internet. The protocol that is most often used to dynamically assign IP layer addresses and its security implications will be discussed in Part III. For now we will concentrate on the security implications of whether an IP address is static or dynamic. First we need to look at who assigns IP addresses. Since IP addresses of machines directly connected to the Internet need to be globally unique, they are assigned by address authorities. From a security standpoint these assignments can be useful to try and identify the sender of a packet. However, we will see later in this chapter and throughout the book that addresses can be changed in an attempt to fool the receiver. With dynamic assignment it is more difficult to tie the sender to a computer, and some security mechanisms rely on that mapping. From an overall security standpoint the method of IP address assignment has little effect on the security of a system once the correct address has been assigned. The method used to discover the destination address may vary depending on the application. The destination address can be hard-coded or configured into the application. The user may be asked to provide the destination address. The application may also ask another application for the address. From a security standpoint there are two problems: (1) How do we know the destination is the correct one? (2) If we use a protocol to determine the destination address, can we trust the results? Both of these issues will be discussed in detail in Part II.

The application address (port number) assignment is much less controlled than the hardware address assignment or the IP layer assignment. Once we know the address of the destination computer, we need to know the address of the application on the computer. There are several ways the addresses are assigned. The first is using a well-known port; in this case, everyone knows the port number of the application. For example, the well-known port for a web server is 80. The application can ask a service on a well-known port to tell it the port number of a given application, or the port numbers can be configured into the application. There is not much of a security issue with the assignment of application addresses. The biggest security issue is how the applications are authenticated, which will be discussed in Part III.

The host name address assignments are more complex because they are often political. As everyone who uses the Internet knows, services are addressed by using a host name. The host names are assigned by a set of registration authorities who help maintain order in the name assignments. These names are then mapped to an IP address using a protocol called Domain Name Service (DNS) [6]. There are many security issues with DNS, which will be discussed in Part II.

Definitions

Address.

Used to identify a computer, network device, application, protocol layer, or any other entity within a network.

Application address.

The address used to identify and distinguish between different network applications running on a computer.

Domain Name Service (DNS).

A system used to convert the name of a computer on the Internet to the address of the computer.

Dynamic address.

An address that can change and is often obtained during system start-up, or by asking a third party.

Hardware address.

The address used to identify the hardware interface connected to the physical network.

Internet service provider (ISP).

An organization, typically for profit, that provides access to the Internet for commercial or private users.

Port number.
An address used to identify an Internet application within a computer system.
The port number is the name given to the application address in the Internet.
Static address.
An address that does not change unless someone changes it. This address is
often set during the initial configuration of the computer system.

2.3   Headers

As discussed earlier, network protocols carry address information, along with
information that enables the protocol to function. This information is encapsulated
within each packet using headers. The headers are defined as part of the protocol
specification. Depending on the requirements, headers can come in two forms:
fixed packet type and freeform. When the data is transmitted in packets, the
headers are often appended to the front of the packet, and in some cases are also
at the end, often called a trailer. Figure 2.4 shows a typical header and trailer
in a packet. The header consists of two parts, the fixed part and an optional
or variable part. The fixed part contains information that is needed to process
every packet, like addresses, control information, etc. The optional part contains
information that is often used as part of the first few packets to negotiate a set of

Fixed	Options	Payload	Trailer

Fixed:
- Addresses (Layer addresses and payload type)
- Payload data
- Control data
- Header data

Options:
- Extended fixed data
- Optional control data
- Optional Payload control

Payload: Content is not a concern of the header

Trailer:
Optional field often used for error control

Figure 2.4:   Packet header/trailer.

```
<Start Header>
<Data type = application 7>
<Data length = 400>
<Data encoding = ASCII>
</End Header>
<Start Data>
(the data)
</End Data>
```

Figure 2.5:   Freeform header.

parameters needed to communicate. To speed up the processing of the packets, the field lengths are often a fixed size. The layer can examine any part of the header independent of the other parts; so, for example, the address field can be examined to determine if the packet is destined for the layer without parsing any other part of the header. The payload of the packet contains the data passed in from the layer above. In the case of control packets, the payload is not included.

   A freeform header is often found at the application layer when the data flow is a stream of data and not a series of packets. The freeform header is more complex to parse, but allows an endless number of possibilities, and can therefore create complex application protocols. An example of a freeform header is shown in Figure 2.5. As we see in the figure, the freeform header is not completely freeform; it follows a structure and has a set of rules that dictate the construction of the headers.

   From a security standpoint, both header types are subject to the same types of attacks, which are described in Chapter 4.

Definitions

Fixed form packet header.
A packet header where the fields are fixed in both location and size within the header.

Freeform header.
A header where the data is not in a fixed format, and therefore the header must be interpreted.

Packet payload.
The data part of the packet, where the data is defined as the information received or sent to the upper layer.

Homework Problems and Lab Experiments

Homework Problems

1. Describe the process a proposed standard goes through to become an RFC.

2. How many RFCs have been assigned?

3. How many RFCs are related to security?

4. Find one or more nonserious RFCs. (Hint: Search for "electricity over IP.")

5. How many different Ethernet standards can you find, and why are there so many?

6. Estimate the number of different network standards that are used.

7. What would happen if two computers had the same IP address?

8. What would happen if two computers had the same Ethernet address:

   a. If they were on the same network?

   b. If they were on different networks?

Lab Experiments

1. Find the following in the lab and place them in a table. (This table will be useful in the future.)

   a. The machine's name

   b. The IP addresses

   c. The hardware addresses

2. Look up the vendor code for each hardware address you found in lab experiment 1 and describe how this code could be used by a network administrator.

References

[1] Alvestrand, H. T. 2004. *A mission statement for the IETF*. RFC 3935.

[2] Postel, J. 1981. *Internet protocol*. RFC 791.

[3] Comer, D. E. 1995. *Internetworking with TCPIP*. Vol. 1. *Principles, proto-cols and architecture*. Englewood Cliffs, NJ: Prentice Hall.

[4] Spurgeon, C. E. 2000. *Ethernet: The definitive guide*. Sebastopal, CA: O'Reilly Media.

[5] Reynolds, J. K., and J. Postel. 1990. *Assigned numbers*. RFC 1060.

[6] Mockapetris, P., and K. J. Dunlap. 1988. Development of the domain name system. *SIGCOMM Computer Communication Review* 18:123–33.

Chapter 3

The Internet

This chapter provides an overview of the Internet and describes several key components that are important to our understanding of security. Throughout the remainder of the book, many of the protocols and critical security implications will be discussed in greater detail. The first step is to define the Internet.

The Internet is a collection of devices that are interconnected using network protocols [1–3]. Some of the interconnected devices run applications and interface with users; others are used to provide the connectivity between devices and networks. Figure 3.1 provides a representation of the hierarchical structure of the Internet. Figure 3.1a shows the user's view of the Internet. As far as a typical user is concerned, the Internet is a connection point that he plugs his computer into and then he can talk to anyone else connected to the Internet. Users view the Internet as a black box. From a security standpoint, we can sometimes view the Internet as a black box where the attacks come from, and we do not care about how the Internet is constructed. This is the most common view of the Internet, since we are more often concerned about attacks against the end system and networks and not the Internet itself. One reason this is true is that the end users have no real control of the Internet and no ability to mitigate attacks against the parts of the Internet they do not control. However, many organizations have networks that are as complicated as parts of the Internet, and therefore understanding the composition of the Internet and the protocols used will help mitigate attacks.

Another view of the Internet is shown in Figure 3.1b, where the Internet consists of interconnected Internet service providers (ISPs). These ISPs have an informal hierarchy in that national, international, and large regional ISPs are interconnected to create what is often referred to as the backbone. These ISPs are interconnected using high-speed dedicated connections and carry the bulk of the traffic. Connected to the backbone are other ISPs or large organizations, and this hierarchy continues with smaller ISPs and organizations connected to the mid-tier ISPs. Finally, the end user or organization is connected. As we also see in Figure 3.1b, an ISP consists of a set of interconnected devices. These devices can also be attacked along with the computer systems and networks connected to the Internet.

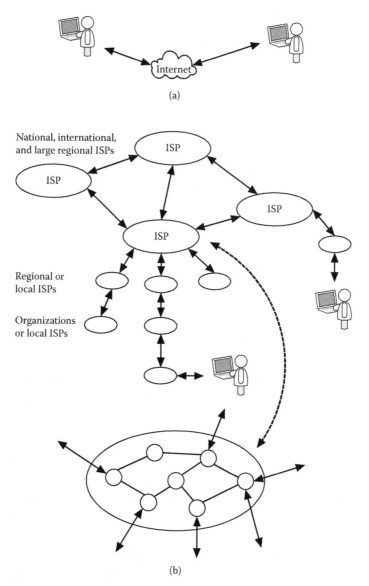

(a)

(b)

Figure 3.1:   Representation of the Internet.

From a security viewpoint, each device and protocol used in the Internet can be vulnerable and is a potential source or target of attack. Therefore, each device or protocol needs to be viewed with a security focus. Before we begin a detailed look at various protocols, we need to understand a few key concepts used in the Internet that are fundamental to security. These concepts are addressing and routing, which are at the heart of the Internet, and one can argue that they are the two most critical aspects of the Internet from a security standpoint. First, we will look at addressing. Then we need to understand the client-server model used throughout the Internet, followed by a discussion of Internet routing.

3.1 Addressing

In Chapter 2 we saw how addresses are used by the layers within the network to identify devices, protocols, and applications. The Internet uses addresses in the same way. It is important to understand which addresses can be changed by an attacker, which addresses are local to a single network, and which are global within the Internet.

If we summarize the addressing used in the Internet, we can see there is a logical division between the applications view of Internet addressing and the lower layers view of Internet addressing. The user and application view the Internet as a method to get data from one user or application to another. Figure 3.2 shows the user and application layers views of addressing.

As we see in Figure 3.2, the user's and application's view of addressing is analogous to the view of addressing that a person has when he or she uses the postal system. The user provides the application the address of the destination computer. The user may also provide the address of the destination application, although most times this is set by the application. The user may also provide the address of the destination user or destination file. The application will provide address information so the destination application can send data back to the sending application. As far as the user and the application are concerned, the Internet is something you push data into, and it will get to the correct destination. They do not worry about how the data gets there or what devices handle the data during its travels. Again, this is like the postal system, where the letter sender does not worry about how the letter gets to the destination.

Figure 3.3 expands on Figure 3.2 by showing two devices connected using the Internet, and by showing the lower layers needed for the data transfer [4]. Figure 3.3 also shows the different layer addresses that are utilized to pass the data from device to device. For now, we will ignore how traffic is routed across the Internet and how address discovery is handled. User A on computer C1 wants to send the message "hello" to user B on computer D1. As we see in Figure 3.3, user A sends the message "hello" into application A1 on computer C1. We will assume the sending application does not need to provide an address within the

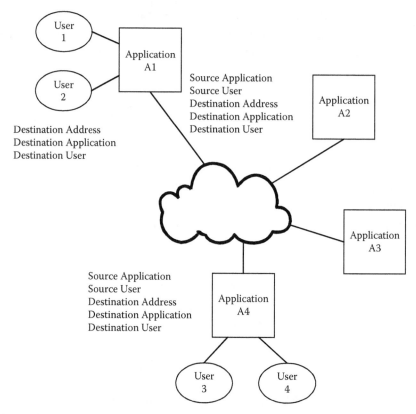

Figure 3.2: Application addressing.

destination application, like a URL or email username. If it did, then the sending user would also need to provide that address to the sending application. The user, or in some cases the application, provides the address of destination computer D1. The sending application uses an application port number to identify the remote application. The Transmission Control Protocol (TCP) layer uses the application port number in order to identify which incoming TCP packets are associated with that application. The application on computer C1 will need to know the application port number for the application on computer D1. As we will see later, this can be provided by the user, or it can be something the applications agree on as part of their configuration. So in summary, the application and the user provide the destination port number, the destination IP address, and the user data (payload) to the TCP layer.

The TCP layer will send the packet to the IP layer with the port numbers of the source and destination application, the user data, and TCP control information as

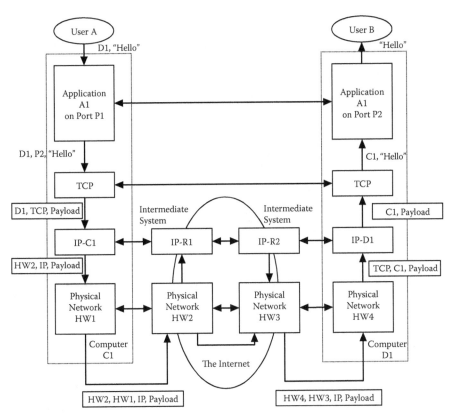

Figure 3.3: Internet addressing.

part of the payload. The address (transport protocol type) to identify TCP as the protocol used by the application, the source IP address of computer C1, and the destination IP address [5, 6] of computer D1 are added to the IP layer header. The destination IP address is obtained from the TCP layer (provided by the user), and the source IP address is obtained from the IP layer. The IP layer passes the packet down to the physical network layer along with the destination hardware address of the next device and the network protocol ID to the IP layer. The physical network layer adds its source address.

The packet that is sent on the network to the next device contains several addresses, as shown in Table 3.1. The table also shows who provided the address.

The packet is delivered to the next device, which in this case is a router. The router does not care about the transport or application layers. The router will

TABLE 3.1:   Internet Addresses

Address		User	Application	TCP	IP	Network
User or file	SRC	X	X			
	DST	X				
Computer address	SRC				X	
	DST	X				
Application ID (port number)	SRC			X		
	DST	X	X			
Transport protocol					X	
IP address	SRC				X	
	DST	X	X			
Network layer protocol ID					X	
Hardware address	SRC					X
	DST				X	

receive the packet because the destination hardware address matches the router's hardware address. The physical network layer of the router will examine the network layer protocol ID to see what type of packet it is. If it is an IP packet, then it will strip off the physical network layer header and pass the remainder of the packet to the IP layer of the router. The IP layer of the router will examine the source and destination IP addresses to determine where to send the packet next. The router will then pass the IP packet down to the physical network layer, which will add a new source and destination hardware address and set the network layer protocol ID to IP. Note that devices like routers often have multiple physical network interfaces, and each interface has its own physical network protocol layer. The packet will continue to be passed from router to router until the packet arrives at the destination computer D1. When the packet arrives at computer D1, the source hardware addresses will match the address of the last router, and the destination hardware address will match the hardware address of computer D1.

When the packet is received by computer D1, the packet's network layer protocol ID will be examined and the packet will be passed to the IP layer. The IP layer will examine the destination IP address to see if it matches the IP address of computer D1. If there is a match, the IP layer will examine the transport protocol ID to determine if that packet should be passed to the TCP layer or to a different transport protocol. The TCP layer will examine the destination application port number to determine which application should get the packet. Finally, the word "hello" will be passed to application A1 running on computer D1.

If the application on computer D1 wishes to send a packet back to the application on computer C1, it can use the source application port number from the packet it received as the identifier for the application on computer C1 and the source IP from the packet it received as the identifier for computer C1. A packet would be formed in the same manner as the packet sent by computer C1, as shown in Figure 3.2. As we see, the packets that are exchanged between the two applications on the two computers have four addresses that uniquely identify the packets flowing in each direction. The two IP addresses and the application port numbers create a globally unique identifier that is used to separate different packet streams from each other. This is how you can have two browser windows open to the same web site at the same time. Each browser window has a different network connection, and therefore a different unique identifier.

3.1.1 Address Spoofing

What we have seen in Figures 3.2 and 3.3 is that addressing is used to direct traffic to the correct layer and device within the Internet. In many cases, addresses are also used to indicate from where and whom the data came. We often use these various addresses as a way to verify the sender and the receiver of the data—just like we use postal addresses to ensure a letter gets to the correct person and the return address tells us where it came from. And just like with the postal system, there is no verification of the validity of these addresses. You can put a letter into a mailbox with any return address you want and the letter will still be delivered. Putting a fake destination address does not work as well since the letter will get sent to whatever address is placed on the envelope. The same thing can happen in the Internet. The use of fake source addresses is called address spoofing [7, 8]. Figure 3.4 shows an example of address spoofing.

As we see in the figure, the first example of addressing spoofing is the packet sent by computer C to computer A. The source address is computer D, so when computer C gets the packet it will think the packet came from computer D. This can lead to potential problems if, for example, computer A trusts computer D, and thus treats the packet as a trusted one. The second example shown in the figure shows the user Alice sending a message to the user John. Alice sets the sending address to be the user Mary, so when John gets the message, he will think it came from Mary. We will see in later chapters that in some cases it is easy to spoof an address, and in other cases it can be difficult or impossible.

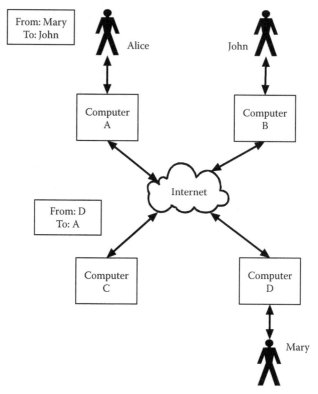

Figure 3.4: Address spoofing.

3.1.2 IP Addresses

The IP address is designed to be a globally unique address within the Internet. The IP address consists of two parts: the network and the host. Therefore, one way to look at the Internet is as a collection of networks, each with an address and each containing some number of hosts. In version 4 of the IP protocol the address space is 32 bits in length. IP addresses are written as four numbers separated by dots. This was done to make it easier to use the number and to make it easier to understand routing and classes. Each of the four numbers represents 8 bits of the 32-bit address.

When the IP protocol was first deployed, there were a very small number of computing devices envisioned on the network. The address space was allocated on a first come, first served basis. The network part of the address is assigned to the requesting organization, and it assigns the host part of the address space. An organization can also divide its address space into smaller networks. To help with routing, a netmask was developed as a way to tell which part of an address

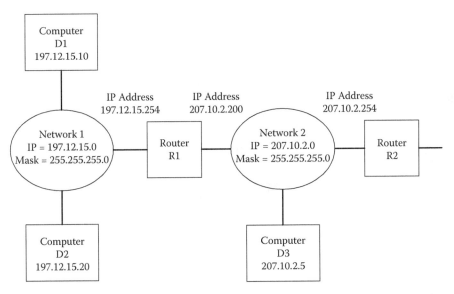

Figure 3.5: Networks in the Internet.

is the network and which part is the host. The netmask is specified like an IP
address with four numbers separated by dots. When converted to its 32-bit binary
value, the bits that are a 1 represent that part of the address that is the network.
For example 255.0.0.0 has the upper 8 bits being 1s, and therefore would be the
netmask for a class A network. Figure 3.5 shows a typical set of networks within
the Internet with their network addresses and netmasks.

3.1.3 Host Name to IP Address Mapping

Most users do not use IP addresses to specify the servers or applications they wish
to connect with. Instead, they use host names and domain names. For example,
when a user sends an email message, he or she uses a domain name as the destination address (e.g., admin@vulcan.dougj.net). When the email application sends
the email message into the network, the IP packet header needs to have the destination IP address in the 32-bit format. The conversion between the domain name and
the IP address takes place using a distributed application called Domain Name
Service (DNS). The application uses a local DNS application to communicate
with the distributed DNS servers to make the translation between the full name
of a host (host name + domain name) and its IP addresses. If we look at a typical
name of a device on the Internet (like a web server), we will see that the name

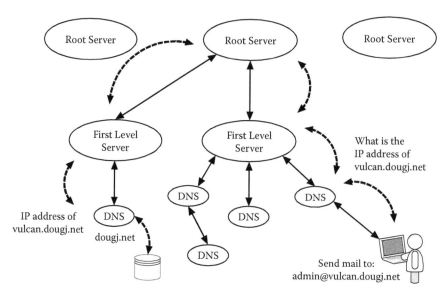

Figure 3.6:   DNS model.

is made of several parts. For example, vulcan.dougj.net is a full name of a host. The name of the computer is vulcan, and the name of the domain is dougj.net. The DNS model is shown in Figure 3.6 [9].

As shown in Figure 3.6, the user wants to send an email message to admin@ vulcan.dougj.net. The email application will query the local DNS application, which in turn will query the next DNS server. The DNS system is laid out in a tree structure with a set of root DNS servers that have knowledge about the location of all of the first-level domain servers. A first-level domain server has information about the IP addresses of every host within its domain or knows which DNS server within its domain to ask. The hierarchical approach allows a DNS server to distribute the knowledge based on administrative control of the name to IP address mapping. We will discuss the security of the DNS protocol later in the book. For now, we just need to know that when a machine wants to know the IP address of a host given the machine name, it asks its DNS server, which in turn will get the answer. The answer may already be in its cache, or it may have to ask the root server where to find the answer. As Figure 3.6 shows, the request (represented by the dashed lines) propagates through the root server to the DNS server that knows the answer, and the response propagates back.

Definitions

Address spoofing.

Changing the source address of the packet to a value that does not belong to the device that is sending the packet.

Domain name.

The name of an organizational unit that consists of one or more networks with one or more hosts attached. Domains must be unique within the Internet.

Domain Name Service (DNS).

A collection of distributed servers that is responsible for converting full domain names into IP addresses.

Full domain name.

The combination of the host name and domain name used to create a unique device identifier within the Internet.

Host name.

The name of the device in a domain. The host name must be unique within the domain.

IP address.

The address used to uniquely identify every device on the Internet.

Netmask.

A 32-bit value that is used to indicate which part of an IP address represents the network and which part represents the host.

Network layer ID.

An identifier placed in the header of the physical network layer to indicate which upper-layer protocol is contained in the payload.

Subnet.

This occurs when a range of IP addresses are divided into multiple networks using a router.

3.2 Client-Server Model

A concept that is pervasive throughout the Internet is one of a client application talking to a server application, which is called the client-server model [1, 10]. The client-server model is more of a definition than a standard. In the Internet a server is defined as an application that waits for another application to connect. The

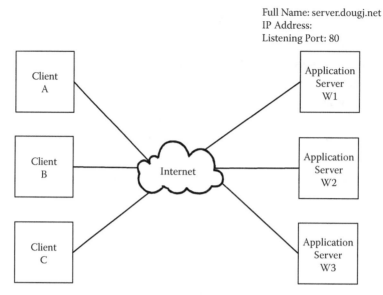

Figure 3.7:   Client-server model.

server often waits on a well-known port number for a client to connect [1, 5, 6]. Figure 3.7 shows several client applications using the Internet to connect to server applications.

As shown in Figure 3.7, the server applications are located on computers with full host names and IP addresses, and the applications are assigned application addresses (listening port numbers). In the figure the three applications are each waiting on port 80 (the same port used by web servers). The client application will initiate the connection with a waiting server by specifying the destination IP address and destination port number. The client may use the DNS system to convert the full domain name of the server into the IP address of the server.

To initiate the waiting for a connection, a server application will ask the operating system to open a connection to the TCP layer (a socket) and to listen for incoming connections that are destined for a certain port number (the listening port). Figure 3.8 shows two clients and two servers and the process they go through to start communications. Each server on the same host listens on a different port, and the clients must specify the destination port number along with the destination IP address when making the connection. The socket is a name given to the connection between the application and the operating system and is defined by the listening IP address and port number. Only one application can listen on a given port that is associated with a given destination IP address. If there

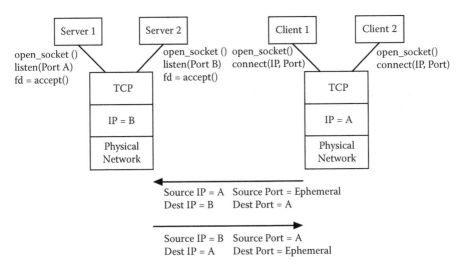

Figure 3.8: Client-server model connections.

are multiple IP addresses associated with the computer, the application needs to indicate the destination IP address on which it is listening.

As we see in Figure 3.8, servers 1 and 2 each open a socket and tell the TCP layer what port they wish to listen on, and then wait for a connection from a client. When the client connects to the server, the accept call will return with an open connection to the client. The server will use this open connection to send and receive data from the client application.

The client also needs to interact with the operating system in order to start a connection. The client will open a socket and can either pick its source port number or let the operating system pick a source port for it. When the operating system picks the source port for the client, it is called the ephemeral port. Just as with the server, only one client application can use a given source port at a time. The client specifies both the destination IP address and the destination port number of the application it wishes to connect to.

The client initiates the connection by sending the first packet with the destination IP address that matches the server host and the application port number matching the server application. Table 3.2 shows the IP addresses and port numbers for packets from the client to the server and the packets returning. These four numbers (IP addresses and ports) for the two types of packets (client to server and server to client) are intended to be globally unique within the Internet.

If a packet arrives at the destination and there is no application waiting, the packet is rejected. How the packet is rejected will be discussed in a later chapter.

TABLE 3.2:   Packet Addressing

<table>
<tr><td colspan="2" align="center">Packets from Client to Server</td></tr>
<tr><td>Source IP</td><td>Client's IP address</td></tr>
<tr><td>Destination IP</td><td>IP server's IP address</td></tr>
<tr><td>Source port</td><td>Ephemeral port</td></tr>
<tr><td>Destination port</td><td>Server's port number (often well known)</td></tr>
<tr><td colspan="2" align="center">Packets from Server to Client</td></tr>
<tr><td>Source IP</td><td>Server's IP address</td></tr>
<tr><td>Destination IP</td><td>Client's IP address</td></tr>
<tr><td>Source port</td><td>Server's port number (often well known)</td></tr>
<tr><td>Destination port</td><td>Ephemeral port</td></tr>
</table>

A question should come to mind. If only one application can open a given port number, then how does an application server like a web server support multiple connections, even from the same client? To understand this, we need to first examine how the server handles incoming connections. When a connection arrives, the operating system returns a new connection to the operating system that the server will now use to communicate with the client. This is shown in Figure 3.8 as the accept function, which is returning a new connection identifier. The server can then spawn off (create) a new process to handle the connection with that client. The parent server application will wait for another connection from a client.

To see how the same client application from the same host makes multiple connections to the same server application, we need to look at how the client application handles multiple connections. Each connection from a client on a given host would be given a different ephemeral port number by the operating system. So for a client application with two connections open to the same server, the two packets would have different ephemeral ports. A good example of this is two windows open in the same web browser to the same web site. As stated earlier, every client and server connection is unique and is distinguished from every other connection by the 4-tuple consisting of IP addresses and port numbers. Figure 3.9 illustrates several clients connecting to a couple of web servers whose well-known port is 80.

There are five connections shown in Figure 3.9, with each connection consisting of a different 4-tuple as shown in Table 3.3. Notice how the 4-tuple for each packet that is destined for the server is different, and therefore each return packet will

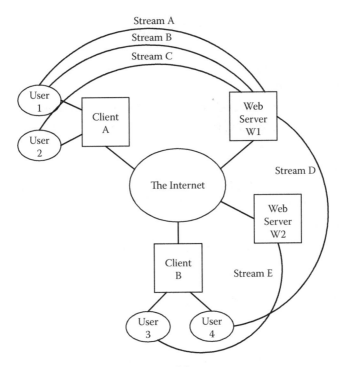

Figure 3.9: Multiple client-server model.

be different. Also notice that the ephemeral ports used by client B do not have to be different than the ephemeral ports used by client A since the source IP addresses are different.

We will see later in the book that this 4-tuple can be used by network-based security devices to help keep track of the connections and to help filter traffic-based active connections.

TABLE 3.3: Stream Addresses

Stream	Source IP	Destination IP	Source Port	Destination Port
A	A	W1	Ephemeral A1	80
B	A	W1	Ephemeral A2	80
C	A	W1	Ephemeral A3	80
D	B	W1	Ephemeral B1	80
E	B	W2	Ephemeral B2	80

Definitions

Client.

The application that initiates the connection to a waiting server.

Connection 4-tuple.

Four addresses that uniquely identify each connection in the Internet. It consists of the source and destination IP addresses and the source and destination port numbers.

Ephemeral port.

The port number provided by the operating system typically to a client as its source port number.

Listening port.

The port number used by a server application to wait for a connection from a client.

Server.

The application that waits for a client application to connect with it. A server typically provides services to the client.

Socket.

A connection between the application layer and the TCP layer that allows a server to specify the IP address and port number to wait on, and allows a client to specify the destination IP address and port number.

Well-known port.

The same as the listening port, but a port number that is the default port number of the server application and is known by all client applications that interact with the server. For example, port 80 is the well-known port for web traffic.

3.3 Routing

One key function of the Internet is its ability to route packets from the source to the destination across multiple networks, each owned or controlled by different organizations. There have been numerous research projects and articles written about routing and how to efficiently route traffic [11]. For the purpose of this book, we will deal with routing as a simple function provided by a set of interconnected devices called routers. We will assume the routers have methods to determine where to send a packet in order to get the packet to the destination. There are attacks on the protocols routers use to determine the route of the packet, and we will discuss those in a later chapter. Before we look at routing in the Internet it would be useful to look back at the early networks.

The first networks were based on the same concepts as the telephone system, where a route was established between the source and destination before any traffic could pass, and all traffic followed the same path. This connection-oriented network made it easy to send and receive data since the data arrived in order. The complexity in this type of network comes from the requirement of a global view of all devices in order to establish the route. The intermediate devices do not need to know anything about the network and only react to commands given by the global network management system.

The Internet uses a connectionless approach where each packet is handled separately by each router. Packets are sent from the source device to the next device that can handle the packet. That device then looks at its local route table and determines where to send the packet next. Note that even a computer connected to the Internet needs to know how to route traffic and therefore has a route table. These local route tables can be static or dynamic [12]. A static route table is set up when the device is configured and does not change unless the device is reconfigured. Static routes are most commonly found in the computers connected to a network and in networks with only one route out of the network. In a dynamic route table there are protocols that update the table based on various factors. The dynamic route table is beyond the scope of this chapter. Whether the route tables are updated dynamically or are static, routing still works the same way. The benefits of dynamic versus static routing can best be shown in Figure 3.10.

As we see in Figure 3.10, host H1 would not benefit from a dynamic route since there is only one path to leave the network, and that is through router R1. Likewise, router R1 only has a couple of paths and may not benefit from a dynamic route. If we look at other routers in the diagram we see there are multiple paths to get a packet across the network. In this case a dynamic route table would make sense.

Every device connected to a network has a route table that shows each possible destination it could send the packet to next. The next hop is specified by an IP address and an interface (routers, for example, might have two or more interfaces). At first glance this might seem to make the table very large if every possible destination needs to have an entry. The best way to look at the routing table is by looking at the possible destinations for the packet. The destination is represented by a network address, which consists of an address and a network mask. Figure 3.11 shows a network and the routing tables for several devices.

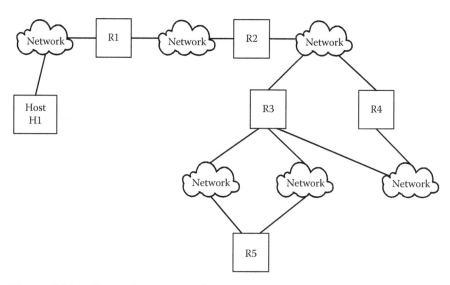

Figure 3.10: Dynamic versus static routing.

As we see in Figure 3.11, the computer connected to network 1 has two choices for destinations: computers connected to network 1 and everywhere else. The routing table has two entries. The first entry is for a destination address matching any computer on network 1. The computer can send a packet directly to any

Destination	Next Hop
Network 1	Direct
Default	Router R1

Destination	Next Hop
Network 1	Direct
Network 2	Direct
Default	Router R2

Figure 3.11: Routing example.

computer on network 1 without a router. The second choice is any computer not on network 1. The choice is referred to as the default route and is the route taken when all other destinations do not match. In this case the default route is through router R1.

If we look at router R1 it has three possible destinations: computers on network 1, computers on network 2, and everywhere else. Therefore, there are three entries in the table corresponding to the three choices. For this example the tables have been simplified; a more detailed discussion of routing and how it relates to security will occur in Part II of the book.

Definitions

Default route.
The route that is taken when the destination address does not match any of the destinations in the route table.

Dynamic route.
A route table or route table entry that changes based on external information obtained using special protocols.

Route table.
A list of possible destinations for a packet to be sent by a device. The destinations are typically either a device or a router.

Routing.
The act of moving packets from one device to another through a series of networks interconnected with routers.

Static route.
A route table or entry in a route table that only changes when the system is configured or reconfigured.

Homework Problems and Lab Experiments

Homework Problems

1. Find one or two maps of the topology of the Internet. Comment on their accuracy.

2. Approximately how many well-known ports have been specified in the Internet?

3. Does this number represent all of the unique applications on the Internet?

4. What would happen if a client application uses the wrong port number to identify the server application?

5. What happens if a server application is waiting on a port other than the well-known port?

6. Does an application have to use the well-known port that it has been assigned?

7. Can you think of any reason why a server application would want to use a port other than its well-known port number?

8. Identify each of the components of an address (hardware, computer [name and IP address], application, and user) for each item below (indicate which address components do not apply). Also indicate how you can determine the value of the address components you may not know.

   a. Email address of admin@dougj.net

   b. Web address of http://www.dougj.net

   c. Web address of http://129.186.215.40

   d. FTP address of vulcan.dougj.net

9. Can you think of any reason why you may want to spoof the hardware address (change the hardware address of the device)?

10. What is the total number of IP version 4 addresses?

11. Find the IP addresses of the root DNS servers.

12. Does every packet between two applications have to take the same route? Explain your answer.

13. What are some advantages in using a connectionless approach to routing within the Internet?

Lab Experiments

1. Develop a list of at least five web sites and five email servers that you think are geographically dispersed across the Internet.

2. Using DNS (a program called nslookup or dig), look up the IP addresses of each of the sites from experiment 1. For the email servers you will need to set the DNS query type to MX. See the man page for running the program.

3. Using the same program, look up the names of machines with an IP address close to the IP addresses of the web sites (use the same first three octets of the IP address and vary the last octet). How could an attacker use this process?

4. Using the program traceroute on a UNIX-based computer or tracert on a Windows-based computer, find the path from a host on your network to the servers listed in experiment 1.

   a. Using the data returned, draw a diagram of the paths out to these sites.

   b. Can you determine the geographical region of where these sites are located?

   c. How many of the routers are part of your organization's network?

   d. Can you determine the name of your Internet service provider (ISP)?

5. Using the program ping, determine the average round-trip time for packets going to the servers listed in experiment 1.

   a. Comment on propagation time versus your distance from the servers.

   b. Comment on why some servers may not have answered the ping request.

6. The command "netstat -a" will show all connections on your computer. Use the command to identify the 4-tuple used to identify each client-server connection.

References

[1] Comer, D. E. 1995. *Internetworking with TCP/IP*. Vol. 1. *Principles, protocols and architecture*. Englewood Cliffs, NJ: Prentice Hall.

[2] Calvert, K. I., M. B. Doar, and E. W. Zegura. 1997. Modeling Internet topology. *IEEE Communications Magazine* 35:160–63.

[3] Subramanian, L., et al. 2002. Characterizing the Internet hierarchy from multiple vantage points. In *INFOCOM 2002: Proceedings of the Twenty-First Annual Joint Conference of the IEEE Computer and Communications Societies*, 2. New York, NY.

[4] Kurose, J. F., and K. W. Ross. 2003. *Computer networking: A top-down approach featuring the Internet*. Reading, MA: Addison-Wesley.

[5] Postel, J. 1981. *Assigned numbers*. RFC 790.

[6] Postel, J. 1981. *Internet protocol*. RFC 791.

[7] Heberlein, L. T., and M. Bishop. 1996. Attack class: Address spoofing. In *Proceedings of the 19th National Information Systems Security Conference*, Baltimore, MD: 371–77.

[8] Bellovin, S. M. 1989. Security problems in the TCP/IP protocol suite. *ACM SIGCOMM Computer Communication Review* 19:32–48.

[9] Mockapetris, P., and K. J. Dunlap. 1988. Development of the domain name system. *SIGCOMM Computer Communication Review* 18:123–33.

[10] Stevens, W. R., and T. Narten. 1990. Unix network programming. *ACM SIGCOMM Computer Communication Review* 20:8–9.

[11] Huitema, C. 1995. *Routing in the Internet*. Upper Saddle River, NJ: Prentice-Hall.

[12] Halabi, B., S. Halabi, and D. McPherson. 2000. *Internet routing architectures*. Indianapolis, IN: Cisco Press.

Chapter 4

Taxonomy of Network-Based Vulnerabilities

In this chapter we introduce the taxonomy to classify network vulnerabilities and to help understand the types of attacks that can be used against the various protocols discussed throughout the remainder of the book. There are many different ways we can categorize the types of attacks and vulnerabilities seen in computers and networks. As we examine the vulnerabilities for each protocol discussed in the remaining chapters, we will place them into one of four categories. By providing categories of vulnerabilities and attacks we can start to group the defense mechanisms in hope that a single defense mechanism will mitigate multiple attacks.

4.1   Network Security Threat Model

Before we develop the taxonomy, we need to look at a network threat model that will show the possible points of attack in the network. If we take another look at the layered model of the network, as shown in Figure 4.1 we can see that each layer receives information from the layer below it and passes information to the layer above it. As shown in Figure 4.1, the packet received by a layer is treated as input to a program (the layer), and the input is processed and the layer produces output. That output may go up to the next layer, may go back down to the lower layer, or may do both. As we also saw earlier, the payload of each packet is not analyzed by the layer and is just passed on to the next layer. This allows an attacker to insert data into any layer by packaging up the data as payload and encapsulating the payload in the appropriate headers. In this model even the user is considered a layer that will receive data from the application layer (the lower layer) and process that data.

Figure 4.2 shows a more complete version of the concepts shown in Figure 4.1. Figure 4.2 shows the network protocol stack of two computers connected via the Internet. As we saw earlier in the book, there are numerous protocols that must cooperate in order for the network to function. Any of these protocols can be attacked. Attackers use their knowledge of the protocol and the protocol

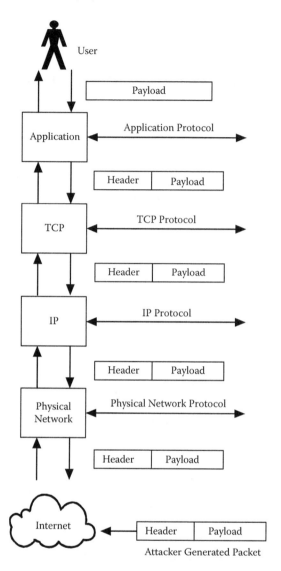

Figure 4.1:　Layered model of attack data.

implementation to create the attacks. An attacker can create and send a packet to any open application on the Internet or target any of the layers. For example, an attacker might create a packet that the IP protocol does not understand and that causes certain implementations of the protocol to crash. Or an attacker might violate the application protocol, thus causing the application to fail. An attacker might create data for the user that causes the user to violate security. We can view every protocol layer as a program that accepts input in the form of packets

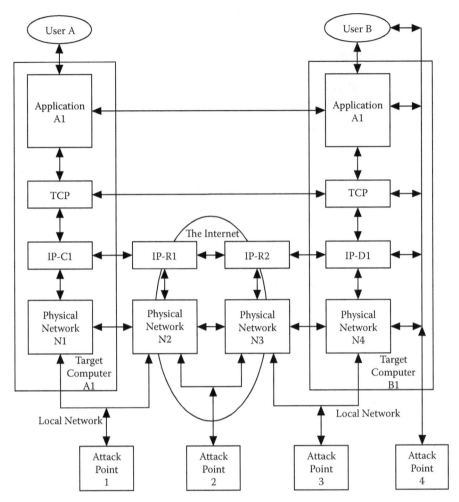

Figure 4.2: Network security threat model.

and produces output. An attacker can interact with the victim's protocol layer by sending a packet to the layer.

Figure 4.2 also shows possible attack points when two computers are communicating. These attack points depend on where the two computers are located and where the attacker is located. An attacker can be located on the local network of either of the two computers, as shown in attack points 1 and 3. In this case, the attacker can attack any layer of a computer located on the same network. So, for example, attack point 1 can attack all four layers on the target computer A1. Attack point 2 shows an attacker on the Internet, in which case the attacker can attack the TCP and application layer protocols of computers A1 and B1, and can attack the IP layer of all devices between the attacker and the target computer.

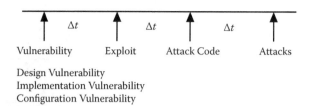

Figure 4.3: Relationship between vulnerabilities, exploits, and attacks.

Another attack point is where the attacker has taken over the target computer. This is shown as attack point 4 in Figure 4.2. Most of the attacks launched by an attacker from attack point 4 are beyond the scope of this book and deal with the security of the computer and operating system. From a network security standpoint, attack point 4 looks like using any computer on the Internet to attack the target. A big difference is that if an attacker has gained access to one of the two computers used to communicate, then the attacker could bypass many of the security protocols. For example, if the data transfer between computer A1 and computer B1 is encrypted, an attacker on the network would not be able to read the data; however, if the attacker has gained access to computer B1 and all of its files, then the encrypted file transfer would not protect the storage of the file.

In Figure 4.2 we outlined several possible attacks and attack points. In order for an attack to be successful, the protocol or application must be vulnerable to the attack. There are several terms that are used in computer and network security that we need to understand. Vulnerabilities are weaknesses in the design or implementation of a protocol or application that an attacker can use to his or her advantage [1–3]. An exploit is a method to take advantage of the vulnerability, and an attack is using the exploit against the vulnerable protocol or application. Figure 4.3 shows the relationships among vulnerabilities, exploits, attack implementation, and attacks.

As we see in Figure 4.3, vulnerabilities can exist in the design, implementation, or configuration. Often the vulnerabilities in the protocol or application design exist because of the nature of the way protocols are created and written, as we discussed in Chapters 1 and 2. In some cases there is a design flaw in the specification itself. Design vulnerabilities often cannot be easily mitigated in the protocol itself, and often we rely on the higher-layer protocols to mitigate the vulnerability [4]. Fixing design vulnerabilities in applications requires a new version of the application that may also prove to be difficult to deploy. A design flaw might also be just an oversight concerning the security implications of the protocol or not designing security into the protocol.

Implementation vulnerabilities exist when during the implementation of the protocol or application there was either an error in the code, a misinterpretation in the specification, or maybe an unforeseen method of attack was discovered. There have been cases where the specification itself had conflicts and, depending on which part of the specification was used for the implementation, vulnerabilities were introduced. Implementation vulnerabilities can be very difficult to find, but often are easy to fix once discovered.

Configuration vulnerabilities occur when the user either configures the system incorrectly or uses the system defaults. The most common are authentication problems when the system default passwords are not changed. There are several web sites where you can get lists of default passwords for many devices.

Vulnerabilities may be present for years before someone discovers them [5, 6]. Even if the vulnerability is discovered, there may not be an easy way to exploit it. The time between when a vulnerability is discovered and an exploit is designed can take anywhere from days to months. Once the exploit has been devised, there may be a period of time before the attack code is created. Sometimes the exploit is demonstrated as attack code, and therefore the time between exploit and attack code is zero. The time between attack code and widespread attacks can also vary, depending on the type and distribution methods of the attack code. In many cases the exploit has been demonstrated but the attack code exists in very rough form and is not widely available. There is something called a zero-day exploit, which is where the exploit and corresponding attack code are used before the vulnerability is widely known [7].

Attack code will often be made available on the Internet, where other users will modify and improve the code. Sometimes there is a time delay between when the attack code is first made public and widespread usage occurs. Attack code is like any other code that goes through changes and enhancements. The attack code itself may also have vulnerabilities.

In Figure 4.3 we see a correlation between vulnerabilities and the attacks. However, an attacker does not need to know about the correlation and can use the attack code against any device on the Internet. The Internet has made attack code readily available to anyone who wants to use it.

We have seen the number of attacks increase over time. Figure 4.4 provides a timeline of attacks, and while this list is not meant to be exhaustive, it should give the reader some idea of issues facing network and computer administrators [8]. As we see in the figure, early events occurred with a lower frequency than current events. The first widespread network-based attack was in 1988. In the 1990s we saw an increase in network-based viruses that targeted applications like email. In

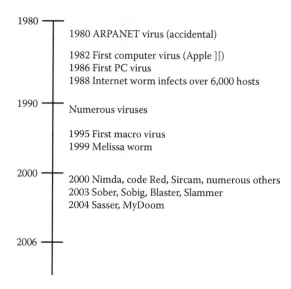

Figure 4.4: Attack timeline.

the 2000s we have seen an increase in the number of attacks transported by the network. We have also seen attack codes change rapidly over time in an effort to avoid detection. We leave it up to reader to study the history and frequency of different types of attacks.

One misconception is that the attackers are sophisticated computer programmers that have a deep understanding of computers and networks. While there are a number of these people creating attacks, there are also a larger number of people that just use attack code created by others. The users of the attack code do not need to understand the vulnerability, the exploit, or the code itself. These types of attackers are often called script kiddies. The attack code can be launched against devices that do not have the underlying vulnerability, and in most cases the attack will cause no damage to the targeted device. There are cases where attack code will cause unexpected side effects that can cause damage. Most often the damage is a large increase in network traffic that can slow down the network. As we will see in Part IV of the book, when we talk about network-wide security solutions, these script kiddie attacks often make it more difficult to detect the attacks that do target vulnerabilities on our systems.

Before we discuss the taxonomy, we should talk about risk assessment [9–14]. Risk assessment is a process where you decide how important something is and how hard you are going to work to protect it. The idea is that not every device needs to be protected at the same level. There are numerous books and other resources dedicated to risk assessment, and there are consulting firms that make a business out of performing risk assessment of organizations. The goal of this book is not to provide an in-depth study of risk, but to give the reader insight into the existence of and the need for risk assessment. The risk associated with a given device is made up of several factors. A common description of risk is a combination of threats, vulnerabilities, and impact.

The concept of threats deals with the measure of how likely it is that the device or application will be attacked. For example, the web server placed on the public Internet has a high probability of being attacked, while an internal server that cannot be accessed from the Internet would have a lower probability of being attacked by an attacker from the Internet. Threat can be a very hard factor to quantify and depends on what type of attack is of concern. For example, looking at an internal server, we stated the threat is low from an Internet-based attack; however, the threat might be high if you consider that an employee may be determined to steal information.

The impact is a nebulous factor that is based on the overall impact a security breach would have on the organization. Again, looking at the external public web server, the impact of losing the web server might be considered low since the data is all public. However, the impact of losing data that consists of employee or customer records would be very high.

A relationship between the factors can be shown in Figure 4.5. The figure is meant to be a representation of the relationship between the three factors, and as you might imagine, finding the best solution can be very complex. As you can tell from the brief discussion, an analysis of the risk of each device can be a complex process.

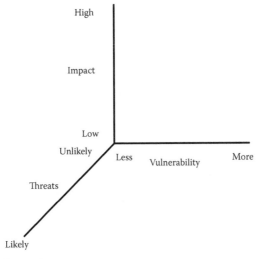

Figure 4.5: Risk graph.

Definitions

Attack code.

A program or other implementation of an exploit used to attack the vulnerability in a system.

Attacks.

The use of the attack code against a device.

Exploit.

A method to take advantage of the vulnerability in a device; the method has not been implemented.

Impact.

A measure of what would happen if the device or object was compromised as the result of a security breach.

Risk.

A measure of how critical something is based on several metrics.

Risk assessment.

A process or procedure to determine the level of risk associated with a device or object.

Threat.

A measure of how likely it is that a device or object will be attacked.

Vulnerability.

A weakness in a protocol, application, or other aspect of the network that can be used to attack the device.

Zero-day exploit.

Where the attack code is used to attack a system before the vulnerability or exploit is known outside the developers of the attack code.

4.2   The Taxonomy

Now that we have looked at possible attack points in the network it would be tempting to classify attacks based on the protocol, layer, or application they targeted. There have been many different types of taxonomies proposed over the years with different goals in mind [15–19]. Some of them have been designed to help study the evolution of attacks and to classify attack code. For the purpose of this book, the author proposes another taxonomy that focuses on network security.

This network security taxonomy consists of four categories of vulnerabilities that can be played out against any layer or protocol: header based, protocol based, authentication based, and traffic based. These categories are defined in the following sections with simple examples. Following the description of the taxonomy is a short discussion on how to apply it.

4.2.1 Header-Based Vulnerabilities and Attacks

Header-based vulnerabilities are when the protocol header is created in violation of the standard, such as using invalid values in a field in a header. As we saw in a previous chapter, each layer adds a header to the data it receives (the payload) from the upper layer. This header is used by the layer to carry out the function of the protocol and to communicate with its corresponding layer. For example, one attack would be setting all of the bits to zero in a control field when the standard calls for at least one bit being set. An attacker could also create invalid headers, where the header is too long or too short. This is often seen in freeform headers. Most protocol specifications do not cover the intentional corruption of packet headers, and therefore the consequences of these attacks often are implementation dependent. Different implementations of a protocol will handle these header violations differently.

One of the more famous header-based attacks was the ping of death [20]. Someone discovered that certain operating systems did not handle invalid values in the IP header. The problem was with the way the IP protocol handled segmentation and reassembly. In the IP header there is a length field that indicates the length of the IP packet and an offset field that indicates where the segmented packet is to be placed during reassembly. The operating system allocates a buffer that is 64K in length (the maximum length of an IP packet). As shown in Figure 4.6, the attack contained an invalid packet with an offset of 65528, which is the maximum value for the offset. If the length of the packet was greater than 7, then the packet would not fit into the reassembly buffer. All the attacker had to do was send one packet with the offset set to 65528 and the length greater than 7. When packets arrive out of order, the IP protocol handles the packets by placing them in a reassembly buffer based on the offset. In the case of this attack, the last packet arrives first and the IP layer places it in a reassembly buffer. In some implementations the segmented packet payload was copied into the reassembly buffer without checking to see if it would fit and the data was copied past the end of the buffer. This caused some computers to crash. The protocol specification stated that the maximum packet is 64K in length. The implementation did not consider that the offset and length

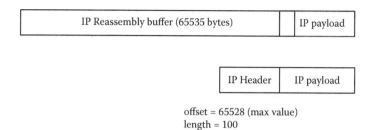

Figure 4.6:   Ping of death example.

could be used to create a packet that was longer than allowed, and the programmers never checked to see if the end of the reassembly buffer had been reached.

Header-based attacks are often easy to fix once discovered, but are difficult to discover since they rely on finding mistakes in the implementation of the protocol.

4.2.2   Protocol-Based Vulnerabilities and Attacks

Protocol-based vulnerabilities are where all of the packets are valid, but they violate the procedural aspect of the protocol. As we saw earlier in this chapter, a protocol consists of a series of packets that are exchanged in a certain order to carry out a function. There are several ways for a protocol-based attack to be carried out, including:

Sending packets out of order

Sending packets too fast or too slow

Not sending packets

Sending valid packets to the wrong layer

Sending valid packets to the wrong multiplexed packet stream

Sending packets out of order can involve sending the wrong packet in response to a packet. An example would be sending an open connection packet in response to a closed connection packet. Another example of out-of-order packets is sending a packet that was not expected, like sending an open connection when the connection is already open. Most of these out-of-order packets are covered in either the protocol specification or during implementation. The most common solution is to just drop the out-of-order or unexpected packet.

The case where packets arrive too fast or too slow is often handled during the implementation and is typically treated as an out-of-order packet or unexpected packet. This type of attack is difficult to carry out on the Internet since the end systems have little control over the speed of the packets. A too-slow attack would be the most common and might be best used on shared applications where you keep the application busy waiting for a packet. These types of attacks are not common, and we do want to make a distinction between sending packets too fast and overwhelming a network with too many packets. Attacks that simply send too much network traffic are categorized in a separate classification in the taxonomy.

The missing packet protocol violation is the most difficult one to handle, since in some cases we do not know how long to wait for a response. Think about the telephone protocol, for example. When you call someone, you expect the called party to say something when they pick up the phone. There is no specified amount of time to wait for them to say something.

One classic protocol-based attack violates the TCP open connection protocol. When TCP opens a connection, the protocol uses what is called a three-way handshake. A simple description of the three-way handshake is when the client sends the first packet requesting a connection with the server, and the server responds with a packet indicating it can accept the connection. When the server does this, it must allocate enough memory to maintain the connection. When the client receives the open acknowledgment from the server, it will send back an acknowledgment and the connection is opened. This is shown in Figure 4.7.

The classic attack (called the SYN flood attack) against the three-way hand-shake is shown in Figure 4.8 [21]. In the SYN flood attack, the attacker sends the open request (called a synchronize [SYN] packet) and the server responds, but the attacker never finishes the three-way handshake by acknowledging the server. This leaves the server in a pending open state waiting for the client acknowledge packet. The attacker sends another open request and does not respond to the server acknowledgment. The attacker continues making requests until all of the server buffer space is allocated and the server cannot accept any additional connections. This is where the name of the attack comes from: the attacker floods the server with SYN packets. There is a timeout specified in the standard for how long to wait for the client to respond to the open connection acknowledgment, but the attacker sends enough requests before the timeout that all of the resources are allocated. This is much more complex to fix, since the time it takes the client to respond is not known and can vary. One fix is to limit the number of connection attempts between a single computer and the server. The attackers circumvented that defense by launching the attack from multiple clients in a coordinated

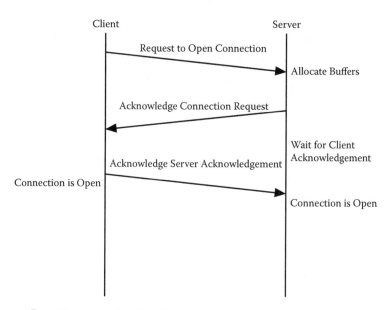

Figure 4.7:   Three-way handshake.

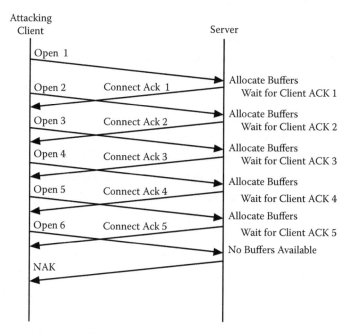

Figure 4.8:   SYN flood attack.

attack. This brings up another issue—that attackers are able to adapt to mitigation methods.

4.2.3 Authentication-Based Vulnerabilities and Attacks

Authentication is the proof of one's identity to another. Authentication is often thought of as a username and password. In network security, authentication is where one layer relies on the identity of another layer to carry out its functions. We have already discussed spoofing, which really is an attack on the authentication of a layer. Before we look at categories of authentication we should look at the parts of the network protocol stack that can rely on authentication. Figure 4.9 shows a network protocol stack with the several possible places where authentication would be needed.

Starting with the user we can see that a user might want to prove who he or she is to another user, which is often called user-to-user authentication. User-to-user authentication is where two or more users prove their identity to each other. This is often done with encryption keys and certificates. This form of authentication is most often found in email and secure documents. This type of authentication can be used as a solution to some network-based attacks. The use of user-to-user authentication will be discussed as a solution where appropriate.

The user may also need to prove who he is to an application, host, or protocol layer before he can gain access, which is often called user-to-host authentication. User-to-host authentication is what everyone thinks about when they look at authentication. The most common form is a username and password that allows the user to prove his identity to the resource requesting authentication and gain access to a server, application, or data. This type of authentication is attacked all of time using many different methods, ranging from trying to break the passwords to guessing the passwords. For the purpose of this book, we will not look at user-to-host authentication except where it is part of the network. For example, in wireless security there is a password used to gain access to a secure wireless network.

In the two previous examples a person was responsible for providing the authentication information. In both cases the network is often used to carry the authentication information and is beyond the scope of this book. However, we will see cases where, because we are using a network to carry authentication information, we introduce a security risk. In those cases we will examine methods to mitigate the risk.

Two other types of authentication involve an application, host, or network as the object providing the authentication.

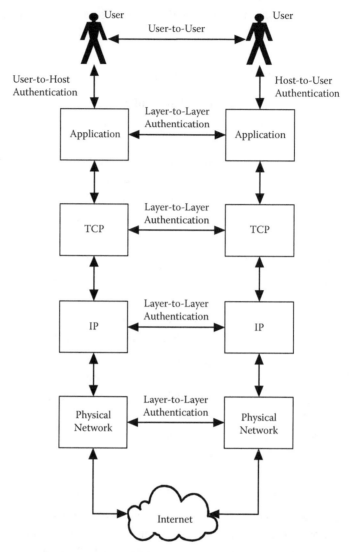

Figure 4.9: Network authentication.

As shown in Figure 4.9 and as we have discussed in the earlier chapters, two layers communicate with a protocol and implied in the communication is the fact that each layer knows the identity of the other. Authentication between two applications, hosts, or network layers is referred to as host-to-host authentication. Host-to-host authentication is where two hosts authenticate each other in order to carry out a function. This is often done using the host or application addresses, like the IP address or hardware address. This form of authentication can be weak because, as we have seen, addresses can be changed.

The final type of authentication is where an application, host, or network layer provides proof to a user of its identity. This is called host-to-user authentication, which allows the user to prove the identity of the host he or she is connecting to. This is often used when a user connects to a secure web site. However, we will see that in many cases the user does not authenticate the host, or the authentication is done using the IP or hardware address, which can cause security problems. We will look at several attacks based on nonexistent or flawed host-to-user authentication.

4.2.4   Traffic-Based Vulnerabilities and Attacks

Traffic-based vulnerabilities and attacks focus on the traffic on the network, either having too much traffic on the network or an attacker being able to capture the traffic and steal the information.

Traffic-based vulnerabilities occur when too much data is sent to a layer or layers and they cannot keep up with the incoming data, which can cause the layer to drop packets or stop handling packets all together. These attacks can be the most devastating to a network and can be caused by a single attacker or by multiple attacking devices working together. We will look at traffic-based attacks throughout the remaining chapters since each layer responds differently to too much traffic. Also, depending on the type of traffic, sending a single packet can cause multiple packets to be sent in response, thus creating a flood of traffic. One example of a single-packet traffic-based vulnerability is where the attacker would send a directed broadcast packet into a remote network that required a response. A broadcast packet is one that is received by all devices on a network. As shown in Figure 4.10, the attack code sends a broadcast packet into a network, and every device on the network gets the request and responds back through the router. If the network is large, a single inbound packet could create hundreds of outbound packets. If the attacker floods the network with the inbound requests, then tens of thousands of outbound packets would be generated per second, which would cause the victim's network to become flooded and make it unusable.

Another type of traffic-based vulnerability is packet sniffing. Packet sniffing is where you capture all of the traffic on a network. Traffic sniffing can be carried

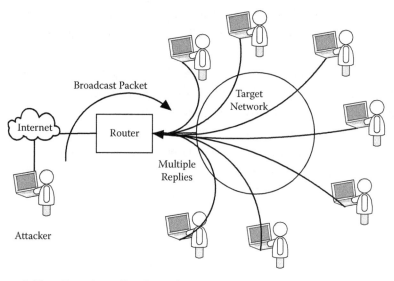

Figure 4.10:   Broadcast flood attack.

out against almost every protocol used in the Internet. The vulnerabilities due to traffic sniffing depend on the protocol.

4.3   Applying the Taxonomy

There are a few comments that can be made about using the taxonomy to classify vulnerabilities and attacks. To start with, the four categories do appear to have some overlap, since authentication-based attacks deal with a goal as well as a method. Header-based, protocol-based, and traffic-based attacks are methods of attack. The best way to help tell the difference is if the goal of breaking authentication is accomplished using one of the other three methods, then it is not classified as an authentication-based attack. For example, if a header-based attack causes the attacker to gain access to a computer, it would be tempting to call that an authentication-based attack, but the method used was header based.

The more complex categorization is when the attacker uses the payload to attack the authentication. This would be classified as an authentication-based attack. Think of it as the method, which in this case would be authentication, which also happens to be the goal.

Another comment on the taxonomy is where the payload is handled and where it fits in the taxonomy. The payload in most cases is the data that is given to the layer above. There are cases, however, when the payload can cause a problem in the lower layers. This often occurs when the payload is too large or contains data that is incompatible with the layer. These types of attacks can be classified as protocol based since the protocol often specifies the size and structure of the payload.

One final comment: No taxonomy can cover all possible attack methods or types of vulnerabilities, and since this taxonomy is designed for network-based attacks, there are many other attacks that do not fit into the taxonomy.

Definitions

Authentication.

Proof of identity.

Authentication-based vulnerability.

A vulnerability in the authentication between applications, hosts, or network layers.

Broadcast packet.

A single packet that can be sent to every host on a network.

Header-based vulnerability.

A vulnerability caused by an invalid header or invalid values in the header.

Host-to-host authentication.

When an application, host, or network layer proves its identity to another application, host, or network layer.

Host-to-user authentication.

When an application, host, or network layer proves its identity to a user.

Ping.

A name given to a protocol that is used to query a device on the network to see if it will respond.

Ping of death.

A well-known header-based attack that uses invalid values in the header of a ping packet.

Protocol-based vulnerability.

A vulnerability using valid packets in a way that violates the protocol between layers.

SYN flood attack.

A well-known attack that violates the three-way handshake, which disables network access for the target system.

Three-way handshake.
An exchange of three packets between a client and server that is often used for establishing a connection.
Traffic-based authentication.
A vulnerability based on the network traffic volume or capturing of network traffic.
User-to-host authentication.
When a user proves his or her identity to an application, host, or network layer.
User-to-user authentication.
When one user proves his or her identity to one or more other users.

Homework Problems and Lab Experiments

Homework Problems

1. Using sites on the Internet, find the default password for several network devices (e.g., wireless access points, routers, firewalls).

2. Develop a more detailed timeline of network-delivered attacks with estimates of the number of systems affected, and also show any relationships between the attacks.

3. Search the Internet for attack tools and list several in a table. Categorize the tools based on the layer that they attack and, if possible, how they apply to the taxonomy.

4. There are several sites on the Internet that contain vulnerability databases. Find the location of the CVE database and determine how many vulnerabilities are in it. Comment on how the database could be used for good and for attacking.

5. If a vendor discovers a vulnerability in its code, does it always need to fix the vulnerability? Explain your answer.

6. Can a vendor always find a fix for every vulnerability? Explain your answer.

Lab Experiments

1. Using the IDS connected to your test network, determine how many attacks have been launched against your network in the past day, week, and month.

2. Look up the five most common attacks found by the IDS in the CVE database and determine if there is a pattern. Also comment on if the attacks could have worked in the test network.

3. Using Nessus, perform a vulnerability scan of the test network and comment on what was found.

References

[1] Chien, E., and P. Ször. 2002. Blended attacks, exploits, vulnerabilities and buffer-overflow techniques in computer viruses. *VIRUS* 1.

[2] Whalen, S., M. Bishop, and S. Engle. 2005. *Protocol vulnerability analysis*. Technical Report CSE-2005-04, Department of Computer Science, University of California, Davis.

[3] Ramakrishnan, C. R., and R. Sekar. 2002. Model-based analysis of configuration vulnerabilities. *Journal of Computer Security*, 10:189–209.

[4] Schneier, B. 1998. Cryptographic design vulnerabilities. *Computer* 31:29–33.

[5] Shuo, C., et al. 2003. A data-driven finite state machine model for analyzing security vulnerabilities. In *Proceedings of 2003 International Conference on Dependable Systems and Networks*. San Francisco, CA.

[6] Ritchey, R. W., and P. Ammann. 2000. Using model checking to analyze network vulnerabilities. In *Proceedings of IEEE Symposium on Security and Privacy 2000*, Oakland, CA: 156–65.

[7] Crandall, J. R., Z. Su, and S. F. Wu. 2005. On deriving unknown vulnerabilities from zero-day polymorphic and metamorphic worm exploits.

In *Proceedings of the 12th ACM Conference on Computer and Communications Security*, Alexandria, VA: 235–48.

[8] Zakon, H. R. 2006. *Hobbes Internet timeline* v8.2, www.zakon.org/robert/internet/timeline/

[9] Gilliam, D., J. Kelly, and M. Bishop. 2000. Reducing software security risk through an integrated approach. In *Proceedings of the Ninth IEEE International Workshops on Enabling Technologies: Infrastructure for Collaborative Enterprises*, Gaithersburg, MD, June, 141–46.

[10] Hoo, K. J. S. 2000. *How much is enough? A risk management approach to computer security*. Stanford, CA: Stanford University.

[11] Stoneburner, G., A. Goguen, and A. Feringa. 2002. *Risk management guide for information technology systems*, 800–30. NIST Special Publication.

[12] Hinde, S. 2003. The law, cybercrime, risk assessment and cyber protection. *Computers and Security* 22:90–95.

[13] McDermott, J., and C. Fox. 1999. Using abuse case models for security requirements analysis. In *Proceedings of 15th Annual Computer Security Applications Conference (ACSAC '99)* Scottsdale, AZ: 55.

[14] Arbaugh, W. A., W. L. Fithen, and J. McHugh. 2000. Windows of vulnerability: A case study analysis. *Computer* 33:52–59.

[15] Venter, H. S., and J. H. P. Eloff. 2003. A taxonomy for information security technologies. *Computers and Security* 22:299–307.

[16] Ali, A., S. Abdulmotaleb El, and M. Ali. 2006. A comprehensive approach to designing Internet security taxonomy. In *Canadian Conference on Electrical and Computer Engineering (CCECE '06)*. Ottawa, Canada, 1316–1319.

[17] Chakrabarti, A., and G. Manimaran. 2002. Internet infrastructure security: A taxonomy. *IEEE Network* 16:13–21.

[18] Irvine, C., and T. Levin. 1999. Toward a taxonomy and costing method for security services. In *Proceedings of the 15th Annual Computer Security Applications Conference (ACSAC '99)*.

[19] Welch, D., and S. Lathrop. 2003. Wireless security threat taxonomy. In *IEEE Systems, Man and Cybernetics Society Information Assurance Workshop.* Washington, DC: 76–83.

[20] Templeton, S. J., and K. Levitt. 2001. A requires/provides model for computer attacks. In *Proceedings of the 2000 Workshop on New Security Paradigms*, Ascona, Switzerland: 31–38.

[21] Garber, L. 2000. Denial-of-service attacks rip the Internet. *Computer* 33:12–17.

Part II

Lower-Layer Security

In Part II we will examine the lower three layers of the Transmission Control Protocol/Internet Protocol (TCP/IP) stack (physical network layer, IP layer, TCP layer). We will provide a brief introduction to the protocols and their vulnerabilities and possible attacks against the protocols. We will also examine general countermeasures for each vulnerability and attack, along with some countermeasures common to vulnerabilities. The lower three layers are common to all the devices interconnected across the Internet, and since they are also part of the operating system, they make good targets for attackers.

Chapter 5

Physical Network Layer Overview

As we saw in Chapter 1, the physical network layer is the lowest layer in the Transmission Control Protocol/Internet Protocol (TCP/IP) stack and is used to provide connection to the network. The services provided by this layer are simple and consist of sending and receiving packets. The TCP/IP protocols are designed to operate on any type of network, and therefore assume a minimal level of service provided by the layer. Even though the physical network layer provides a minimal set of services, the implementation can be complex and subject to attack. We can group the physical network protocols into categories based on the physical medium used to interconnect the devices. The two broad categories are wired and wireless. At the heart of the physical network layer is a network access controller, which is implemented in hardware and used to connect the device to the network medium [1–3]. Figure 5.1 shows a block diagram of a typical physical network layer.

As we see in Figure 5.1, there is a hardware and software component to the layer. The hardware controller, such as the network card in a personal computer, is responsible for the interface to the physical medium, such as network cable, and the conversion from bytes of data to bits to the actual signals sent across the medium on the transmit side, and from the signal back to bytes on the receive side. The hardware controller is also responsible for interfacing with the computer system so the software can move data into the hardware controller, as well as for controlling access to the medium when more than one device wants to talk at once. As you can imagine, there are several vendors of hardware controllers for each physical network layer protocol. And while there may be vulnerabilities with a particular hardware implementation, it is beyond the scope of this book to explore those flaws.

The software section of the layer provides services to the upper layers and maintains the buffers to store the packets waiting to be sent and the received packets. The software also provides the device driver that interfaces with the hardware. The device driver is often provided by the vendor of the hardware controller and provides a standard interface between the hardware and the operating

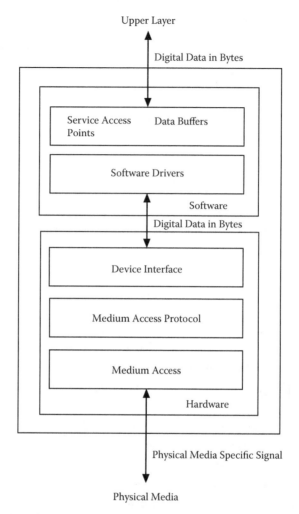

Upper Layer

Digital Data in Bytes

Service Access Points

Data Buffers

Software Drivers

Software

Digital Data in Bytes

Device Interface

Medium Access Protocol

Medium Access

Hardware

Physical Media Specific Signal

Physical Media

Figure 5.1: Physical network layer block diagram.

system. There have been examples of vulnerabilities and attacks against the device drivers and controlling software. These attacks are vendor and implementation specific and are rare. When they do occur, they are typically handled by fixing the code. Attacks against the software drivers are beyond the scope of this book.

In Chapter 5 we will examine the most commonly used wired and wireless protocols in the Internet, which are based on the same basic protocol, called Ethernet. Before we begin the discussion of the protocols there are some common attack methods that are independent of the physical network layer protocol. In the next section we will examine several common attack methods. We will examine methods to mitigate these attacks when we discuss each of the protocols and their vulnerabilities, since the mitigation method is often protocol dependent.

5.1 Common Attack Methods

Even though there are a large number of physical network protocols in existence, there are a few common methods of attack that are independent of the protocol. In this section we will examine three common attack methods that can be used against a physical network layer. The methods to mitigate the attacks are often dependent on the physical network protocols and will be discussed in the following sections.

5.1.1 Hardware Address Spoofing

If we look at the physical network layer packets from a security viewpoint, we need to ask what the destination knows for sure about the identity of the sender and what the sender knows about the identity of the destination. In order to answer that question, we need to look at the source and destination hardware addresses and determine who could have generated the packet with those addresses. If we look at the hardware addresses, the destination knows that a device on the same network actually transmitted the packet. This is because each router that receives a packet and passes it along the way on the Internet rewrites the hardware addresses, as we see in Figure 5.2. Therefore, a destination device knows the packet it just received had to be sent by a device on the same physical network. This does not mean, however, that the originator of the packet was on the same physical network, just that the last device to send the packet was on the same physical network.

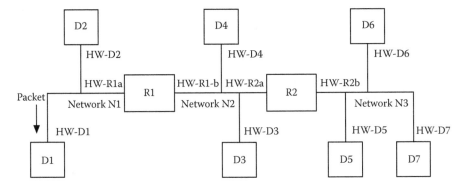

Figure 5.2: Hardware addressing.

If we look at the addresses used in the packet, there is a source address and a destination address. The source address is used to indicate the sender of the packet. For the most part, the source address has no real function in the physical network. One might think that the source address would be used to know how to send a reply packet. However, typically any reply packet will get its source and destination addresses using higher-layer protocols. We will see that sometimes the source hardware address is used by the network to authenticate the device wishing to gain access to the network.

So, for example, Figure 5.2 shows device D1 on network N1 receiving a packet. That packet must have been transmitted by another device on the same network, like device D2 or router R1. If the packet was originated by a device on the other side of router R1 (like device D6), the packet arriving at device D1 will still have the source address of router R1. The destination address is used to determine which device should read the packet from the media. In most local area networks all devices on the network can receive packets that are destined for other devices, and they use the destination address to filter out unwanted packets. So, as shown in Figure 5.2, the packet being read by device D1 will also be received by device D2, but since the destination address does not match, it will be discarded.

So if the attacker wants to spoof the source hardware addresses he or she must have access to the physical network [4, 5]. In other words, a device on another network cannot send a packet with a fake or invalid hardware address to a device on a different network. Figure 5.3 shows several possible outcomes of spoofing the hardware address. In Figure 5.3 there are three networks and three attackers.

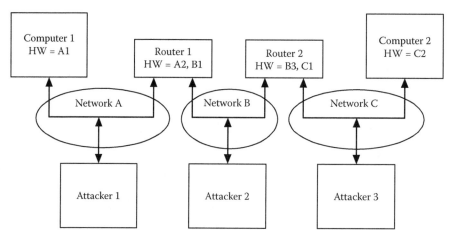

Figure 5.3: Hardware address spoofing and sniffing.

Each device shown in Figure 5.3 has a device hardware address. The device hardware address is used as the source address when the device sends packets into the network, and as a filter to determine which packets the device should read from the network. As we also see in Figure 5.3, some devices (e.g., the routers) have multiple hardware addresses.

Attacker 1 can create packets with any source hardware address it wants. There are some network protocols that use the source hardware to verify the sender as being a valid device on the network. Therefore, an attacker could pretend to be another device on the network. However, if the real device is running at the same time as the fake device (the attacker), the network might not function correctly, which could lead to problems such as preventing both devices from using the network. As we mentioned in Chapter 2, the hardware address is often assigned by the hardware vendor. This may lead one to believe that is it difficult to change the hardware address of a device. In most devices the hardware address is written into the hardware controller when the system boots and can be changed using software.

When creating a fake destination address we know that in order for devices on the network to read the packets, the destination address must match the hardware address of the device. Therefore, in order for any of the devices to read a packet from attacker 1, the attacker must create a packet with a destination address that matches a device on the network. There are a few attacks where using invalid destination addresses could cause network problems. Attacker 1 could create packets where the destination address does not match any machine to possibly confuse a switch or just to generate a large amount of traffic. These types of attacks will be discussed later. Attacker 1 can send packets to network B by sending packets to router 1, but the source hardware address of the packets sent to network B will be the hardware address of router 1, since router 1 will rewrite the hardware addresses. As we saw in Figure 3.3, the destination hardware address is provided by the software using the physical network layer.

5.1.2 Network Sniffing

Most hardware network access controllers use the destination address to tell which packets on the network should be read and sent on to the physical network layer software. This filtering function keeps the device from receiving packets that are not meant for the device. This design was not put in place for security as much as it was devised to reduce the traffic that a device needs to process. It is possible for a network access controller to ignore its destination address and read every packet it receives, which is often called sniffing.

If we refer back to Figure 5.3, we can see that attacker 1 can sniff the traffic on network A, but not the traffic on network B or C. An interesting question is: What about sniffing traffic on an intermediate network like network B? Attacker 2 on network B could sniff any traffic that it can see on network B. If that traffic was between computer 1 and computer 2, then attacker 2 could sniff the traffic between computer 1 and computer 2. This leads to the question: Can attackers sniff traffic on the Internet? Typically the backbone network is physically protected, which makes sniffing the backbone very difficult. In general we do not worry about sniffing once the traffic enters an Internet service provider (ISP). The most common place for packet sniffing is in wireless networks like those located in coffee shops with free wireless Internet access.

5.1.3   Physical Attacks

The network used to interconnect devices is subject to physical attacks [6, 7]. While physical attacks and their mitigation techniques are beyond the scope of this book, it is worth looking at a couple of commonplace physical attacks. For our discussion we will categorize physical attacks into two groups: accidental and deliberate. The deliberate attacks are somewhat obvious and involve physical destruction of the network. The attacks can be against the network cabling or the devices used to interconnect the networks (e.g., routers). Mitigation of deliberate attacks can be difficult and, of course, require some type of physical security. In the case of protection against loss of network connectivity to an ISP, many organizations run multiple connections to multiple ISPs. To be safe, they will make sure the connections take multiple paths leaving the building.

Accidental attacks can be just like deliberate attacks involving the destruction of a device or network such as a cut network cable, a power outage to a router, etc. If they are accidental, then you might not even call them attacks, but they have the same outcome as a deliberate attack and cause the same type of outages. What may be of more interest are accidental physical attacks that come from misconfiguration, or miswiring, or some other nondestructive event. Again, we will not go into much detail about these types of attacks or the mitigation methods. There are a few accidental physical attacks that are worth discussing since they are common (at least the author has seen them several times):

1. Bad network cable is a problem that seems to occur out of nowhere. A seemingly good cable can fail, and it is often the cable used to connect a critical device.

2. A network cable loop happens when you plug both ends of a network cable into the same device, like a network switch. The author has seen cases when the amount of traffic generated can take down the entire network.

3. Bad network controllers can cause problems either by not allowing the device to communicate with the network or, in some cases, generating bad packets that can cause some network devices to fail.

4. Two network controllers with the same hardware address can cause problems. This can occur if the network controller is reprogrammed with a different hardware address. There are times when it makes sense to change the hardware address, but if this is done incorrectly, it can cause strange problems.

This list is by no means exhaustive, but these problems can make it difficult to deal with the physical network layer and security. Some of these events are caused when the network changes, like when you install a new device, such as a security device. There is not much we can do to prevent these events, but knowing they can occur can help keep the network running.

Definitions

Ethernet.
The most common protocol used in a local area network. Ethernet defines the physical medium and the method that multiple devices can use to share the physical media.

Hardware address spoofing.
Creating packets with a source hardware address that is different than the source address of the sending device. Often the spoofed address is the same as another device on the network.

Network access controller.
The hardware part of the network device that interfaces the device with the physical network.

Network sniffing.
Capturing the packets on a network independent of their destination address. When a device is configured to sniff the traffic, it is placed in what is often called a promiscuous mode.

Wired network.
A network of devices that are interconnected using physical cabling that can be twisted pair, coaxial cable, fiber optics, etc.

> **Wireless network.**
> A network of devices that are interconnected using a transmitter and receiver that operate in free space. The most common transmission method is radio waves. Other methods include microwave and light.

5.2   Wired Network Protocols

There have been numerous wired network protocols introduced over the past 30 years. They have ranged from protocols that work over the phone lines to high-speed fiber optic networks. As we have discussed, the Internet consists of millions of interconnected networks using other networks. What has happened over the past decade is that we have seen wired networks divided based on usage. There are a set of wired network protocols that are used primarily by ISPs to provide high-speed connectivity between networks, and there are network protocols used to provide connectivity in smaller networks, often called local area networks (LANs). The network protocols used by ISPs vary based on the speed of data transfer, distance between nodes, and environment. These networks are often called wide area networks (WANs). For the purpose of this book, we will not examine the wide area networks and protocols. However, many of the attacks that could be used against local area networks can also be used against wide area networks.

5.2.1   Ethernet Protocol

There have been several protocols proposed over the years for local area networks, but the Ethernet protocol has emerged as the dominant protocol and is the most common interconnection method for local area networks in use today. In this section we will discuss the Ethernet protocol and the various technologies that are used to implement an Ethernet local area network.

Ethernet is available in several different data rates and media formats. A naming convention was developed to help classify different types of Ethernet. Ethernet is part of the IEEE 802 standard [3]. IEEE 802.3 is wired Ethernet, and IEEE 802.11 is wireless Ethernet. Wireless Ethernet will be discussed in Section 5.3. For wired Ethernet the naming convention is (speed in Mbps)base(wire type). Table 5.1 shows some of the common Ethernet names [8].

The wire types specified in the table are coax, which is center conductor surrounded by a wire mesh. This type of wire is most often seen today in video

TABLE 5.1: Common Ethernet Types

Name	Speed	Wire Type	Maximum Distance between Devices
10Base2	10 Mbps	Coax	185 m
10BaseF	10 Mbps	Fiber	500 m
10BaseT	10 Mbps	Twisted pair	100 m
100BaseT	100 Mbps	Twisted pair	100 m
100BaseFX	100 Mbps	Fiber	1,000 m
1000BaseX	1,000 Mbps	Fiber or coax	Depends on cable type

systems. Coax provides high data rates. Fiber is a glass cable used to transmit light. Fiber provides very high data rates over very long distances. Twisted pair is two conductors twisted together and provides data rates that are lower than the other two methods and over shorter distances.

In the early days of Ethernet, coax cable was used to connect devices. This created a single cable for each network, which had problems when new devices were added or removed since the cable needed to be disconnected. The network speed was 10 million bits per second (Mbps). The wired Ethernet uses a "listen before talking" protocol. For this protocol to work, every device needs to be able to "hear" every other device on the same network. Coax cabling worked well for this protocol since every device can receive the packets transmitted by every device on the same network. Figure 5.4 shows a typical coax cable–based Ethernet network. In Figure 5.4 we see devices D1 to D7 and router R1 are connected with coax cable. Figure 5.4 also shows device D6 transmitting a packet and the packet traversing the cable in both directions.

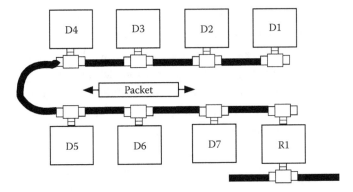

Figure 5.4: Coax cable Ethernet.

The Ethernet protocol is simple in design, and its primary function is to provide access to the shared medium in a manner that will try to give equal access to all devices connected to the same shared medium. The protocol used by wired Ethernet is called Carrier Sense Multiple Access with Collision Detection (CSMA/CD) [9]. The idea behind the protocol is to have the network controller listen to the medium to determine if any other device is transmitting (carrier sense). If no other device is transmitting, then the device will transmit its packet.

Since it is possible for two or more devices to detect silence on the network at the same time, a device that is transmitting must continue to listen while it is transmitting to determine if any other device tries to transmit during the same time, which is referred to as a collision (collision detection). All devices that are transmitting during a collision must continue transmitting for a preset amount of time to ensure that all devices on the network see the collision. Once the colliding devices have finished, they will wait to try again. To ensure they do not all try again at the same time, they pick a random wait time before trying to transmit again. Note that collisions only occur within the shared medium and are not propagated across network devices like routers. This is often defined as a collision domain. Figure 5.5 shows a flowchart of the CSMA/CD Ethernet protocol. As we see in Figure 5.5, the transmitting device will listen while sending, and if there is a collision, the device will send more data and then pick a random number between 1 and N. N will double each time there is a collision for the same packet until N reaches 16. If N reaches 16, then the Ethernet controller will quit trying to send that packet.

A problem with Ethernet is that as the number of devices connected to the same shared media increases, so does the probability of a collision, which can reduce the overall performance of the network. This is also true if there are several devices with a large amount of traffic.

As electronic technologies improved, there was a push to create an Ethernet network where the connections between each device were made directly back to a central point. This enabled easier insertion and removals of devices, and simplified wiring in general, since they moved from coax cable to twisted pair wiring. As discussed earlier in this chapter, in order for the Ethernet protocol to function, each device needs to hear the other devices. To enable this in the early twisted pair systems a device called a hub was used. The hub recreated what existed in a coax cable system by letting every device listen to the traffic from every other device connected to it. In addition, hubs can be cascaded to create a large tree of devices. Figure 5.6 shows a typical configuration using a hub. The first hub-based Ethernet networks had a speed of 10 Mbps. As technology improved, the speed

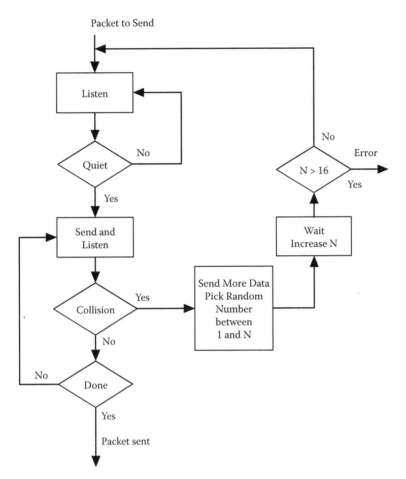

Figure 5.5: CSMA/CD Ethernet protocol.

increased to 100 Mbps. From a security standpoint there was no real difference between hub-based and coax-based systems. In either method every device on the network could listen to the traffic from every other device on the same network. This makes a sniffing attack easy for any device connected to the network.

The next step in the evolution of Ethernet was the introduction of a network switch. The network switch placed intelligence in the device that physically interconnected the computer to the network. The switch was an active part of the Ethernet protocol and created what looked like an individual Ethernet network between each device and the switch. An Ethernet switch maintains a table with the hardware address of every device that is associated with each port on the switch. The Ethernet switch will examine the received packets, and if the destination

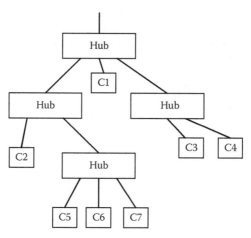

Figure 5.6: Hub configuration.

address matches an address in the table, the packet is only sent to the devices on that port. If there is no match in the table, the packet is sent out on every port, and therefore to every device. Figure 5.7 shows a typical switch configuration with the port tables. Ethernet switches greatly improve the performance of the Ethernet network since collisions (when two or more devices try to talk at once) are reduced and traffic is only sent to the devices that need it.

As we see in Figure 5.7, if device C7 on switch 4, port P4 sends a packet to device C6 on port P3, device C5 will not see the packet. The packet will not be passed to switch 2. If device C7 sends a packet that is destined for router R1, devices C6, C5, C2, and C1 and switch 3 will not see the packet. In addition to isolating traffic, an Ethernet switch can allow the simultaneous transmission and reception of data, which is called full duplex. A hub is half duplex since only one device can talk at a time and all others listen to what is being transmitted. A full-duplex network performs better than a half-duplex network. Ethernet switches have an impact on security and network management. Since a device only sees the traffic that is destined for it, it makes eavesdropping on other devices very difficult. It is not impossible to sniff traffic in a switched network since there are ways of fooling the tables within the switches.

One difficultly that has occurred because of the use of switches in most local area networks is there are times when the network administrator needs to listen to all of the traffic on a network for network diagnostics or performance monitoring. From a network security standpoint, several devices (like intrusion detection systems) need to see all of the traffic on the network to function correctly. This can be

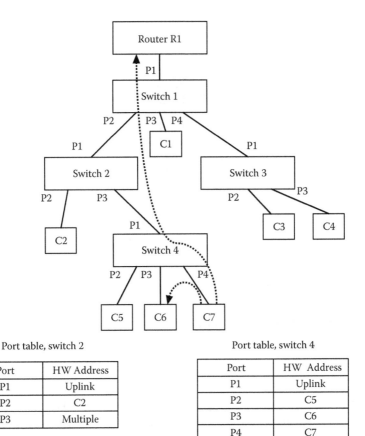

Figure 5.7: Ethernet switch configurations.

Port table, switch 2

Port	HW Address
P1	Uplink
P2	C2
P3	Multiple

Port table, switch 4

Port	HW Address
P1	Uplink
P2	C5
P3	C6
P4	C7

accomplished in several different ways, as shown in Figure 5.8. Many switches
support what is called a spanning port or a mirrored port. A copy of all packets is
sent out on this port. The primary problem is the speed. For example, if every port
on a 16-port switch is 100 Mbps, the spanning port would only be able to pass
100 Mbps, or 1/16 of the total possible traffic. A solution would be to use a hub
with a switch. This also creates a problem since hubs peak out at 100 Mbps half
duplex and Ethernet switches have speeds of up to 10 Gbps. The third solution is a
network tap, which is a device that is inserted inline of the traffic flow and makes
an electronic copy of the data. In a full-duplex network the tap will provide two
output ports. The problem with a tap and a hub is being able to see all traffic. As
shown in Figure 5.8, the tap and hub can only see the traffic between the switch
and the router. This works well for monitoring traffic as it enters and leaves an

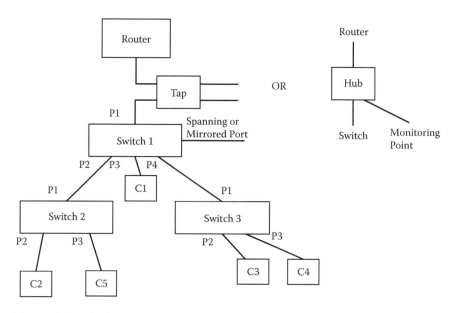

Figure 5.8:   Switch tap points.

organization, but does not provide monitoring of intraorganizational traffic. The functions of each field of the Ethernet packet are described below.

The Ethernet protocol uses a simple packet format, as shown in Figure 5.9. The Ethernet controller is given a frame that consists of the destination address, source address, type/length field, and data. The Ethernet controller will add the other fields of the packet and will likewise strip them off of the received packet. Several of the fields in the Ethernet frame are added by the network controller (preamble, start frame delimiter [SFD], frame check sequence [FCS]). These fields are also stripped off by the receiving network controller. The network controller is the lowest layer in which packets can be extracted from the network by an attacker (or anyone monitoring the network). It should be noted that the packets extracted from the network do not contain the preamble, SFD, or FCS, so when packets are presented to the physical network layer software by the hardware controller, they start with the destination address.

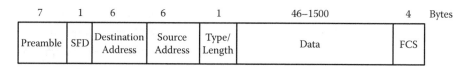

Figure 5.9:   Ethernet frame format.

Preamble: The preamble is a sequence of 7 bytes that are used by the receiver to synchronize its clock to the Ethernet frame. This field is inserted by the hardware controller when the frame is transmitted.

Start frame delimiter (SFD): SFD is 1 byte long and is used to indicate when the preamble is done and the destination address starts. This field is inserted by the hardware controller when the frame is transmitted.

Destination address: A 6-byte value used to identify the destination. This field is supplied to the hardware controller. This is used by the receiving hardware controller to determine if the frame should be read. If it does not match the address of the controller, the remainder of the frame is ignored.

Source address: Address of the sending device is 6 bytes long. This field is supplied to the hardware controller.

Type/length field: A 1-byte value used to identify the lower-layer protocol that should process the packet. This field has two meanings, depending on its value. This was a compromise between two competing standards. If the value in the field is 1,536 (0x600) or greater, then it is a type field and the value indicates the protocol type contained in the data part of the frame. Table 5.2 shows several common values, and as we see, they are Internet protocols. If the value is less than 1,518, then the value is the length of the data field. The most common protocols that use the length field are router protocols.

Data: The data field contains the data. The data field length is limited to 1,500 bytes. This is to help ensure equal access to the media. Ethernet also has a minimum data length, which is 46 bytes. This is needed to make sure the collision detection works. If the upper layer's payload is less than 46 bytes, it must be padded out to 46 bytes. It is the responsibility of the upper layer to handle adding and deleting the pad bytes.

Frame check sequence (FCS): This field is used to help verify that the frame has not been corrupted during transmission. It uses what is called a cyclic redundancy check code. Note that the

Ethernet protocol does not deal with retransmission of frames. When a frame arrives with a bad FCS, the frame is discarded and the receiving hardware controller does not notify the upper layer.

Table 5.2 shows several common values for the type field in the Ethernet frame. Several of these protocols will de discussed in Chapter 6.

TABLE 5.2:   Common Type Field Values

Value in Hex	Protocol
0x800	IP
0x806	ARP
0x86dd	IP version 6

As we saw in Figure 5.9, Ethernet contains two address fields, and as we discussed in Part I of the book, addresses within the same network need to be unique. This is referred to as the hardware address domain. Within the hardware address domain all Ethernet addresses need to be unique. As we saw earlier, devices like routers rewrite the addresses, and therefore create separate hardware address domains.

The Ethernet address is 6 bytes long, and there are three different address types. The most common type is the unicast address, which is used to uniquely identify a single device. The second type is a multicast address, which is used to identify a group of devices. The multicast address is used as a destination address only. In order for multicasting to work, there are protocols that create the groups of devices and assign addresses to the groups. A device will still have its unicast address in addition to any optional multicast addresses. The last address type is the broadcast address, which is only used as a destination address. A frame with the broadcast address as the destination address will be received by every device within the hardware address domain. Table 5.3 shows the values of the three different address types. Note that the common way to represent an Ethernet address is as six hex values separated with colons.

As we discussed before, Ethernet needs to make sure every address within the hardware address domain is unique, which is handled by assigning a unique address to each Ethernet network controller produced. This is done by assigning the upper 3 bytes of the address to the vendors of the hardware controllers, and then allowing the vendors to allocate the lower 3 bytes. The upper 3 bytes can be useful in determining the type of hardware controller used, which can help

TABLE 5.3: Ethernet Address Types

Address Type	Value
Unicast	Upper bit is a 0
Multicast	Upper bit is a 1
Broadcast	FF:FF:FF:FF:FF:FF

diagnose a network problem. However, as we discussed earlier, the hardware address used by the Ethernet controller is stored in read-only memory and is copied into the controller using software at system boot time. This means that the Ethernet address can be changed using software, which enables address spoofing.

There are several vulnerabilities in the Ethernet protocol. These are categorized using the taxonomy and described below along with any countermeasures. It should be noted that many of the countermeasures will actually involve upper-layer protocols and will be discussed in greater detail in later chapters. Also, as discussed in Chapter 3 and in this chapter, attacks against the Ethernet protocol need to take place within the address domain of the Ethernet network. This makes attacks against wired Ethernet somewhat rare.

5.2.2 Header-Based Attacks

Since there are only three fields in the Ethernet header that are not handled by the hardware controller, there are a limited number of header-based attacks. One type of attack is setting the source and destination addresses to be the same. Some network switches have had problems with this in the past. There is no real countermeasure to this attack, other than better security of the devices, since this attack must be played out using a device on the network. Another type of attack is to create packets with the data field either too short (less than 46 bytes) or too long (greater than 1,500 bytes). First, the hardware controller would not allow these packets onto the network, but let us say somehow they did get on the network. The receiving hardware will toss all packets that are either too long or too short.

5.2.3 Protocol-Based Attacks

The wired Ethernet protocol is very simple, and since it is primarily implemented in hardware, it does not have any protocol-based vulnerabilities. The only real protocol-based vulnerability is if a device violates the CSMA/CD protocol. This could happen if the hardware controller fails, which would not be considered an

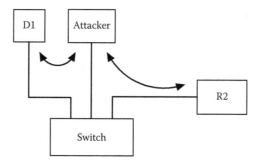

Figure 5.10:   ARP poisoning.

attack. We mention it here only because the behavior of the network with a faulty controller could cause complete network failure and might appear to be an attack.

5.2.4   Authentication-Based Attacks

If we look at the possible places for an authentication-based attack, we focus on the source and destination Ethernet addresses. The destination Ethernet address authenticates the physical network controller connected to the network that should receive the frame. If an attacker could convince a device that the hardware address for the intended destination is the attacker's Ethernet address, then all frames could be read by the attacker. This would work well if the attacker could convince the target device it was the router, and then would route the traffic for the target. This would have the same effect as sniffing the traffic, but could be done in a switched environment. Figure 5.10 shows a possible attack scenario where the attacker becomes the router.

In this example the attacker convinces device D1 that its hardware address is the hardware address of the router R1, and therefore the traffic from D1 to R1 goes to the attacker. Note that since the devices are connected using an Ethernet switch, the attacker would not be able to sniff the traffic from D1. But by making the traffic go to the attacker, it would be able to capture all of the traffic between D1 and the router. The attacker would only need to copy all of the traffic to the router. The attacker also needs to make sure it convinces the router it is D1. This attack is possible because the destination hardware address is obtained using a protocol called the Address Resolution Protocol (ARP), and this attack is called ARP poisoning. ARP is the protocol used by the IP layer to determine the hardware address of the destination device. We will discuss the ARP protocol in more detail in Chapter 6.

There is no good countermeasure for ARP poisoning [10–13]. In order for this attack to work, the attacker must have access to the physical network. There are some physical network layer encryption protocols that could mitigate this attack. These will be discussed in the section on general countermeasures, since they can mitigate several authentication and sniffing attacks.

The source Ethernet address has not traditionally been used for authentication; however, there are several newer security methods that use the source address to authenticate the sender. One of these is called network access control (NAC), which is designed to ensure only valid computers are allowed access to the network. We will discuss NAC in the general countermeasures section of this chapter.

The source address is also used to authenticate a device connected to an ISP. This is common with ISPs that use the cable TV system to provide Internet access. They use the source hardware address to register the device connected to their network. This is done to help ensure no one installs his or her own cable modem without paying the ISP, and in some cases to enable charging for multiple computers in one house. This might be considered a very simple form of NAC. Using the source address to control the number of devices connected to the ISP does not work since most routers available for the consumer market can change their source address. So all a user needs to do is copy the registered Ethernet address to the router.

Another source address authentication-based attack is to send packets with different source addresses in an attempt to either fill an Ethernet switch's tables or to convince the switch to send the packets for another device to you. This attack is specific to the switch vendor. Some switches might default to passing all traffic when their tables fill, or if two ports on the switch have the same source address.

In the case of an attacker using the source address of a device on another port of the switch, some switches might just pass the traffic to both ports, which would enable the attacker to sniff the traffic, or the switch might change the table and the traffic would be sent out the last port where the source address appeared. This, of course, would cause problems since packets from the same upper-layer protocol might get split between two ports. Mitigation of this type of attack is also difficult. There is software that can be used to try and monitor the mapping of the hardware address to ports and devices. Also, the NAC methods can help mitigate this attack.

Another attack that can occur is to set the source address of a device to the same address as another device in the same Ethernet hardware address domain. Ignoring the problems this might cause with switches, as discussed above, can cause problems with the upper-layer protocols. What happens is that when a packet is sent to the destination address of the two machines, they both might respond. This typically will cause both devices with the matching hardware addresses to have problems using the network. This is not an effective attack other than to disable another device on the network; however, that can happen by accident if users change their Ethernet addresses to bypass NAC. There is no good mitigation for this attack other than to try and disable the user's ability to change the hardware address. This problem is also very difficult to track down if it occurs on the network. Some higher-end switches can tell you what source addresses are attached to what ports, and this can be used to track down the problem.

In general, wired Ethernet authentication-based attacks are difficult to implement for an attacker and only work if they have access to a device on the network.

5.2.5   Traffic-Based Attacks

The most common traffic-based attack against Ethernet is traffic sniffing. This is easy to do since most Ethernet hardware controllers can be placed in promiscuous mode, which enables them to read all traffic independent of the hardware address. There are several mitigation methods that can be deployed to prevent sniffing.

Using a switched network environment can reduce the effect of sniffing to only the devices on the same port (typically only one device per port). We saw in the discussion on authentication-based attacks that there are ways to cause switches to pass other traffic to the port, which would enable sniffing traffic of the other devices on the network. Another mitigation method is to use what are referred to as virtual local area networks (VLANs). This is a method to keep traffic segregated into virtual networks so you could only see traffic in your virtual network. This is a common countermeasure for both wired and wireless local area networks and will be discussed later.

Using encryption can also reduce the effect of sniffing since the attacker cannot read the data. Encrypted traffic can occur at many different layers within the TCP/IP protocol stack. Wired Ethernet layer encryption is not common. It is more common to see encryption at the upper layers or in wireless Ethernet, and therefore we will discuss these protocols later.

The second type of traffic-based attack is to flood the network with excess traffic, which can cause a decrease in the amount of real traffic that can be sent across the network, and in some cases actually reduce the real traffic to zero. One way this can be accomplished is through the broadcast address. When a broadcast packet is sent, every machine within the Ethernet hardware address domain will receive the packet and will have to process it. If an attacker can generate enough broadcast traffic, the devices on the network would slow down and the overall amount of real traffic would be reduced. This type of attack can be carried out by a machine directly connected to the network. Mitigation of this attack is difficult and requires securing the devices on the network. If an attacker has access to a device, he or she can carry out this attack.

There are methods to carry out this attack through the Internet. This requires using a protocol that requires broadcasting. The ARP protocol requires broadcasting and can be activated across the Internet. We will discuss this attack in Chapter 6 since the mitigation methods need to take place in the IP layer.

Definitions

Broadcast address.

An address used to a send a packet to all devices within a network.

Broadcast domain.

The set of devices that can receive a broadcast address from a device within the same domain.

CSMA/CD.

Carrier Sense Multiple Access with Collision Detection. The protocol used by Ethernet to manage access to the shared media. Often called a "listen before talk" protocol because device waits for silence on the network before talking, and if multiple devices talk at once, they all quit and wait until the media is free again.

Collision domain.

The set of devices that can be part of a given Ethernet collision.

Ethernet.

A local area network protocol used to allow multiple devices to share access to the same physical network. The protocol was developed in 1973 and is the most widely used local area network protocol.

Ethernet hub.

A network device that is used to interconnect Ethernet devices using twisted pair cabling. A hub creates a large shared network.

Ethernet switch.

A network device that is used to interconnect Ethernet devices. A switch treats each connection (called a port) as a separate Ethernet collision domain. A switch will only send traffic to the port where the destination device is located, thus reducing the overall traffic to each device.

Ethernet tap.

A device that sits between two Ethernet devices and copies all traffic onto another Ethernet segment. A tap can only read traffic.

Hardware address domain.

The set of devices that are interconnected via a network where the hardware addresses need to be unique in order to identify each possible device.

Local area network.

A network of devices within a small space, typically a room or a small number of rooms. Local area networks are interconnected via routers.

Multicast address.

An address used to send a packet to a group of devices.

Promiscuous mode.

A state in which a hardware controller can be placed to force it to read all packets that appear on the network. Used for sniffing of network traffic.

Spanning or mirrored port.

A port on an Ethernet switch that is designed to allow monitoring of traffic. The switch will copy traffic from one or more standard ports to the spanning or mirrored port.

Unicast address.

An address used to identify a single device. Always used as a source address.

Wide area network.

A network typically used to interconnect local area networks. These networks span a larger geographic area.

5.3   Wireless Network Protocols

Wireless network protocols have been gaining in popularity due to the low cost of implementation and the widespread use of portable devices. The most common wireless protocol is Ethernet. For wireless Ethernet the naming convention is 802.11(a through z), where the letter indicates the version number [14–17]. The primary difference between versions is the carrier frequency used and the data rate. The frequencies used by wireless Ethernet are not dedicated to wireless Ethernet only. A problem that occurs is with the protocols that use 2.4 GHz, which is a common frequency for portable telephones. Often it is the telephones that have a problem working in the presence of a conflicting Ethernet frequency. Table 5.4 also shows some of the common wireless names and data rates.

TABLE 5.4: Common Wireless Ethernet Protocols

Name	Frequency	Data Rate	Maximum Distance between Devices
802.11a	5 GHz	54 Mbps	30 m
802.11b	2.4 GHz	11 Mbps	30 m
802.11g	2.4 GHz	11–54 Mbps	30 m
802.11n	2.4 GHz	200–500 Mbps	50 m

It should be noted that the distances specified in Table 5.4 are based on certain conditions, and that the actual distance can be much less or, in some cases, much greater. This has a security implication, as we will see later, in that, unlike wired Ethernet, where the network traffic is confined to the wire, in a wireless network the traffic is not confined. The wireless network signal is affected by objects such as walls. The signal will tend to pass through objects that are at right angles to the source and will reflect off an object as the angle deviates from 90 degrees. Figure 5.11 shows an example signal reflection.

As shown in Figure 5.11, this variability in signal strength will cause security problems because while you may have a weak signal inside rooms in a building, you might have a strong signal in the parking lot right outside the window. Short of spending large amounts of money to shield a building, there is not a lot that can be done to mitigate stray signals. There are some directional antennas that

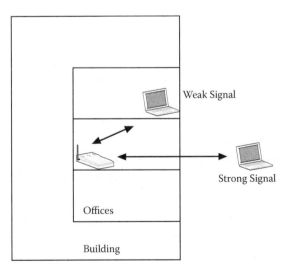

Figure 5.11: Signal reflection.

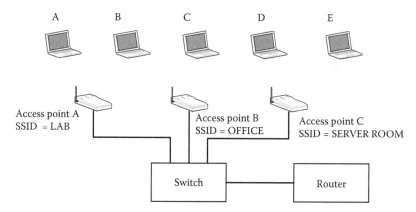

Figure 5.12:   Wireless network environment.

could reduce the signal strength in certain directions, but they are often hard to calibrate. As we will see, network sniffing is the largest security vulnerability in wireless networks.

Wireless networks can also be used to go much longer distances (several miles) by using special antennas. This is used in rural areas where it is difficult to get wired network service from an ISP. There are also special antennas that can be used to pick up weak wireless signals. The use of these antennas will be discussed in more detail as a traffic-based attack.

The wireless Ethernet protocol is based on the wired Ethernet protocol. The primary difference between the wired Ethernet protocol and the wireless Ethernet protocol is that since wireless cannot detect collisions, the wireless packets need an acknowledge packet sent back in response to a transmitted packet. Before we look at the protocol, we need to look at the technologies used to implement the protocol. Unlike wired Ethernet, where every device implements the same protocol and no device is special, wireless Ethernet needs to have a device that is in charge of the network. This device is called an access point (AP), and it serves two primary functions. The first is to create the wireless network and help manage access to the network. The second is to provide access to the wired network. It should be noted that there is also an ad hoc wireless Ethernet where no device is in charge and the devices create a network among themselves. For the purpose of this book, we will not examine the ad hoc Ethernet protocol. However, the security problems will be the same. Figure 5.12 shows a wireless network with three access points and several wireless devices.

In Figure 5.12 we see three wireless networks and five wireless devices. There are several steps that a device must go through to become part of a wireless

Ethernet network. The first step is to discover what wireless access points are available to the device. This can be done by either listening for an access point to transmit its network identity, called the service set identity (SSID), or by knowing the SSID ahead of time. The second step is to join the network by telling the access point you want to be part of the network. The third step is using the Ethernet protocol to send traffic between the device and the access point.

As we see in Figure 5.12, the access points all have an SSID. Assume access points A and B are broadcasting their SSIDs and access point C is not. The process of broadcasting the SSID is called a beacon. The mobile devices can listen for beacons to indicate the available access points. When a wireless device is ready to associate itself with an access point, it can send out a probe packet and the access points will respond with a probe response. The probe response packet returns the same information as the beacon packet. The use of beacons and probes allows a device to develop a list of available access points. This is the discovery step.

The joining step starts when the wireless device picks the wireless access point and sends an association request packet to the selected access point. Note that if the wireless device already knows the access point it wants to connect to, it can send an association request packet without sending a probe, thus skipping the discovery step. The access point will respond to an association request packet with an association response packet. At this point the wireless device will be associated with the access point. Note that the beacon, probe, association request, and association response packets all contain information about the devices and their capabilities. It is beyond the scope of this book to examine the details of these packets. Figure 5.13 shows the discovery and joining process for the devices shown in Figure 5.12.

As we see in Figure 5.13, device C wants to join a wireless network. The figure shows the device receiving beacon packets from access points A and B, each with their respective SSID. Device C can also send out a probe packet asking for an access point to respond. Once device C has chosen access point B, it can send the association request packet and wait for the association response packet. Once device C receives the response packet, it is associated with access point B. As we will see later, there may be additional authentication required to associate with an access point.

Once the wireless device is associated with an access point, it can start communicating. All communications (even the discovery and joining packets) use the same protocol. The wireless devices use the Carrier Sense Multiple Access with Collision Avoidance (CSMA/CA) protocol to communicate with the access point [18–20]. A simplified version of the protocol is shown in Figure 5.14.

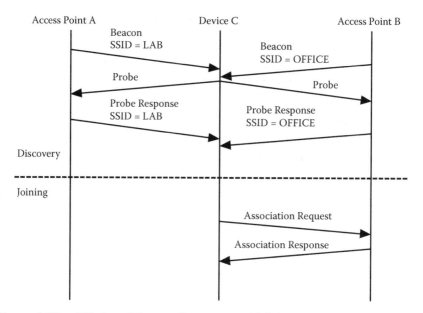

Figure 5.13:   Wireless Ethernet discovery and joining protocol.

The CSMA/CA protocol is similar to the CSMA/CD protocol, except that collision detection cannot be done on wireless. Figure 5.14 shows the protocol is similar to the CSMA/CD protocol if the network is free, in that the device can transmit the packet, but in wireless it will wait for an acknowledgment packet. If the device gets an acknowledgment packet, the device has successfully transmitted the packet. The difference from the CSMA/CD protocol occurs if the medium is not free. The wireless device will wait a random number of time slots and will only decrement the time slot counter if the medium is free. In other words, if the medium continues to stay busy, a device will continue to wait, and when the medium becomes free, the device will wait additional time. This keeps the devices from all transmitting once the medium becomes free. If the device fails to transmit the packet enough times in a row, then the packet will not be transmitted.

When the device is sending data what role does the access point play? The access point can serve as the physical network layer destination of the packets or as a pass-through device, in which case the wireless device will send packets directly to the end device, and the access point simply acts as a relay creating an extended network. The most common implementation is where the access point is the physical network layer destination. This is commonly referred to as a wireless router. A wireless router is an access point that also has a router built in. With a wireless router the wireless network is a separate network and traffic

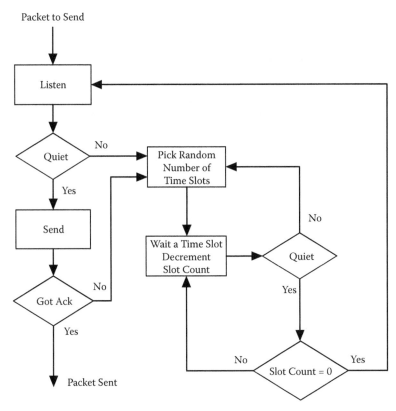

Figure 5.14: CSMA/CA Ethernet protocol.

is routed across the router like between any two networks. Figure 5.15 shows the differences between using an access point to extend the network and using an access point in combination with a router.

As we see in Figure 5.15, an extended network uses the access point to create a larger Ethernet network. So, for example, if wireless device C wishes to send a packet to wired device D, it will send the packet to the access point. The destination address of the packet will be the access point. The packet also contains the hardware address of the final destination on the wired network. The access point will take the packet it received from device C and create a wired Ethernet packet and send it to the final destination. When the wired device D sends a packet to a wireless device C, it will send the packet with the destination address of the wireless device, and the access point will relay it to the wireless device. An access point configured in this manner is transparent to the wired network and can create security problems, which will be discussed later.

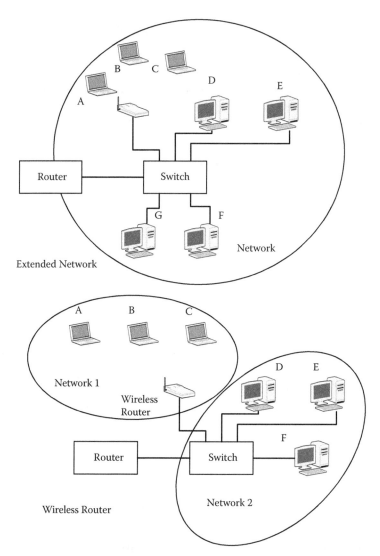

Figure 5.15:   Access point configurations.

The second configuration is where the access point is part of the router that creates two separate hardware address domains. In Figure 5.15, when device C wishes
to send a packet to device D, it will send the packet to the access point that looks
like a router to device C. The access point will route the packet to device D. When
device D wishes to send a packet to the wireless device C, it will send the packet to
the wireless router. The wireless router will in turn send the packet to the destination using the access point. As far as the wired network is concerned, the wireless

2	2	6	6	6	2	6	0–2312	4 bytes
Frame Control	Duration ID	Addr 1	Addr 2	Addr 3	Seq Control	Addr 4	Data	FCS

Figure 5.16:   Wireless Ethernet frame format.

router looks like any other router. From a security standpoint, the wireless router often has additional security features built in and can provide better isolation between wireless and wired networks. We will discuss the security features provided by routers in Chapter 6 when we discuss router security. Security issues associated with the wireless network will be discussed in the following subsections.

Before we look at security issues with wireless Ethernet, it would be useful to understand the frame format used in wireless Ethernet. The wireless Ethernet frame format is more complex than the wired frame format since the access protocol is more complex. The difference in frame formats between wired and wireless Ethernet is minor and does not affect security from the standpoint of header-based attacks. Figure 5.16 shows the wireless Ethernet frame format minus the preamble. Each field is described below.

Frame control: A 2-byte value used to identify the frame type and other frame specific information.

Duration/ID: A 2-byte value used to manage the access control protocol.

Address 1: A 6-byte value used to identify the destination of the transmitted packet. This is used by the hardware controller to determine if the frame should be read. If it does not match the address of the controller, the remainder of the frame is ignored.

Address 2: The 6-byte address of the transmitting device.

Address 3: A 6-byte value used when the access point is part of an extended network where the access point will relay the traffic.

Address 4: A 6-byte value used when the access point is part of an extended network where the access point will relay the traffic.

Sequence control: A 2-byte value used by the acknowledgment process.

Data: The data field contains the data. The data field length is limited to 2,312 bytes. Wireless Ethernet does not have a minimum data length.

Frame check sequence (FCS): This field is used to help verify that the frame has not been corrupted during transmission. It uses what is called a cyclic redundancy check code. Note that the Ethernet protocol does not deal with retransmission of frames. When a frame arrives with a bad FCS, the frame is discarded and the receiving hardware controller does not notify the upper layer.

There are more known vulnerabilities in the wireless Ethernet protocol than in the wired protocol. Several of the known vulnerabilities are categorized using the taxonomy and are described next, along with any countermeasures. It should be noted that some of the countermeasures will actually involve upper-layer protocols and will be discussed in greater detail in later chapters. Also as discussed in Chapter 3 and this chapter, attacks against the Ethernet protocol need to take place within the address domain of Ethernet. Unlike wired Ethernet, where direct access to the medium is often difficult, wireless Ethernet allows anyone with an antenna and close proximity to the transmitter access to the packets. This makes attacks against wireless Ethernet much more commonplace than attacks against wired Ethernet.

5.3.1 Header-Based Attacks

Like with wired Ethernet, most of the fields in the wireless Ethernet frame are handled by the hardware controller, and there are a limited number of header-based attacks. Most header-based attacks result in the attacking device being unable to communicate. An attacking device could set values in the frame control to confuse other wireless devices. This will often cause devices to lose access to the network by losing association with the access point. There is no real countermeasure to these types of attacks since it is hard to stop devices from transmitting signals.

5.3.2 Protocol-Based Attacks

The wireless Ethernet protocol is more complex than the wired Ethernet protocol. Since an attacker can interject packets into the medium, there are some protocol-based attacks that could be carried out. However, since the protocol is also primarily implemented in hardware, the protocol-based attacks would be complex to implement.

One attack that can be considered a protocol-based attack is using the access points' broadcasting of the SSID to determine the location and availability of access points. This process is called wardriving [21–24]. While wardriving does not violate the actual protocol, it does use the protocol in a way that it was not intended to be used. When an access point broadcasts its SSID, any computer with a wireless access controller can pick up the signal. This is designed to help devices find an access point to connect to. In wardriving the goal is to find access points and map their locations, which by itself is not really an attack. It is when someone uses that information to connect to an access point he or she is not authorized to use that it becomes an attack. There is public domain software that can record the SSID of all access points that it can hear, and if there is a GPS connected to the computer, it can record the location of the computer where it found the access point. In addition, an attacker can add a low-cost external antenna to the computer and increase the range of detection to several miles. The author has captured over 500 SSIDs in the 40-mile trip from Ames to Des Moines, Iowa, using public domain software and an external antenna.

There are several methods to mitigate wardriving. However, the first question to ask is: Does it need to be mitigated? If the access point is intended for public use, then broadcasting the SSID is appropriate. Even if the access point is not public, broadcasting the SSID may still be necessary. This is true if there are multiple access points and the user needs to chose which one to use. If there is no need to broadcast the SSID, then broadcasting can be turned off in the access point. A more common method to mitigate wardriving is to use encryption or network access control (NAC). When an access point uses encryption, the SSID broadcast message will contain an indication that the access point requires encryption. A wardriver will still see the access point, but it will be marked as encrypted. If the wardriver wants to use the encrypted access point, he or she will need to overcome the authentication/encryption mechanism of the access point. This turns the attack into an authentication-based attack. We will discuss wireless encryption methods in the section on traffic-based attacks since encryption also mitigates traffic-based attacks.

Another interesting aspect of broadcasting the SSID is what people use as the SSID name. The author has seen SSIDs that are names of people, home addresses, business names, etc. This information could be used to help an attacker identify a possible target. While this is not really a network-based attack, this information is provided by the user configuration of the wireless access point.

There could also be attacks carried out against the CSMA/CA protocol, which would result in denying network access for the device under attack. For example, an attacker could transmit on top of the signals in order to force a device to not receive an acknowledgment. This is called jamming. Jamming the wireless signal could keep devices from gaining access to the network. There are some attacks against the encryption protocols used by wireless Ethernet to prevent sniffing of traffic. These attacks will be discussed in the section on encryption protocols.

5.3.3 Authentication-Based Attacks

There are two aspects of wireless authentication: device authentication and access point configuration authentication. Device authentication is where a wireless device authenticates the access point (access point authentication) to know if it is connecting to a valid access point. An access point might want to authenticate the wireless device (wireless device authentication) connecting to the network and, in some cases, might also want to authenticate the user of the wireless device. Access point configuration authentication is where an attacker gains access to the configuration menus of the access point and disables or modifies the network security features of the access point.

In access point authentication there are two primary types of attacks that are very similar, but have two different goals. The first is where a valid network user installs a wireless access point without knowledge of the organization. This is called a rogue access point [25–27]. The second is where an attacker installs an access point that pretends to be a valid access point. This is called a fake access point [28, 29]. Figure 5.17 shows a rogue access point, and Figure 5.18 shows a fake access point.

In Figure 5.17 a user could connect an access point to the organization's internal network. Depending on the sophistication of the user, he or she may turn off the broadcasting of the SSID, which creates a hidden rogue access point. Even if he or she enables the SSID broadcast, it still might be difficult to determine if a rogue access point has been installed. There are several security risks associated with the installation of a rogue access point. First, the installation might not be secure and could provide an attacker access to the internal network. Even if the rogue access point uses wireless security protocols, they have weaknesses and an attacker could still gain access. Another security threat is that the rogue network might allow users to bypass other internal security methods, like network access control, thus weakening the overall security of the network.

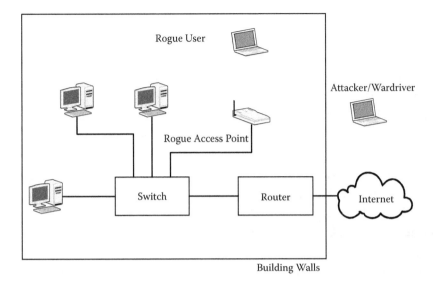

Figure 5.17: Rogue wireless access point.

Mitigation of rogue access points is very difficult since they can be hard to locate, especially if the organization has wireless networking. One method to mitigate rogue access points is by the same methods used to stop unauthorized wired devices, like NAC or other upper-layer security protocols. This will keep

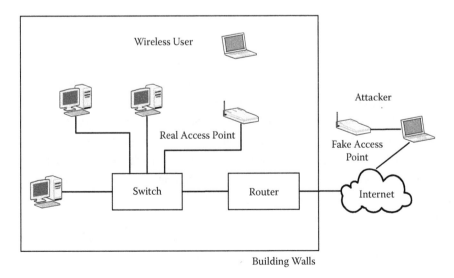

Figure 5.18: Fake access point.

the access point from gaining access to the wired network, or might at least keep unauthorized users from accessing the wired side of the network. Another method is to scan for rogue access points by looking for the wireless signals. You can look for the SSID broadcast messages. You can also sniff the traffic and look for packets between access points and wireless devices. This can be complex to set up and would require monitoring of all wireless traffic. This would be very difficult if you are in an office complex with other organizations with wireless networks.

The second access point authentication attack, as shown in Figure 5.18, is where an attacker installs a fake access point and pretends to be one of the valid access points in an organization.

This attack would allow the attacker to capture all traffic from the wireless device. This attack has several problems that need to be overcome to make it successful. The first problem is if you get a wireless device to attach to the fake access point, you need to provide it access to a network. It would be to difficult set up a fake access point that looks like it is inside a secure network unless the attacker had access to a secure network. If the attacker is inside the organization's network, then it looks like a rogue access point, but the goal is to capture traffic.

Another issue is that this only works if the fake access has no wireless encryption (unless the attacker knows the encryption key of the real access point). So if this attack only works with unencrypted access points, it would be easier for the attacker to just capture the packets between the wireless devices and the already existing access point. This attack then becomes a traffic-based attack. Mitigation of a fake access point can be done with wireless encryption protocols or with upper-layer security protocols.

Access point configuration authentication is where the attacker gains access to the control software of the access point. Access to the control software can be done via the wireless network. The control software is password protected. If an attacker can gain access to the control software for an access point, he or she can change the encryption keys, read the encryption keys, disable encryption, and add additional encryption keys, along with many other malicious attacks against the access point. To mitigate this attack, the user should change the default password to the access point and disable access to the configuration menus from the wireless network (if possible). It should be noted that there are web sites that provide lists of the default passwords for most network devices.

As with wired Ethernet, mitigation of authentication-based attacks requires additional protocols and, in some cases, relies on the upper layers to provide the solution.

5.3.4 Traffic-Based Attacks

The most common traffic-based attack is sniffing of wireless network traffic. As we have seen, wireless signals cannot be controlled, and sometimes can be picked up over distances greater than the standard specifies as a maximum distance. Just like wired Ethernet, the wireless Ethernet network controller can be configured to ignore the destination address (promiscuous mode) and can capture all traffic. Of course, unlike wired Ethernet, the wireless signals are easy to pick up. To mitigate this type of attack, the wireless Ethernet standards added encryption to keep an attacker from being able to decode the data in a wireless packet. The most common mitigation method for authentication-based attacks against wireless networks is also using encryption. In this section we will examine two common methods for providing both authentication and encryption in a wireless network. These encryption protocols encrypt the traffic between the wireless device and the access point and do not provide end-to-end encryption. There are other higher-layer protocols that provide end-to-end encryption that will be discussed in later chapters.

The first of these protocols is called Wired Equivalent Privacy (WEP); it was designed to provide simple authentication and encryption [30–32]. The WEP standard was established in 1997 and was designed to provide simple security and comply with encryption export laws. Figure 5.19 shows WEP being used between an access point and a wireless device.

In Figure 5.19 the access point and wireless device have a shared secret key that is used to encrypt the data frames. The key size is either 40 or 128 bits. Authentication is accomplished through the knowledge of the shared key. The wireless device sends a message encrypted in the shared key to authenticate itself before sending an associate request. This is not very strong authentication and cannot authenticate a user. An access point may support only a small set of keys (often only one key is enabled), so a single key is often used by all devices accessing the network through the same access point. The only thing the authentication proves is that a wireless device that knows the encryption key is sending packets, and that an access point that knows the key is sending packets. WEP encryption can be broken using several public domain software packages. WEP is not considered to be a very strong protocol. In spite of these weaknesses WEP is still used today.

A stronger and newer protocol is called Wi-Fi Protected Access (WPA), developed in 2002 [33–37]. WPA uses both authentication and encryption to provide security. WPA is designed to work in a home environment where the authentication

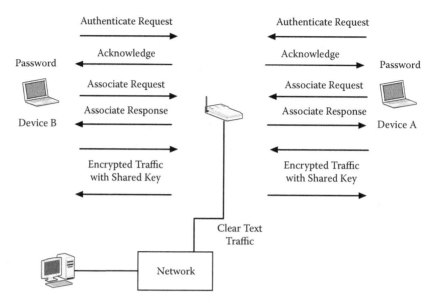

Figure 5.19: WEP.

process is self-contained or in a corporate environment where the authentication can be tied to the corporate user-based authentication system. Figure 5.20 shows WPA in a home environment.

In the figure, in the home environment the wireless device and the access point still share a common password, but that password is used for authentication and is not the encryption key. The wireless device will first associate with the access point, and then will send the password as a one-way hash. The password is used to authenticate the user and the device. All devices and users using the access point share the same password. Once the wireless device has authenticated with the access point, then the two devices negotiate a session encryption key that is used for the packets exchanged between the wireless device and the access point. The session key is randomly chosen for each wireless device and is valid until the device disassociates with the access point. In the figure, the two wireless devices each have their own key even though they have the same password. This makes it difficult to break the encryption and discover the session key, and even if the session key is discovered, it is only valid for one wireless device and only for a short period of time. The length of a session key is 128 bits.

In a corporate environment it is useful to authenticate each user and not just the device. WPA is designed to interact with an authentication server. Figure 5.21 shows WPA in an enterprise environment.

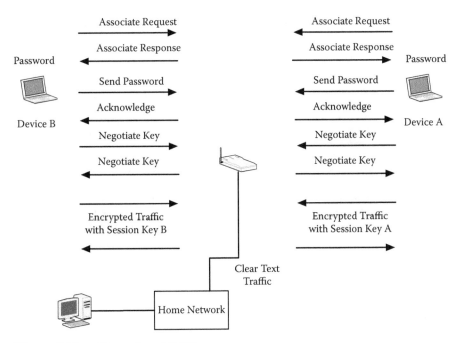

Figure 5.20:   Home-based WPA.

In the figure the wireless device first associates with the access point, but the access point does not provide access to the corporate network. The wireless device user will present the authentication information to the access point, and the access point will verify the authentication information. If the wireless device user is not authorized to use the network, the access point will continue to block access to the corporate network. If the wireless device user is authorized to use the network, then the wireless device and access point negotiate a session encryption key. Note that the session key negotiation and distribution is the same in the home version as the corporate version. The session key is used to encrypt the data between the wireless device and the access point.

Weaknesses in WPA are similar to those found in WEP. The encryption keys can still be discovered if an attacker can see enough traffic. Since those keys are only valid for a short time, the impact of key disclosure is minimal. In the home environment there is still a password, but since it is not used as the encryption key, it is harder to break. An attacker could capture the authentication session and use public domain tools to try to guess the password. If the authentication password is discovered, an attacker could then connect to the access point and gain access to the network. In a corporate environment it is much more difficult

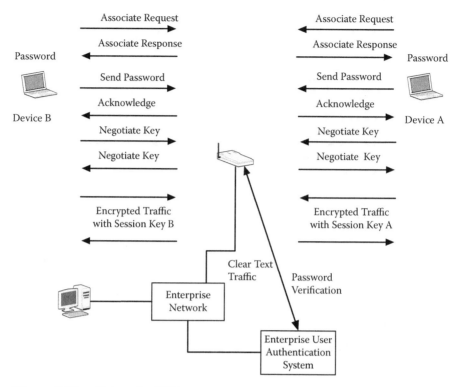

Figure 5.21: Enterprise WPA.

to guess the password. In spite of these weaknesses, WPA is still recommended to mitigate sniffing and authentication-based attacks.

Wireless networks are subject to flooding attacks that can either keep devices from accessing the network or reduce the overall data rate. Not all wireless flooding is an attack. Excess traffic can be due to multiple access points in close proximity to each other. If the flooding is malicious, then that attack is almost impossible to stop. There is also the possibility of an attacker jamming the wireless signals. This is a physical attack and also very hard to stop.

In general it is recommended to use WPA for a private wireless network. Even though there are weaknesses, WPA still makes it difficult for an attacker to sniff the traffic. Although, if there is still a concern about sniffing data, there are other protocols that can be used as part of the upper layers or the applications. These protocols will be discussed in later chapters.

Definitions

Access point.

A wireless device that connects other wireless devices to a wired network. The wireless devices share the media under the control of the access point.

Access point authentication.

Proving the access point is the correct one.

Access point configuration authentication.

Authorizing access to the control software of the access point.

Ad hoc wireless network.

A wireless network where each device is a peer, and they create a network among themselves.

CSMA/CA.

Carrier Sense Multiple Access with Collision Avoidance. This protocol is used by the wireless Ethernet protocol to allow multiple devices to share access to the media.

Fake access point.

An access point set up by an attacker to mimic the access points installed within an organization.

Hidden rogue access point.

A rogue access point that is not broadcasting its SSID.

Jamming.

Transmitting signals to interrupt the communications between an access point's wireless devices.

Rogue access point.

An access point that is installed inside a network without the knowledge of the organization.

SSID.

Service set identifier. This is a name used by the access point to identify the network. The access point will use the SSID to know which network a wireless device wishes to connect to.

Wardriving.

Using a wireless computer and software to find wireless access points and logging the SSID, access point type, and location of the computer when the access point is found.

WEP.

Wired Equivalent Privacy. A protocol designed to provide authentication and encryption between an access point and wireless devices. It uses a shared key.

Wireless device authentication.

Proving the wireless device wishing to connect with the access point is authorized to use the access point.

Wireless router.

An access point that is connected to a router. Together they create a wireless network that is separated from the wired network via a router.

WPA.

Wi-Fi Protected Access. A protocol designed to provide authentication and encryption between an access point and wireless devices. The authentication is based on shared information, but the encryption key is negotiated for every association.

5.4   Common Countermeasures

As we saw in this chapter, similar attacks can be played out against both wired and wireless networks. The differences in attacks are more a matter of ease of implementation and ease of mitigation. There are a few common countermeasures that can be deployed to help mitigate physical network attacks. Some of the countermeasures are actually upper-layer protocols, and therefore will not be discussed in this chapter. For example, there are protocols that perform end-to-end encryption of traffic. These protocols can mitigate both sniffing attacks and some authentication attacks. In this section, we will look at some common countermeasures that are part of the physical network layer and are typically targeted to mitigate sniffing and authentication attacks.

5.4.1   Virtual Local Area Networks (VLANs)

The first common countermeasure is called a virtual local area network (VLAN) [38–39]. The goal behind a VLAN is to create logical networks out of a physical network of switches. If you remember, in a switched environment we already have isolation of the network traffic. This isolation does not extend to broadcast traffic. In a VLAN the broadcast traffic is restricted to that VLAN. Figure 5.22 shows a simple VLAN with three switches and two VLANs.

As we see in Figure 5.22, each device is connected to a port on the switch, and each port has been assigned to one of the two VLANs. All traffic from VLAN 1 will be separated from VLAN 2. If D2 wishes to talk to D1, it must use the router. This creates two virtual networks that logically look like Figure 5.23.

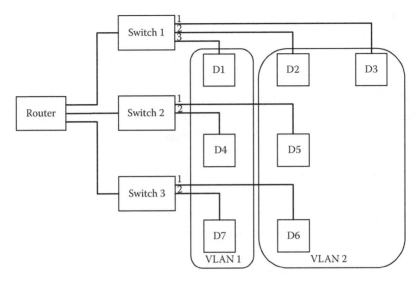

Figure 5.22: VLAN.

There are two types of VLANs. A static VLAN is based on fixed port assignment, and a dynamic VLAN is based on the hardware addresses of the devices. A static VLAN is shown in Figure 5.22, where any device connected to port 3 of switch 1 will be in VLAN 1. From a security standpoint a static VLAN provides some protection from ARP poisoning and from attacks against the port-mapping tables within the switches. However, as shown in Figure 5.23, all a VLAN does is create smaller networks, but each network still has the same problems.

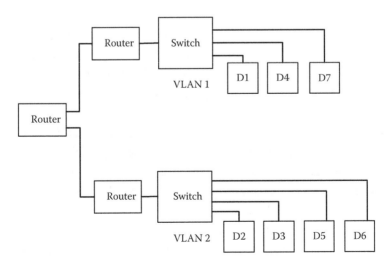

Figure 5.23: Logical view of VLANs.

A dynamic VLAN assigns the VLAN based on the hardware address of the device. This provides a small amount of additional security by keeping only devices with known hardware addresses on the network. You can configure most dynamic VLAN systems to place unknown devices into a VLAN with limited or even no access. From a security standpoint, a dynamic VLAN provides additional protection by adding authentication of the device based on the hardware address. Since the hardware address can be changed, dynamic VLANs add limited additional security.

In both types of VLANs there is a potential for added security because all traffic between VLANs must go through a router, which can include additional security features, as will be discussed in Chapter 6. VLANs are also used as a network management tool since they can create logical networks on top of physical networks.

Protecting wireless networks is one way to utilize a VLAN. The access points could all be placed into one or more VLANs, which would allow you to force the wireless traffic to go through its own router and any other security devices. As shown in Figure 5.24, the access points are placed on a VLAN, and their traffic is routed through one or more devices that implement additional security. These would be the same types of devices that implement security between the Internet and the main network. At this point we are not ready to talk about these devices, but the VLAN does give us a way to create an internal network that is treated as an external network.

5.4.2 Network Access Control (NAC)

Another general countermeasure is referred to as network access control (NAC) [38, 39]. NAC is a relatively new term in network security. However, the concept has been around for some time. The basic idea is to authenticate every device on the network based not only on the user, but also on the configuration of the device, and in some cases, to continue to monitor the device to determine if it should remain on the network. There are no universally accepted standards for the implementation of a NAC environment. There are several vendor-based solutions that each have a different take on implementation. For the purpose of this book, we will look at just the general concepts behind NAC. Figure 5.25 shows the general framework of a NAC environment.

When a device attaches to the network, it authenticates itself. This can happen as part of the user authentication. Device authentication is based on the policies of the organization and often consists of information about the device. This

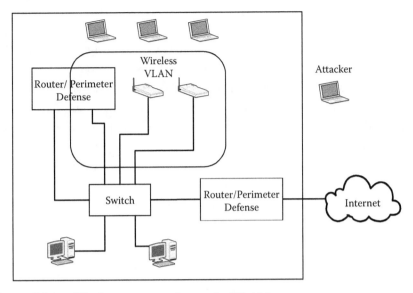

Figure 5.24:   Wireless access points and a VLAN.

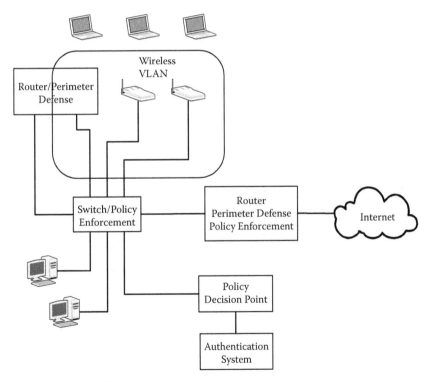

Figure 5.25:   NAC framework.

common device information is typically the version and patch level of the operating system and application software. Based on the result of the user and device authentication, the NAC will decide what network access rights the device has. A NAC environment typically uses dynamic VLANs to enforce the policies by segregating the devices based on the policies. This is different than the user-based authentication we will discuss later in the book, since with a NAC, if the device is unauthenticated, it will not be allowed access to the network or may be segregated to an isolated network.

The security provided by NAC is focused on protecting a network from misconfigured or infected devices. While this is a good goal, NAC has not gained widespread use. This is due in some part to the complexity of implementation and a questionable return on investment, especially if the organization does not use VLANs or equipment from a vendor that supports NAC.

Definitions

Dynamic VLAN.

A VLAN where the virtual local area networks are created based on information provided by the devices. Typically this is the hardware address of the device.

Network access control (NAC).

A system where access to the network is controlled and is based on user authentication, system configuration information, or both. Unauthorized devices are either denied access to the network or are segregated into isolated networks.

Static VLAN.

A VLAN where the virtual local area networks are created based on the network ports of the switches and often do not change.

Virtual local area network (VLAN).

A system using switches to segregate devices into separate local area networks even when they share switches.

5.5   General Comments

The physical network layer, from a security standpoint, provides limited security services and functions. The biggest security issue with the physical network layer is that access to the medium provides access to the data through network sniffing.

As we saw, this can be mitigated using several different methods; however, they have some limitations. The bottom line is that physical network layer security is important, but it does not solve the overall problem of network security. We need to rely on the upper layers to provide additional security to overcome the problems with the physical network layer. We will also see that the upper layers cannot rely on the physical network layer to provide the security needed to protect them.

Homework Problems and Lab Experiments

Homework Problems

1. Develop a list of common network protocols used in the Internet for both LANs and WANs.

2. If the type/length field in the Ethernet frame is a type field, how does the upper layer know the length of the frame?

3. Ethernet addresses are designed to be globally unique. Is this needed and why?

4. Why is there a minimum length to the wired Ethernet frame?

5. What is the maximum cable length for 100 Mbps and Gigabit Ethernet?

6. How could the maximum length be extended?

7. Why do most protocols try to avoid using broadcast packets?

8. Search the Internet for tools that will allow you to change the source Ethernet address and sniff network traffic. Comment on how these tools could be used for both defending and attacking.

9. Search the Internet for tools that can detect hardware address spoofing.

10. Search the Internet for tools that allow you to wardrive, and comment on how these tools could be used for both defending and attacking.

11. What makes the WPA protocol more secure than the WEP protocol?

12. Why are WPA and WEP hard to use in a public wireless network, and would they provide much security if implemented?

13. How would you detect a rogue access point?

14. Using the Internet, research the NAC market and determine the primary vendors and market size. Comment on what you have found and where you think the market is going.

Lab Experiments

1. Log in to a computer in the test lab and determine the Ethernet hardware address of that computer.

2. Using tcpdump or wireshark find the Ethernet addresses and the vendor ID for each machine in the test network.

3. Using tcpdump or wireshark determine the number of broadcast packets in the test network during a 10-minute period and compare that to the total number of packets during that time.

4. If your test lab has wireless, try sniffing wireless traffic. Sniff both encrypted and unencrypted traffic and see what you can tell from each.

5. Using a wardriving program, see how many wireless access points you can find and what percentage are unencrypted.

Programming Problem

1. Download the file netdump.tar from ftp://www.dougj.net. The program is base code for a simple packet sniffer. There will be programming problems in some of the following chapters that will expand on the program developed in this problem. Extract the files into a directory and type "make" to create the program netdump. To run the program, you will need to use the command "run_dump." Note: There are C and Unix tutorials located on a web site described in Appendix B. Perform the following:

   a. Run the program to capture traffic in a text file. Look at the format of the traffic stored in the file.

   b. Modify the file netdump.c and add code to decode the Ethernet header and print the header in a readable format. Print the addresses in hex with ":" between each byte (e.g., DA = 00:16:22:F3:33:45, SA = 00:FF:34:78:CD:22). Print the type/length field as Type = (hex value) or Len = (in decimal).

   c. If the type field indicates the payload is IP (0x800), then print Payload = IP. If the type field indicates the payload is ARP (0x806), then print Payload = ARP.

d. Add a set of counters to the code to count the number of broadcast packets, the number of IP packets, and the number of ARP packets. Add code
to print the values of these counters to the subroutine program_ending().
Note the subroutine already prints the total number of packets.

References

[1] Zimmermann, H. 1980. OSI reference model—The ISO model of architecture for open systems interconnection. *IEEE Transactions on Communications* 28:425–32.

[2] Comer, D. E. 1995. *Internetworking with TCP/IP.* Vol. 1. *Principles, protocols and architecture.* Englewood Cliffs, NJ: Prentice Hall.

[3] IEEE 802 standards. http://www.ieee802.org/.

[4] Simon, D., B. Aboba, and T. Moore. *IEEE 802.11 security and 802.1 x,*
p. 802.11-00.

[5] Templeton, S. J., and K. E. Levitt. 2003. Detecting spoofed packets. Paper
presented at Proceedings of DARPA Information Survivability Conference
and Exposition. Washington, DC: 164–176.

[6] Medhi, D. 1999. Network reliability and fault tolerance. In *Wiley Encyclopedia of Electrical and Electronics Engineering.* New York: John Wiley &
Sons.

[7] Shake, T. H., B. Hazzard, and D. Marquis. 1999. Assessing network infrastructure vulnerabilities to physical layer attacks. In *22nd National Information Systems Security Conference,* Arlington, VA: 18–21.

[8] Held, G. 2003. *Ethernet networks: Design, implementation, operation, management.* New York: Wiley.

[9] Lundy, G. M., and R. E. Miller. 1993. Analyzing a CSMA/CO protocol
through a systems of communicating machines specification. *IEEE Transactions on Communications* 41:447–49.

[10] Whalen, S. 2001. An introduction to ARP spoofing [online]. *Node99*, April.

[11] Wagner, R. 2001. *Address resolution protocol spoofing and man-in-the-middle attacks*. www.sans.org

[12] Kwon, K., S. Ahn, and J. W. Chung. 2004. Network security management using ARP spoofing. Paper presented at Proceedings of ICCSA. Assis: Italy.

[13] Crow, B. P., et al. 1997. IEEE 802.11 wireless local area networks. *IEEE Communications Magazine* 35:116–26.

[14] O'Hara, B. 2004. *The IEEE 802.11 handbook: A designer's companion.* IEEE Standards Association. Piscataway, NJ.

[15] Brenner, P. 1992. *A technical tutorial on the IEEE 802.11 protocol.* Breeze-Com Wireless Communications. San Jose, CA.

[16] Ramanathan, R., J. Redi, and B. B. N. Technologies. 2002. A brief overview of ad hoc networks: Challenges and directions. *IEEE Communications Magazine* 40:20–22.

[17] Calì, F., M. Conti, and E. Gregori. 2000. IEEE 802.11 protocol: Design and performance evaluation of an adaptive backoff mechanism. *IEEE Journal on Selected Areas in Communications*, 18(9).

[18] Carney, W., W. N. B. Unit, and Texas Instruments. 2002. *IEEE 802.11 g new draft standard clarifies future of wireless LAN.* Texas Instruments.

[19] Wardriving home page. http://www.wardriving.com/.

[20] Shipley, P. 2003. Open WLANs: The early results of wardriving. www.dis.org-filez-openlans.

[21] Kim, M., J. J. Fielding, and D. Kotz. 2006. Risks of using AP locations discovered through war driving. In *Proceedings of the 4th International Conference on Pervasive Computing (Pervasive 2006)*, Dublin, Ireland: 67–82.

[22] Freeman, E. H. 2006. Wardriving: Unauthorized access to wi-fi networks. *Information Systems Security* 15:11–15.

[23] Maxim, M., and D. Pollino. 2002. *Wireless security*. New York: McGraw-Hill/Osborne.

[24] Beyah, R., et al. 2004. Rogue access point detection using temporal traffic characteristics. In *IEEE Global Telecommunications Conference (GLOBE-COM'04)*, Dallas, TX: 4.

[25] Welch, D., and S. Lathrop. 2003. Wireless security threat taxonomy. In *IEEE Systems, Man and Cybernetics Society Information Assurance Workshop*. Washington, DC: 76–83.

[26] Fleck, B., and J. Dimov. 2003. Wireless access points and ARP poisoning. Online document (accessed October 12, 2001). www.cigital.com

[27] Lim, Y. X., et al. 2003. Wireless intrusion detection and response. In *IEEE Systems, Man and Cybernetics Society Information Assurance Workshop*. Washington, DC: 68–75.

[28] Cam-Winget, N., et al. 2003. Security flaws in 802.11 data link protocols. *Communications of the ACM* 46:35–39.

[29] Miller, S. K. 2001. Facing the challenge of wireless security. *Computer* 34:6–18.

[30] Craiger, J. P. 2002. 802.11, 802.1 x, and wireless security. www.sans.org/reading-room/whitepapers/wireless/171.php

[31] Arbaugh, W. A. 2003. Wireless security is different. *Computer* 36:99–101.

[32] Wong, S. 2003. The evolution of wireless security in 802.11 networks: WEP, WPA and 802.11 standards. 28:5. http://www.sans.org/rr/whitepapers/wireless/1109.php.

[33] Edney, J., and W. A. Arbaugh. 2004. *Real 802.11 security: Wi-fi protected access and 802.11 i*. Reading, MA: Addison-Wesley Professional.

[34] Boland, H., and H. Mousavi. 2004. Security issues of the IEEE 802.11 b wireless LAN. In *Canadian Conference on Electrical and Computer Engineering*, 1. Sashatdon, Sashatchewan, Canada.

[35] Moen, V., H. Raddum, and K. J. Hole. 2004. Weaknesses in the temporal key hash of WPA. *ACM SIGMOBILE Mobile Computing and Communications Review* Philadelphia, PA: 8:76–83.

[36] Bridges, V. IEEE p802. 1ap/d3. 0.

[37] Zhu, M., M. Moile, and B. Brahman. 2004. Design and implementation of application-based secure VLAN, *29th Annual IEEE Conference on Local Computer Networks CLCN '04*. Tampa, FL: 407.408.

[38] Shi, L., and P. Sjodin. 2007. A VLAN Ethernet backplane for distributed network systems. In *Workshop on High Performance Switching and Routing (HPSR '07)*. New York, NY: 1–4.

[39] Ferraiolo, D. F., D. R. Kuhn, and R. Chandramouli. 2003. *Role-based access control*. Boston, MA: Artech House.

Chapter 6

Network Layer Protocols

The network layer is designed to provide interconnection between multiple networks and to allow devices to connect to networks [1, 2]. There have been several network layer standards developed over the years, and these standards can be categorized into two types. The first type is used to connect a device to a network that is responsible for the end-to-end transfer of data. This end-to-end network is often a closed network that is maintained by a single organization, like a telephone-based network. This type of network is called a network access protocol network. The second type of network layer protocol is called an internetwork protocol [3–5]. This is where the same network layer protocol is part of every device within the network. Figure 6.1 shows the difference between the two.

As we see in the Figure 6.1a, the network access protocol is used to connect a device or network to an end-to-end network. The network access protocol controls the interaction between the device and the private network. The private network is treated as a direct path to the final destination. The private end-to-end network is responsible for getting the data to the final endpoint of the network. There is a separate network access protocol used to connect a remote device with the private end-to-end network. The network access protocol provides the private end-to-end network with the address of the destination, and the private end-to-end network handles all routing of the traffic. This configuration was originally designed to create large networks similar to what the Internet is today. These networks still exist and are used to create private networks, and are also used to interconnect networks within the Internet. From a security standpoint, we often treat the private end-to-end network as a point-to-point connection between the devices since it is controlled and managed by a single organization.

Figure 6.1b shows the second type of network layer, where a common network layer protocol is part of every device in the network and the network layers work together to create an end-to-end flow of data. This type of network layer protocol is used in the Internet (called the Internet Protocol [IP]). As we see in Figure 6.1b, each device has a network layer that is responsible for routing the packets from the source device to the destination device, which makes it a prime target for attacks. The network layer is also responsible for interfacing with the various types of

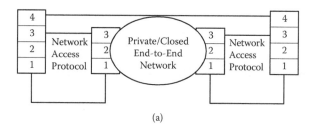

(a)

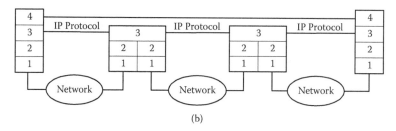

(b)

Figure 6.1: Network layer protocols.

physical networks. As we saw in Chapter 5, there are several different types of physical networks, and each type has its own unique characteristics. In order to provide end-to-end transfer of data, the network layer needs to compensate for the differences between the various physical network layers. Some of these differences are shown in Table 6.1, along with the compensation to be provided by the network layer to handle the differences.

TABLE 6.1: Differences between Networks

Differences	Compensation
Physical network layer addressing schemes	The network layer needs to adapt to the different physical layer addressing types. This is more difficult in devices like routers.
Maximum and minimum packet sizes	The network layer needs to implement segmentation and reassembly.
Network access methods	The network layer needs to provide buffering that handles different access methods, especially in a router.
Error and flow control	The network layer needs to handle lost and delayed packets.
Machine and user authentication	The network layer needs to provide authentication to the physical network if required.

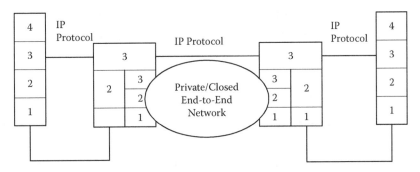

Figure 6.2: Using a private end-to-end network in the Internet.

As mentioned earlier, the network access protocol can be used to interconnect networks within the Internet. Figure 6.2 shows how the network layer within the Internet (IP layer) treats the network access layer as a physical network layer, thus treating the end-to-end network as a point-to-point physical network. Security of the network access layer is typically controlled and managed by the network provider. From an Internet security standpoint, we typically do not worry about the network access protocol.

Definitions

Internetwork layer.
A network layer that is common across all devices connected to the same global network. An example is the IP layer in the Internet.

Network access layer.
A network layer that is used to connect devices or networks to a private end-to-end network.

Private end-to-end network.
A network controlled and managed by a single organization like a telephone company. Access to the network is controlled along with the physical devices that comprise the network.

6.1 IP Version 4 Protocol

This section will examine the IP protocol (version 4) and the supporting protocols that are used in the Internet [6]. Also, the newest version of the IP protocol (version 6) will be examined. From a security standpoint, the two versions have the same issues. There is a security extension for version 6 of the IP protocol that has also been adapted to version 4 and will be discussed along with other general countermeasures.

6.1.1   IP Addressing

The IP address is designed to be a globally unique address, so before we look at how packets are moved through the Internet, we need to understand how IP addresses are allocated and assigned [7]. The IP address consists of two parts: the network and the host. Therefore, one way to look at the Internet is as a collection of uniquely addressed networks, each containing some number of uniquely addressed hosts. In version 4 of the IP protocol the address space is 32 bits in length. IP addresses are written as four numbers separated by dots. This was done to make it easier to use the IP address. Each of the four numbers represents 8 bits of the 32-bit address. Figure 6.3 shows two networks and the address allocations for the networks and hosts.

Figure 6.3 shows network 1 with an IP address of 197.12.15.0. Networks are given addresses as a way to refer to the network. You do not address the network, and the network address does not show up in any packets. Network 1 can have 254 devices connected to it, ranging in address from 197.12.15.1 to 197.12.15.254. The host address of 0 is not allowed, and the host address of 255 (all 1s) is a reserved address. Likewise, the figure shows 254 possible host addresses for network 2. It should also be noted that the addresses assigned to adjacent networks have no numerical relationships with each other.

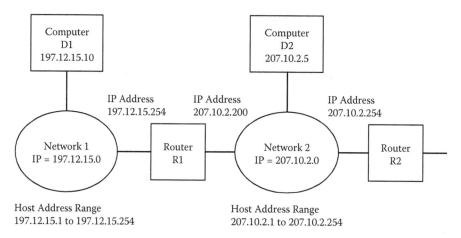

Figure 6.3:   Example IP addresses.

TABLE 6.2: IP Address Space Allocation

Class	First Network	Last Network	Number of Networks	Number of Hosts per Network
Class A	1.0.0.0	126.0.0.0	126	16,777,214
Class B	128.0.0.0	191.255.0.0	16,384	65,534
Class C	192.0.0.0	223.255.255.0	2,097,152	254
Class D	224.0.0.0	239.0.0.0	Multicast	
Class E	240.0.0.0	255.255.255.254	Reserved	

Not all network addresses have the same number of hosts associated with them. As shown in Figure 6.3, each network can have up to 254 hosts. The IP address space was envisioned to consist of a large number of small networks. To accommodate this arrangement, the IP address space was divided into five classes, where each class has a different breakdown between the network part and the host part. In addition, there are several IP address ranges that were allocated for specific purposes. Not all IP addresses within these classes are open for use; several ranges have been reserved for private IP addresses and will be discussed later. In addition, several IP address ranges and individual addresses have been reserved as shown in Tables 6.2 and 6.3. Table 6.2 shows the five address classes for IP version 4. It should be noted that in version 6 of the IP protocol the address space is much larger (128 bits).

The class A address space was designed for Internet service providers, and the class B address space was designed for large organizations. The class C addresses were designed for smaller organizations. Figure 6.4 shows how the address space was originally designed to be allocated.

TABLE 6.3: Reserved IP Addresses

Network Part	Host Part	Purpose
Network	All 0s	Network address—Not used in the packet.
Network	All 1s	Directed broadcast—Destination address only.
All 1s	All 1s	Broadcast address—Destination address only.
All 0s	All 0s	This host on this network—Source address only.
All 0s	Host	A specific host on this network—Destination address only.
127	Any	Loopback address

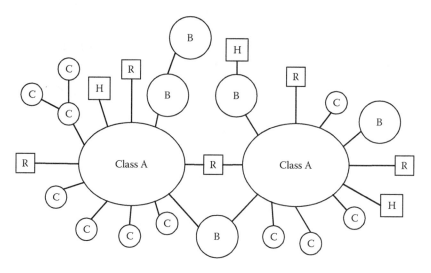

Figure 6.4:   IP address space.

As we see in Figure 6.4, the intent was to have the class A networks serve as the backbone to the Internet, with the class B and C networks interconnected using class A networks. Individual hosts can be connected to any of the networks. While this is generally how the Internet is configured, there are many cases when class B and C networks are connected together without going through a class A network. The routing within the Internet does not depend on the hierarchical approach shown in Figure 6.4. It should also be noted that there is no correlation between the assigned addresses of one class and the networks that are connected to them. In other words, a class B address connected to one class A network may have the address 129.188.0.0, and the network with the next class B address (129.189.0.0) may be connected to a different class A network.

As was mentioned earlier, not all IP addresses are open for use in the Internet, and some can only be used in special cases, as shown in Table 6.3. From a security standpoint these addresses are of interest because they can cause problems if used improperly.

As we see in Table 6.3, two of the addresses (with the host part all 1s) are used for broadcasting to all devices in a network. Broadcast packets can be used to carry out traffic-based attacks against the network. The full broadcast packet is not routed and can only affect the network where the sending device is connected. The directed broadcast can be routed across the Internet, and therefore can be sent into a network from anywhere in the Internet. There have been attacks that

TABLE 6.4: Netmask Values

Class	Netmask
A	255.0.0.0
B	255.255.0.0
C	255.255.255.0

have utilized directed broadcast packets to get multiple machines to respond to a single packet. The reserved address that is all zeros is used by protocols where the sender does not know its own IP address. The loopback address is used to test the protocol stack within the host. When an application specifies this address as a destination, the packets will flow down to the IP layer and the IP layer will forward them back up the protocol stack to the transport layer.

When the IP protocol was first deployed there were a very small number of computing devices envisioned on the network. The address space was allocated on a first come, first served basis. The network part of the address is assigned to the requesting organization, and it in turn assigns the host part of the address space. An organization can also divide its address space into smaller networks. To help with routing, a netmask is used as a way to tell which part of an address is the network and which part is the host. The netmask is specified like an IP address with four numbers separated by dots. When converted to its 32-bit binary value, the bits that are a 1 represent that part of the address that is the network. For example, 255.0.0.0 has the upper eight bits being 1s, and therefore would be the netmask for a class A network.

A question that should come to mind is why we need a netmask when there are already classes that define the split between the network and the host. The primary reason is to support splitting a network into subnetworks. For example, a class B network could be divided into 256 class C subnetworks. This would be done to improve performance and make the network more manageable. Table 6.4 shows the netmask for each of the classes of networks.

Figure 6.5 shows an example of a class B network divided into multiple class C networks. The netmask is 255.255.255.0 for each of the subnets shown in Figure 6.5. Also note that the networks are given an address in the figure. For example, 172.16.1.0 is the address of one of the networks. Note that even though a network can be given an address, the network itself is not a destination for traffic. A subnet does not need to be the size of a class; it can be smaller. For example, a class C network can be divided into multiple subnets. ISPs often assign addresses to

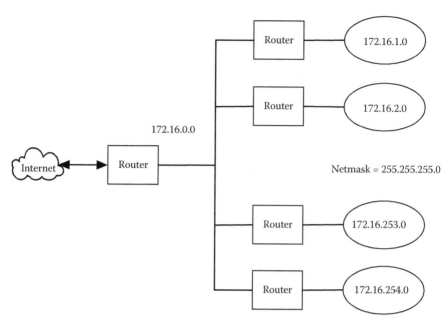

Figure 6.5: Subnetworks.

individuals with a netmask of 255.255.255.254, which means the individual has one address in his or her subnet.

Another way to specify the network is using a concept called Classless Inter-domain Routing (CIDR) [8]. Each CIDR address is represented by the address in dot notation followed by a slash, /, and a number that indicates the number of bits in the network part of the address. In the section on routing we will see examples where the netmask or CIDR address is used. Table 6.5 also shows the CIDR address for each class.

Table 6.6 shows the number of networks and hosts for several common CIDR values.

TABLE 6.5:   CIDR Values for Each IP Address Class

Class	Netmask	CIDR	Example CIDR Address
A	255.0.0.0	/8	15.35.26.234/8
B	255.255.0.0	/16	129.186.34.54/16
C	255.255.255.0	/24	192.168.1.30/24

TABLE 6.6: Common CIDR Values

CIDR	Number of Class C's	Number of Hosts per Network
/30	1/64	4
/29	1/32	8
/28	1/16	16
/27	1/8	32
/26	1/4	64
/25	1/2	128
/24	1 (class C)	256
/23	2	512
/22	4	1,024
/21	8	2,048
/20	16	4,096
/19	32	8,192
/18	64	16,384
/17	128	32,768
/16	256 (class B)	65,536
/15	512	131,072
/14	1,024	262,144
/13	2,048	524,288

6.1.2 Routing

Now that we understand how IP addresses are defined we need to see how packets can be delivered across the Internet using the addresses. IP addresses of the devices in the Internet have no relationship to the physical location of networks or to the interconnection of the networks. Therefore, there needs to be a distributed routing method used by every device within the Internet. This routing method is based on every device within the Internet knowing where a packet will be sent next to get to every possible destination. This is done using a route table that shows each possible destination a device could send the packet and which device (next hop) will help get the packet to the destination. The next hop is specified by an IP address and an interface (routers, for example, might have two or more interfaces). The fields in a route table needed to route a packet are shown in Table 6.7.

A device wishing to send a packet to a destination first searches the destination field of the route table to find a match. The CIDR is used as a mask when searching the destination field. When a match is found, the device sends the packet to the device specified in the next hop field using the interface specified in the interface

TABLE 6.7:   Route Table Fields

Destination	CIDR/Netmask	Next Hop	Interface
The IP addresses of every possible destination on the Internet	The CIDR or netmask used to help search the route table	The IP address of the next device that will get the packet in order to route the packet to the final destination	The interface on this device that is used to reach the next hop

field. It should be noted that a given operating system may place additional values in the route table or may show additional values when the route table is displayed. This will become evident during the lab assignments at the end of this chapter.

At first glance it might seem that we need a very large table if every possible destination needs to have an entry. The best way to look at the routing table is by looking at the possible next hop destinations for the packet. This is called next hop routing. As we saw in Table 6.7, the destination entry in the route table is represented by an IP address and a network mask or CIDR value. Figure 6.6 shows the possible next hop destination for a typical network.

Figure 6.6 shows three networks and a host (H1). From the viewpoint of the host (H1) there are three choices of where to the send the packet next. The H1

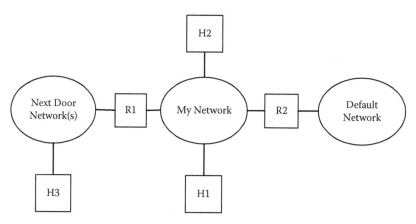

Figure 6.6:   Next hop routing.

can send the packet to a destination (host H2) on "my network." In that case, H1 can directly send the packet to the destination without help from another device. The host can send a packet to a host (H3) on a network it knows about (next-door network). In this case it needs to send a packet to router R1, which handles getting the packet to the destination. The final case is where H1 does not know how to get to the destination (the destination network is not in the route table). This is called the default route and is represented by router R2. Host H1 sends all packets where the destination address does not match any entry in the table to the default router. It should be noted that in many cases a host will not have any next-door networks specified, so the route table will have entries "my network" and the default route in the table.

Now that we have seen a generic example of a routing table in a simple network, we can look at a specific example as shown in Figure 6.7. There are two different scenarios in Figure 6.7: one showing hosts (H1 and H2) without any known next-door network and one where the hosts (H3 and H4) have a next-door network. Scenario 1 involves host H1, which has two choices for the destination network. It can either send the packet to devices (like host H2) that are directly connected to the same network (no router needed), or it can send packets to devices not connected to its network by sending them to router R1 (default router). Therefore, the routing table for host H1 has two entries, one for every device on its network (indicated by a destination address of 192.168.1.0/24) and the default route (indicated by the destination address of default), which goes through router R1. There is a third entry shown in the routing table that is the loopback address (127.0.0.1), which was described earlier in this chapter and will not be discussed further. It should be noted that different operating systems may have addition entries in the route table. For example, some operating systems add entries for the devices on the same network to the table as it discovers them.

Looking at the first entry in the route table for host H1 we see the destination address is specified as a CIDR address. So any destination address of 192.168.1.1 through 192.168.1.255 will match the first entry in the table. The next hop field for the first entry in the table has the IP address of host H1, which indicates that the destination device is on the same network as host H1. When a host needs to send a packet, it first compares the destination address to each entry in the destination column of the route table using the netmask or CIDR for each entry. So if host H1 wants to send a packet to host H2 (with IP address of 192.168.1.25), it looks in its route table and compares the destination address with each entry in the table after applying the netmask to the addresses. In this example the first entry is the network 192.168.1.0/24, so when 192.168.1.25 is masked using the 24-bit CIDR,

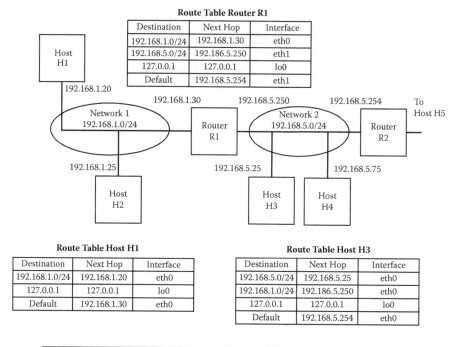

Route Table Router R1

Destination	Next Hop	Interface
192.168.1.0/24	192.168.1.30	eth0
192.168.5.0/24	192.186.5.250	eth1
127.0.0.1	127.0.0.1	lo0
Default	192.168.5.254	eth1

Route Table Host H1

Destination	Next Hop	Interface
192.168.1.0/24	192.168.1.20	eth0
127.0.0.1	127.0.0.1	lo0
Default	192.168.1.30	eth0

Route Table Host H3

Destination	Next Hop	Interface
192.168.5.0/24	192.168.5.25	eth0
192.168.1.0/24	192.186.5.250	eth0
127.0.0.1	127.0.0.1	lo0
Default	192.168.5.254	eth0

Packet Address Table

Entry	Source/Destination IP		Packet	Hardware Addresses	
	Source	Destination		Source	Destination
1	H1	H2	1	H1	H2
2	H1	H3	1	H1	R1
			2	R1	H3
3	H1	H5	1	H1	R1
			2	R1	R2
4	H3	H4	1	H3	H4
5	H3	H1	2	H3	R1
			1	R1	H1
6	H3	H5	2	H3	R2

Figure 6.7: Routing table example.

the address is 192.168.1.0, which matches the first entry in the table. Since the next hop (IP address) for the first entry is host H1 (itself), then the host knows it needs to send the packet directly to the destination and not through a router.

Now that host H1 knows the next hop where the packet needs to go, it sends the packet out on the interface specified in the route table to the host H2. The next question is how host H1 obtains the destination hardware address of the host H2 given that all it knows is the IP address of the host H2. For an Ethernet network, the Address Resolution Protocol (ARP) is used to ask devices on the local network what their hardware address is. The protocol sends a broadcast packet to all devices on the network asking if any device on the local network has the requested IP address. When a device receives the ARP request it checks the IP address in the request, and if the IP address matches, the host must respond with its hardware address. We will discuss this protocol in detail later in this chapter, but for now all we need to know is that the protocol exists. Once the host H1 obtains the hardware address of the host H2, it can send the packet. The packet is sent with the source hardware address equal to the hardware address of host H1, and the destination hardware address equal to the hardware address of host H2. This is shown as entry 1 in the packet address table in Figure 6.7. The next packet that is sent from host H1 to host H2 still uses the route table, as described above. The only difference is the ARP request is only needed once for each packet destined for the same device since the ARP results are cached. We will see that the ARP cache entries time out after a certain amount of inactivity. The routing process can be illustrated using a flowchart, as shown in Figure 6.8.

Figure 6.8 shows the steps outlined above plus an additional step if the device does not reply to the ARP request. The absence of an ARP reply indicates the destination device is not responding. The device that sends the ARP request will try to let the originator of the packet know that the packet could not be delivered. This is done through a special protocol that will be discussed later.

Referring back to Figure 6.7, the second part of the first scenario is where host H1 wishes to send a packet to host H3. Host H1 looks in the route table and compares the destination address of host H3 (192.168.5.25) against 192.168.1.0/24, and since 192.168.5.0 does not match 192.168.1.0, it checks the next entry, which is default. Default matches all addresses that have not been already matched and is the last entry checked. The next hop field contains the IP address of router R1, and therefore host H1 needs to send the packet to router R1 using the hardware address of R1 and keeping the source and destination IP addresses unchanged. Host H1 may have to use the ARP protocol to obtain the hardware address of router R1. When router R1 receives the packet from host H1, it checks to see if the packet is meant for the router. If the packet does not match the router's IP addresses, the router checks the route table to see if the address matches any of the entries in the table. The first entry in the table does not match since 192.168.5.0 does not match 192.168.1.0/24. The second entry in the table will match and indicates that the host H3 is directly connected to the same network (next hop address in the route table is the router's IP address on interface eth1). The router sends the packet to host H3 with the source and destination IP addresses unchanged. The destination hardware address is the hardware address of host H3, and again,

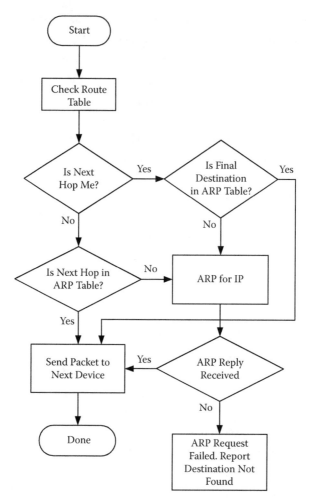

Figure 6.8: Routing process flowchart.

the router may have to use the ARP protocol to obtain the hardware addresses of
the host H3. The source hardware address is the hardware address of interface 2
on router R1. These two packets are shown as entry 2 in the packet address table
in Figure 6.7.

If the final destination of the packet sent by host H1 is not on network 1 or
network 2 (host H4, for example), then router 1 routes the packet to router 2
(its default route). Router 2 tries to route the packet to the next router, and this
continues until the packet reaches the final destination. These two packets are
shown as entry 3 in the packet address table in Figure 6.7. Note that as far as host
H1 is concerned, the route is the same to host H3 or to any device past router R1.

If a router is unable to route a packet to the destination, the router will send a packet back to the sender indicating a problem in the route.

The second scenario is using host H3 as the source of the packets. The route table for host H3 has three entries since it has three choices of where to send the packet next, network 2, network 1 (through router R1), and default (through router R2). There is a difference in the method used to send packets between scenario 2 and scenario 1. The route table is larger since host D3 knows about two networks instead of just one. The flowchart in Figure 6.8 still applies. In the packet address table shown in Figure 6.7 entries 4 to 6 show the packets for host H3 to send packets to hosts H4, H1, and H5.

Routing throughout the Internet is handled in the method described above. It should be noted there are numerous protocols that are designed to create and update the routing tables based on information obtained from the network and from external input. These routing protocols, often used in large networks, are interesting to study and do have some security implications. Routing protocols can cause problems for the Internet if they are successfully attacked. However, for the purpose of this book we will not discuss these protocols since they are often difficult to attack and are closely monitored.

Before we examine the vulnerabilities of the IP protocol we need to examine the IP packet format and two supporting protocols, ARP and the Internet Control Messaging Protocol (ICMP).

6.1.3   Packet Format

For the purpose of this text we will briefly examine the fields of the packet header. The IP packet consists of a fixed-size header that is 20 bytes long followed by an optional header and then a variable-length payload. Figure 6.9 shows the IP packet header.

VER	HLEN	Type of Service		Total Length	
ID			Flags	Offset	
Time to Live		Protocol		Checksum	
Source IP Address					
Destination IP Address					
Option(s)					
Data					

Figure 6.9:   IP header format.

The fields of the IP packet header are:

Version number (4 bits): This is the version of the IP protocol. The two values are 4 and 6. Version 4 is the protocol used across the Internet. However, version 6 is being pushed by several groups, and the goal is to replace version 4. Version 6 will be discussed later in this chapter.

Header length (4 bits): This is the length of the IP header in 4-byte words. The default value is 5.

Type of service (8 bits): This field was designed to be used to pick different networks based on a level of service. The original thought was that there would be different networks, each offering certain services, and packets would be routed based on the type of service. This field is not generally used and is typically set to all zeros.

Length (16 bits): This field is used to indicate the length of the payload in bytes.

Identifier (16 bits): This field contains an identifier that is used to uniquely identify each packet that originates from a device. This field is used to support segmentation and reassembly. When a packet is segmented, each segment maintains the original id value so when the segments reach the destination they can be reassembled.

Flags (3 bits): These three bits contain two flags. The first bit is reserved and is set to zero. The second bit is the "don't fragment" (D) flag. When this bit is set to 1 by the originator of the packet, then the packet cannot be fragmented by the routers as it traverses the Internet. If the router needs to fragment the packet because of the size limitation of lower layers and the D flag is set, the packet is discarded and a message is sent back to the sender. The third bit is the "more" (M) flag. When this bit is set to 1 it indicates that the packet is part of a set of segmented packets and it is not the last packet in the segment. If the M flag is set to zero, then the packet is the last packet in the segment. The M flag is set to zero if there are no fragments.

Offset (13 bits): This field is used to indicate where the fragment should be placed in the reassembly buffer. The offset value is multiplied by 8 to get the actual offset in the buffer. Figure 6.10 shows an IP packet that is fragmented and the values of the length, flags, and offset fields. All other fields from the original packet are copied to the fragments.

As we see in Figure 6.14, the original packet was fragmented into two fragments. Fragment 1 is 1,480 bytes long, which is divisible by 8. The length of all fragments except the last fragment must be divisible by 8 since the offset value is multiplied by 8 to indicate the position in the reassembly buffer. The offset for fragment 2 is 185 (1,480/8). Notice the total length in the header of each fragment is changed to represent the new length. This means that the total length of the original packet is no longer found in the header and can only be determined when all of the fragments are reassembled. We also see that fragment 1 has the M bit set to 1, and that fragment 2 has it set to zero, indicating it is the last fragment. Figure 6.10 shows fragment 1 is further fragmented into 1a and 1b. Again, the length of the fragments must be divisible by 8. When the three fragments arrive at the destination, they may arrive out of order. They are placed into a reassembly buffer based on the value of the offset. We know the total length when the last fragment arrives, and we know the packet is done when the buffer has all of the holes filled. The id field is used to match the fragments up to the buffer.

Time to live (TTL) (8 bits): This field is used to prevent packets that cannot reach a destination from traversing the Internet indefinitely. Every router that processes an IP packet decrements the TTL field in the header by 1. The router that decrements the TTL to zero deletes the packet and sends a message back to the device that originated the packet, indicating the TTL expired. This field can also be used to determine the addresses of the routers used to reach a destination. The process is called a traceroute [9–11]. To perform a traceroute the originator sends a packet to the destination with the TTL set to 1, and the first router decrements the value to zero and returns an error message. The originator sends another packet with the TTL set to 2.

Fields	Original Packet	Fragment 1	Fragment 2	Fragment 1a	Fragment 1b
Ver/HLEN	4/5	4/5	4/5	4/5	4/5
Type	0	0	0	0	0
Length	2520	1500	1040	980	540
ID	2356	2356	2356	2356	2356
Flags	0	0 0 1	0 0 0	0 0 1	0 0 1
Offset	0	0	185	0	120
TTL	150	Computed	Computed	Computed	Computed
Protocol	TCP	TCP	TCP	TCP	TCP
Checksum	Computed	Computed	Computed	Computed	Computed
Source IP	IP1	IP1	IP1	IP1	IP1
Dest IP	IP2	IP2	IP2	IP2	IP2
Data Len	2500	1480	1020	960	520

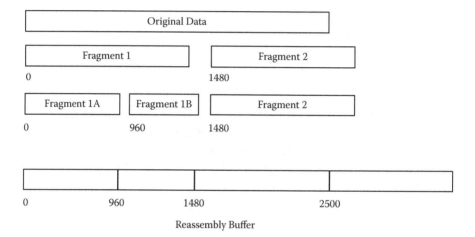

Figure 6.10:   IP fragmentation.

The next router in line decrements the TTL to zero and returns an error. This continues until the final destination is reached and it returns a response to the originator. By default, traceroute uses the Internet Control Message Protocol, which will be discussed later. Attackers have used other protocol types in order to defeat countermeasures to achieve the same effect.

Protocol (8 bits): This field indicates the upper-layer protocol that will handle the packet. There are numerous values defined. The most common values are 1 for ICMP, 6 for TCP, and 17 for UDP.

Checksum (16 bits): This field is used for error detection and is a checksum over the entire packet. This does cause a problem in that the router changes the header, and therefore must recalculate the checksum. Also, if the packet is fragmented, the checksum will be recomputed for each fragment. This takes time, and as networks become larger and faster, the routers start to become a bottleneck. We leave it up to the reader to refer to the references for the method of computing the checksum value.

Source IP address (32 bits): This field contains the IP address of the sender.

Destination IP address (32 bits): This field contains the IP address of the destination.

Options (variable): The option field for IP is seldom used, and therefore will not be discussed in the context of this book. While there may be vulnerabilities and attacks against the option fields, they are rare and are mitigated using the same methods as the fixed part of the header.

Data (variable): The data can contain any value and has a maximum length of 65,536 minus the header length.

6.1.4   Address Resolution Protocol (ARP)

As we discussed in the section on IP routing, the ARP protocol is used to find the hardware address of a device knowing only the device's IP address. The ARP protocol is designed to work with different physical network layers. The most common physical layer network protocol is Ethernet and will be the focus of this discussion. Since the requesting device does not know the hardware address of the destination, it must use an Ethernet broadcast packet to send the ARP request to every device on the network. When a device receives an ARP request packet it compares the IP address in the header with its own IP address, and if there is a match, the device sends an ARP reply packet back to the device that sent the ARP request. The ARP reply packet is not a broadcast packet. When the requesting device receives an ARP reply, it places the result in an ARP cache. As long as the device is sending data to a destination that is in the cache, the cache remains valid. This helps reduce the number of broadcast packets on the network. If the

ARP Header

Hardware Type		Protocol Type	
HLEN	PLEN	Operation	
Sender Hardware Address (bytes 0-3)			
Sender HW Address (bytes 4-5)		Sender IP (bytes 0-1)	
Sender IP (bytes 2-3)		Target HW Address (bytes 0-1)	
Target Hardware Address (bytes 2-5)			
Target IP Address (bytes 0-3)			

ARP Request

Ethernet Header			Data	
Broadcast	SRC HW	0×806	ARP Header	Padding

ARP Reply

Ethernet Header			Data	
DST HW	SRC HW	0×806	ARP Header	Padding

Figure 6.11:　ARP packet format.

device quits sending data for a period of time, then the cache times out and the entry is cleared. The typical timeout value for the cache is 5 minutes.

If there is no response to the ARP request after a certain amount of time, the sender tries again. After so many attempts the sender gives up and reports back that the destination device cannot be found. The timeout value and the number of retries are device specific. The ARP packet has a simple format, as shown in Figure 6.11.

Figure 6.11 shows the ARP header and how the ARP header is encapsulated into an Ethernet packet. As we can see in the figure, the ARP header is designed to support multiple physical network protocols. The fields of the packet are:

Hardware type (16 bits): The type of physical network that the ARP protocol is used on. Ethernet has the value of 1.

Protocol type (16 bits): The protocol that is using the ARP protocol. IP uses a value of 0x800.

Hardware length (8 bits): The length of the hardware address fields in the header in bytes. Ethernet uses a value of 6.

Protocol length (8 bits): The length of the upper-layer protocol addresses. IP version 4 uses a value of 4.

Operation (16 bits): Indicates whether the packet is a request (value = 1) or reply (value = 2).

Sender hardware address (variable): Hardware address of the sender of the packet. Ethernet uses 6 bytes for this field.

Sender protocol address (variable): IP address of the sender. IP version 4 uses 4 bytes for this field.

Target hardware address (variable): Hardware address of the target device. Ethernet uses 6 bytes for this field. In the ARP request this field is all zeros.

Target protocol address (variable): IP address of the target. IP version 4 uses 4 bytes for this field.

Figure 6.11 also shows the ARP packet as payload in an Ethernet frame. As we see, the ARP request has the destination Ethernet address set to broadcast and the source hardware address is the address of the requester. The Ethernet type field is set to 0x806. The reply placket uses the source and destination hardware addresses of the sender and receiver. The figure also shows padding at the end of the ARP header. This is needed since the length of the ARP header is smaller than the minimum Ethernet packet size.

One interesting use of the ARP request is to determine if two devices have the same IP address. When a device first enables its IP protocol stack it should send an ARP request asking for the hardware address of any device with its IP address. The device should not get any responses to the ARP request. If the device receives a response to the ARP request, the device reports an error. The device that sent the ARP reply should also note the error since it should never see an ARP request with the sending IP matching its IP. When a device detects an address conflict, its action depends on the implementation. Some devices halt all network access for some period of time and then try again. Other devices ignore the error. This can make for an interesting attack. If the attacker has access to the network, he or she could create ARP request packets that make other devices think there is an address conflict, which could cause a denial of service. Of course, if the two devices (device A and device B) do have conflicting IP addresses and both continue to function, then results can be strange. You might talk to device A because the ARP reply gave you the hardware address of device A, while another device may end up talking to device B because it got the ARP reply from device B.

This should get you to think about other ways to use ARP replies to trick senders into sending packets to the wrong place [12–14]. This is called ARP spoofing or ARP cache poisoning and can be carried out by attackers on the same network as the victim. We will discuss this in more detail as an authentication-based attack.

6.1.5   Internet Control Messaging Protocol (ICMP)

The Internet Control Messaging Protocol (ICMP) is used to make queries of other devices running IP and to report errors that occur during the routing or delivery of IP packets. ICMP is described as part of the IP protocol in that it helps IP function. However, the ICMP packets are carried as payload in an IP packet. From that standpoint, ICMP looks like an upper-layer protocol. We will introduce several common ICMP message types and discuss their impact on security. The vulnerabilities and attacks will be discussed while looking at the vulnerabilities of the IP layer [15]. Figure 6.12 shows the format of the ICMP packet and how it is encapsulated into the IP packet.

As we see in Figure 6.12, the ICMP packet has an 8-bit type field and an 8-bit code field used to indicate what type of ICMP message is being used. The type field distinguishes between several types of ICMP packets, and each type may have one or more functions designated by the code field. The checksum is used for error checking, and the remainder of the header is divided into a parameter and data section that is based on the particular message type. Table 6.8 shows the values for the common ICMP messages, which are discussed in more detail next.

VER	HLEN	Type of Service		Total Length	
ID			Flags	Offset	IP Header
Time to Live		1		Checksum	
Source IP Address					
Destination IP Address					
Type		Code		Checksum	
Parameter					ICMP Header
Information					

Figure 6.12:   ICMP packet format within an IP packet.

TABLE 6.8: ICMP Messages

Type	Code	Parameter	Data	Name
		Common Query Messages		
0	0	Id (16) + Seq Number (16)	User specified	Echo reply
8	0	Id (16) + Seq Number (16)	User specified	Echo request
13	0	Id (16) + Seq Number (16)	Original timestamp (32 bits) Receive timestamp (32 bits) Transmit timestamp (32 bits)	Timestamp request
14	0	Id (16) + Seq Number (16)	Original timestamp (32 bits) Receive timestamp (32 bits) Transmit timestamp (32 bits)	Timestamp reply
		Common Error Messages		
3	1–15	0	Original IP header plus 8 bytes of payload	Destination unreachable
11	0 or 1	0	Original IP header plus 8 bytes of payload	Time exceeded
5	0–3	IP address of new router	Original IP header plus 8 bytes of payload	Redirection

6.1.5.1 ICMP Echo Request (TYPE = 8) and Reply (TYPE = 0)

The echo request and reply messages are used to probe a device to see if it will answer. These messages are more often called ping request and ping reply. Ping is the name of the application used to send and receive the ICMP echo packets. The ping request uses an id number that is unique to that set of ping requests. That way, if two or more instances of the ping application are running on the same host, the packets will be different. The sequence number is used to distinguish each packet sent by a given application. Each packet sent has the sequence number increased by 1. The echo request supports a user-defined payload, and the echo reply packet returns the payload. The ping command uses the echo request and echo reply packets to measure the amount of time it takes for a packet to make a round-trip. The ICMP echo messages are very useful to diagnose network problems and

TABLE 6.9: ICMP Destination Unreachable Code Values

Code	Reason
0	Network unreachable
1	Host unreachable
2	Protocol unreachable on the target host
3	Port unreachable on the target host
4	Fragmentation needed and "don't fragment" bit is set
5	Source route failed

tell if a host is running. The ICMP echo messages are also used by attackers to determine if a host is running. There is debate among security experts about allowing the echo requests packet to enter a network from the Internet since they can be used to see how many hosts are running. As a lab experiment, the reader can ping several popular web sites to see how many respond.

6.1.5.2 ICMP Timestamp Request (TYPE = 13) and Reply (TYPE = 14)

The ICMP timestamp request and reply messages work just like the echo request and response, except they place time values in the data field to determine the time to reach the destination and the time to return. These ICMP messages are not as common in the Internet.

6.1.5.3 ICMP Destination Unreachable (TYPE = 0)

The destination unreachable message is used to indicate that the packet cannot reach its destination. The code field contains the reason the packet could not get to the destination, and the data field contains the IP header plus 8 bytes of payload of the IP packet that could reach its destination. Table 6.9 shows some of the common code values and describes the reason that corresponds to the code.

6.1.5.4 ICMP Time Exceeded (TYPE = 11)

If the code field is zero, the time exceeded message indicates that the time-to-live field was decremented to zero and the packet was deleted. If the code field is 1, then the packet was fragmented and the receiving device did not get all the fragments before a timer expired. In both cases the IP header plus 8 bytes of payload of the original packet is returned in the data field of the ICMP packet.

The ICMP time exceeded message is used by the traceroute program to get the IP addresses of the routers along the path. As was described earlier, the traceroute program sends packets with the time to live starting at 1 and increasing until the destination is reached. When the traceroute program receives the ICMP time exceeded message it extracts the IP of the device that sent the ICMP time exceeded message from the IP packet header. The standard version of traceroute sends ICMP echo request messages, but since the echo request packets are sometimes blocked, there have been versions created that use other packets.

6.1.5.5 ICMP Redirection (TYPE = 5)

The redirect message is used by a router to tell a host on the same local network that there is a better router to use to get to the destination. Unlike the other ICMP error message, the packet is not discarded by the router. The parameter field contains the IP address of the router that should be used. The code fields are listed in Table 6.10, along with their meanings. The IP header plus 8 bytes of payload of the original packet is returned in the data field of the ICMP packet.

6.1.6 Putting It All Together

Now that we have seen the IP protocol and the supporting protocols, it would be helpful to look at an example with multiple scenarios that illustrates how the protocols are used and what the packets look like on the network. Figure 6.13 shows a network that is similar to the one we used as an example when looking at IP routing.

In Figure 6.13 we see three networks interconnected with routers plus the Internet. For each scenario we will look at the number of packets that need to be generated and the address fields of the packets. For this example we will assume that host H1 will be sending a single ICMP echo request to each host (H2, H3, H4, and H5) in that order. We will also assume that the ARP caches for every device are clear when H1 starts, and that entries placed in the ARP caches will stay in cache for the remainder of the scenarios. The last two scenarios show ICMP echo requests that are destined for hosts that do not exist, one on network 1 and one

TABLE 6.10:   ICMP Redirection Code Values

Code	Meaning
0	Network-based redirect
1	Host-based redirect
2	Network-based redirect of the type of service specified
3	Host-based redirect of the type of service specified

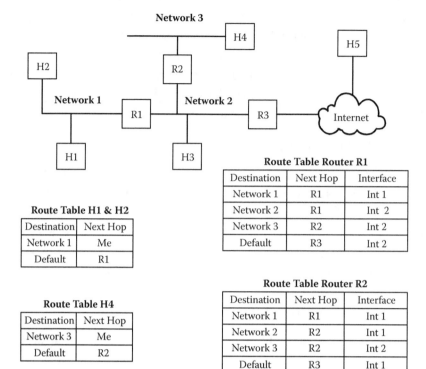

Figure 6.13:   IP layer example.

on network 2. The route tables for the devices are also shown in the figure. Note that the loopback entry has been removed from all route tables, and the interface column has been removed from the host route tables.

6.1.6.1   Scenario 1 (H1 to H2)

Figure 6.14 shows the packets sent across network 1 in order for host H1 to send an ICMP echo request to host H2, and for host H2 to respond to the request with an ICMP echo reply packet. Figure 6.14 also shows the contents of the relevant ARP tables at various times during the packet flow.

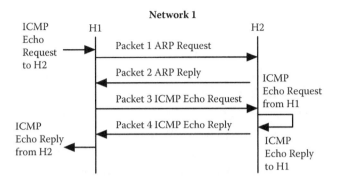

Packet	Hardware Addresses		IP Addresses		Payload
	DST	SRC	DST	SRC	
1	Broadcast	H1	N/A	N/A	ARP
2	H1	H2	N/A	N/A	ARP
3	H2	H1	H2	H1	ICMP
4	H1	H2	H1	H2	ICMP

ARP Table for H1

Time	Destination	HW Address
Start	Empty	Empty
After P2	H2	H2

ARP Table for H2

Time	Destination	HW Address
Start	Empty	Empty
After P1	H1	H1

Figure 6.14: Scenario 1 packet flow.

As we see in Figure 6.14, host H1 assembles an ICMP echo request packet with a destination IP address of H2 and a source IP address of H1. The IP layer in host H1 uses its route table to look up the next hop that is used to reach the destination address of H2. The route table indicates that the packet can be delivered directly to the destination, and therefore the destination hardware address needs to be the hardware address of H2. Since the ARP cache for host H1 does not contain an entry for host H2, host H1 broadcasts an ARP request packet to all devices on network 1 (packet 1). Host H2 receives the ARP request and determines that the ARP request is asking for its hardware address. Host H2 sends an ARP reply directly back to H1 (packet 2). Host H2 also adds the hardware address of host H1 to its ARP cache. When host H1 receives the ARP reply, it can finish creating the ICMP echo request packet by filling in the destination hardware address with the value received from the ARP reply. H1 also adds the hardware address of host H2 to its ARP table. Host H1 sends the ICMP echo request to host H2 (packet 3). Host H2 receives the ICMP echo request packet, and using the IP header, it extracts the IP address of host H1 and uses that as the destination address for the ICMP echo reply packet. Host H2 creates an ICMP echo reply packet and checks its routing table to see where to send the packet. The route table indicates that host H2 can send the packet directly to host H1. Host H2 sends the ICMP echo reply (packet 4). Note that H2 does not need to ARP for the hardware address of host H1 since it was able to add the entry for host H1 into its ARP cache from the information contained in the ARP request from host H1.

In this scenario four packets were transmitted across network 1. From a security standpoint this traffic will not leave network 1, and therefore can only be sniffed by devices on network 1. It is virtually impossible for a device outside of network 1 to disrupt the traffic between host H1 and host H2.

6.1.6.2   Scenario 2 (H1 to H3)

Figure 6.15 shows the packets sent across network 1 and network 2 in order for host H1 to send an ICMP echo request to host H3, and for host H3 to respond to the request with an ICMP ARP reply packet.

As we see in Figure 6.15, host H1 assembles an ICMP echo request with the destination IP address of host H3. Host H1 checks its route table and discovers that the next hop is router R1 (the default case). Host H1 checks its ARP table, and since there is no entry for R1, it sends an ARP request to all devices on network 1 (packet 1). When router R1 receives the ARP request packet it inserts the address information for host H1 in its ARP cache. Router R1 responds to the ARP request with an ARP reply (packet 2), with the destination hardware address set to the hardware address of host H1. Host H1 inserts the address information from the ARP reply into its ARP table, sets the destination hardware address of the ICMP echo packet to the hardware address of router R1, and sends the packet to router R1 (packet 3). Note that the IP addresses used for the ICMP echo request packet are the originator IP (host H1) and the final destination IP (host H3).

Router R1 receives the ICMP echo request packet and determines, based on the destination IP address, that the packet is not destined for router R1, and therefore it should be routed somewhere else. Router R1 decrements the time-to-live field and determines if the packet has reached its maximum number of hops. If the packet has reached its end of life, the packet is discarded and an ICMP time exceeded packet is sent back to H1 by the router. The router sets the destination IP address to the address of host H1, and the source IP address is set to the IP address of router R1 on interface 1. The payload of the ICMP time exceeded packet contains the IP header of the packet that was discarded plus 8 bytes of the packet's data.

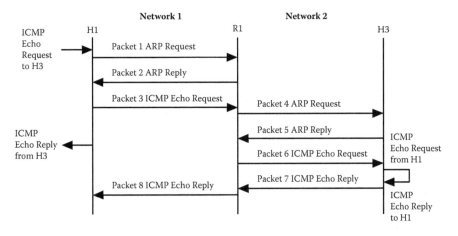

Packet	Hardware Addresses		IP Addresses		Payload
	DST	SRC	DST	SRC	
1	Broadcast	H1	N/A	N/A	ARP
2	H1	R1 (Int 1)	N/A	N/A	ARP
3	R1 (Int 1)	H1	H3	H1	ICMP
4	Broadcast	R1 (Int 2)	N/A	N/A	ARP
5	R1 (Int 2)	H3	N/A	N/A	ARP
6	H3	R1 (Int 2)	H3	H1	ICMP
7	R1 (Int 2)	H3	H1	H3	ICMP
8	H1	R1 (Int 1)	H1	H3	ICMP

ARP Table for H1

Time	Destination	HW Address
Start	H2	H2
After P2	R1	R1 (Int 1)

ARP Table for H3

Time	Destination	HW Address
Start	Empty	Empty
After P4	R1	R1 (Int 2)

ARP Table for R1 (int 1)

Time	Destination	HW Address
Start	Empty	Empty
After P1	H1	H1

ARP Table for R1 (int 2)

Time	Destination	HW Address
Start	Empty	Empty
After P5	H3	H3

Figure 6.15: Scenario 2 packet flow.

Assuming the time to live did not expire, router R1 checks its routing table to determine where to send the packet next. The route table indicates that host H3 is directly connected to network 2, and that router R1 can access network 2 using interface 2. Router R1 checks the ARP table for interface 2 and determines it needs to send an ARP request to the hosts on network 2 (packet 4). When host H3 receives the ARP request it inserts the address information for router R1 into its ARP table and responds back to router R1 with an ARP reply (packet 5). Router R1 inserts the address information into its ARP table and forwards the ICMP echo request packet to host H3 (packet 6) using the hardware address of host H3. Host H3 receives the ICMP echo request and creates an ICMP echo reply packet destined for host H1. Host H3 checks its route table to determine the next hop. It finds the next hop is router R1, and that the ARP table has the hardware address for R1. Host H3 sends the ICMP echo reply packet to R1 (packet 7), and R1 routes the packet back to H1 (packet 8).

In this scenario four packets were transmitted across network 1 and four packets were transmitted across network 2. From a security standpoint this traffic can be seen by devices on networks 1 and 2. An attacker with access to either network could sniff the traffic and disrupt the traffic between H1 and H3. We can also see that a device from one network can cause several packets to be generated by sending just one packet into that network.

6.1.6.3 Scenario 3 (H1 to H4)

Figure 6.16 shows the packets sent across networks 1, 2, and 3 in order for host H1 to send an ICMP echo request to host H4, and for host H4 to respond with an ICMP echo reply packet. This scenario assumes the ARP caches are populated with the values from the first two scenarios.

As we see in Figure 6.16, host H1 creates an ICMP echo request with a destination IP address of host H4. Host H1 checks its route table and discovers that the next hop is router R1 (the default case). Host H1 checks its ARP table and gets the hardware address for router R1 from the table. Host H1 sets the destination hardware address of the ICMP echo request packet to the hardware address of router R1 and sends the packet to router R1 (packet 1).

Router R1 receives the ICMP echo request packet from host H1 and determines, based on the destination IP address, that the packet is not destined for router R1, and therefore it should be routed somewhere else. Router R1 decrements the time-to-live field and determines if the packet has reached its maximum number of hops. Assuming the time to live did not expire, router R1 checks its routing table to determine where to send the packet next. The route table indicates that the host H4 is accessed using router R2 through interface 2. Router R1 checks its ARP table for interface 2 and determines it will need to send an ARP request to the hosts on network 2, asking for the hardware address of router R2 (packet 2). Router R2 inserts the address information from the ARP request into its ARP table and responds back to router R1 with an ARP reply (packet 3). Router R1

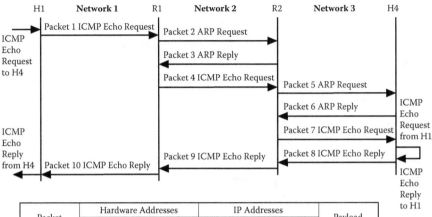

| Packet | Hardware Addresses | | IP Addresses | | Payload |
	DST	SRC	DST	SRC	
1	R1 (Int 1)	H1	H4	H1	ICMP
2	Broadcast	R1 (Int 2)	N/A	N/A	ARP
3	R1 (Int 2)	R2 (Int 1)	N/A	N/A	ARP
4	R2 (Int 1)	R1 (Int 2)	H4	H1	ICMP
5	Broadcast	R2 (Int 2)	N/A	N/A	ARP
6	R2 (Int 2)	H4	N/A	N/A	ARP
7	H4	R2 (Int 2)	H4	H1	ICMP
8	R2 (Int 2)	H4	H1	H4	ICMP
9	R1 (Int 2)	R2 (Int 1)	H1	H4	ICMP
10	H1	R1 (Int 1)	H1	H4	ICMP

ARP Table for H1

Time	Destination	HW Address
Start	H2	H2
	R1	R1 (Int 1)

ARP Table for H4

Time	Destination	HW Address
Start	Empty	Empty
After P5	R2	R2 (Int 2)

ARP Table for R1 (int 1)

Time	Destination	HW Address
Start	H1	H1

ARP Table for R1 (int 2)

Time	Destination	HW Address
Start	H3	H3
After P3	R2	R2 (Int 1)

ARP Table for R2 (int 1)

Time	Destination	HW Address
Start	Empty	Empty
After P2	R1	R1 (Int 2)

ARP Table for R2 (int 2)

Time	Destination	HW Address
Start	Empty	Empty
After P6	H4	H4

Figure 6.16: Scenario 3 packet flow.

inserts the address information into its ARP table and forwards the ICMP echo request packet to router R2 (packet 4).

Router R2 receives the ICMP echo request and determines the packet needs to be routed to host H4 (assuming the time to live has not expired). Its ARP table indicates router R2 needs to send an ARP request for the hardware address of host H4 (packet 5). The ARP request allows host H4 to add the address information to its ARP table and to respond back to router R2 with an ARP reply (packet 6). Router R2 inserts the address information into its ARP table and forwards the ICMP echo request to host H4 using the hardware destination address obtained from the ARP reply (packet 7). Host H4 receives the ICMP echo request and extracts the IP address of host H1 from the IP header. Host H4 creates an ICMP echo reply packet that is destined for host H1. Host H4 checks its route table to determine the next hop and then checks its ARP table for the hardware address of the next hop. It finds the next hop is router R2, and that the ARP table has the hardware address for router R2. Host H4 sends the ICMP echo reply packet to router R2 (packet 8), and router R2 routes the packet back to router R1 (packet 9), which routes the packet to host H1 (packet 10).

In this scenario two packets were transmitted across network 1 and four packets were transmitted across networks 2 and 3. From a security standpoint, the traffic between host H1 and host H4 can be seen by devices on networks 1, 2, and 3. An attacker with access to any of these networks could sniff and disrupt the traffic between H1 and H4. This shows the importance of securing access to the networks that carry traffic between other networks.

6.1.6.4 Scenario 4 (H1 to H5)

Figure 6.17 shows the packets sent across networks 1 and 2 in order for host H1 to send an ICMP echo request to host H5, and for host H5 to respond to the request with an ICMP echo reply packet. This scenario assumes the ARP caches are populated with the values from the first three scenarios.

As we see in Figure 6.17, host H1 creates an ICMP echo request with the destination IP address of host H5. Host H1 checks its route table and discovers that the next hop is router R1 (the default case). H1 checks its ARP table and gets the address of router R1 from the ARP table. Host H1 sets the destination hardware address of the ICMP echo request packet to the hardware address of router R1 and sends the packet to router R1 (packet 1).

Router R1 receives the ICMP echo request packet from host H1 and determines, based on the destination IP address, that the packet is not destined for router R1, and therefore it should be routed somewhere else. Router R1 decrements the

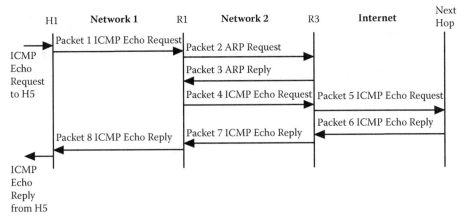

Packet	Hardware Addresses		IP Addresses		Payload
	DST	SRC	DST	SRC	
1	R1 (Int 1)	H1	H5	H1	ICMP
2	Broadcast	R1 (Int 2)	N/A	N/A	ARP
3	R1 (Int 2)	R3 (Int 1)	N/A	N/A	ARP
4	R3 (Int 1)	R1 (Int 2)	H5	H1	ICMP
5	Next hop	R3 (Int 2)	H5	H1	ICMP
6	R3 (Int 2)	Next hop	H1	H5	ICMP
7	R1 (Int 2)	R3 (Int 1)	H1	H5	ICMP
8	H1	R1 (Int 1)	H1	H5	ICMP

ARP Table for H1

Time	Destination	HW Address
Start	H2	H2
	R1	R1 (Int 1)

ARP Table for H4

Time	Destination	HW Address
Start	Empty	Empty
	R2	R2 (Int 2)

ARP Table for R1 (int 1)

Time	Destination	HW Address
Start	H1	H1

ARP Table for R1 (int 2)

Time	Destination	HW Address
Start	H3	H3
	R2	R2 (Int 1)
After P3	R3	R3 (Int 1)

ARP Table for R3 (int 1)

Time	Destination	HW Address
Start	Empty	Empty
After P2	R1	R1 (Int 2)

Figure 6.17: Scenario 4 packet flow.

time-to-live field and determines whether the packet has reached its maximum number of hops. Assuming the time to live did not expire, router R1 checks its routing table to determine where to send the packet next. The route table indicates that the host H5 is accessed using router R3 through interface 2 (the default case). Router R1 then checks the ARP table for interface 2 and determines it needs to send an ARP request to the hosts on network 2, asking for the hardware address of router R3 (packet 2). Router R3 inserts the address information from the ARP request into its ARP table and responds back to router R1 with an ARP reply (packet 3). Router R1 inserts the address information into its ARP table and forwards the ICMP echo request packet to router R3 (packet 4).

Router R3 sends the packet into the Internet. We are assuming router R3 knows how to get the packet to the next hop and that the packet will be routed through the Internet until it reaches host H5. Host H5 uses the source IP address from the received IP packet (host H1) to create an ICMP reply packet that is routed back to router R3 (packet 6). Router R3 forwards the packet to router R1 (packet 7), and router R1 forwards the packet to host H1 (packet 8).

In this scenario two packets were transmitted across network 1 and four packets were transmitted across network 2. From a security standpoint this traffic can be seen by devices on networks 1 and 2. An attacker with access to any of these networks could sniff and disrupt the traffic between host H1 and host H5. Another aspect of security that is shown in the four scenarios is the placement of network security devices. If we wanted to monitor the traffic for all four scenarios we would need to place multiple monitors (typically one per network) since there is no single place all of the traffic can be monitored.

6.1.6.5   Scenario 5 (H1 to No Host on Network 1)

Figure 6.18 shows the packets sent across network 1 in order for host H1 to attempt to send an ICMP echo request to a nonexistent host on network 1. This scenario assumes the ARP caches are populated with the values from the first four scenarios.

As we see in Figure 6.18, host H1 assembles an ICMP echo request packet with a destination IP address of host H6 (assume that the address of host H6 is on network 1, but there is no device with the address of H6) and a source IP address of host H1. The IP layer uses the route table to look up the next hop needed to reach the destination IP address of host H6. The route table indicates the packet can be delivered directly to the destination, and therefore the destination hardware address of the ICMP echo request packet needs to have the hardware address of host H6. Since the ARP cache for host H1 does not contain an entry

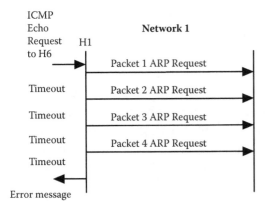

Packet	Hardware Addresses		IP Addresses		Payload
	DST	SRC	DST	SRC	
1	Broadcast	H1	N/A	N/A	ARP
2	Broadcast	H1	N/A	N/A	ARP
3	Broadcast	H1	N/A	N/A	ARP
4	Broadcast	H1	N/A	N/A	ARP

ARP Table for H1

Time	Destination	HW Address
Start	H2	H2
	R1	R1 (Int 1)

Figure 6.18: Scenario 5 packet flow.

for host H6, host H1 broadcasts an ARP request to all devices on network 1 (packet 1). When host H1 does not receive a response to the ARP request (after a certain amount of time), host H1 retransmits the ARP request. After some number of retries (packets 2 and 3), host H1 quits trying and indicates that host H6 is not available. This notification is sent to the application that tried to send the packet. Most applications, upon getting this notification, stop trying to send the packet.

In this scenario we show four ARP request packets being transmitted across network 1 before the host H1 determines that there is no host H6. From a security standpoint the issue is a potential flood of broadcast packets, which can affect the performance of the network and the hosts attached to the network. This is not a very effective attack since the attacker is on the same network as the targets and can be located. In a large network, though, it may be difficult to track down the sender of ARP requests if the IP address has been stolen. There are programs that can monitor the ARP requests and create log messages when the IP address to hardware address mapping has changed.

6.1.6.6   Scenario 6 (H1 to No Host on Network 2)

Figure 6.19 shows the packets sent across networks 1 and 2 in order for host H1 to attempt to send an ICMP echo request to a nonexistent host on network 2.

As we see in Figure 6.19, host H1 assembles an ICMP echo request packet with a destination IP address of host H7 and a source IP address of host H1 (assume that the address of H7 is on network 2, but there is no device at the address of H7).

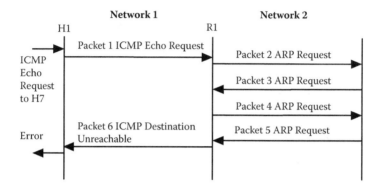

Packet	Hardware Addresses		IP Addresses		Payload
	DST	SRC	DST	SRC	
1	R1 (Int 1)	H1	H7	H1	ICMP
2	Broadcast	R1 (Int 2)	N/A	N/A	ARP
3	Broadcast	R1 (Int 2)	N/A	N/A	ARP
4	Broadcast	R1 (Int 2)	N/A	N/A	ARP
5	Broadcast	R1 (Int 2)	N/A	N/A	ARP
6	H1	R1 (Int 1)	H1	R1	ICMP

ARP Table for H1

Time	Destination	HW Address
Start	H2	H2
	R1	R1 (Int 1)

ARP Table for R1 (int 2)

Time	Destination	HW Address
	H3	H3
Start	R2	R2 (Int 1)
	R3	R3 (Int 1)

ARP Table for R1 (int 1)

Time	Destination	HW Address
Start	H1	H1

Figure 6.19:   Scenario 6 packet flow.

Host H1 checks its route table and discovers that the next hop is router R1 (the default case). Host H1 checks its ARP table and gets the hardware address of router R1 from the table. Host H1 sets the destination hardware address of the ICMP echo packet to the hardware address of router R1 and sends the packet to router R1 (packet 1).

Router R1 receives the ICMP echo request packet and determines, based on the destination IP address, that the packet is not destined for router R1, and therefore it should be routed somewhere else. Router R1 decrements the time-to-live field and determines if the packet has reached its maximum number of hops. Assuming the time to live did not expire, router R1 checks its routing table to determine where to send the packet next. The route table indicates that host H7 is directly connected to network 2, and that router R1 can access network 2 using interface 2. Router R1 then checks the ARP table for interface 2 and determines it will need to send an ARP request to the hosts on network 2 (packet 2) asking for the hardware address of host H7. When router R1 does not receive a response to the ARP request (after a certain amount of time), router R1 retransmits the ARP request. After some number of retries (packets 2 to 3), router R1 indicates that the host H7 is not available.

Router R1 may create an ICMP destination unreachable packet and send it back to the host H1 (packet 4). Not all routers are configured to return the ICMP destination unreachable packet, in which case the sender may not stop sending packets. If host H1 gets an ICMP destination unreachable packet, then the application typically stops sending packets.

In this scenario we see that the single ICMP echo and an ICMP destination unreachable packet are transmitted across network 1. We see four ARP request packets being transmitted across network 2 before router R1 determines that host H7 does not exist. From a security standpoint the issue is the same as in scenario 5, except the device (host H1) that caused the creation of the ARP request packets is on a different network. This scenario shows how a remote computer can send one packet into a network and cause multiple broadcast packets to be generated. Since the ARP table of the router never gets filled, every request from the outside will cause an ARP request.

This can really be a problem when multiple attackers are sending packets to a network with multiple nonexistent hosts. For example, if an attacker is sweeping through an address range of a network with a small number of hosts compared to open addresses, then there will be a large number of ARP request packets generated. If multiple attackers all target the same network, the result could be an ARP flood within a network.

As we will see, there are several vulnerabilities and attacks that target the IP layer and the supporting protocols (ARP and ICMP). Several of the attacks involve the interaction between the various protocols, while other attacks target the specific protocol. The next four sections will use the taxonomy to examine the attacks against these protocols.

6.1.7   Header-Based Attacks

There are several header attacks that can be carried out against the IP protocol. The fields that cause the most trouble are the length, flags, and offset fields. Many of the other fields cause the packet to be rejected if they are invalid. Since any device on the Internet can create an IP packet and have it delivered to a given host, this makes header-based attacks potentially harmful. From a security standpoint we can divide the fields of the IP header into two categories. The first category (endpoint fields) consists of fields that are used primarily by the endpoint and are not examined while the packet is in transit. The second category (transit fields) consists of fields that are examined by each router and possibly modified in transit. The endpoint fields are length, id, flags, offset, protocol, and the source IP address. Even though a router can change the values of the length, flags, and offset fields if it needs to fragment the packet, they are considered endpoint fields, since most attacks using these fields target the endpoint. An attack against the transit fields often causes the packet to be dropped by the routers.

The most well-known attack against the endpoint fields is the ping of death, which was described in Chapter 4 [16–18]. Attacks using the source and destination addresses often fall into the authentication attack category. There have been attacks against some devices where the source and destination addresses have been set to the same value, which caused the device to crash. There have also been attacks where the source address has been set to a broadcast address that is not allowed in the standard.

Mitigation of header-based attacks can be difficult with network-based security devices. The individual end devices need to mitigate header-based attacks. For example, the ping of death was fixed by changing the implementation of the reassembly code in the affected operating systems.

There are fewer header-based attacks against the ARP and ICMP protocols. In the case of the ARP protocol, any header-based attacks would have to be carried out by devices on the same network as the target. Invalid ARP packets are typically discarded by the devices. The ICMP headers are very simple, and there are not many attacks against these headers.

6.1.8   Protocol-Based Attacks

The IP and ICMP protocols are simple in that there is no packet exchange between devices to move the data through the network. Most protocol-based attacks against IP and ICMP focus on the routing of the packets and efforts to cause the packets to be misrouted. There are attacks against the routing tables using various routing protocols. These attacks tend to focus on the large networks used as the backbone of the Internet. These attacks are beyond the scope of this book. As it turns out, there are relatively few attacks against the IP protocol itself. Most attacks use the IP packet to carry attack payload, which is targeting a higher-layer protocol.

The traceroute program might be considered a protocol-based attack since it uses the IP and ICMP protocols to find routes to target machines. As was previously discussed, traceroute has a valid use. Using the TTL function in the IP protocol to discover the path to a destination cannot be mitigated. Even if the ICMP echo request is blocked, an attacker could use any valid IP packet to trace the route since the time-to-live function is an integral part of the IP protocol.

There have been some attacks where the attacker uses the ICMP error messages to cause a denial of service or to redirect traffic to the wrong place. These attacks require that the attacker be able to sniff the traffic along the path to see the IP packets. The attacker then creates an ICMP error message based on the header information found in the sniffed packet. For example, if the attacker sniffed the IP packets from Alice to Bob, it could send an ICMP destination unreachable message to Alice telling her computer that the destination computer is unreachable.

The ARP protocol can be attacked by devices on the same network as the victim. A common attack is where an attacker who sees an ARP request responds with an ARP reply that is not valid. This can cause the ARP cache to be filled with wrong information. Since ARP requests are broadcast packets, every device on the network will see the request. The attacker needs to send the ARP reply back to the victim before the real reply can arrive. Some hosts will detect multiple ARP replies with conflicting results and flag that as a warning. The resulting attack is that an invalid hardware address is placed in the ARP cache of the victim, which will prevent the victim from contacting the destination. Another result is when the attacker sends the bogus ARP reply with the hardware address set to the attacker. This can cause the device that receives the ARP reply to send its packets to the wrong host. This is often called ARP cache poisoning. If the attacker forwards the packet from the victim to the correct destination, it could set itself up to have traffic to and from the victim sent through it, which will allow the attacker to capture all traffic from the victim. Even though this attack is using

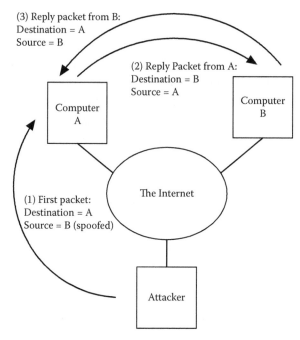

Figure 6.20:   IP address spoofing.

the ARP protocol incorrectly, it is better classified as an authentication-based attack.

6.1.9   Authentication-Based Attacks

The IP address is the unique identifier that is used to distinguish one device from another in the Internet. As is the case with any identifier, we tend to use it as a way to authenticate devices. Many applications use the IP address as the method to authenticate a device before providing service. The source and destination IP addresses are inserted into the packet header by the sending device and remain unchanged as they traverse the Internet. At this time we are not going to consider devices that translate IP addresses; these will be discussed as a common countermeasure in this chapter. Since it is up to the sender to insert the IP addresses into the packet, the destination must trust the sender. It is possible for a device on the Internet to create a packet with a source IP address that is different than its own (IP address spoofing) [19–22]. Figure 6.20 shows IP address spoofing.

As we see in Figure 6.20, the attacker sends a packet to computer A with the return address of computer B. Depending on the upper-layer protocol, computer

B may try to send a packet back to the originator of the packet. Computer A creates a packet with the destination address of computer B. This can create some very interesting attacks.

One type of IP spoofing attack that can cause problems is when the attacker sends an ICMP echo request packet into a network with a spoofed IP address. This causes the target computer to send an ICMP echo reply packet to the spoofed IP address (the victim). While one packet may not be a problem, there are several ways attackers can amplify the attack. One way is to send multiple requests from one attacker or from multiple attackers. Another way is to send a directed IP broadcast packet. In this case, if the router handles inbound broadcast packets, it takes the spoofed ICMP echo request packet and broadcasts it to devices in the target network. The computers then all respond with an ICMP echo reply packet back to the victim computer. This attack has been mitigated by routers that are configured to not allow inbound broadcasts, or by not allowing certain ICMP protocols to come from the outside. Still, this type of attack using IP spoofing can be carried out using other protocols. The key to making this attack work is finding a protocol that causes an IP packet to be returned in response to a single IP packet.

One misconception is that is it possible to use IP address spoofing to steal the identity of a device in an effort to either hide your true identity or to make it look like another device is responsible for the connection. This is often called IP session spoofing. In order for two devices to communicate, they need to exchange packets. Looking back at Figure 6.20, we can see the problem with carrying out a multipacket exchange with a spoofed IP address. We can get the first packet to the destination, but the response will not get back to the attacker. IP spoofing can be done if the attacker has access to the same network as the victim. In that case, the attacker convinces the router that it is a device with the victim's IP address, often using the ARP protocol. As we saw earlier, this method has some problems if the victim's computer is active. A more common scenario is to just steal an unused IP address within a network that you have access to. As was discussed in the chapter on wireless networks, this is a concern for unsecured wireless networks. If the attacker has physical access to the network, it is difficult to mitigate without using something like network access control, as discussed in Chapter 5. We will see in Chapter 7 that there is a method to hijack a transport layer connection using IP session stealing in combination with a protocol-based attack at the transport layer. However, as we will see, this attack requires that the attacker is able to see the traffic.

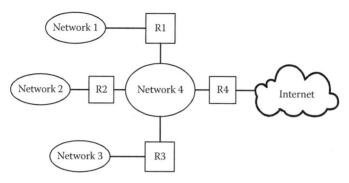

Figure 6.21:   IP address spoofing mitigation.

The same problem happens with the application port number because a source port can also be spoofed. So the real question again is: What does the destination know when it gets a packet? The destination device knows that the packet was sent by a device on the same network that either created the packet itself or forwarded the packet from another device on the Internet. The destination also knows that a device created an IP packet with a source IP address and source port number. The destination, however, cannot be certain which device created the packet.

What we have just described may seem to be poorly designed. However, we have been using a system very similar to this for over 200 years. The U.S. Postal Service allows the sender to create the entire message, including the return address. We do not know how far the letter has traveled, nor do we know for sure where the letter entered the system. The postal system does cancel the stamps, which will place the name of the post office that canceled the stamp. This can give the recipient an idea of the origin of the letter. We do not know the path the letter took to get to us, and unless we see the mail carrier place the letter in our mailbox, we cannot even be sure the letter traveled through the postal system.

There have been some efforts made to make IP address spoofing harder. Most routers are configured to check the sending IP address of devices on a direct network. This only works for devices directly connected to the router, or if devices are all behind a common router. Figure 6.21 shows how routers can mitigate IP spoofing.

As we see in the figure, routers R1, R2, and R3 can stop any outbound packets where the source IP address does not match the corresponding network. Likewise, router R4 can stop any packets whose source IP address does not match one of the subnets inside the organization. The problem with this is that once a packet has entered the Internet, these checks can no longer be performed. This also requires

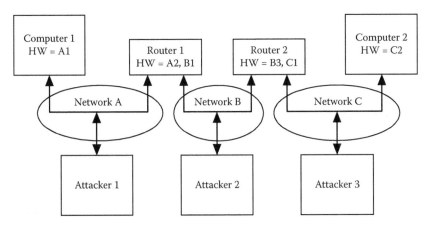

Figure 6.22: IP sniffing.

that all routers are configured this way and can be trusted. This, of course, is not the case in the Internet. This mitigation technique does not stop an attacker inside the network from using the IP address of another computer within the same network.

Another authentication problem with IP packets is that many devices use the IP address as a way to authenticate a device on the network. For example, a server may use the IP address to determine if a device can access the server. Network-based security devices may also use the IP address to allow network access or to provide reports on network activity. As we will see in the next section, dynamic assignment of IP addresses makes this even more difficult.

As far as ICMP is concerned, there is no authentication of the sender. Since it uses the IP protocol to move the data, it is subject to the same types of attacks against the IP layer. The most difficult attacks to mitigate are spoofed ICMP error messages. As we discussed earlier, these can cause denial of service. The ARP protocol is also unauthenticated, and as we have seen, this can cause problems. Authentication-based ARP attacks are limited to the network the attacker is on, and therefore any mitigation is at a local network level.

6.1.10 Traffic-Based Attacks

A sniffing-based attack at the IP layer is more complex than a sniffing attack against the local network, and in some cases is beyond our control. Figure 6.22 shows an example of IP sniffing.

Attacker 1 can sniff the traffic on network A, but not the traffic on network B or C. An interesting question is: What about sniffing traffic on an intermediate network like network B? Attacker 2 on network B could sniff any traffic that it can see on network B. If that traffic was between computer 1 and computer 2, then attacker 2 could sniff the traffic between computer 1 and computer 2. This leads to the question: Can attackers sniff traffic on the Internet? Typically the backbone network is physically protected, which makes sniffing the backbone very difficult. In general, we do not worry about sniffing once the traffic enters an ISP. The most common place for packet sniffing is in wireless networks, like those located in coffee shops with free wireless Internet access.

IP layer sniffing is often used by network-based security devices to monitor traffic and determine if the traffic contains attacks. These devices are typically placed at the network egress point, and as we discussed in Chapter 5, there are several methods that can be used to allow these devices to sniff the network traffic. One interesting thing we will see is that one of the mitigation methods proposed at the end of this chapter involves encryption of the IP payload, which can disable the security function of many of the network-based security devices. This has led to a debate among security experts about encryption and what should be encrypted. On one hand, from a sniffing standpoint, encryption can prevent others from seeing the data. On the other hand, encryption can prevent the monitoring of traffic to determine if the data contains confidential material that should not leave the organization or contains material that should not be accessed by users (i.e., inappropriate web content).

Flooding can be a problem since the IP layer allows an attacker to send packets to a target network or target host. In the simplest case, an attacker could just send a large amount of traffic into a network in an effort to overwhelm the routers or the target host. In some cases this can happen by accident. For example, a web site that becomes very popular can get so many requests that the router or host cannot handle the traffic. There is little that can be done to mitigate these attacks. There are devices that reduce the amount of traffic coming into a network based on traffic characteristics. These devices typically interact at the transport layer. There have also been cases where a large number of attackers have targeted a network or a host within a network. The attack created so much traffic that some of the routers between the attackers and the target were affected. The Internet routing protocols try to redirect traffic to even out the load across routers, but in some cases it is not possible to redirect the traffic. It is very difficult for an end user to mitigate an attack that causes a router within the Internet to stop functioning, and therefore shuts down his or her Internet access. This sometimes happens during a widespread attack like Code Red or other network-based worms [23–25]. It is left up to the reader to study some of the effects of these Internet-wide attacks.

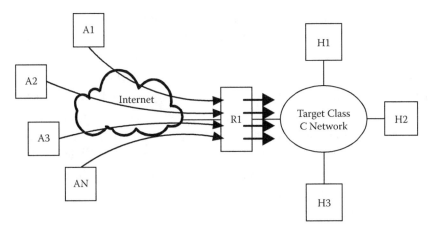

Figure 6.23:   ARP broadcast flood attack.

There are some flooding-based attacks using the IP broadcast address. The most common was discussed earlier and is when the attacker sends an IP broadcast packet into a remote network and gets all of the hosts to reply. The goal is to get a large number of devices within the network to respond in an effort to flood the network. This has been mitigated by not allowing directed broadcasts to enter through a router.

Another flooding attack is to use the ARP protocol. We have already seen that an attacker can cause problems using the ARP protocol on the same network he or she is connected to. There is an attack where an attacker can remotely cause an ARP broadcast flood. Figure 6.23 shows an example of an ARP broadcast flood.

In Figure 6.23 we see that the target network is a class C network with a small number of hosts. As we saw in the section that described IP routing and the ARP tables, every time a packet comes in from another network destined for a host on the target network, the router checks its ARP table to see if it needs to send an ARP request for the destination. If an attacker sends a packet to each address in the target network, the ARP table for the router will contain four entries after the attacker is done. Since there are 254 possible hosts, the router could send as many as 253 ARP requests. Of those 253 ARP requests, 249 are unanswered and the router typically retries four times for each request. This causes close to 1,000 ARP requests to be generated. This in itself might not be a problem. But now let us say the attacker continues to sweep through the address space of the target, sending a packet to each possible host. Each sweep through the target network could cause the router to send 1,000 ARP requests. Now let us say there are multiple attackers targeting the same network in the same way. This could cause thousands of broadcast packets to be generated.

This attack can be a consequence of another attack. For example, a distributed attack that comes from thousands of attackers, each sweeping through hundreds of target networks, could end up causing an ARP request flood on a network that is lightly populated. The author has seen this type of attack cripple a network when it received thousands of ICMP echo requests per second across every address in the network. The ICMP echo requests were sent as part of another attack, but the result was that their network was shut down. They were able to mitigate the attack by disabling incoming ICMP echo request packets at the router.

There are some general mitigation methods that can be implemented by routers or other network devices that limit the number of packets entering a network. This can help with flooding-based attacks; however, what often happens is that when these devices throttle or block excess traffic, some legitimate traffic may be affected. In general, traffic-based attacks are difficult to stop.

Definitions

ARP cache poisoning.

When an attacker uses ARP spoofing to put bogus values in the victims ARP table.

ARP spoofing.

When an attacker detects an ARP request packet on the network and responds pretending to be the host with the IP address in question.

Classless Interdomain Routing (CIDR).

Like a netmask, but uses a number to indicate the number of bits in the network part of the address.

Default network.

The default network is the network where all packets are sent when the destination IP address does not appear in the router table.

Direct network.

A direct network is the network the device is connected to, and therefore it is responsible for delivering any packets to devices on the direct network.

IP loopback address.

This is a reserved address (127.0.0.1 typically) that is used to test the internal IP protocol stack. A packet sent to this address is returned to the application by the IP stack. This address is not a valid address for packets on the network.

IP spoofing.

Sending a packet with a false IP source address.

Netmask.

A netmask is used to indicate which part of the IP address represents the network. For example, 255.255.255.0 indicates the first 24 bits identifying the network.

Next-door network.

A next-door network appears in the routing table, and therefore the device knows which router to send the packet to.

Ping.

Ping is a program that sends and receives ICMP echo packets and is used to determine if a device is active on the network.

Route table.

Every device on the Internet has a route table that is used to determine where to send the packet next to get it to the destination.

Subnetworks.

When a network is divided into smaller networks using routers, the resulting smaller networks are called subnetworks of the larger network.

Traceroute.

Traceroute is a program that determines the IP addresses of the routers used to get a packet from the source to the destination.

6.2   BOOTP and DHCP

As we have seen, IP addresses are globally unique identifiers that are assigned to devices in the Internet. We have seen that addresses are assigned in blocks to organizations, which in turn assign the addresses to individual devices. We also saw that the assignment of the address blocks is controlled and allocated by a few groups. What we have not discussed is how a device within a network gets an IP address assigned to it. There are two methods for IP address assignment. The first is static, where the address is assigned to the device and the device is typically manually configured with the assigned address and assigned netmask. The second method is dynamic, where the address is discovered using a protocol.

In the early days of the Internet almost all devices had statically assigned IP addresses, and many network-savvy users often used the IP address to access devices without using the device name and the Domain Name Service. The only devices that had dynamic IPs were diskless devices that did not have any way to remember their IP address when they were powered off. And even in this case, every time they started and retrieved their IP address, they got the same address. This was common for printers and diskless workstations. During this era the mapping between IP addresses and physical devices was useful in tracking down problems or handling security issues. When the network administrator saw an IP address, he or she knew exactly where the device was located. Of course, the biggest problem with static IP address assignment is that someone needed to maintain the list of assigned IP addresses and handle additions and deletions. Network administrators also had to spend time configuring devices to access the Internet.

Today networks have grown larger and the number of devices continues to increase. We have also seen an increase in mobile computing, where devices come and go from a network. This has led to the large-scale adoption of dynamic IP assignment. Most computers come configured to use dynamic IP assignment by default, and therefore can connect to the network without user configuration. We will see there are two protocols used to support dynamic IP address assignment. The first is an older protocol called BOOTP and is not used much. The newer protocol, called Dynamic Host Configuration Protocol (DHCP), is widely used today. Both protocols are discussed in the following sections [26–28].

It should be noted that there is still a debate about whether is it easier to administrate a statically assigned network or a dynamically assigned network. Some network administrators find it easier to troubleshoot and secure a static network since they know where every device is located based on the IP address. Certain network security devices provide better reporting in a static IP assignment environment because the IP address can be linked to the same IP address every time. Others think the ease of configuration that a dynamic assignment method provides overrides any troubleshooting savings. Even when using dynamic address assignment, certain devices never change their assigned IP addresses. These are often public servers, printers, and routers.

6.2.1 BOOTP Protocol

The BOOTP protocol was designed to support diskless workstations and network printers. It assigns the same IP address to the same device each time. The assignment is based on the hardware address of the device requesting the IP address. The BOOTP protocol requires a BOOTP server, which has a configuration file with the hardware addresses and the corresponding IP addresses of the devices it serves. In addition to the IP address of the device, the BOOTP server can also

TABLE 6.11: Sample BOOTP Configuration

BOOTP Entry	Description
hp255:\	Name of the entry
:ht=ether:vm=rfc1048:\	Network type of Ethernet
:ha=080000105634:\	Ethernet address of the printer
:ip=192.168.5.7:\	IP address of the printer
:sm=255.255.255.0:\	Netmask
:gw=192.168.5.254:\	IP address of the default router
:lg=192.168.5.200:\	IP address of a log server
:T144="hp.printer"	Name of a file that can be transferred using Trivial File Transfer Protocol (TFTP)

provide the network mask, the IP address of the router, and the IP address of a domain name server, along with several other parameters. Table 6.11 shows a sample BOOTP configuration entry for a printer.

The BOOTP protocol is designed to be simple and uses the User Datagram Protocol (UDP) transport protocol. We will discuss UDP in the next chapter. For the purposes of this chapter, we can view UDP as a way to use the IP protocol directly. The UDP protocol has port numbers that are used to identify the application that is using the protocol. Figure 6.24 shows the BOOTP protocol and the values used in some of the packet headers.

As we see in Figure 6.24, the device wishing to get an IP address (client) will send a broadcast UDP packet from port 68 to port 67 that contains the BOOTP packet as its payload. The packet has the destination IP and destination hardware addresses set to broadcast. Every device in the network will receive the packet. Only a device with a BOOTP server application waiting for data on port 67 will accept the packet. All of the other devices just toss the packet. The BOOTP server responds to the BOOTP request with the information from the configuration file in a BOOTP response packet. The BOOTP response packet is placed in a UDP packet with the destination hardware address set to the address of the device requesting the IP address assignment. Note that the ARP table of the BOOTP server does not contain the address of the device requesting the IP address assignment. The server cannot use ARP for the hardware address of the device requesting the IP address assignment since it does not have an IP address. Therefore, the server needs to extract the hardware address of the client from the BOOTP request packet it received.

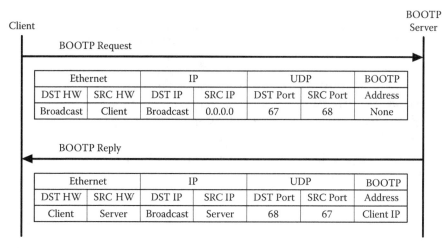

Figure 6.24: BOOTP protocol.

Since the BOOTP request packet is sent as a hardware broadcast packet, it is limited to the network the requesting device is connected to. This would imply that you need to have a BOOTP server on each network that has a device that needs to talk to a BOOTP server. To fix this limitation, a BOOTP relay was designed. Figure 6.25 shows a setup with a BOOTP relay. It should be noted that the DHCP protocol will function with a BOOTP relay, so the same relay is used for both protocols.

As we see in Figure 6.25, the BOOTP relay picks up the BOOTP request (packet 1) and forwards the packet to the BOOTP server using its IP address to the BOOTP server (packet 2). The BOOTP server responds to the BOOTP relay, assuming the relay is the device asking for the IP address (packet 3). The BOOTP relay then responds to the BOOTP client as if it were the server (packet 4). You need one relay per network, but one BOOTP server with a single configuration file can serve multiple networks.

Since the packet format of the BOOTP protocol is the same as the packet format of the DHCP protocol, we will wait and discuss it in the next section.

From a security standpoint, BOOTP can be attacked, but only by devices that are on the same network. Since it is a broadcast protocol, it is easy for any device on the network to see the packet and respond. This could cause problems if an attacker could change the IP addresses of devices. However, this attack requires the attacker to be on the same network as the target.

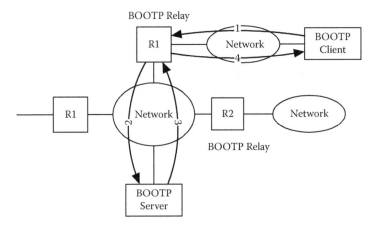

	Ethernet		IP		UDP		BOOTP
Packet	DST HW	SRC HW	DST IP	SRC IP	DST Port	SRC Port	Address
1	Broadcast	Client	Broadcast	0.0.0.0	67	68	None
2	Server	Relay	Server	Relay	67	68	None
3	Relay	Server	Relay	Server	68	67	Client IP
4	Client	Relay	Broadcast	Relay	68	67	Client IP

Figure 6.25:   BOOTP relay.

6.2.2   DHCP Protocol

The problem with the BOOTP protocol is that the mapping between IP and
hardware addresses is static. The BOOTP protocol still requires a network administrator to configure the server and to know the hardware addresses of all the
devices. This protocol would not work with mobile devices or networks where
devices are constantly being added and removed. The Dynamic Host Configuration Protocol (DHCP) is designed to support true dynamic assignment of IP
addresses. A DHCP server supports the BOOTP protocol, and the DHCP protocol supports IP address assignment where the same device always gets the same
IP address.

DHCP has two pools of IP addresses it can assign to clients. The first pool
is the static pool, which acts just like BOOTP. If the hardware address of the
requesting device matches an entry in the static pool, it is given that IP address.
The second pool is a dynamic pool that is assigned to devices that request an
address. Addresses from the dynamic pool can be assigned to devices where
the hardware address is unknown. Unlike the static pool, a device is assigned
a dynamic IP address for a short period of time as determined by the server

configuration. This is referred to as a lease. When the lease expires, the client must ask for the address to be renewed, and if the server rejects the renewal, the device must give up the IP address. Figure 6.26 shows the DHCP protocol.

As we see in Figure 6.26, the DHCP client and server use the same port numbers as the BOOTP client and server. The DHCP client issues a DHCP discover packet that is broadcast across the network. Any DHCP server on the network can respond with a DHCP offer packet. This packet indicates an offer to lease an IP address. The DHCP offer packet contains the lease time. A DHCP server locks the IP address when it sends an offer. If the client does not receive an offer within 2 seconds, it sends another DHCP discover packet. The client sends up to five DHCP discover packets before it gives up. The client can try again after 5 minutes.

If the client gets one or more offers, it chooses one offer and sends a DHCP request packet to the DHCP server. The DHCP server responds with a DHCP ACK packet. This tells the client it can now use the address. The client uses the packet for 50% of the lease time, at which time it will ask for a lease renewal by sending a DHCP request packet. If the DHCP server responds with a DHCP ACK packet, the client resets its lease timer. If the server responds with a DHCP NAK packet, the client must give up the IP address. If the client gives up the IP address, it must send a DHCP discover packet if it wants another IP address. If the DHCP server does not respond to the DHCP request packet, the client sends another DHCP request after 87.5% of the lease time has expired. If the lease expires before the client can renew the lease, it must give up the IP address. A client can also give up the IP address at any time by sending a DHCP release packet. The DHCP packet format is shown in Figure 6.27.

Most of the fields are self-explanatory. The DHCP packet type is part of the options field.

6.2.3   Header-Based Attacks

The header is designed to be simple, and since it is carried as payload in a UDP packet, there are not any header-based attacks.

6.2.4   Protocol-Based Attacks

Protocol-based attacks are limited to the network where the client is located. The protocol for BOOTP is very simple, so the only real attacks are when an attacker sends false messages to the client pretending to be the server. These attacks are better classified as authentication based. The DHCP protocol is more complicated

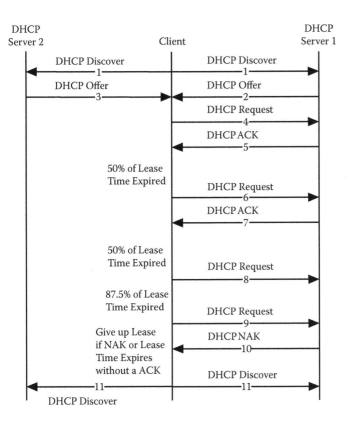

	Ethernet		IP		UDP		DHCP
Packet	DST HW	SRC HW	DST IP	SRC IP	DST Port	SRC Port	
1	Broadcast	Client	Broadcast	0.0.0.0	67	68	Discover
2	Client	Server 1	Broadcast	Server 1	68	67	Offer
3	Client	Server 2	Broadcast	Server 2	68	67	Offer
4	Server 1	Client	Server 1	0.0.0.0	67	68	Request
5	Client	Server 1	Broadcast	Server 1	68	67	ACK
6	Server 1	Client	Server 1	Client	67	68	Request
7	Client	Server 1	Broadcast	Server 1	68	67	ACK
8	Server 1	Client	Server 1	Client	67	68	Request
9	Server 1	Client	Server 1	Client	67	68	Request
10	Client	Server 1	Broadcast	Server 1	68	67	NAK
11	Broadcast	Client	Broadcast	0.0.0.0	67	68	Discover

Figure 6.26:   DHCP protocol.

Op Code	Hardware Type	Hardware Len	Hop Count
ID			
Number of Seconds		Flag + Unused	
Client IP Address			
Client IP Address (used in reply packet)			
Server IP Address			
Gateway IP Address			
Client Hardware Address (16 bytes)			
Server Name (64 bytes)			
Boot File Name (128 bytes)			
Options (contains DHCP message types)			

Figure 6.27:   DHCP/BOOTP packet format.

and involves resource allocation. The DHCP protocol is also subject to false reply messages that will be discussed as an authentication-based attack.

There are several possible attacks against the server. One possible attack is to send multiple discover packets using fake hardware addresses with a goal of getting the DHCP server to consume all of the IP addresses in the dynamic pool. Remember that the DHCP server reserves an IP address when it gets a DHCP discover packet. Since the DHCP server will time out and start to release the reserved IP addresses, an attacker needs to continue to send discover packets. An attacker could reply to the offer and accept the lease. This would force the server to give out all of its IP addresses to the attacker. This is an interesting attack and could possibly cause a denial of service. This attack would have to be carried out by someone with access to the network. The attacker would not need to be able to sniff the traffic to carry out this attack. Where this attack would be most effective is in a wireless public network site. An attacker could shut down the site. This attack would be very difficult to mitigate.

Another attack is to send a DHCP release packet to the server pretending to be one of the clients that got a lease. This requires that the attacker is able to see the DHCP discover packet and then uses that information to determine which victims to target. The attacker also needs to be able to see the DHCP offer to know the IP address of the client. When the server releases the IP address, it becomes available for other clients. This attack could cause the same IP address to be given out to more than one computer. If the attacker is not able to see the DHCP offer packet, it could just send DHCP release packets from each of the addresses in the dynamic pool. It could also send its own DHCP discover packet to help guess the address that was offered since most DHCP servers offer addresses in order. This attack would cause chaos on the network and would be very hard to mitigate. Again, like the previous attack, this would be very effective in an open wireless network. Once an attacker has access to a network, it would be difficult to stop these attacks.

6.2.5 Authentication-Based Attacks

The BOOTP and DHCP protocols are not authenticated. As far as the servers are concerned, they respond to requests from any client. In the case of BOOTP or static DHCP, they only respond if the hardware address matches a value in the configuration table. If we are concerned about assigning addresses to unauthorized clients, then the typical solution is using network access control, as was discussed in Chapter 5. The other type of authentication attack is where the identity of the server cannot be verified. It is possible for an attacker to respond to BOOTP and DHCP requests from a client pretending to be a valid server. This is often referred to as a rogue DHCP server.

The BOOTP server needs to find a match in the configuration file before it responds, which allows for multiple BOOTP servers on the same network. Since DHCP servers respond to a request from devices without matching an entry in a configuration file, if there are multiple DHCP servers on the same network, a client may receive multiple responses. This is normally not a problem if all of the DHCP servers are legitimate and are handing out valid nonoverlapping addresses.

A rogue DHCP server could assign an address to a client that is not valid for the network. When the client accepts a lease for an invalid address from the rogue server, it is unable to communicate. This can happen with an attacker whose intent is to disrupt network service or because of a misconfigured DHCP server. Since the request is a broadcast packet, a rogue DHCP server does not need to be able to see all of the traffic to carry out this attack. An attacker could also send fake reply packets in response to the client requesting the continuation of the lease. The attacker needs to be able to see the DHCP request packet from the client in order to carry out this attack.

These attacks point out the problems with an authenticated protocol. Mitigation of these attacks is very difficult without a total redesign of the protocol. In order to add authentication, there needs to be some type of password or key exchange. Authentication could work in a closed environment, but is difficult in something like an open wireless network.

6.2.6   Traffic-Based Attacks

Sniffing of the DHCP packets can aid in the implementation of several of the authentication attacks described earlier. However, since the information exchanged between the client and the server is not really a secret, sniffing is not a major concern for DHCP. There are not many effective flooding attacks. An attacker could try to flood the server with requests, but again, the attacker needs access to the network where the DHCP server is located.

Definitions

DHCP lease.

An IP address is given to a client for a period of time called a lease time. The client must request renewal of the address before the lease time has expired.

Dynamic DHCP pool.

A set of IP addresses that are assigned to any device that requests a packet.

Rogue DHCP server.

A DHCP server that answers DHCP requests and provides invalid answers.

Static DHCP pool.

A set of IP addresses that are assigned to devices based on their hardware address.

6.3   IP Version 6 Protocol

Version 4 of the IP protocol has limitations that are causing problems in the Internet today. The primary limitation is the address space. When version 4 was created there were a small number of computers in the world, and personal computers were very limited. As we know, the number of computers today is growing, and the unallocated address space is limited. Also as we saw, there are several fields in the header that are not used or are seldom used. This has led to a redesign of the IP protocol and the release of IP version 6 [29–31]. The designers of IP version 6 also decided to add security to the protocol to mitigate many of the authentication and traffic-based attacks that have been used against IP version 4. The designers also added the capability for different traffic types (voice, video, etc.) based on their need for real-time transmission.

Of course, as is often the case with any new protocol, it takes time to adopt the changes. Given the very large number of devices using IP version 4 and the amount of legacy code used in these devices, the transition from IP version 4 to IP version 6 has been slow. There have also been several workarounds that have been deployed that minimize the shortcomings of IP version 4. The widespread use of private network address space has reduced the burden on the IP version 4 address space. We will discuss this technology as a general mitigation technique. The security features of IP version 6 have been adapted to IP version 4 and will also be discussed as a general mitigation technique.

For the purpose of this book, we will briefly introduce the IP version 6 protocol and packet header. We will also examine the ICMP version 6 protocol and packet format. The attacks used against IP version 6 are the same as the attacks used against IP version 4, and therefore we will not compare IP version 6 against the taxonomy. This is assuming IP version 6 is not using the optional security headers.

6.3.1   Packet Format

One of the biggest differences between IP version 6 and IP version 4 is the header. In version 6 the header contains a base header and optional extension headers. The base header is designed to be used for the basic routing functions of the protocol. The extension headers are designed to be used by the two end devices. There are some extension headers that are intended to be examined by the routers. The use of a base header is designed to speed up the routing function by minimizing the amount of calculation required by the router. In IP version 4 the router must compute a new checksum for every packet. This has caused problems as the network speed and total traffic volume have increased. Figure 6.28 shows the IP version 6 header.

As we see in Figure 6.28, the base header only has a few fields:

Version (4 bits): Indicates the version number of the IP packet. For IP version 6 the value is 6.

Priority (4 bits): This 4-bit field is used to indicate the priority of the packet. This replaces the type of service field in version 4. This is used to determine what to do with multiple packets from the same source. If a packet must be discarded due to congestion of the network, the packet with the lowest priority is discarded. Values 0 through 7 are reserved for traffic where the upper-layer protocol can compensate for discarded packets, as shown in Figure 6.28. This traffic is called congestion controlled. Values 8 to 15 are reserved for traffic where

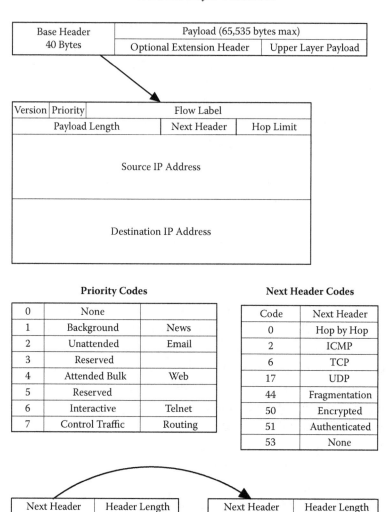

Figure 6.28:   IP version 6 header format.

the upper-layer protocol does not retransmit discarded packets. This non-congestion-controlled traffic would be for real-time protocols like voice and video.

Flow label (24 bits): The flow label is used to identify a stream of traffic that routers will treat the same. The flow label and the source IP address create a unique flow through the routers. In order for this to work, the routers need to support some type of reservation protocol that will set up the characteristics of the flow. These protocols are not widely used and are beyond the scope of this book.

Payload length (2 bytes): Total length of the IP packet, not including the base header.

Next header (1 byte): Indicates what type of data the packet contains. This is like the protocol field in IP version 4, except it is also used to indicate if there are extension headers.

Hop limit (1 byte): This field performs the same function as the time-to-live field in IP version 4.

Source address (16 bytes): Globally unique source address of the packet.

Destination address (16 bytes): Globally unique destination address of the packet.

As we see in Figure 6.28, the IP addresses are 16 bytes in length. This is approximately 3.4×10^{38} addresses. The addresses are written as eight 2-byte hexadecimal values, each separated by a colon.

For example, an address would look like this:

A234:BF33:00DD:1324:57FF:3366:DDDD:011F

Leading zeros can be removed to make the address look like this:

A234:BF33: DD:1324:57FF:3366:DDDD: 11F

In addition, multiple fields of zeros can be reduced; for example,

2DD3:0:0:0: FF34:0:0:45DD

can be written as

2DD3:: FF34:0:0:45DD

Note that we can only remove one set of zeros. IP version 6 also supports CIDR addresses. Just like in IP version 4, the address space is divided into groups. The upper bits indicate which group the address space is divided into. We will leave it up to the reader to explore the various address types. There is a provider-based unicast packet that is intended to support a majority of the addresses on the Internet. The provider-based address space is shown in Figure 6.29.

As we see in Figure 6.29, the provider-based address space is divided into 32 registry groups, each of which has about 65,000 address blocks to allocate to various providers (like ISPs). There are 2^24 possible subscribers for each

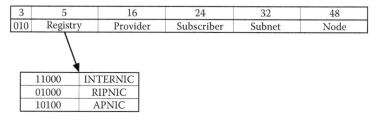

Figure 6.29:   Provider-based address space.

provider, and each subscriber could be allocated a set of subnets ($2 \hat{\ } 32$ possible). The remaining 48 bits are used to identify the device on the subnet. This is the same length as the Ethernet address, and the idea is to use the Ethernet address as the node address. This would eliminate the need for the ARP protocol. As we will see, the ARP protocol has become part of the ICMP protocol in IP version 6. There are a number of reserved addresses, including the loopback address and private addresses, similar to what is supported in IP version 4. From a security standpoint, we will not discuss these other addresses. They have the same security issues as IP version 4. The use of the hardware address as part of the IP address can lead to potentially interesting situations. For example, it might enable better tracking of the actual device that is sending data. Assuming the hardware address has not been spoofed, the IP packet contains information that identifies the sending device. This could be used in civil or criminal prosecution. It could also reduce privacy since with DHCP-assigned IP addresses, web sites, or other servers on the Internet cannot use the IP address to track the usage of a device. With the IP address containing the hardware address, it would be easy to track access to a server on a device-by-device basis.

As we saw in Figure 6.28, the extension headers are used to support options. For example, fragmentation is an extension header. In IP version 6 only the source can fragment the packet. Two headers of interest for security purposes are the authentication header and the encrypted security payload header. These will be discussed as a general countermeasure. The reader is encouraged to study the IP version 6 packet format in more detail.

6.3.2   ICMP Version 6 Protocol

The ICMP version 6 packet format is the same as IP version 4. The number of ICMP packet types has been reduced. The error reporting packet remains the same in IP version 6 as it was in IP version 4, with the exception of the elimination of the source quench, which was used to slow down the sender. Also added is a packet type called "packet too big," which is sent by a router that needs to fragment a packet. In IP version 6 fragmentation by a router is not allowed.

The number of ICMP query packets has been reduced in IP version 6. The timestamp messages and the address mask request messages have been eliminated. ARP as an ICMP neighbor solicitation and advertisement message has been added. The idea is the same as in IP version 4, but the packet format has changed. The same security issues exist in IP version 6 as with the ARP protocol in IP version 4.

This section provided a brief introduction to the IP version 6 protocol, and from a security standpoint, the issues are the same between version 4 and version 6. As version 6 becomes more widespread and implementations start to be widely deployed, there may be new attacks that only work on IP version 6 or on certain implementations of IP version 6.

Definitions

IP V6 base header.

The primary header for IP version 6 that is used by the routers to move the packets through the Internet.

IP V6 extension header.

A header used to identify the payload of the IP version 6 packet. There may be multiple extension headers in a packet.

Provider-based IP V6 address.

The primary IP version 6 address format for the Internet.

6.4 Common IP Layer Countermeasures

In this section we will examine four different countermeasures that are designed to address several of the vulnerabilities described in this chapter. Two of the countermeasures are used to protect a network from attacks (IP filtering and network address translation) and two are used to provide end-to-end encryption and authentication of the IP packets (virtual private networks and IP security).

6.4.1 IP Filtering

IP filtering is the concept of blocking IP traffic based on values in the IP header [32–35]. This is typically done at the router and is available in most routers. The most common fields used as filtering criteria are the IP addresses, port numbers, and protocol type. Typically the criteria are specified as a list of values to be blocked (often called a blacklist). It is common to block applications and protocols. For example, blocking incoming ICMP echo requests prevents someone in the Internet from determining which IP addresses are active. Another common protocol to block is UDP. For most organizations the only UDP traffic that is needed to pass through into the Internet is to support the Domain Name Service (DNS). So, many organizations block all UDP except for packets that are carrying the Domain Name Service protocol. A DNS packet is determined by the port number in the UDP header.

This means that filtering routers need to examine the payload of the packets, which adds to the processing time for each packet. In addition, port numbers are set by the sender of the packet. So even though the router may only allow the DNS port (port 53), that does not mean that the packet is carrying DNS as its payload. Port blocking is not perfect; for example, many rogue applications (i.e., peer-to-peer applications) can use any port, making it difficult to block them based on port number. We will discuss these applications in Chapter 12.

The problem with filtering based on IP addresses is determining which addresses are bad. There are groups that produce lists of bad IP addresses that can be loaded into a router's blacklist. Since attackers move around, the lists are always out of date; in addition, sometimes legitimate IP addresses can get placed on the blacklist. Generally most organizations do not use large IP blacklists. Sometimes an administrator may add an IP address to the list if he or she detects an attack or a large number of packets coming from a certain address or addresses. Another way to use an IP blacklist is if any internal machine appears to have been compromised. Then an administrator could cut off all access to the outside world to make sure the attacker can no longer access the machine he or she attacked.

Generally we use IP filters at the router as the first line of defense, and this does not replace other network defenses like firewalls.

6.4.2   Network Address Translation (NAT)

As we discussed earlier, there are various address ranges reserved for special purposes. Three address ranges have been reserved as private. These addresses do not appear on the public Internet and are designed to allow organizations to create private networks. These private networks can be connected to the public Internet using a process called network address translation (NAT) [36–39]. Figure 6.30 shows the concept of a private network connected to the public Internet.

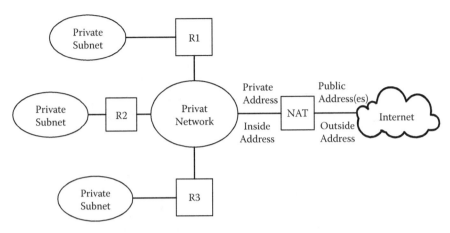

Figure 6.30: Private network.

As we see in Figure 6.30, the private network can be complex, consisting of multiple routers and multiple devices. The private network is connected to the public Internet through a device that looks like a router but actually translates the addresses between the public and private address ranges. To the devices inside the private network, the NAT looks like a router, and to any device in the Internet, the NAT looks like the final destination. The private address ranges are shown in Table 6.12.

A NAT was not originally designed as a security device. However, it can provide some level of security and is often coupled with a firewall to provide additional security. The primary goal of a NAT is to allow a large number of devices to share a small number of public addresses. There are two types of NATs. A static NAT is where there is a one-to-one mapping of outside addresses and inside addresses. Static NATs are not very common since they do not reduce the number of public addresses required. The second type of NAT is called dynamic and is used when there are more inside devices than public IP addresses.

TABLE 6.12: Private IP Address Ranges

Range		
Network	**Host**	**Purpose**
10.0.0.0 to 10.255.255.255	Any	Private class A address
172.16 to 172.31	Any	Private class B addresses (16 of them)
192.168.0 to 192.168.255	Any	Private class C addresses (256 of them)

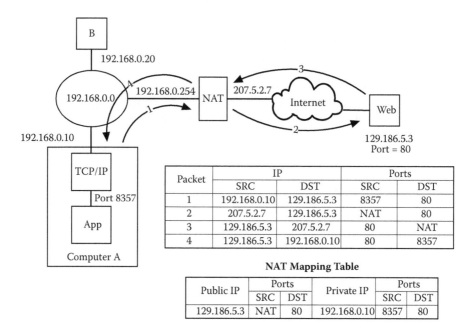

Figure 6.31:   Sample private network.

In order for the NAT to function, it maintains a table to map packets between the inside addresses and the outside addresses. In order for this to work, the NAT uses the port numbers that are part of the TCP or UDP headers to make the mapping succeed. We have not yet discussed the transport protocols, so we need to briefly look at how port numbers are used. In TCP and UDP every packet has a source and destination port that identifies the source and destination applications that are communicating with each other. The port numbers combined with the source and destination addresses uniquely identify the communication between two applications. Figure 6.31 shows a sample private network with a NAT.

As we see in Figure 6.31, there are two computers inside the private network. If computer A wishes to communicate with a web server in the public Internet, it needs to send a packet to the server. To do this, it creates an IP packet with the source IP address of 192.168.0.10 and the destination IP address of the web site (129.186.5.3). It also picks a source port number (assume 8357) and uses the destination port number of the web server (80). This is shown as packet 1 in Figure 6.31. Computer A handles the IP packet by routing it to the default router since the destination IP address is not on the 192.168.0.0 network. The NAT looks like a router to the private network. When the NAT receives a packet to be routed out to the public Internet, it creates an entry in the NAT mapping table that contains the source and destination IP addresses and the source and destination port numbers. The NAT then picks a new source port number (it could be the same as the original source port). The NAT creates a new IP packet with the same destination IP address and destination port. It uses its public IP address as the source IP and the new source port number. This is shown as packet 2 in Figure 6.31. It places the new port number in its table along with the original addresses, as shown in Figure 6.31.

The web server receives the packet and creates a reply packet with the source and destination IP addresses and port numbers reversed, as shown in Figure 6.31 as packet 3. When the NAT receives a packet it looks in its table to determine how to create the internal packet. The NAT uses the data from the mapping table to create packet 4, which is returned to computer A. As far as the web server is concerned, the NAT sent the packets. As far as computer A is concerned, it was talking directly to the web server. Neither the web server nor computer A knows about the NAT.

An issue with using a NAT is how to handle inbound connections where the first packet comes from the Internet. In that case, there is no entry in the mapping table. This is only an issue when there are server applications inside the private network. If the private network has only client applications (i.e., web browsers, email clients), then there is no special configuration needed at the NAT since all connections will be started by the devices inside the NAT.

NOTE

This is very common for home users, and many devices like wireless access points operate as a NAT and create private networks. This is how NATs are often used for security. Since they block all incoming packets that are not in the mapping table, an attacker cannot send packets to the private network. The device that functions as a NAT is often coupled with a firewall to provide additional security. We will discuss firewalls later in the book. NATs can be configured to allow specific inbound connections, as described below.

If an organization needs to have servers accessed from the public Internet, there are several ways to handle these servers. The first is to put the servers on the public Internet and the rest of the organization behind the NAT, as shown in Figure 6.32.

As we see in Figure 6.32, computers A and B and the NAT each have a public IP address that can be accessed from the Internet. The public network with computers A and B is sometimes referred to as the Demilitarized Zone (DMZ), and the hosts are sometimes called sacrificial hosts. Computers in the private network

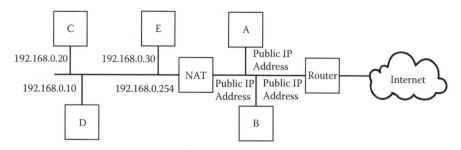

Figure 6.32:   Public servers and a private network.

can also access the public computers using the NAT. However, if the computers in the public network wish to connect to the private network, they need to have the NAT configured to allow incoming packets. This is called a tunnel and is shown in Figure 6.33.

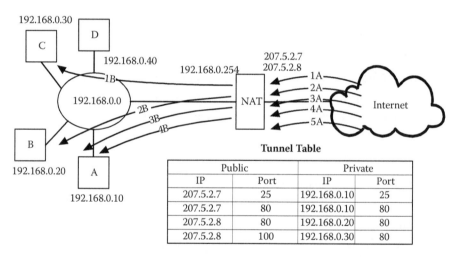

Tunnel Table

Public		Private	
IP	Port	IP	Port
207.5.2.7	25	192.168.0.10	25
207.5.2.7	80	192.168.0.10	80
207.5.2.8	80	192.168.0.20	80
207.5.2.8	100	192.168.0.30	80

Packet	IP		Ports	
	SRC	DST	SRC	DST
1A	Internet	207.5.2.8	8357	100
1B	Internet	192.168.0.30	8357	80
2A	Internet	207.5.2.8	7384	80
2B	Internet	192.168.0.20	7384	80
3A	Internet	207.5.2.7	2345	80
3B	Internet	192.168.0.10	2345	80
4A	Internet	207.5.2.7	2554	25
4B	Internet	192.168.0.10	2554	25
5A	Internet	207.5.2.7	6623	22

Figure 6.33:   Tunneling through a NAT.

As we see in Figure 6.33, the NAT has two public IP addresses (as we saw earlier, an NAT can have multiple public IP addresses). The idea behind the tunnel is to map a public IP address and port number to a private IP address and port number. When a packet arrives at the NAT on a port that has been tunneled, the NAT takes the inbound packet and rewrites the IP addresses and port numbers and sends the packet to the computer in the private network based on the values in the tunnel table.

Figure 6.33 shows four entries in the tunnel table and what happens to an inbound packet that matches each entry in the tunnel table. Packet 1A shows an inbound packet that has a destination IP address of 207.5.2.8 on port 100. The source of the packet is from a device on the public Internet. The tunnel table indicates that the packet should be sent to the device with the private IP address of 192.168.0.30 on port 80. The NAT rewrites the destination IP address and the destination port. The packet is sent to the destination as shown in packet 1B. The destination responds to the packet by using the IP addresses and ports in the packet. The NAT rewrites the destination IP address and port number and sends the packet back to the device in the Internet. As far as the device in the Internet is concerned, the end device is the NAT, and it never sees the private IP address as part of the IP headers. As far as the server in the private network is concerned, it is talking to the device on the network and the NAT does not exist, except as a router. Figure 6.33 also shows a case where the public port matches the private port. This is more typical since most applications use predefined port numbers. Packets 2 and 3 show a device in the Internet connecting to web servers that are on the private network using port 80 on the public Internet. There is a limitation with tunneling. If you wanted to connect to multiple private machines using public IP addresses and ports, there can only be one private device per public IP address and port number combination.

Figure 6.33 also shows packet 5 coming from a device in the Internet that has a destination address of the NAT and a destination port that is not in the tunnel table. Depending on how the NAT is configured, it could just drop the packet, or it might send back an ICMP destination unreachable packet. Either way, the packet will not enter the private network.

We have shown a NAT as a two-network interface device where traffic passes through the NAT. There is a configuration where the NAT sits on the network like any other computer. In this configuration we can have public and private addresses on the same network. This configuration is called pass-by and is shown in Figure 6.34.

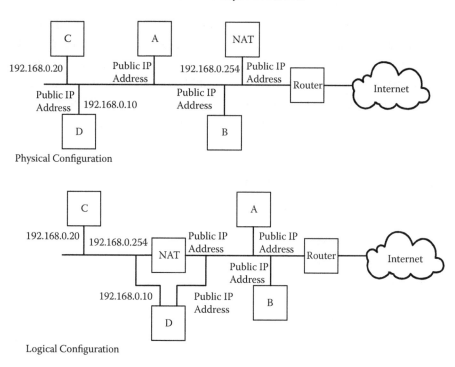

Figure 6.34:   Pass-by NAT.

Figure 6.34 shows a router and several computers with public IP addresses (A, B, D, and the NAT) that can be accessed from the Internet. The NAT is shown with one connection to the network. The NAT could have two network connections connected to the same physical network. This configuration logically looks like the diagram shown in the figure and behaves the same way as the network shown in Figure 6.32. Devices on the private network need to use the NAT to access the Internet. One difference between this configuration and Figure 6.32 is that it is possible for a device to have two IP addresses (one public and one private). This is shown as computer D in the figure. Computer D has full access to all computers on the private network and the public Internet and is not limited by any tunnels. While this may offer flexibility and can reduce security, if an attacker gains access to computer D, he or she could bypass the NAT and have full access to the private network. The private network shown in Figure 6.32 is not compromised if the public hosts are compromised. In addition, if any of the public-only computers are compromised, an attacker might be able to access the private network by adding a private IP address. They would be able to sniff the traffic of the private network.

6.4 Common IP Layer Countermeasures 203

Generally speaking, the configuration shown in Figure 6.34 is not considered very secure.

The NAT technology is widely used today and is included as part of most home routers and wireless access points. They are typically coupled with firewalls and IP filters. NATs provide network security and help mitigate inbound attacks and prevent attackers from accessing the devices inside the NAT. Like all security devices, NATs are part of the solution.

6.4.3 Virtual Private Network (VPN)

A virtual private network (VPN) is used to provide encrypted and authenticated communication channels between two devices [40–43]. There are several different types of VPNs based on how two devices are connected. There are multiple protocols defined that support the concept of a VPN. There are several standards for encryption and authentication that can be used by VPNs. Some companies have created proprietary protocols. The next section will discuss a common protocol that is used for an IP layer VPN. We will look at transport layer end-to-end encryption in the next chapter. IP layer VPNs can be divided into three categories: network to network, client to client, and client to network. Figure 6.35 shows an example of the network-to-network VPN.

The first configuration shown in Figure 6.35 is where two networks are connected using a VPN. The two networks can be disjointed, with separate address ranges, or the remote network could be a subnet of the main network. The VPN provides encryption between the two VPN nodes. The VPN nodes typically require authentication to prevent unauthorized connections. A network-to-network VPN is typically implemented as two hardware devices.

The typical configuration is for all traffic between the two networks to go through the VPNs, shown in Figure 6.35 as traffic between computers A and B. All other Internet traffic will be handled by each network, shown as the traffic between computers A and C.

Another method to configure a VPN is to have the remote network be an extension of the main network. This is shown in Figure 6.35 as the remote subnet. In this case the remote network uses the VPN to become part of the main network, and all traffic from the remote network passes through the main network. In this scenario the main network provides the connection to the Internet for both networks. The remote network looks like it is part of the main network to the outside world. The main network can control, monitor, and secure all traffic for both networks.

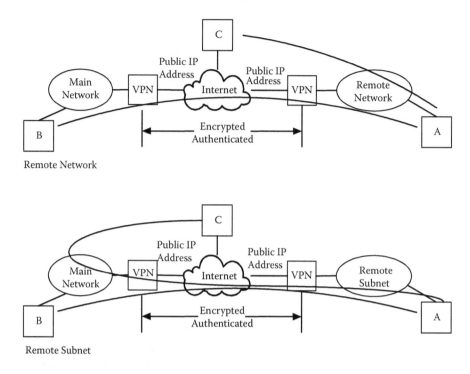

Figure 6.35:   Network-to-network VPN.

The next type of VPN is called client to client and is shown in Figure 6.36. As shown in the figure, the client device is running a VPN client that allows it to communicate with a remote VPN server that gives it access to the remote device. All traffic is encrypted between the two devices. The VPNs require additional authentication to establish the connection between the two devices. This method is not very common at the IP layer. There are transport and application protocols

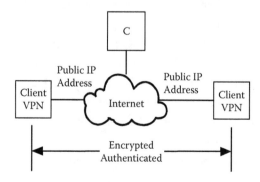

Figure 6.36:   Client-to-client VPN.

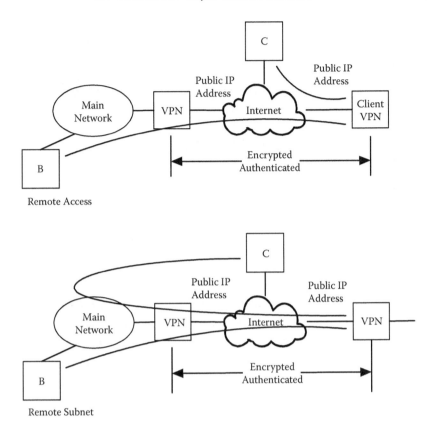

Figure 6.37: Client-to-network VPN.

that also provide computer-to-computer encrypted communications, which will be discussed later. A more common VPN connection for the client is called a client-to-network VPN, shown in Figure 6.37.

As shown in Figure 6.37, the client-to-network VPN is a combination of the last two VPN configurations. The remote client uses the VPN to connect to the main network. This connection provides remote access to the main network and makes the remote client appear to be located on the main network. The remote client can have two configurations. The first configuration is where the remote client has two IP addresses: the original address on the Internet that was used to make the VPN connection and the address the client has for the main network. Any traffic to devices in the main network uses the VPN, and any traffic for devices not on the main network uses the Internet. The scenario mimics the remote network VPN shown in Figure 6.35.

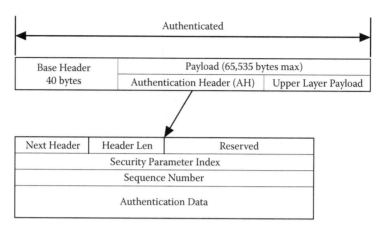

Figure 6.38:   Authentication of an IP version 6 packet.

The second configuration is where all of the traffic from the client goes into the main network, and then if its destination is in the Internet, the main network routes the traffic. This configuration mimics the remote subnet VPN shown in Figure 6.35. In this scenario the client computer is subject to all of the security policies that apply to any computer in the main network.

The VPN helps mitigate sniffing and authentication. Client-based VPNs are useful in public wireless networks. The VPN also provides access to a controlled network since the main network can be configured to only allow VPN traffic. This allows any authorized device to gain access to the network as if it were inside the network.

6.4.4   IPSEC

IPSEC is a protocol that was developed for IP version 6 that supports encryption and authentication [44–47]. IPSEC can be used as the protocol for a VPN. IPSEC uses one header to support authentication and one to support encryption and authentication. IPSEC does not specify the encryption algorithms or methods to manage the encryption keys. Figure 6.38 shows the authentication header used in IP version 6.

As shown in Figure 6.38, the authentication header is an extension header and is used to authenticate the data. It ensures that the data has not been altered. This is done by taking a hash of the entire packet (except for the IP fields that change) and then encrypting the hash using a security key. When the receiver gets the packet, it decrypts the hash value and computes the hash of the received packet

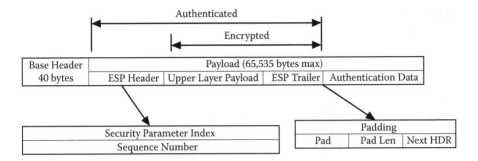

Figure 6.39: ESP in an IP version 6 packet.

to see if it matches the hash sent with the packet. If the two hash values match, then the receiver knows that a device that knows the security key sent the packet. The authentication header shown in the figure has several fields, including the security parameter index that is used to identify all packets that are part of the same data flow. The sequence number is used to prevent the replay of packets. Every packet that is sent has a different sequence number. The authentication data field is where the encrypted hash is stored. It should be noted the authentication header does not prevent sniffing. For IP version 4 the authentication header is part of the payload since IP version 4 does not support the extension headers. The authentication protocol is not widely used since the encryption protocol supports both authentication and encrypted traffic.

The second header supports encryption of the payload and also supports authentication. The encryption protocol is called Encapsulating Security Payload (ESP) and is shown in Figure 6.39.

As we see in Figure 6.39, the ESP consists of a header and a trailer plus authentication data. The ESP header is shown and consists of some of the same parameters as the authentication header. The payload is encrypted with the security key along with the ESP trailer, which is used to pad out the payload for the encryption algorithm and has the next header information. The authentication data is the hash of the ESP header, the payload, and the ESP trailer. Again, the ESP header is part of the payload for IP version 4.

IPSEC can mitigate sniffing and authentication attacks. The real problem with implementation is the distribution of keys. IPSEC works well in VPNs where keys can be distributed easily. If we wanted to use IPSEC for all communication across the Internet, then every device would have to have an encryption key that is known by everyone else. This is the idea behind the public key infrastructure

(PKI). PKI is beyond the scope of this book and has many social and political implications.

Definitions

DMZ.

A network that is outside the security perimeter.

IP address blacklist.

A list of IP addresses to be blocked by the router.

IP filter.

A process carried out by the routers of filtering-out packets based on the contents of the IP header and some of the transport header.

NAT tunnel.

A method to allow inbound packets to be routed to internal devices inside the private network.

Private network.

A network whose address range is one of the three reserved private addresses ranges. A NAT is needed to connect the private network to the Internet.

Sacrificial hosts.

Hosts that sit outside the security perimeter.

Homework Problems and Lab Experiments

Homework Problems

1. How many total public IP addresses are available for assignment?

2. Why are ARP request packets sent as an Ethernet broadcast packet and replies sent as directed packets?

3. Why do values in a host machine's internal ARP table expire after several minutes?

4. Research IP layer attacks and comment on how they have been mitigated (or not).

5. Figure 6.40 shows a small network. Create the route tables for each of the devices in the figure. (Show the destination, next hop, and interface values.)

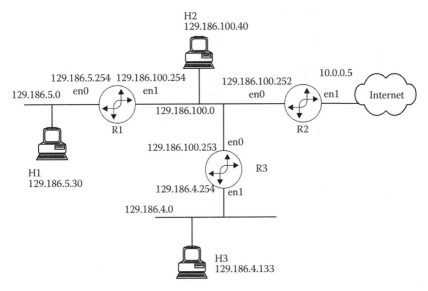

Figure 6.40: Homework problem 5.

6. Given Figure 6.41, fill in the following table. An IP packet with 2,700 bytes of user data needs to be sent across an Ethernet network from machine M1 to machine M2, and therefore needs to be fragmented. Show the pair of fragments for the network segment between the two routers (fill in all blank parts of the table; for the data field indicate the length of the data). Assume the first fragment is made as large as possible for an Ethernet network.

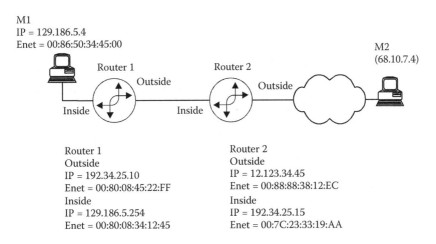

Figure 6.41: Homework problem 6.

Layer	Field Name	Original	Fragment 1	Fragment 2
	Destination	N/A		
Ethernet	Source	N/A		
	Type field	N/A		
	Ver/IHL	4 5		
	Type	0		
	Len			
	Id	3486		
	Flags	0 0 0		
IP	Offset	0		
	TTL	150		
	Protocol	17		
	Checksum	Computed	Computed	Computed
	Source IP			
	Destination IP			
Data		2,700 bytes		

7. Describe what happens in the following conditions (including any packets generated by the condition):

    a. The TTL expires.

    b. The ARP cache is "poisoned" by a hacker with the HW address of the hacker.

    c. A packet reaches a router that does not know how to route the packet any further.

    d. An IP packet arrives at a router and is too big to fit on the data link of the outgoing network.

    e. The destination does not receive all of the fragments to an IP packet.

    f. A machine "sees" an ARP request with the source IP address the same as its IP address.

8. Which category or categories in the taxonomy does each of the following mitigate?

    a. IPSEC or VPN

    b. NAT

    c. WEP

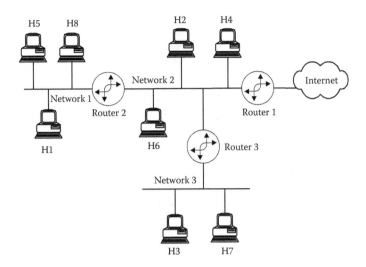

Figure 6.42: Homework problem 9.

9. Using Figure 6.42, answer the following questions.

Assume the following addresses:

Name IP		Name IP	
H1	129.186.5.4	Router 2	129.186.5.254 (for the network 129.186.5.0)
H2	129.186.4.10	Router 2	129.186.4.100 (for the main network)
H3	129.186.10.20	Router 1	129.186.4.254 (for the main network)
H4	129.186.4.25	Router 1	10.0.0.5 (for the Internet side)
H5	129.186.5.34	Router 3	129.186.4.253 (for NET 2)
		Router 3	129.186.10.254 (for NET 3)

H2 is the DNS server for the entire 129.186.0.0 network.

a. Assume H1 sent a message to H2, H3, H4, H5, and a machine on the Internet (ibm.com). How many entries would be in H1's ARP table due to these messages?

b. For the next three parts assume all caches are cleared before machine H3 sends a single ping request to machine H1 (the command = ping H1).

c. How many packets are transmitted on the network segment NET 1 (including the ping request and reply)?

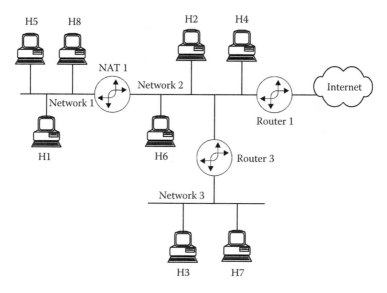

H5   H8

H2   H4

NAT 1

Network 2

Internet

Network 1

Router 1

H1

H6

Router 3

Network 3

H3   H7

Figure 6.43: Homework problem 12.

    d. How many packets are transmitted on the network segment NET 3 (including the ping request and reply)?

    e. How many packets are transmitted on the network segment NET 2 (including the ping request and reply)?

    f. Answer the same questions for hosts H6 and H7, again assuming caches are all clear before starting.

10. Under what conditions are static IP address assignments desirable in a DHCP environment?

11. Research the adoption of IPv6 and the estimated number of IPv6 hosts.

12. Use Figure 6.43 to complete the following.

    Assume the following addresses:

H1 192.168.168.5	Nat 1 192.168.168.254 (for NET 1)
H3 129.186.10.20	Nat 1 129.186.4.100 (for NET 2)
Router 3 129.186.4.253 (for NET 2)	Router 1 129.186.4.254
	(for NET 2)
Router 3 129.186.10.254 (for NET 3)	Router 1 10.0.0.5
	(for the Internet side)

Assume the NAT is dynamic and that 192.168.168.0 is the internal network.

Assume the following request packet is delivered to the IP layer from the TCP layer on host H1 with an intended destination of H3.

TCP source port = 5240

TCP destination port = 80

Assume all ARP and DNS tables are current.

For each of the points in the network listed below, show the values for the following fields in the packets. (If the value for a field is not specified, you can assume a value.) Show the fields in the reply packet at each of the points in the network.

	Request			Reply		
	Net 1	Net 2	Net 3	Net 1	Net 2	Net 3
TCP layer						
Source port						
Destination port						
IP layer						
SRC IP address						
Dest IP address						

13. Research commercial VPNs and develop a table comparing the types of VPNs based on encryption type, hardware versus software based, and client versus network based.

Lab Experiments

1. Determine the network address for the test laboratory and the netmask value.

2. Use the test lab and nslookup to find the IP address for each of the following machines.

   a. www.nasa.gov

   b. www.iac.iastate.edu

   c. www.cnn.com

   d. www.iseage.org

    e. www.iastate.edu

    f. A machine in the test lab

3. Use the command "ping" to find an average time delay to get to each of the machines in experiment 2.

4. Dump the route table for the machine you used in step 3 (netstat -r -n) to determine the address of the gateway (if one was needed) that was used to send packets to each of the hosts in experiment 2.

5. Use the command "arp -a" to determine the Ethernet address of the host or gateway in the previous question.

   Include all of the information from questions 2 to 5 in a table.

6. Use nslookup to find the IP addresses of the mail servers for the domains listed in experiment 2. This can be done by doing the following steps:

   $ nslookup

   set type=MX Tell nslookup to look for Mail records

   domain name lookup the mail server for the domain

   d Exit nslookup

7. Use nslookup to find the machine name of several IP addresses.

8. Use the program traceroute to determine the addresses of the first five routers between the test lab and www.cnn.com. Use ping to find the average delays to each of the routers that are used to talk to www.cnn.com. This can be done using the following commands:

   sudo ping −s 50 −c 100 address

   sudo ping −s 500 −c 100 address

   sudo ping −s 1000 −c 100 address

   The first number is the packet size and the second number is the number of packets. Check with your lab setup for the password for the sudo command. You may not need to use the sudo command, but if you do, sudo will ask you for a password.

   Provide a table of average delays for each packet size to each machine.

   Comment on the results.

Programming Problems

1. Use the code you downloaded for Chapter 5. Add code to perform the following:

   a. Decode and print the ARP request and reply packets. Print the IP addresses in standard IP address notation. Print all other values in the data format that makes it most readable.

   b. Decode and print the IP header. Print the IP addresses in standard IP address notation. Print all other values in the data format that makes it most readable.

   c. Decode and print the ICMP header. Print the IP addresses in standard IP address notation. Print all other values in the data format that makes it most readable.

   d. Add to the set of counters a counter for the number of ICMP packets. Add code to print the values of these counters to the subroutine program_ending(). Note the subroutine already prints the total number of packets.

References

[1] Zimmermann, H. 1980. OSI reference model—The ISO model of architecture for open systems interconnection. *IEEE Transactions on Communications* 28:425–32.

[2] Day, J. D., and H. Zimmermann. 1983. The OSI reference model. *Proceedings of the IEEE* 71:1334–40.

[3] Forouzan, B. A., and S. C. Fegan. 1999. *TCP/IP protocol suite*. New York: McGraw-Hill Higher Education.

[4] Comer, D. E. 1995. *Internetworking with TCPIP*. Vol. 1. *Principles, protocols and architecture*. Englewood Cliffs, NJ: Prentice Hall.

[5] Leiner, B., et al. 1985. The DARPA internet protocol suite. *IEEE Communications Magazine* 23:29–34.

[6]   Postel, J. 1981. *Internet protocol.* RFC 791.

[7]   Reynolds, J. K., and J. Postel. 1990. *Assigned numbers.* RFC 1060.

[8]   Fuller, V., et al. 1993. *Classless inter-domain routing (CIDR): An address assignment and aggregation strategy.* RFC 1519.

[9]   Dall'Asta, L., et al. 2006. Exploring networks with traceroute-like probes: Theory and simulations. *Theoretical Computer Science* 355:6–24.

[10] Periakaruppan, R., and E. Nemeth. 1999. Gtrace—A graphical traceroute tool. Paper presented at Proceedings of the 13th Systems Administration Conference. Seattle, WA. (LISA 1999).

[11] Branigan, S., et al. 2001. What can you do with traceroute? *IEEE Internet Computing* 5(5).

[12] Altunbasak, H., et al. 2004. Addressing the weak link between layer 2 and layer 3 in the Internet architecture. In *29th Annual IEEE International Conference on Local Computer Networks*, Tampa, FL: 417–18.

[13] Kumar, S. *Impact of distributed denial of service (DDOS) attack due to ARP storm.* Lecture Notes in Computer Science. Berlin Springer-Verlag, V. 3421/2005, 997–1002.

[14] de Vivo, M., O. Gabriela, and G. Isern. 1998. Internet security attacks at the basic levels. *ACM SIGOPS Operating Systems Review* 32:4–15.

[15] Lau, F., et al. 2000. Distributed denial of service attacks. In *IEEE International Conference on Systems, Man, and Cybernetics*, Nashville, TN: 3.

[16] Richards, K. 1999. Network based intrusion detection: A review of technologies. *Computers and Security* 18:671–82.

[17] Lippmann, R. P., et al. 1998. The 1998 DARPA/AFRL off-line intrusion detection evaluation. Paper presented at the First International Workshop on Recent Advances in Intrusion Detection (RAID). Louvain-La-Nueve, Belgium.

[18] Hariri, S., et al. 2003. Impact analysis of faults and attacks in large-scale networks. *IEEE Security and Privacy Magazine* 1:49–54.

[19] Tanase, M. 2003. IP spoofing: An introduction. *Security Focus* 11.

[20] Harris, B., and R. Hunt. 1999. TCP/IP security threats and attack methods. *Computer Communications* 22:885–97.

[21] Hastings, N. E., and P. A. McLean. 1996. TCP/IP spoofing fundamentals. In *Conference Proceedings of the IEEE Fifteenth Annual International Phoenix Conference on Computers and Communications*, 218–24.

[22] de Vivo, M., et al. 1999. Internet vulnerabilities related to TCP/IP and T/TCP. *ACM SIGCOMM Computer Communication Review* 29:81–85.

[23] Moore, D., and C. Shannon. 2002. Code-red: A case study on the spread and victims of an Internet worm. In *Proceedings of the Second ACM SIGCOMM Workshop on Internet Measurement*, Marseille, France: 273–84.

[24] Berghel, H. 2001. The code red worm. *Communications of the ACM* 44: 15–19.

[25] Moore, D., et al. 2003. Inside the slammer worm. *IEEE Security and Privacy Magazine* 1:33–39.

[26] Droms, R. 1999. Automated configuration of TCP/IP with DHCP. *IEEE Internet Computing* 3:45–53.

[27] Perkins, C. E., and K. Luo. 1995. Using DHCP with computers that move. *Wireless Networks* 1:341–53.

[28] Schulzrinne, H. 2002. *Dynamic host configuration protocol (DHCP-for-IPv4) option for session initiation protocol (SIP) servers*. RFC 3361.

[29] Deering, S., and R. Hinden. 1995. *Internet protocol, version 6 (IPv6) specification*. RFC 1883.

[30] Hinden, R., and S. Deering. 2003. *Internet protocol version 6 (IPv6) addressing architecture*. RFC 3513.

[31] Bound, C. J., M. Carney, and C. E. Perkins. 2000. Dynamic host configuration protocol for IPv6, DHCPv6. Internet draft, draft-ietfdhc-dhcpv6-15.txt.

[32] Peng, T., C. Leckie, and K. Ramamohanarao. 2003. Protection from distributed denial of service attacks using history-based IP filtering. In *IEEE International Conference on Communications (ICC'03)*, Anchorage, AK: 1.

[33] Ferguson, P., and D. Senie. 1998. *Network ingress filtering: Defeating denial of service attacks which employ IP source address spoofing*. RFC 2267.

[34] McCanne, S., and V. Jacobson. 1993. The BSD packet filter: A new architecture for user-level packet capture. In *Proceedings of Winter '93 USENIX Conference*. San Diego, CA.

[35] Chapman, D. B. 1993. Network (in) security through IP packet filtering. In *Proceedings of the Third UNIX Security Symposium*, Baltimore, MD: 63–76.

[36] Tsirtsis, G., and P. Srisuresh. 2000. *Network address translation–protocol translation (NAT-PT)*. RFC 2766.

[37] Srisuresh, P., and M. Holdrege. 1999. *IP network address translator (NAT) terminology and considerations*. RFC 2663.

[38] Srisuresh, P., and K. Egevang. 2001. *Traditional IP network address translator (traditional NAT)*. RFC 3022.

[39] Senie, D. 2002. *Network address translator (NAT)-friendly application design guidelines*. RFC 3235.

[40] Braun, T., et al. 1999. Virtual private network architecture. In *CATI— Charging and Accounting Technologies for the Internet*, 1.

[41] Carugi, M., and J. De Clercq. 2004. Virtual private network services: Scenarios, requirements and architectural constructs from a standardization perspective. *IEEE Communications Magazine* 42:116–22.

[42] Guo, X., et al. 2003. A policy-based network management system for IP VPN. In *International Conference on Communication Technology Proceedings (ICCT 2003)*, Beijing, China: 2.

[43] Ferguson, P., and G. Huston. 1998. What is a VPN? Paper presented at Workshop on Open Signaling for ATM, Internet and Mobile Networks (OPENSIG'98). Toronto, Canada.

[44] Doraswamy, N., and D. Harkins. 1999. *IPSEC: The new security standard for the Internet, intranets, and virtual private networks.* Englewood Cliffs, NJ: Prentice Hall.

[45] Blaze, M., J. Ioannidis, and A. D. Keromytis. 2002. Trust management for IPSEC. *ACM Transactions on Information and System Security* 5:95–118.

[46] Elkeelany, O., et al. 2002. Performance analysis of IPSEC protocol: Encryption and authentication. *IEEE International Conference on Communications (ICC 2002)*, New York, NY: 2.

[47] Keromytis, A. D., J. Ioannidis, and J. M. Smith. 1997. Implementing IPSEC. In *IEEE Global Telecommunications Conference (GLOBECOM'97)*, Phoenix, AZ: 3.

Chapter 7

Transport Layer Protocols

The transport layer is responsible for the end-to-end transfer of user data [1–3]. The transport layer is the common programming interface for application developers. The transport layer provides error control and is responsible for reliable data transfer. The transport layer protocol can be complex and is subject to a wide range of security threats. As we will see, the vulnerabilities of the transport layer are often coupled with the vulnerabilities of the physical network layer and the IP layer. In this chapter we will examine the common transport protocol used in the Internet. We will also examine a connectionless transport protocol, and we will look at the protocol that is responsible for converting names into IP addresses. Additionally, we will look at common countermeasures that can be used to mitigate the threats against the transport layer protocols.

7.1 Transmission Control Protocol (TCP)

The Transmission Control Protocol (TCP) is the connection-oriented transport protocol used throughout the Internet [4, 5]. TCP supports reliable end-to-end transfer of user data. The TCP layer provides the basic function of data transfer and the ability to establish connections between two applications. The TCP layer offers several services to the application layer, as described next. The TCP protocol will be described later.

7.1.1 Multiplexing

The TCP layer supports multiple applications using the layer at the same time (called multiplexing). This is accomplished by giving each application an identifier called a port. The port number and an IP address create a socket. The TCP layer provides a connection between two sockets. As we saw in Chapter 6, the source and destination port numbers and the source and destination IP addresses

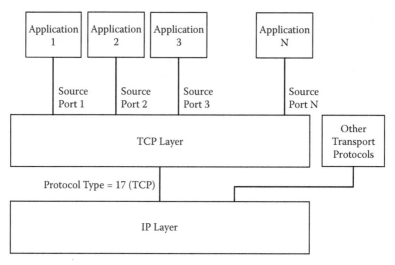

Figure 7.1:   TCP multiplexing.

create a unique identifier for each packet within the Internet. The transport layer uses the port numbers to sort out the packets and determine which application will receive the data from which packets. Figure 7.1 shows multiplexing between multiple applications.

As we see in Figure 7.1, each application has a source port associated with its connection to the TCP layer. When the application sends data, the TCP layer places the source port in the TCP header and also places the destination port provided by the application into the header. The application also provides the destination IP address. When a packet arrives from the IP layer, the TCP layer examines the destination port number in the TCP header to determine which application gets the data.

A client wishing to connect to an application needs to know the port number of the destination application. There are a large number of default port numbers that have been assigned to application protocols. Table 7.1 shows a few of these default port numbers.

The port numbers shown in Table 7.1 are recommended port numbers and are used by legitimate application protocols. Network-based security devices often use the port number as a way to filter out unwanted traffic or to determine which traffic should be allowed into a network. For example, a network-based filter might allow all inbound port 80 traffic (web traffic). The assumption is that only web traffic uses port 80. However, a user inside the network could install a rogue application that accepts connections on port 80. An external user would not be

TABLE 7.1: Default Port Numbers

Port	Protocol	Port	Protocol
20	FTP (data)	21	FTP (control)
22	SSH	23	TELNET
25	SMTP (email)	53	DNS
80	HTTP (web)	110	POP (remote email)
143	IMAP (remote email)	443	HTTPS (secure web)

blocked by the network filter when connecting to the rogue application. This technique is used by some peer-to-peer applications.

7.1.2 Connection Management

TCP is a connection-oriented protocol, and as part of connection management, TCP provides three services: connection establishment, connection maintenance, and connection termination. Connection establishment is where one application requests a connection with another application. In order for the connection to be established, the receiving application must be ready for the connection. There cannot be another connection with the same source and destination port and source and destination IP addresses. There must also be enough resources for TCP to maintain the connection. Typically the resource is memory.

Connection maintenance provides for the exchange of application data. This is described as a separate service. Connection termination typically occurs when one of the parties sends a message to the other indicating it is done. This is a graceful termination. TCP also supports an abrupt termination, where the one application can just terminate the connection without telling the other application. Data may be lost with an abrupt termination.

7.1.3 Data Transfer

TCP provides for an ordered and reliable transfer of data between two applications. TCP also provides flow control, which enables the receiver to reduce the speed of the transmission if it is unable to keep up with the data flow. TCP does handle data differently than the lower layers. TCP provides a stream-oriented service to the application layer. This allows the application to just send data to the TCP layer as a stream of bytes. Figure 7.2 shows the stream service and how TCP interacts with the application layer and the IP layer.

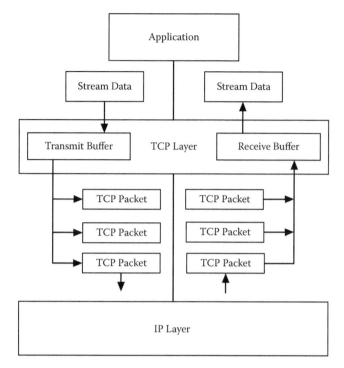

Figure 7.2:   TCP stream service.

As we see in Figure 7.2, the application will send a stream of bytes into the TCP layer. The TCP layer decides when to create a packet out of the data based on both the amount of data and the time since the last packet was sent. When the TCP layer has enough data, it adds its header and sends the data to the IP layer as a packet. On the receiving side, when TCP gets a packet from IP, it will place it in a buffer, and when the application reads data from the TCP layer, the TCP will move data from the receive buffer to the application. Chapter 8 will discuss how the application layer uses the stream service.

7.1.4   Special Services

TCP supports a special service called data stream push, which is where the application layer can request that the data in the TCP transmit buffer be pushed into a packet and sent. The receiving TCP layer detects the push packet and tries to push the receive buffer to the application. The push is often used by applications that send a character at a time, like a remote terminal application. Another special service is the urgent data signal, where the application can mark data as urgent and the TCP layer indicates that in the header of the packet.

7.1.5 Error Reporting

TCP reports errors that occur. These errors may come from the TCP layer or from a problem with the lower layers.

7.1.6 TCP Protocol

The TCP protocol is fairly complex. For the purposes of this book, we will look at several of the critical aspects of the protocol. We will leave it up to the reader to examine the full protocol. Here we will discuss three parts of the protocol: connection establishment, data transfer, and connection termination.

TCP must establish a connection before data can be transferred. The connection establishment phase allows the two TCP layers to coordinate starting header values. The application that is receiving the connection (server application) does not have to accept the connection. The TCP protocol uses an acknowledgment by the server application to indicate the acceptance of the connection. Figure 7.3 shows the packets exchanged during the connection establishment phase of TCP.

As we see in Figure 7.3, the application wishing to make the connection (the client) sends a SYN packet. This packet contains a starting sequence number that is used during the data transfer phase. The packet also contains the destination port number, which indicates which application the client wishes to connect to. When the server TCP layer receives a SYN packet, it allocates buffer space to handle the steaming data and then it notifies the server application that there is an incoming connection. If the server application accepts the connection, it responds to the TCP layer indicating it wishes to accept the connection. The server TCP layer sends a SYN+ACK packet to the client TCP layer. This packet contains the starting sequence number to be used by the server and the acknowledgment that

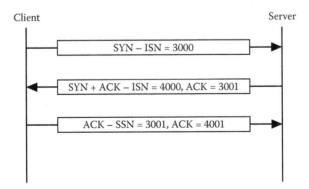

Figure 7.3:   TCP connection establishment.

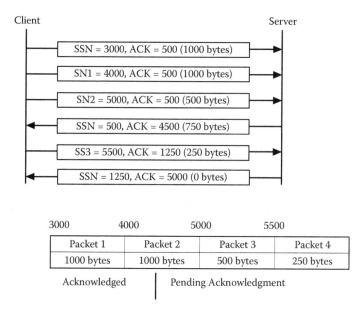

Figure 7.4: TCP data transfer.

the server accepts the connection. When the client TCP layer gets the SYN+ACK packet it notifies the client application that the connection has been accepted and sends an ACK back to the server TCP layer. The server TCP then notifies the server application that the connection has been established. This protocol is called the three-way handshake.

The data transfer part of the TCP protocol uses a sequence number to represent the number of bytes. The best way to think of the sequence number is the index into the receive buffer of where to put the data. The acknowledgment number is used to indicate how much of the data has been accepted by the receiver. Figure 7.4 shows the concept behind the data transfer method used by TCP.

As we see in Figure 7.4, each packet has a sequence number and an acknowledgment number. In Figure 7.4 the first packet starts with the initial sequence number (ISN) and contains 1,000 bytes. The next packet has a sequence number of ISN + 1,000. As the receiving TCP layer gets the packets, it places them into a receive buffer and at some point it acknowledges the data it has received. If the receiving TCP layer has data to send, it can send the data and set the acknowledgment number to acknowledge the data received. In Figure 7.4 we see packet 4 acknowledging the first 500 bytes of data. We also see in packet 6 that the receiving side can acknowledge received data without sending its own data. Figure 7.4 provides a simple overview of the transfer part of the protocol.

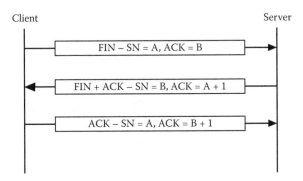

Figure 7.5: Graceful termination.

Connection termination can be handled through an exchange of packets that ensures that all data in transit is received (graceful termination). The connection can also be terminated by sending a single packet, which may cause the loss of data (abrupt termination). Figure 7.5 shows the packet exchange used in a graceful termination.

As we see in Figure 7.5, the side wishing to terminate the connection sends a FIN packet. The FIN packet can contain data. The other side responds with a FIN+ACK packet with the acknowledgment number equal to the received sequence number plus 1. The FIN+ACK can also contain data. The side requesting the termination sends an ACK packet with the acknowledgment number set to the received sequence number plus 1.

A connection can be abruptly terminated at any point by sending a reset packet (RST) to the other side. The TCP layer that receives the RST packet must terminate the connection. As you might imagine, this could lead to some attacks. We will also see that the RST packet can be used by security devices to terminate unwanted connections.

For the purpose of this book we will not examine the flow and error control mechanisms of TCP. These are complex and support lost packets and retransmission of packets. From a security standpoint there have been attacks against the data transfer protocol, but not many attacks against the error control mechanism. Attacks against the data transfer typically require the attacker to sniff the traffic.

It would take many pages to fully describe the TCP protocol. For the purposes of network security, most of the attacks against TCP can be understood given this overview of the protocol. The reader is encouraged to read more about the TCP protocol.

Source Port	Destination Port
Sequence Number	
Acknowledgment Number	
Hdr-Len	Reserved	Flags	Window Size
Checksum		Urgent Pointer
Options			

Flags

URG	ACK	PSH	RST	SYN	FIN

Flag	Function
URG	Packet Contains Urgent Data
ACK	Acknowledgment Number is Valid
PSH	Data Should be Pushed to the Application
RST	Reset Packet
SYN	Synchronize Packet
FIN	Finish Packet

Figure 7.6:   TCP header format.

7.1.7   TCP Packet Format

The TCP header is shown in Figure 7.6. As we see in the figure, the header is 20 bytes long without any options. The fields are described below:

Source port number (16 bits): Used to identify the sending application.

Destination port number (16 bits): Used to identify the destination application.

Sequence number (32 bits): Used to support data transfer plus flow and error control.

Acknowledgment number (32 bits): Used to support data transfer plus flow and error control.

Hdr-Len (4 bits): Length of the TCP header in 4-byte words.

Reserved (6 bits): Reserved, typically set to zero.

Flags (6 bits): The flags indicate the type of packet. The figure shows the values for each of the flags.

Window size (16 bits): Used to support flow control. From a security standpoint the interesting part about the window size is that the initial value was not defined in the standard and is left up to the implementation of the operating system. It is sometimes possible to determine the type of operating system by looking at the initial window size. Knowing the type of operating system could be used to help attack the system.

Checksum (16 bits): Computed using part of the IP header plus the TCP header and data.

Urgent pointer (16 bits): Used to indicate where the urgent data is located within the packet.

Options (up to 40 bytes): Optional information.

Most of the fields within the header are used to support the flow and error control mechanisms. The next sections will examine the vulnerabilities of the TCP protocol. Many of the vulnerabilities are the same types of vulnerabilities found in the IP layer, and some of the mitigation methods discussed in Chapter 6 can help mitigate some of the attacks against the TCP layer.

7.1.8 Header-Based Attacks

There have been several header-based attacks against the TCP layer [6–9]. We can divide the attacks into two categories. The first is where the attacker sends invalid header information with the goal of disrupting the TCP layer implementation. The second is where the attacker uses responses to send invalid headers as a method to determine the operating system (called a probing attack). An attacker can use the information from a probing attacker to develop an attack plan against the device. We will also see that there are protocol-based attacks that are also used to help determine the operating system.

The most common field to attack in the TCP header is the flag field. One type of attack is to create packets that contain flag combinations that are not specified in the standard. For example, an attacker could set all of the flags to 1 or 0. In the past some operating systems had problems with invalid flag combinations and would quit or drop all connections. The problem has been fixed in all current versions of most operating systems. Other attacks involve sending invalid sequence numbers during an already open connection. This attack typically only disrupts the single connection.

In probing attacks using the TCP header, there are many different fields that can be used. A common probing attack is to send invalid flag combinations to determine how the operating system responds. Probing attack software uses a list of characteristics that are unique to a particular set of operating systems. For example, the attacker might know which ten operating systems respond to an invalid flag combination in a certain way. It would use other header information to further narrow the list. Other probing attacks use initial sequence numbers. Some operating systems use a pattern for determining the initial value of the sequence number. By opening multiple connections (or at least sending multiple SYN packets), the attacker might be able to determine a pattern in the initial sequence number assignment. The starting window size can also help narrow the list of possible operating systems. The TCP standard does not specify a value for the initial window size, so different operating systems use different values.

There are several public domain tools that an attacker can use to implement these probing attacks. These tools also carry out protocol-based probing attacks that will be discussed in the next section. Probing attacks are very difficult to mitigate since they use the characteristics of the operating system's implementation of the TCP protocol. There is nothing invalid with the implementation. The problem is that the standard does not specify all possible combinations of header values.

7.1.9   Protocol-Based Attacks

The TCP protocol is the most complex protocol we have examined so far. Due to the complexity of the protocol, there have been a large number of attacks designed to exploit it. Mitigation of many of these attacks can also be complex. We can divide the TCP protocol-based attacks into two categories. The first category is where the attacker is at the endpoint and communicates with the target incorrectly. The second category is where the attacker can sniff the traffic and inserts packets into the TCP protocol stream. We consider these types of attacks to be protocol based even though they use a traffic-based attack (sniffing) to carry out the protocol-based attack.

The endpoint protocol attacks typically involve sending packets out of sequence or not completing a handshake. Sending packets out of sequence typically will only disrupt the current connection, and therefore is not very useful for an attacker. He or she can use out-of-sequence packets to help determine the operating system. For example, sending a reset (RST) to a port where an application is waiting for a connection but the reset does not match an open connection will cause some

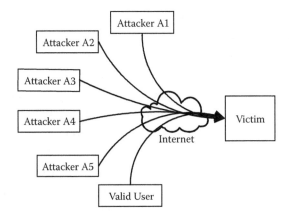

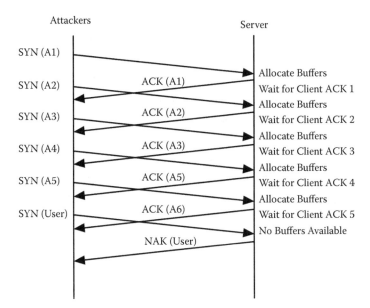

Figure 7.7: SYN flood attack.

operating systems to respond with a packet. The same is true with sending a finish (FIN) packet to an open port where there is no connection. Just like with the header-based probes, these are very difficult to mitigate, and again, there are tools that will send these types of packets to determine the operating system type.

A well-known endpoint attack involves the connection establishment protocol in TCP. We briefly discussed this attack in Chapter 4. The attack is called a SYN flood and is shown in Figure 7.7 [10–13].

As we discussed earlier, the TCP three-way connection protocol starts with a SYN packet that forces the server to allocate buffer space. The goal of this attack is to consume all of the TCP resources, thus forcing TCP to reject other connection attempts. As we see in Figure 7.7, if the attacker sends enough SYN packets without sending the ACK packets, it can cause the TCP protocol stack on the server to reject new connections. These connection attempts are often referred to as half-open connections. The mitigation method was to limit the number of half-open connections from the same source IP address. The attacker can also carry out this attack from multiple locations, which makes it even harder to mitigate. A successful SYN flood attack can take a server offline and prevent anyone from connecting to it. One possible mitigation method would be to implement a network-based filter at the entrance to the network that would try to detect the attack. The problem is that if the attack is distributed, the network-based filter will not be able to tell good connection attempts from bad connection attempts.

The second category of protocol-based attacks takes place when the attacker can see the traffic. These attacks are different than normal packet sniffing, where the attacker is trying to read the data from the network. In this attack the attacker inserts packets into the protocol stream with the goal of either shutting down the connection or stealing the connection.

It turns out that if the attacker can see the traffic, it is very easy to shut down the connection by spoofing the IP addresses and sending reset (RST) packets to both parties [14–16]. Figure 7.8 shows the use of reset packets to shut down the connection.

In Figure 7.8 we see the attacker is connected to the network, so it can see the traffic between the victim and the server. Even though the figure shows the attacker and victim on the same network, the attacker can be connected to any network where it can see the traffic. When the attacker wishes to terminate a connection, it creates a TCP reset packet and sends it to the victim with the source IP address set to the IP address of the server, and to the server with the source IP address set to the IP address of the victim. Both the server and victim will terminate the connection immediately upon receiving a reset packet.

The attacker needs to set the hardware destination address to the appropriate address so that the packet can be delivered to the correct device. In the figure we show a router between the victim's network and the Internet. The attacker needs to set the hardware address of the reset packet destined for the server to the hardware address of the router. The destination hardware address of the reset packet destined for the victim needs to be set to the hardware address of the

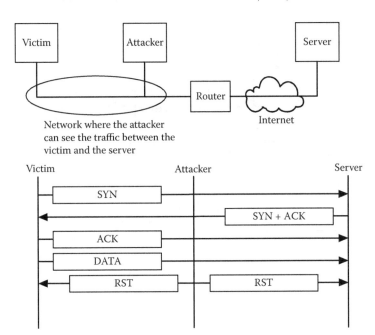

Figure 7.8: RST connection shutdown.

victim. The attacker does not need to spoof the source hardware address since neither the victim nor the router checks the source hardware address.

It should be noted that until recently the sequence number and acknowledgment number in the reset packet were not checked by the TCP implementation; therefore, the attacker could just send a reset packet. This led to some attacks where the attacker did not need to see the traffic, but would guess the source and destination IP addresses and source and destination port numbers. This type of attack was very difficult to carry out with any precision. The attacker would often just sweep through a range of addresses and port numbers. More recent implementations of the TCP protocol require the sequence numbers to be within a range that is close to the current sequence numbers. While this has mitigated the attacks where the attacker cannot sniff the traffic, it has not mitigated them where the attacker can see the traffic.

This attack is impossible to mitigate if the attacker can see the traffic and can insert packets into the network. If the attacker also sets the source hardware address to either the victim or the router (depending on which reset packet it is sending), then it is impossible to determine which device is carrying out the attack. This attack could be mitigated with encryption like in the IP layer.

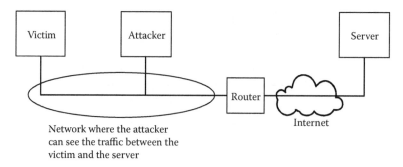

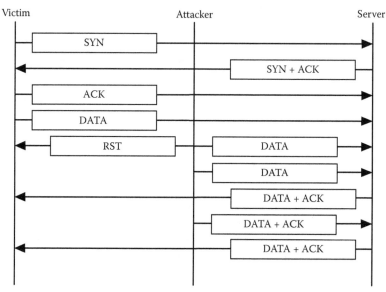

Figure 7.9:   Session hijacking.

However, as we saw in Chapter 6, we typically do not encrypt the traffic within a network.

The next type of protocol-based attack is called session hijacking, which also requires that the attacker is able to see the traffic between the victim and the server [17–19]. The goal of session hijacking is to steal the connection from one of the two parties, and thus pretending to be that device. Figure 7.9 shows how session hijacking works.

As we see in Figure 7.9, the attacker sniffs the traffic between the victim and the server. The attacker monitors the traffic, waiting for a connection to be established between the victim and the server. Typically the attacker looks for certain types of applications where the victim is establishing an authenticated remote access connection to the server. Once the victim has become authenticated with the application, the attacker hijacks the session. This way, when the attacker hijacks the session from the victim, he is connected to the application as if he were the victim.

As we see in Figure 7.9, the attacker waits until he sees the data that signals the attack should start. The attacker sends a reset packet to the victim, pretending to be the server by setting the source IP address to the server's IP address and setting the destination IP address to be the victim. The attacker sends data to the server using the sequence numbers it was able to see in the sniffed traffic. The data packet from the attacker to the server will look like it came from the victim, and the server responds to the victim with its own data. The attacker needs to continue to sniff the traffic to get the data that is destined for the victim. The victim still receives the traffic from the server, but since the connection has been closed, it does not respond.

Just like with the RST connection termination attack, the session hijacking attack is impossible to mitigate without some type of encryption. In this case, however, if we encrypt the TCP payload, the attacker would not be able to send data to the server, even if he hijacked the session. Typically the TCP payload is encrypted by the application. At the end of this chapter we will look at using TCP encryption as a general mitigation technique.

Reset connection termination and session hijacking can be used by security devices to block unwanted connections without having the traffic pass through the security device. These security devices are often called passive network filters. Figure 7.10 shows a security device placed in the network to passively filter connections.

As we see in Figure 7.10, the passive network filter is placed where it can see the traffic leaving and entering the network from the Internet. The filter monitors all network traffic, and when it sees a connection that should be filtered, it terminates the connection using either session hijacking or reset packets. The figure shows both methods of connection termination. In the case of session hijacking, the filter sends data back to the user and terminates the server side of the connection. The data that is sent back to the user is often a message that tells her that she has been blocked due to a violation in the security policy. Notice that in the case of a session hijack, the filter gracefully terminates the connection with the user. The session hijacking method of filtering is commonly used for web traffic or other protocols where the user gets messages back from the server. With many applications the session hijacking method does not work since the user does not see the message. In that case, the filter just terminates the connection using the reset packets.

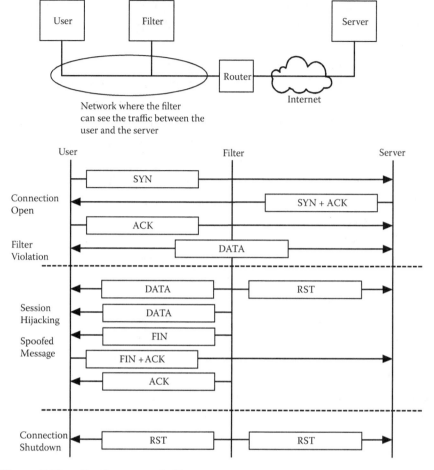

Figure 7.10:   Passive network filter.

Since the filter is only sniffing traffic and no traffic flows through the filter, it does not become a bottleneck on the network. The rules for filtering the connection are often based on the application data. This type of network filter will be discussed when we look at web filters and intrusion prevention devices.

There are other protocol-based attacks that target the window size in order to reduce the amount of traffic. If the attacker sends ACK packets with a reduced window size, the sender reduces the amount of data he sends. This attack is not very useful for an attacker. However, this technique has also been implemented in products called traffic shapers. A traffic shaper is designed to reduce the amount of traffic between low-priority applications. These devices are often placed in the traffic flow like a router. When they are placed inline, they are transparent to the IP layer. These devices can operate as passive devices, like the filter shown in Figure 7.10.

The reader can also imagine several other possible attacks that could be carried out by an attacker that can see the traffic. Most of these attacks would have the same effect as the reset attack, but would be more complex to carry out.

7.1.10 Authentication-Based Attacks

TCP does not support authentication. It uses the IP layer to provide any authentication, and address-based authentication attacks were covered in Chapter 6. Using port numbers might be considered authentication. As we mentioned earlier in this chapter, any application can use any port number it wants. A network-based security device cannot rely on port numbers to authenticate application traffic. Most operating systems restrict which applications can use low-numbered ports (below 1024). These applications need to be run by the administrative user. This still does not prevent rogue devices from running applications on reserved ports.

7.1.11 Traffic-Based Attacks

As we have seen, sniffing can be a problem with TCP in that it allows session hijacking and TCP connection termination attacks. Sniffing can be mitigated using the techniques discussed in Chapters 5 and 6. There are some TCP payload encryption techniques that will be discussed at the end of this chapter.

There are various flooding-based attacks that are targeted at consuming the resources within the TCP layer. We already discussed SYN flood. Since TCP is resource intensive, a large amount of traffic can degrade performance. This may not even be due to an attack. There have been cases where a server becomes overwhelmed due to a popular application. There are techniques to mitigate flooding, whether it is caused by an attack or excessive traffic. The most common method is using network-based devices like the traffic shaper described earlier. The broader term used for these devices is quality of service (QOS). We are not going to discuss the various types of QOS devices on the market today. They all use various criteria to divide the traffic into categories and then allocate bandwidth to each category.

Definitions

Passive network filter.

A device that sniffs traffic from the network and will insert packets to either hijack a connection or terminate a connection based on criteria set by the user. Often used to filter web requests.

TCP abrupt connection termination.

A connection that is terminated with possible loss of data.

TCP graceful connection termination.

A packet exchange that causes the connection to close without any loss of data.

TCP multiplexing.

TCP allows multiple applications to share the IP protocol stack by assigning a port number to each application.

TCP port number.

A unique number assigned to each application using the TCP layer on a given device.

TCP session hijacking.

When an open TCP connection is taken over by a third party and one side of the connection is terminated and the third party pretends to be the device whose connection was terminated.

TCP socket.

A combination of the port number assigned to the application and the IP address of the device creates a socket.

TCP three-way handshaking.

A three packet exchange that consists of a request, a response with acknowledgment, and an acknowledgment.

7.2   User Datagram Protocol (UDP)

The UDP protocol was designed to allow an application to use a connectionless transport layer [20]. UDP has a very simple packet format and does not have an actual protocol. The UDP header is designed to support multiplexing like we saw in TCP. UDP uses port numbers to allow for multiple applications to share the UDP layer. Unlike TCP, UDP is packet based. UDP does not support any end-to-end reliability or any connection establishment. UDP is typically used by applications that need to send one packet and get a single packet response. However, there are applications that use UDP and establish their own concept of a connection using the application protocol. We will briefly describe the UDP packet format and look at the attacks against using the taxonomy.

Source Port	Destination Port
UDP Total Length	Checksum

Figure 7.11: UDP header.

7.2.1 Packet Format

UDP has a fixed-length header that is shown in Figure 7.11. As we see in Figure 7.11, UDP has a source and destination port number. These port numbers are used the same way as TCP port numbers. Since UDP is a separate protocol, the UDP port numbers are separate from the TCP port numbers. There is also a total length field that is the total length of the UDP packet (header plus payload). The checksum is calculated the same way as in TCP.

7.2.2 Header- and Protocol-Based Attacks

The UDP header is simple and there are no header-based attacks, and since there is no protocol, there are no protocol-based attacks.

7.2.3 Authentication-Based Attacks

The UDP protocol has the same problems with authentication as described in the section on TCP. Typically an organization filters out all UDP traffic except for port 53 (DNS).

7.2.4 Traffic-Based Attacks

UDP is subject to sniffing just like TCP. Encryption can mitigate sniffing; however, this would need to be done by the application. Flooding is a not as big a problem since the applications that use UDP are typically slower to respond. It is difficult to generate a large amount of UDP traffic. Most applications that exchange multiple UDP packets use a command response protocol, which means after each packet (command) is sent, the sender must wait for a response.

7.3 Domain Name Service (DNS)

As we discussed in Chapter 3, DNS is used to convert a domain name into an IP address [21–23]. This conversion is done through a series of applications called name servers. From a security standpoint we need to understand how this

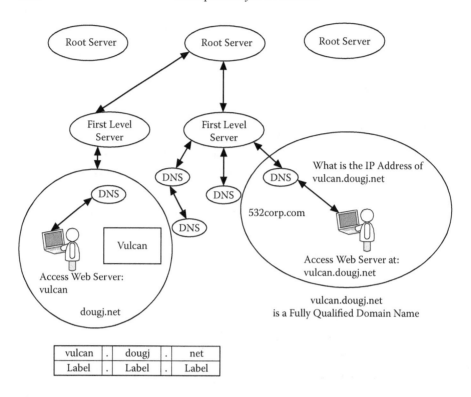

vulcan	.	dougj	.	net
Label	.	Label	.	Label

Figure 7.12:   Hierarchical DNS name space.

conversion takes place and what devices are responsible for providing the answers to the questions being asked by the client. Almost all applications on the Internet are addressed by the user using the domain name instead of the IP address. This makes the process of conversion from a domain name to an IP address a prime target of attackers. If an attacker is able to provide the wrong answer to a client, it could trick the client into going to the wrong IP address. As we will see, DNS is an unauthenticated service.

The idea behind DNS is to divide all of the devices' names in the Internet (the name space) into a hierarchy that is controlled by name servers as shown in Figure 7.12.

As we see in Figure 7.12, a domain name consists of several labels, where each label represents a level of the hierarchy. Each label is separated by a "." and has a maximum length of 63 characters. DNS handles two types of domain names. The first is called a fully qualified domain name (FQDN). An FQDN contains the entire domain from the root of the hierarchy down to the node. You can think of

TABLE 7.2: Common First-Level Domain Names

Label	Usage
com	Commercial use
edu	Educational organization
gov	Government
mil	Military
net	Network support groups
org	Nonprofit organization
biz	Businesses (like .com)

the FQDN as a road map showing which DNS servers should be contacted to find the answer. The second type is called a partially qualified domain name (PQDN). A PQDN contains part of the FQDN and is often used to refer to devices within the same domain. Figure 7.12 shows the hierarchical nature of the name space in the Internet and the use of FQDN and PQDN.

In Figure 7.12 we see two requests being made to discover the IP address of the web server "vulcan.dougj.net." The first request is made from the user in the domain 532corp.com. That request uses the FQDN and the name servers interact to retrieve the answer of the DNS server located in the dougj.net domain. This interaction is described in the next section. The second request is made from a user inside the dougj.net domain. This request uses a PQDN of "vulcan." It should be noted that the user can use an FQDN anytime, but can only use a PQDN when she is referring to a device in a domain she is part of. For example, if the user in 532corp.com tried to access the "vulcan.dougj.net" web server using the domain name of "vulcan," she would not get an answer to the DNS request unless there was a machine inside her domain called vulcan. This, of course, would not be the correct device.

As we see in the figure, there are first-level domains that represent the rightmost part of the domain name. There are several first-level domains defined in the Internet. Table 7.2 shows several common first-level names. In addition to several defined domains, there are first-level domains for each country based on the two-character country code. As we move down the tree, we see the labels to the left of the first-level domain name. Also in Figure 7.12 there are root servers. Root servers do not contain any host domain information. The root servers know how to get to the next-level servers.

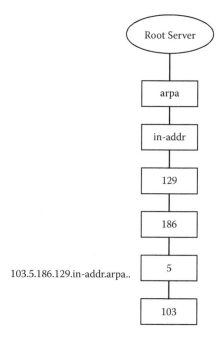

Figure 7.13:   DNS reverse name hierarchy.

Another function of the DNS system is to convert an IP address into a domain name (reverse lookup). The protocol is the same; the only difference is the domain name used in the request. Each octet of the requested IP address can be thought of as a label within a hierarchy. Figure 7.13 shows the reverse name hierarchy.

Figure 7.13 shows a reverse lookup for the IP address 129.186.5.103. As we see in the figure, the domain name is the IP address written backwards, with the first two levels of the domain name set to "in-addr.arpa." The reverse lookup is sometimes used to verify the name of a device given its IP address. As we will see, this form of authentication is only as secure as the DNS system.

7.3.1   DNS Protocol

The DNS protocol is designed to use UDP, where a client sends a request to a name server listening on port 53 and the answer is returned. DNS supports TCP when the answer is longer than 512 bytes. The DNS system consists of several components, as shown in Figure 7.14.

As we see in Figure 7.14, each device has a client application called a resolver. An application on the client device makes a request to the resolver. The resolver makes the request to a DNS server, and when the answer is returned, the resolver

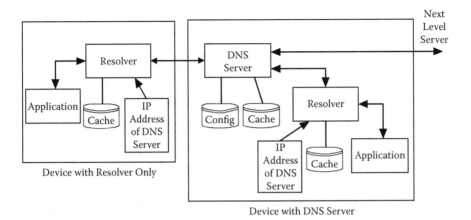

Figure 7.14: DNS system.

places the answer in a cache so when future requests are made, the resolver will have the answer. The resolver needs to know the IP address of at least one DNS server. Note that the resolver cannot use a domain name to find the DNS server. As shown in Figure 7.14, the DNS system also consists of DNS servers that respond to requests from the resolvers. The DNS servers maintain configuration files that hold the information for the domain for which they are responsible. These files contain the IP-to-name and name-to-IP mappings. DNS servers also maintain caches of answers from other DNS servers. The goal of using a cache is to reduce the number of DNS requests. When a server or a resolver gets the answer from a cache, it will mark the answer as being nonauthoritative. The resolvers and servers operate in one of two modes (recursive and iterative), as shown in Figures 7.15 and 7.16.

As we see in Figure 7.15, recursive mode is where the resolver asks its DNS server, which in turn asks the next DNS server. This continues until the requests reach the DNS with the answer. The answer is returned back through the DNS servers that asked the question. The advantage with this method is that each server is able to cache the answer, which could reduce the number of requests. A problem with this method is that all requests go through the root servers. The alternate method reduces the traffic through the root servers.

As we see in Figure 7.16, the client still queries its DNS server; the difference is that the DNS server returns the address of the next DNS server that might provide the answer. The client then asks that server, which either returns the answer or returns the address of the next server. As we see, the total number of packets is the

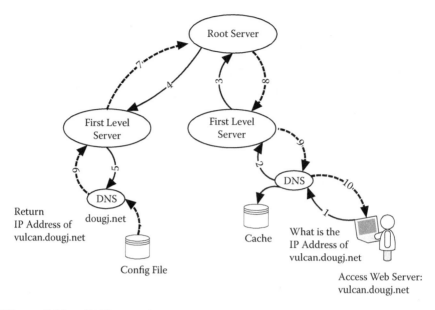

Figure 7.15:   DNS recursive mode.

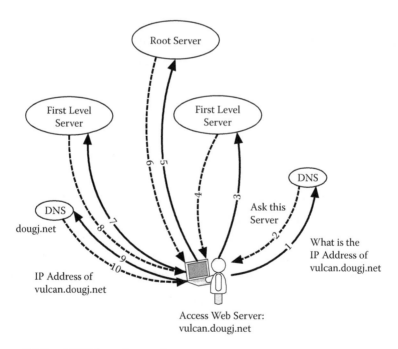

Figure 7.16:   DNS iterative mode.

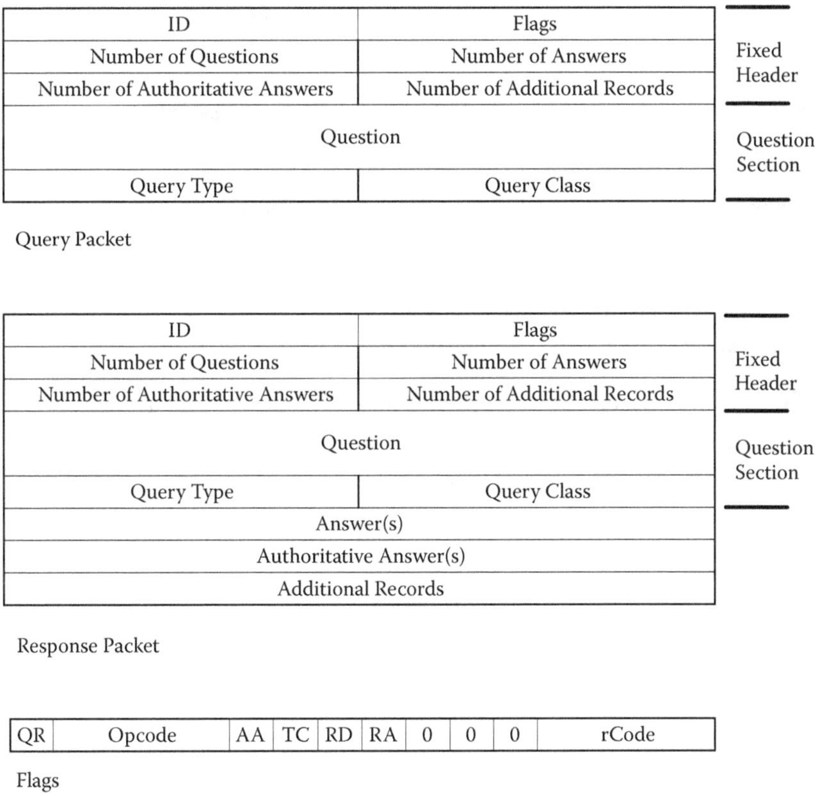

ID	Flags	
Number of Questions	Number of Answers	Fixed
Number of Authoritative Answers	Number of Additional Records	Header
Question		Question
Query Type	Query Class	Section

Query Packet

ID	Flags	
Number of Questions	Number of Answers	Fixed
Number of Authoritative Answers	Number of Additional Records	Header
Question		Question
Query Type	Query Class	Section
Answer(s)		
Authoritative Answer(s)		
Additional Records		

Response Packet

QR	Opcode	AA	TC	RD	RA	0	0	0	rCode

Flags

Figure 7.17: DNS packet format.

same. However, in the iterative mode each DNS server only receives one packet and sends one packet.

7.3.2 DNS Packet Format

There are two message types in the DNS protocol: query and response. The DNS packet header is fixed length and is the same for both the query and response packets. The DNS packet header is shown in Figure 7.17.

As we see in Figure 7.17, the DNS header is 12 bytes. Each packet type also contains the question section, and the response packet contains the answers to the questions. The fields in the header are:

ID (16 bits): Used to correlate the response to the question. Each question issued by a client will get a new id.

Flags (16 bits): As shown in the figure, the flag field has several items, as described below:

QR (1 bit): For a query the value is zero, and for a response the value is 1.

Opcode (4 bits): Defines the type of query or response. A value of zero means a standard request/response.

AA (1 bit): Used in the response packet. A value of 1 means the response is an authoritative response.

TC (1 bit): If the response is larger than 512 bytes, the response is truncated to 512 bytes and the TC flag is set to 1. The client can use TCP to ask the question and get the entire answer.

RD (1 bit): This bit is set to 1 by the client when the client wishes to use recursion.

RA (1 bit): This bit is set to 1 if a recursive response is available. This bit is only set in the response packet.

Reserved (3 bits): These bits are set to zero.

rCode (4 bits): This is the return code that is set in the response message. The values are shown in Table 7.3.

Number of questions (16 bits): Number of questions in the question part of the packet.

Number of answers (16 bits): Number of answers in the answer part of the response packet. Set to zero in the query.

TABLE 7.3:   rCode Values

Value	Error Type
0	No error
1	Format error
2	Name server error
3	Domain reference error
4	Unsupported query type
5	Action not allowed
6–15	Reserved

Number of authoritative answers (16 bits): Number of authoritative answers in the authoritative part of the response packet. Set to zero in the query.

Number of additional records (16 bits): Number of additional answers in the additional part of the response packet. Set to zero in the query.

For the purpose of this book, we will not go into the details of the response packet field or the question section. Figure 7.17 does show the question packet format. The query name is the question that is being asked, and the query type specifies different types of queries that are shown in Table 7.4. The query class is set to 1 for the Internet.

The format of the query name in the question field and the format of the responses are beyond the scope of this book and are left up to the reader to research.

DNS plays a critical role in the operation of the Internet, which makes it a prime target for attacks [24–29]. There are two types of attacks against the DNS system within the Internet. One type is to attack the actual servers in order to take a server offline. These attacks are often carried out using something other than the DNS protocol. There have been successful attacks against the root servers that have caused outages in the DNS system. These attacks against the root servers can be devastating to the Internet. The second type of attacks target the DNS protocol and the lack of authentication. These attacks will be compared against the taxonomy.

TABLE 7.4: DNS Query Types

Value	Abbreviation	Function
1	A	IP version 4 IP address
2	NS	Name server
5	CNAME	Canonical name (an alias)
6	SOA	Start of authority; contains information about a domain
11	WKS	Well-known services
12	PTR	Reverse lookup (IP address to name)
13	HINFO	(Host info) Description of the host
15	MX	Mail exchange
28	AAAA	IP version 6 IP address
252	XFER	Request for a zone transfer
255	ANY	Request for all records

7.3.3   Header-Based Attacks

Even though the DNS header is complex, there are few attacks against the header that would be useful. If the header values are incorrect, the DNS client or server will reject the header. There have been some programs written to use the DNS headers as a method to leak data through a firewall. Since the DNS packets are often not checked, they can make a covert channel. This is a slow method to leak data and is not very effective.

7.3.4   Protocol-Based Attacks

The DNS protocol is very simple, consisting of a query and a response. Since there is no connection, there is not much an attacker can do to the protocol except to send false data pretending to be a DNS server. This type of attack is best classified as an authentication-based attack. There is one type of protocol attack where a rogue application uses the DNS port number to communicate with another rogue application outside the firewall. There have been some attempts at creating peer-to-peer software using the DNS port numbers. Again, since most organizations do not monitor DNS traffic, this rogue communication often travels undetected through the organization.

7.3.5   Authentication-Based Attacks

DNS clients trust the DNS servers to return the correct answer to the question. The only authentication in the DNS system is the IP addresses of the servers. If an attacker could either replace the entries in a DNS server with bogus entries or send his own response to a query, he could trick a client into connecting to the wrong IP address. There are two ways an attacker could insert bogus entries into a DNS server. The first is by gaining access to the server and changing the internal tables that hold the name to IP address mapping. This requires the attacker to break into the machine running the DNS server. The second type of attack is where an attacker sends bad information to a server that has queried another server. This will place a bad entry into the DNS server's cache. This is called DNS cache poisoning. DNS cache poisoning requires that the attacker is able to see the query packet so it can create a bogus response. This requires that the attacker is able sniff the traffic between two servers.

The scope of the damage depends on which server is attacked. Figure 7.18 shows several DNS servers and the scope of damage for different attacks.

As we see in the example shown in Figure 7.18, there are three zones of control. Each of the zones depends on a DNS server to provide answers. In zone 1 there

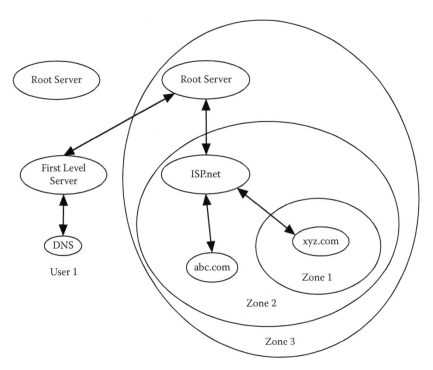

Figure 7.18: DNS attack damage scope.

is a server that has the answers for the domain xyz.com. If the tables in that DNS server were compromised, any request for information about machines in the domain xyz.com would be compromised. If that server was feeding false information about domains outside zone 1, machines inside zone 1 would be affected. In zone 2 we assume the next-level DNS server is compromised (ISP.net). In that case, any domain served by ISP.net would be compromised in that any DNS request that filters through ISP.net would potentially return the wrong answer. The final zone consists of all domains connected through a compromised root server. In this case, there would be the potential for widespread dissemination of false information. Compromising the root servers is the worst-case scenario in DNS. If an attacker could disable or poison the caches of all the root servers, he could disable the entire Internet.

Another attack is to respond to a client query with a bogus response. This attack is like the DNS cache poisoning attack, except it targets a single device. The scope of the damage is the single device. Again, the attacker must be able to see the traffic between the DNS server and the client.

Mitigation of these DNS attacks is difficult without changing the DNS protocol. There have been proposals for a secure DNS protocol that attempts to authenticate the DNS server. These protocols have not been widely adopted.

7.3.6 Traffic-Based Attacks

The most common traffic-based attack against DNS is flooding the DNS server with requests. The DNS server process is simple, and is difficult to flood with requests. If the UDP receive buffers fill up, the UDP layer will just drop packets. This typically does not do much damage since the DNS client will retry several times if it does not get a response back within a certain period.

Sniffing attacks do not cause problems unless they are used to carry out an authentication-based attack. The information provided by the DNS is public information.

DNS remains one of the weak points in the Internet. Most of the mitigation against DNS attacks centers around redundancy of key DNS servers. The root servers are operated by different organizations and are geographically dispersed. The root servers do not all run the same operating systems, which also helps enhance the redundancy.

Definitions

DNS cache poisoning.

Sending false information to a DNS server or to a resolver to get it to put that information into the cache. This will cause future requests to return the false information.

DNS resolver.

The client process that sends a query to the DNS server.

DNS server.

The application that handles requests and returns the IP-to-name or name-to-IP mapping.

Domain name space.

A hierarchical naming convention used to uniquely identify devices within the Internet.

Fully qualified domain name (FQDN).

A domain name that includes every label from the root to the final device.

Partially qualified domain name (PQDN).

A domain name often used within a domain that contains only part of the FQDN. Typically the PQDN is used by a device within a domain to identify other machines in the domain.

7.4 Common Countermeasures

There are not many countermeasures designed for the transport layer. Transport layer security is provided by either the lower layers or the applications. There is one standard that has been developed to provide security across the transport layer: Transport Layer Security (TLS) or Secure Sockets Layer (SSL) [30–33].

7.4.1 Transport Layer Security (TLS)

The Transport Layer Security protocol is actually designed as a separate layer that sits between the application and TCP, as shown in Figure 7.19. The most common use for the TLS/SSL protocol is to provide security for web traffic. The usage of TLS/SSL by a web server and web browser will be discussed in Chapter 10. TLS/SSL is designed to mitigate sniffing and host-based authentication attacks where an attacker is pretending to be another device.

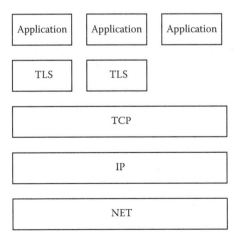

Figure 7.19: TLS stack.

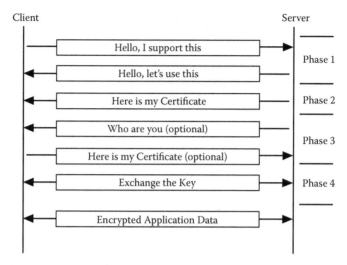

Figure 7.20:   TLS protocol.

The TLS protocol is designed to authenticate the server and optionally the client, and once authentication is complete, the client and server create an encryption key they can use to encrypt the traffic. This is all handled by the TLS/SSL layer and is transparent to the application that uses the layer. The application needs to support the certificate management as described in Chapter 10. Figure 7.20 shows a simplified version of the protocol. For the purposes of this book, it is not critical that we examine the packet formats or the actual message exchange. The format and protocol exchange depends on the authentication method and the encryption protocols.

As we see in Figure 7.20, the protocol has four phases. The first phase is where the client and server agree to the encryption and authentication methods to be used. The second phase is where the server presents its credentials and optionally asks the client for credentials. The optional third phase is where the client presents its credentials. The fourth phase is where the client and server exchange the session encryption key that will be used to encrypt all data between the client and server. TLS/SSL is considered to be secure, and while there have been some attacks against the protocol generally, the only attacks that have worked are man-in-the-middle attacks. In order for the man-in-the-middle attack to work, the attacker needs to present itself as a valid server. This can be difficult if the client and valid server have communicated in the past, or the client has prior knowledge as to the authenticity of the server. If the client has no knowledge of the server, an attacker can pretend to be a valid server and then establish a valid connection with the real server. TLS/SSL will mitigate authentication and sniffing attacks.

Homework Problems and Lab Experiments

Homework Problems

1. Describe a method that could be used to mitigate TCP session hijacking.

2. The TCP sequence and acknowledgment number are used to indicate the number of: bytes or packets?

3. Assume a client uses TCP to send data to a server. The data length is 5 bytes.

   a. Calculate the total number of bytes passed to the IP layer by the TCP layer.

   b. Calculate the total number of bytes passed to the network layer by the IP layer.

   c. Calculate the total number of bytes transmitted on the Ethernet cable (do not include preamble or start frame delimiter).

   d. What is the percentage of overhead for the packet being transmitted on Ethernet (ratio of user data to protocol data)?

4. Repeat problem 3 using 100, 1,000, and 2,000 bytes of payload.

5. Given that we are transmitting over Ethernet, what would be the best data length for TCP to use?

6. TCP has a default MTU size (the size of the payload). Determine what the default value is and comment on why the value is not optimized for Ethernet.

7. Find the location of as many of the DNS root servers as you can. Comment on what it would take to disable the root-level DNS system.

8. How could you mitigate DNS cache poisoning?

9. Research the protocols or methods used to allow DNS to work with Dynamic Host Configuration Protocol (DHCP).

10. Research secure DNS and indicate what attacks it is designed to mitigate.

11. Research any vulnerabilities or attacks against TLS/SSL.

Lab Experiments

1. Using the command "netstat -a," get a listing of all active connections on a computer in the test lab. What can you tell from the list, and how could this be used during an attack?

2. Use tcpdump or wireshark to capture a TELNET session between a computer in the test lab and another computer, and to capture a web or FTP session. Comment on the difference in the packet size between the two types of traffic.

3. Set up tcpdump or wireshark to capture DNS traffic. Run nslookup to query for the IP address of several web sites. Set the debug level to debug (set debug). Also query for the name of a nonexistent web site. Comment on the traffic that is generated. Comment on any differences between the DNS searches and the traffic on the network.

Programming Problems

1. Use the code you downloaded for Chapter 5. Add code to perform the following:

   a. Decode and print the TCP header. Print all other values in the data format that makes it most readable. Print any options as hex values.

   b. Add to the set of counters a counter for the number of TCP packets and for the number of DNS packets. Add code to print the values of these counters to the subroutine program_ending(). Note the subroutine already prints the total number of packets.

References

[1] Zimmermann, H. 1980. OSI reference model—The ISO model of architecture for open systems interconnection. *IEEE Transactions on Communications* 28:425–32.

[2] Halsall, F. 1995. *Data communications, computer networks and open systems*. Redwood City, CA: Addison Wesley Longman Publishing Co.

[3] Forouzan, B. A., and S. C. Fegan. 1999. *TCP/IP protocol suite*. New York: McGraw-Hill Higher Education.

[4] Comer, D. E. 1995. *Internetworking with TCPIP*. Vol. 1. *Principles, protocols and architecture*. Englewood Cliffs, NJ: Prentice Hall.

[5] Postel, J. 1981. *Transmission control protocol (TCP)*. RFC 793.

[6] Schuba, C., et al. 1997. Analysis of a denial of service attack on TCP. In *Proceedings of the 1997 IEEE Symposium on Security and Privacy*, Oakland, CA: 223.

[7] Joncheray, L. 1995. A simple active attack against TCP. Paper presented at 5th USENIX Security Symposium. Salt Lake City, UT.

[8] Harris, B., and R. Hunt. 1999. TCP/IP security threats and attack methods. *Computer Communications* 22:885–97.

[9] Bellovin, S. M. 1989. Security problems in the TCP/IP protocol suite. *ACM SIGCOMM Computer Communication Review* 19:32–48.

[10] Wang, H., D. Zhang, and K. G. Shin. 2002. Detecting SYN flooding attacks. In *Proceedings of the Twenty-First Annual Joint Conference of the IEEE Computer and Communications Societies (INFOCOM 2002)*, New York, NY: 3.

[11] Schuba, C., et al. 1997. Analysis of a denial of service attack on TCP. In *Proceedings of the 1997 IEEE Symposium on Security and Privacy*, Oakland, CA: 223.

[12] Oliver, R. 2001. Countering SYN flood denial-of-service attacks. Invited presentation at the 10th Usenix Security Conference. Washington, DC.

[13] Ricciulli, L., P. Lincoln, and P. Kakkar. 1999. TCP SYN flooding defense. Paper presented at Proceedings of CNDS. San Francisco, CA.

[14] Mutaf, P. 1999. Defending against a denial-of-service attack on TCP. Paper presented at Proceedings of the Recent Advances in Intrusion Detection Conference. West Lafayette, IN.

[15] Garg, A., and A. L. N. Reddy. 2002. *Mitigating denial of service attacks using QoS regulation.* Texas A&M University Tech Report TAMU-ECE-2001-06, 45–53.

[16] Arlitt, M., and C. Williamson. 2005. An analysis of TCP reset behaviour on the Internet. *ACM SIGCOMM Computer Communication Review* 35:37–44.

[17] Dittrich, D. 2000. The dos project's 'trinoo' distributed denial of service attack tool. Technical report, University of Washington. http://staff.washington.edu/dittrich/misc/trinoo.analysis.txt.

[18] Thomsen, D. 1995. IP Spoofing and session hijacking network security, Issue 3. Amsterdam: Elsevier, 6–11.

[19] Cowan, C., et al. 2000. The cracker patch choice: An analysis of post hoc security techniques. Paper presented at Proceedings of the 19th National Information Systems Security Conference (NISSC 2000). Baltimore, MD.

[20] Postel, J. 1980. *User datagram protocol.* STD 6, RFC 768.

[21] IETF. *e. 2000. 164 number and DNS.* RFC 2916. http://www.ietf.org/rfc/rfc2916.txt.

[22] Mockapetris, P. V. 1987. *Domain names—Implementation and specification.* RFC 1035.

[23] Ateniese, G., and S. Mangard. 2001. A new approach to DNS security (DNSSEC). In *Proceedings of the 8th ACM Conference on Computer and Communications Security*, Philadelphia, PA: 86–95.

[24] Householder, A., K. Houle, and C. Dougherty. 2002. Computer attack trends challenge Internet security. *Computer* 35:5–7.

[25] Bellovin, S. M. 1995. Using the domain name system for system break-ins. Paper presented at Proceedings of the Fifth Usenix UNIX Security Symposium, Salt Lake City, UT.

[26] Chakrabarti, A., and G. Manimaran. 2002. Internet infrastructure security: A taxonomy. *IEEE Network* 16:13–21.

[27] Chang, R. K. C. 2002. Defending against flooding-based distributed denial-of-service attacks: A tutorial. *IEEE Communications Magazine* 40: 42–51.

[28] Lewis, J. A., D.C.C.f. 2002. *Assessing the risks of cyber terrorism, cyber war and other cyber threats.* Center for Strategic & International Studies.

[29] Brownlee, N., K. C. Claffy, and E. Nemeth. 2001. DNS measurements at a root server. In *IEEE Global Telecommunications Conference (GLOBE-COM'01)*, San Antonio, TX: 3.

[30] Dierks, T., and C. Allen. 1999. *The TLS protocol version 1.0.* RFC 2246.

[31] Persiano, P., and I. Visconti. 2000. User privacy issues regarding certificates and the TLS protocol: The design and implementation of the SPSL protocol. In *Proceedings of the 7th ACM Conference on Computer and Communications Security*, Athens, Greece: 53–62.

[32] Paulson, L. C. 1999. Inductive analysis of the internet protocol TLS. Paper presented at Proceedings of Security Protocols: 6th International Workshop, Cambridge, UK, April 15–17.

[33] Díaz, G., et al. 2004. Automatic verification of the TLS handshake protocol. In *Proceedings of the 2004 ACM Symposium on Applied Computing*, Nicosia, Cyprus: 789–94.

Part III

Application Layer Security

Part III of the book will look at a cross section of common network applications and their vulnerabilities and possible attacks. We will also examine countermeasures for each application vulnerability and attack. From a networking viewpoint applications can be categorized into three categories: store and forward, bulk transfer, and interactive.

Store-and-forward applications are characterized by the user's data being sent as a single packaged message. Store-and-forward messages are often not time critical. Often the messages are stored on intermediate computers as they traverse the network. Email is a good example of a store-and-forward application.

Bulk transfer applications also move blocks of information for the user, but the data moves between the client and the server, and time is more critical. These applications are the most common. They include file transfer applications, web-based applications, and file sharing applications.

Interactive applications are time critical and the data is broken up into small chunks that are transferred between the client and server. Interactive applications often involve a user interacting with an application directly and expecting a quick response on a keystroke-by-keystroke basis. These applications can generate a large number of small packets on the network. Typical interactive applications include remote access, voice or video streams, and interactive voice.

We will examine at least one application of each type, and since there are so many different applications, by using the taxonomy we can group the vulnerabilities and attacks. Such a grouping should be transferable to other applications not discussed in the book. The first chapter of Part III will provide an overview of the application layer and its interface with the transport layer.

Chapter 8

Application Layer Overview

Interface between the TCP layer and application layer was designed to be simple [1, 2]. The application layer assumes the transport layer will provide a connection-oriented reliable end-to-end transmission of data. There are some applications that are designed to work on top of the connectionless transport service, where the data is transferred using an unreliable service.

Before we look at specific application protocols we will first look at the interface between the application layer and the transport layer in terms of services, functions provided by the transport layer, and the parameters required and provided by the transport layer. This will provide a framework for looking at classifying which vulnerabilities and attacks are common to a large set of applications and which are application specific.

The transport layer is the typical interface between the application and the network. The transport layer is part of the operating system, and therefore has access to system resources. The application layer needs to connect to the transport layer and then use its services to transfer data. The two common transport protocols are User Datagram Protocol (UDP) and Transmission Control Protocol (TCP). UDP is basically a direct connection to the Internet Protocol (IP) layer and provides only an application multiplexing service. The interface between the application layer and UDP is packet based. The TCP layer provides a reliable end-to-end connection between two applications. The TCP layer also provides flow control and error control. One interesting aspect of the interface between the application layer and the TCP layer is the way data is passed between them. TCP provides what is called a stream-oriented service, where the data is not presented as packets, but as a stream of data. TCP then takes the data and puts it in packets to pass to the IP layer. When TCP receives a packet from the IP layer, it places the data in a receive buffer, waiting for the application layer to read the data. An interesting side effect of the stream service is that the application layers need to parse the data to extract the application protocol, as shown in Figure 8.1.

As we see in Figure 8.1, user A wants to send a text message to user B. The application needs to add a header to the message as part of the application

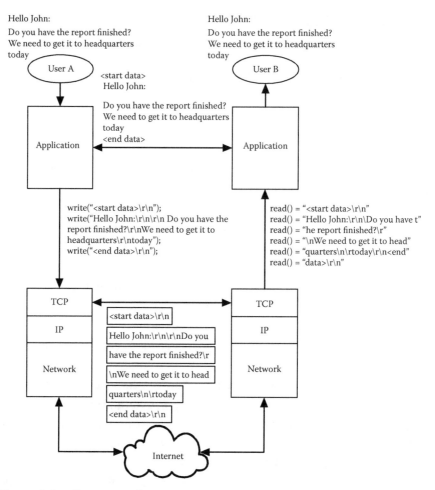

Figure 8.1:   Stream service.

protocol. The header is a freeform header, which consists of <start data> and <end data>. The headers and the message are written to the TCP layer as a stream of data. Figure 8.1 shows the application sending the data that has the application header added to the TCP layer. In this example we assume that the application has already opened a connection to the corresponding application and has established a service connection with the TCP layer. As shown in Figure 8.1, the application layer sends the application to the TCP using three write functions. Depending on how the application is implemented, the application data can be presented to the TCP layer a byte at a time or as multiple bytes, as shown. Figure 8.1 shows the

TCP layer breaking the application data into six packets that are passed to the IP and then physical network layers. (Figure 8.1 does not show the TCP, IP, or physical network headers.)

The TCP layer decides when it has received enough data from the application to create a packet. This is based on the amount of data received and the time since the last data element was received from the application. The application can request that the TCP layer take all of the data it has so far and push it into a packet. This is helpful in application protocols that are interactive, like TELNET, Secure Shell (SSH), or chat applications. Figure 8.1 shows the receiving TCP layer presenting the data to the application via an application read request. TCP will provide the data it has assembled in its buffer when requested by the application layer. This can lead to multiple read requests per message. Figure 8.1 shows six read requests to get all of the data. The application needs to utilize its protocol to tell when the entire message has been received. In this case it looks for the string \r\n<end data>\r\n to tell when the message is finished. The \r and \n are the carriage return and linefeed characters that are generated when a user presses the enter key. In some cases the application protocol will use a length field to indicate the amount of data in the message, and in other cases it will use strings or other data markers. As mentioned above, TCP does support a method to allow the applications to push the data into a packet. This data push method will also cause the receiving TCP layer to push that data to the application during the read request. Because of the way the stream interface works, many of the application protocols are written almost like a conversation.

8.1 Sockets

Before we look at application protocols we need to understand how an application interfaces with the transport layer and how the application port numbering scheme works. As we saw in Figure 8.1, the application layer is provided with a stream service to send data. Before the client application can send data to the server application, it must first establish a connection with the operating system. After the connection has been made with the transport layer, the client application requests a connection with the server application using the TCP connection establishment protocol. The exact details of the programming interface between the application layer and the TCP layer are dependent on the operating system and the programming environment. We will look at a typical programming interface

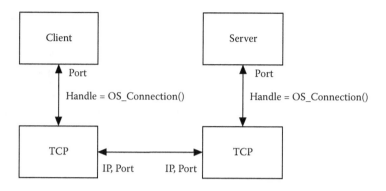

Figure 8.2:   Application-TCP interface.

between the two layers and provide an overview of how the interface works. This interface is often referred to as a socket-level interface [3–7]. Figure 8.2 shows a client and server application where each application is using its respective TCP layer to communicate. The client and server applications have a connection to the TCP layer using the operating system. The operating system helps provide the multiplexing service of the TCP layer. Each application using the TCP layer will have a separate connection to the operating system. A connection to the operating system does not mean there is a connection with another TCP layer or application. A server, for example, will create its connection to the operating system and then wait for a client connection. As shown in Figure 8.2, each application has a port number and an IP address that creates the 4-tuple used to uniquely identify each packet, as discussed in Chapter 3. Once the TCP connection has been established, the application can use the stream service to communicate.

To get a better understanding of the sequence of events involved in establishing a client-server connection, we can refer to Figure 8.3. As we see in the timing diagram, the server starts by opening a connection to the TCP layer using the operating system. Since the server typically picks the port where it listens for a connection, the server will tell the TCP layer it wishes to be bound to a given port number. After binding to a port, the server can wait for the connection from a client. The TCP layer will indicate there is a connection request from a client, and the application can then decide if it will accept the connection.

On the client side of the diagram, we see that the client will also open a connection to the TCP layer. Since the client often does not care what port it uses, it will let the TCP layer choose a port number. Once the client is ready to connect to a server, it will issue a connection request to the TCP layer. The client

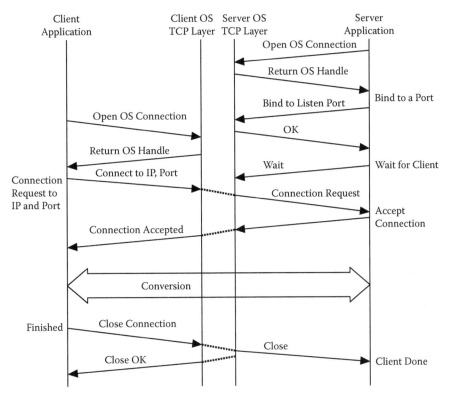

Figure 8.3: Socket protocol diagram.

will pass the IP address of the destination computer and the port number of the destination application to the connection request service call. The client TCP layer will establish a connection with the server TCP layer, and once the connection has been established, the client and server applications can communicate using the stream service. The diagram also shows the closing of the connection, which can be initiated by either application, although it is typically the client that closes the connection.

As we have seen from Figures 8.2 and 8.3, the interface between the application layer and the TCP layer is simple, which makes writing programs that open a connection and send data between each other easy. The complexity is in the application protocol and having the application programs exchange data that can be processed. Given this simple interface, there are not many attacks that can be played out against the interface; most attacks against the application target the protocol used by the application.

Definitions

Buffer overflow.

An attack method where an attacker sends too much data to a program, and when the program copies the data into an internal buffer, it overwrites its internal data.

Stream service.

Applications using TCP send data as a stream of bytes, not as packets.

TCP socket.

A connection between the application and the TCP layer. A pair of sockets is used by two applications to communicate with each other.

8.2   Common Attack Methods

This section will review the taxonomy presented in Chapter 4 as it relates to the application layer and common attack methods. One primary difference between attacks against the application layer and attacks against the lower layers is that the lower-layer attacks often affect all applications and can affect the operating system. An application-based attack can affect that application and sometimes allows the attacker to gain access to the computer system.

8.2.1   Header-Based Attacks

Header-based attacks are often used against the application layer. Since the application layer header is typically freeform, the implementation is often robust. The most common header attack is a buffer overflow. This attack happens when the data received is longer than the data expected. For example, if we refer to Figure 8.1, we see that the application header consisted of <start data>\r\n and <end data>. Let us also assume the designer of the software allocated a fifteen-character buffer to store the header. A buffer overflow occurs if an attacker sends a string that is longer than fifteen characters and the software designer did not check the length of the input. The extra characters are copied into memory and overwrite other variables in the program. Depending on how the other variables are used, the application program would crash, and in some cases the attacker could cause its own program to be executed. This is how worms are propagated through the Internet. Figure 8.4 shows an example of a buffer overflow. As we see

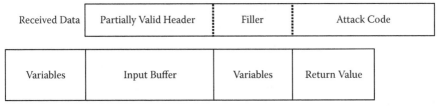

| Received Data | Partially Valid Header | Filler | Attack Code |

| Variables | Input Buffer | Variables | Return Value |

Application Memory

Figure 8.4:   Buffer overflow.

in Figure 8.4, the received data contains the valid header followed by filler data, which is used to position the attack code into the right place in memory so that it can be executed. The length of the filler and the attack code are implementation dependent. This often means that a buffer overflow attack will behave differently on different systems. On one system the attack code may carry out the desired attack, and on another system it may just cause the application to fail, or it may not do anything.

8.2.2   Protocol-Based Attacks

Protocol-based attacks are very application specific. However, there are a few general observations that can be made about a protocol-based attack. Protocol-based attacks at the application layer often are part of an attempt to circumvent the authentication mechanism used by the application. One example would be using the protocol for authenticating an email user to try multiple usernames and passwords to try to gain access. Most protocol-based attacks only affect the application under attack. However, if the application provides remote access to the computer and the attacker gains access, he or she can affect the operation of the computer.

8.2.3   Authentication-Based Attacks

Authentication-based attacks are the most common type of attack against an application that requires authentication. These attacks can be part of a protocol-based or header-based attack. An authentication-based attack is application protocol specific. However, we can classify these attacks into two categories: direct attack and indirect attack.

A direct attack is where the attacker uses the authentication part of the protocol as a way to attack the application. An example of a direct attack is when the attacker responds to the application's request for a username and password.

An indirect attack is where the attacker uses one of the other attack categories (header, protocol, traffic) to circumvent authentication. As we saw in Chapter 4, authentication does not just involve a username and password. Applications might rely on IP addresses for authentication, and in many cases, applications perform no authentication of the user or of the other application. For the purpose of this book, we will focus on indirect authentication attacks. The direct attacks are more of a computer security issue, and the network is only used as a conduit for the attacker.

8.2.4   Traffic-Based Attacks

Traffic-based attacks against the application can cause the application to either quit or reduce its response time. Attacks designed to reduce the application's performance or deny access are called denial-of-service (DoS) attacks. There are some DoS attacks that are focused strictly at the application and operate by sending a large number of requests to the application over an open connection. Another type of DoS attack targets the other layers, but the goal is to deny access to the application.

The remainder of this part of the book will focus on several common network-based applications. We will start with an overview of each application protocol and then examine any security weaknesses in the protocol, followed by a set of possible solutions to the weaknesses. In some cases we will see that there are not any good solutions that can be implemented as part of the application, and that we will need to rely on other methods to mitigate the weaknesses.

Homework Problems and Lab Experiments

Homework Problems

1. In addition to the TCP socket there are local sockets. Research the uses of local sockets and comment on why local sockets are designed to work like TCP sockets.

2. Research buffer overflow attacks and develop a timeline of major attacks. Comment on why the buffer overflow vulnerability still exists.

3. Research the number of programming environments that support a socket interface.

4. Is there a limit on the number of TCP sockets that can be open at one time? What constraints create the limit?

Lab Experiments

1. Using the command "sockstat" (works on UNIX machines), get a listing of all sockets on a computer in the test lab. How can this command be used to help during a network attack?

2. Using the command "netstat -a," get a listing of all TCP sockets. Note that state of the sockets. Comment on the different states of the TCP sockets and how that relates to the state of the application.

3. Use tcpdump or wireshark to capture a web session between a computer in the test lab and another computer on the Internet. Look at the data in the packets to see how the application data is divided into packets.

Programming Problems

1. Download the file sock.tar from ftp://www.dougj.net. There are four source files in the tar file that are example TCP and UDP client and server programs. There will be programming problems in some of the following chapters that will expand on the program developed in this problem. Extract the files into a directory and type "make" to create the four programs. Note: There is a C and UNIX tutorial located on a web site described in Appendix B. There is a description of the programs in sock.tar and a brief tutorial on socket programming located on the web site. Perform the following:

   a. Run the programs tcp_server and tcp_client to see how they work. Modify tcp_server.c to accept and print data to screen indefinitely. Modify the tcp_client program to accept the destination port number as a parameter (flag of -p number). Use TELNET to connect to your tcp_server program, and send it data and comment on what you observe.

   b. Run the programs udp_server and udp_client to see how they work. Modify udp_server.c to accept and print data to screen indefinitely. Also modify the code to print out the IP address of the application that sent the packet. Modify udp_client to allow the user to input a string that will be sent as the packet. Use udp_client from multiple machines to test your code.

c. Modify the program tcp_client to accept a file as a parameter (flag -f filename) and to send the file to the tcp_server application.

References

[1] Forouzan, B. A., and S. C. Fegan. 1999. *TCP/IP protocol suite*. New York: McGraw-Hill Higher Education.

[2] Comer, D. E. 1995. *Internetworking with TCPIP*. Vol. 1. *Principles, protocols and architecture*. Englewood Cliffs, NJ: Prentice Hall.

[3] Comer, D. E., and D. L. Stevens. 1996. *Internetworking with TCP/IP*. Vol. iii. *Client-server programming and applications BSD socket version*. Upper Saddle River, NJ: Prentice-Hall.

[4] Stevens, W. R., and T. Narten. 1990. UNIX network programming. *ACM SIGCOMM Computer Communication Review* 20:8–9.

[5] Toll, W. E. 1995. Socket programming in the data communications laboratory. In *Proceedings of the Twenty-Sixth SIGCSE Technical Symposium on Computer Science Education*, Nashville, TN, 39–43.

[6] Schmidt, D. C., and S. D. Huston. 2001. C++ *network programming*. Reading, MA: Addison-Wesley Professional.

[7] Stevens, W. R., B. Fenner, and A. M. Rudoff. 2004. *UNIX network programming: The sockets networking API*. Reading, MA: Addison-Wesley Professional.

Chapter 9

Email

Email is one of the earliest network applications and one of the first to gain widespread use on the Internet [1–4]. The early email systems were proprietary and did not interoperate with other email systems. They used simple programs to create, send, and read short text messages and not support attachments. An email was sent through a series of servers that stored and forwarded the email as it traversed the network. The email server was used to send the outgoing email to the next server and received and stored the inbound email destined for the users. The users logged into the same computer that ran the email server. The demands on the functions and services offered by the email system grew over time, and today several protocols are involved to create the modern email system. As the email protocols have evolved, so have the vulnerabilities and attacks against email. Figure 9.1 shows the protocols involved to create, send, receive, and read email [5–7].

As shown in Figure 9.1, there are message transfer agents (MTAs), which are mail servers used to store and forward email. They communicate with a protocol called Simple Mail Transfer Protocol (SMTP). SMTP is an application protocol designed to use Transmission Control Protocol (TCP) connections to transfer mail from one server to another. Email can be stored on intermediate servers and then passed on to other servers. Each time the email is transferred from one server to another the SMTP protocol exchange is used. What the destination MTA does with the email once it is received is not part of SMTP protocol and is often implementation specific. The MTA also maintains its own file storage system for inbound mail that has not been picked up by the user and for outbound mail that is waiting for delivery. The MTAs do not authenticate each other and will allow any computer to connect and send email. Some basic authentication can be done to help increase security of the email system.

Another part of the mail system is the user agent (UA). The UA is the application that interfaces with the user and allows the user to create, read, send, and manage his or her email messages. As we see in Figure 9.1, there are two types of user agents (local and remote). Just like in the early email systems, the user agent can be on the same computer as the email server, as in MTA1 in Figure 9.1. In this

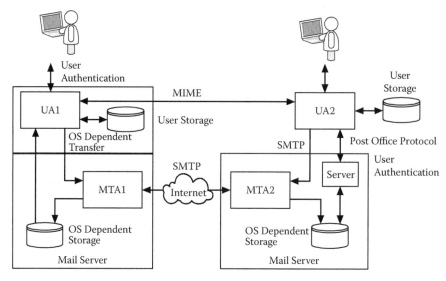

Figure 9.1:   Email system.

case, the interaction between the user agent and the MTA is operating system and implementation dependent and often does not involve the network. The user agent also maintains storage to help the user manage his or her email messages.

The other type of UA is remote from the MTA, as in MTA2 and UA2 shown in Figure 9.1. In this case, the UA uses SMTP to send outbound email messages to the MTA, which will forward the messages on to the next MTA. One difference between the local UA and remote UA is that the remote UA uses a protocol to get the user's email off of the email server. There are several protocols that have been designed to accomplish this transfer. We will look at the Post Office Protocol (POP) and the Internet Message Access Protocol (IMAP). There are also web-based mail systems where the user retrieves his or her email using a web browser.

Another difference between the remote UA and the local UA is user authentication. With the local UA, the user is authenticated by the computer that is running the UA and is not authenticated by the MTA when the mail is read. With the remote UA the post office server authenticates the user before he is allowed to retrieve his email. In neither case is the outbound email authenticated; however, with the local UA the user still has been authenticated in order to gain access to the UA and MTA.

There is another protocol that is used by the UA when creating the email messages. The MTA does not care what is in the email message; it only needs to know the destination address. The user agents can use a protocol that will help them display the message content. The most common format is Multipurpose Internet Mail Extensions (MIME) [8–12]. MIME is used to tell the user agents how the data is encoded and what type of data is in the email message. The email message may contain many different data formats, such as web-based data, pictures, text files, sound, and video. The user agents can display the content in a format that the user can use or see directly. For example, the user agent can display the pictures that were sent as part of the email message. The MIME protocol allows an attacker to send viruses, worms, and other malicious data directly to the user.

The electronic mail system was patterned after the postal mail system, and it helps to understand the email system if we compare it to the postal system. We can think of the MTA that accepts outbound email as the postal box on the corner, and the interaction between the MTAs as the postal system. Just as in the postal system, outbound email is not authenticated, which means anyone can send a letter with any return address by just placing it in the mailbox. Some MTAs do check to see if the return address is valid, but they have no way of telling if the user on the return address matches the actual user that sent the email.

The UAs can be equated to the user's mailbox. The UAs that are part of the MTA can be equated to home delivery of mail. The postal system delivers the mail to a home without authenticating the actual recipient. The assumption is that only people with access to the home have access to the mail. The UA that is remote from the MTA is similar to having your mail delivered to a post office box. In order to gain access to your mail you need to provide authentication (in the form of a key or combination).

The postal system does not open the letters as they are carried from the sender to the receiver, just as the MTAs do not open the contents of the email. There are a few exceptions where the MTA does open the message, such as spam filters and email virus scanners.

Before we examine the specific protocols, it would useful to look at the basic message format used by the mail system. An email message consists of a message header and the message body as shown in Figure 9.2.

The user sends a message that contains a picture and some text. The UA creates the message and adds a MIME header to indicate the email contains a picture and text. The UA can also add a header that contains information about the UA, the subject of the message, date and time the message was sent, and other information that might be useful to the recipient. The first MTA will take the message from the UA. Every time an MTA receives the message it will add a header to the front of the message. This header contains the date and time the message was received by

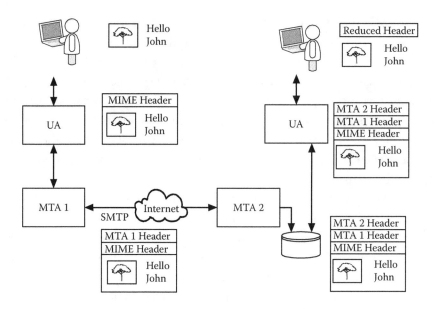

Figure 9.2:   Email message format.

each MTA, the IP address and machine name of the sender, and the email address of the recipient. These headers can be useful in tracking the sender of an email message; however, most UAs will not display the headers in order to make email easier for the user. The user agent will present the picture and the text to the user along with a reduced header that typically consists of the sender's email address, the recipient's email address, and a time and date stamp.

The next sections of this chapter will examine the SMTP, POP/IMAP, and MIME protocols to see how they function, what vulnerabilities are common for each, and possible countermeasures to mitigate the vulnerabilities.

9.1   Simple Mail Transfer Protocol

The Simple Mail Transfer Protocol (SMTP) is designed to operate using the TCP stream service [13]. The email servers listen on well-known application port 25. The header format is freeform and consists of English words. The email message must be in 7-bit ASCII format. There are extended versions of the protocol that support binary data; however, 7-bit ASCII is the most common format. SMTP is

TABLE 9.1: Common SMTP Commands

Command	Action
HELO <domain>	Used by sending system to identify itself HELO machine.foo.bar
MAIL FROM: <path>	Identifies who the message is from MAIL FROM: john@issl.org

RCPT TO: <path>	Identifies who the message should be mailed to;
	    there is a separate RCPT TO for each recipient.
	    RCPT TO: mary

DATA	Indicates that the next transmission contains message text. The message is terminated by <cr><lf>.<cr><lf>.
RSET	Terminate current transaction
VRFY <user>	Returns the full name of the user specified (often not supported)
EXPN <alias>	Returns a list of mailboxes corresponding to the alias provided (often not supported)
NOOP	Returns a response code of "250 OK" and is used to test communication
QUIT	Ends the connection with the mail server
HELP	Shows a list of supported commands
EHLO <domain>	Request extended SMTP mode
AUTH	Authentication request
STARTTLS	Use Transport Layer Security

what is known as a command-and-response protocol. A command-and-response protocol is where one side issues commands (typically the client) and the other side sends a response message to each command. Table 9.1 shows the common commands supported by SMTP, and Table 9.2 shows the response messages. Depending on the implementation and configuration of the SMTP server, not all of these commands will be present or supported. Each command and response is terminated with a carriage return (<cr>) and line feed (<lf>).

SMTP is a command-and-response protocol, and just as the commands are in ASCII, the response codes are also in ASCII. Each response code consists of a three-digit ASCII number and a text field. The first digit of the response code indicates if the command worked or failed, the second digit specifies what type

TABLE 9.2: SMTP Response Codes

Code	Response Status
2XX	Positive completion reply—Indicates the command was successful and a new command can be issued
3XX	Positive intermediate reply—Indicates the command was successful, but the action is held up pending receipt of another command
4XX	Transient negative completion reply—Indicates the command was not accepted; however, the error is temporary
5XX	Permanent negative completion reply—Indicates the command was not accepted

Code	Response Type
X0X	Syntax error or unimplemented commands
X1X	Information—Reply to a request for information
X2X	Connections—Reply to a request for connection
X3X and X4X	Unspecified
X5X	Mail system—Indicates the status of the receiver

of code, and the third digit is used to indicate specific codes. The response code syntax is shown in Table 9.2. Some of the most common response codes are shown in Table 9.3.

Figure 9.3 shows a typical SMTP exchange between two MTAs used to send a message to a single user.

TABLE 9.3: Common SMTP Response Codes

Code	Responses
214	Help message
220	Service ready
250	Requested action completed
354	Start mail input
450	Mailbox busy
452	Requested action failed, insufficient system storage
500	Syntax error—command unrecognized
501	Syntax error in arguments
502	Command not implemented
550	Mailbox not found

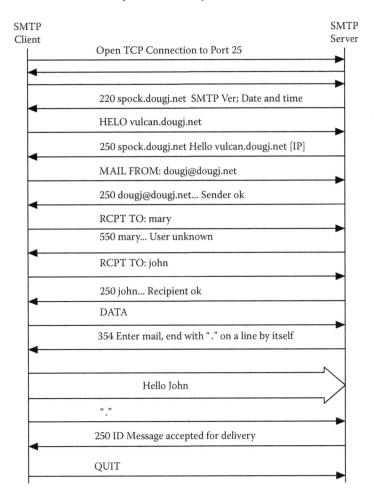

SMTP
Client

SMTP
Server

Open TCP Connection to Port 25

220 spock.dougj.net SMTP Ver; Date and time

HELO vulcan.dougj.net

250 spock.dougj.net Hello vulcan.dougj.net [IP]

MAIL FROM: dougj@dougj.net

250 dougj@dougj.net... Sender ok

RCPT TO: mary

550 mary... User unknown

RCPT TO: john

250 john... Recipient ok

DATA

354 Enter mail, end with "." on a line by itself

Hello John

"."

250 ID Message accepted for delivery

QUIT

Figure 9.3: SMTP message exchange.

The client MTA opens a TCP connection with the server MTA. The server responds with a 220 response code. The text that follows the response code is representative of the response messages, but will vary depending on the implementation. The client then introduces itself using the HELO command and waits for a response code. The client tells the server where the email is coming from and who the email should be delivered to. It is up to the sender to tell the receiving MTA where the email came from. Notice that the command "RCPT TO mary" failed because mary is not a user the server knows about. Also note that the response to the HELO contains the IP address of the client, which was obtained from the TCP layer. Following the DATA command the client sends data until a

"." is on a line by itself. There is no message size indicator. The client can then either send another email message by sending another set of MAIL FROM: and RCPT TO: commands or can quit by sending the QUIT command.

9.1.1   Vulnerabilities, Attacks, and Countermeasures

Even though the SMTP is straightforward, there are several vulnerabilities. Two of the four categories of vulnerabilities and attacks, discussed in Part I, are common.

9.1.1.1   Header-Based Attacks

Header-based attacks are not very common since the headers are simple and any command or response that is invalid is ignored. The early versions of email servers were subject to buffer overflow attacks. The early implementations had a fixed buffer size for the SMTP commands and responses. There have been several well-known attacks that were able to exploit the fixed buffer size by sending commands that were too long. Today most email servers have been patched or designed to accept arbitrarily long input messages. They typically toss all input commands or responses that are over a certain length. However, there is attack code still available that targets SMTP servers using command line buffer overflow. Often a large percentage of attacks that are launched against a particular service or protocol have no chance of working. This makes defending a network even more difficult.

9.1.1.2   Protocol-Based Attacks

Protocol-based attacks are not common in command-and-response-based protocols since the timing and sequence of protocol messages are controlled and any violation is ignored.

9.1.1.3   Authentication-Based Attacks

The most common category of email attack is an authentication-based attack, which is due in large part to the lack of authentication in the SMTP protocol. The most common SMTP authentication attack involves using a fake sender either directly or through a process called relaying. This attack is known as email spoofing. As was shown in Figure 9.3, the client is responsible for telling the server the email address of the sender. There is no process or protocol to verify the sender of the email message. (Several have been proposed, but are not widely adopted.) The only countermeasure widely deployed is to examine the sender's domain to see if it is valid, which can be done using a domain name lookup

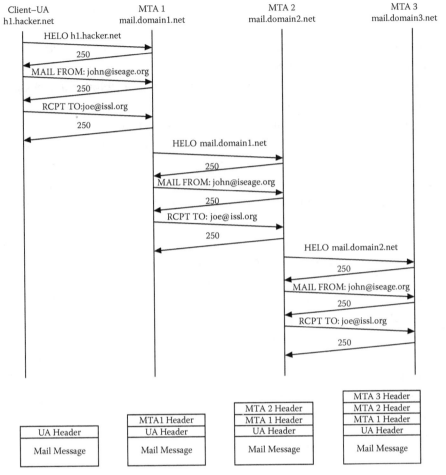

Figure 9.4: Sender and receiver address propagation.

protocol, Domain Name Service (DNS). So looking at Figure 9.4, for example, MTA 1 would check to see if "iseage.org" is a valid domain name [14]. There is no protocol in place to verify the user "john" as being a real user in the domain "iseage.org."

In addition, there is no attempt by MTA 1 to correlate the name of the client computer, h1.hacker.net, with the sender's reported email address, iseage.org. This is due to the fact that the email message may be forwarded through several MTAs before reaching the destination, and each MTA client communicates the "from" and "to" email addresses to the MTA server. In Figure 9.4 we see an email message propagating through several MTAs, each adding its own header and each using the original sender's and receiver's addresses.

Email address spoofing is used for spam email and other malicious email messages. There are several methods that can be used to send email with a spoofed address, including setting the return address on the UA. Spammers use custom software that interacts with the MTA using the SMTP protocol. Since the UA only shows a reduced header to the user, the user cannot easily tell that the message has a spoofed sender's address. The other issue with a spoofed sender's address is if the final recipient's address is invalid, then the mail message is bounced back to the spoofed sender's address. If the address the attacker uses as the return address actually exists, then this could cause excess email traffic to be sent to the spoofed address and could cause the system's disk storage to fill on the spoofed email server. This type of attack could also be considered a traffic-based attack.

Another feature of the email system allows a remote user to spoof the return address. This feature allows remote UAs connected to a single email server to have a return address that is the organization's address rather than the sender's computer address. Figure 9.5 shows a scenario where three user agents are connected to a single MTA for mail handling.

The UAs are running on three different hosts, each with a different machine name and IP address. The goal is to have a consistent view from the outside, so all email looks like it comes from the same main mail server and not from each individual host. For outbound email, the sender's address should be user@iseage.org even though he or she is on a machine that is not iseage.org. Inbound mail would be destined for user@iseage.org, and each user would authenticate with the MTA to pick up his or her mail using a post office protocol. In order to handle changing the sender's address, the MTA is set up to allow forwarding of email messages through a method called relaying. When a message is relayed the MTA forwards the message on to the MTA with the sender's address of user@iseage.org and the recipient's address of user@domain. In Figure 9.5, three users (Mary, John, and Jill) are sending a mail message to john@issl.org. Each UA has been configured to have a return address of user@iseage.org. When the UA sends the email to MTA 1, it uses the RCTP TO: address of john@issl.org. MTA 1 takes the mail and forwards it on to the next MTA for delivery. The detailed header will show that the email is from the UA on the host; however, the "from" address used in the header as the return address is user@iseage.org.

Another aspect of relaying is the ability for the sender to specify the route that the email will take as it traverses the network called source routing. This is used to send the email through a set of internal MTAs. It is not common to specify the source route across multiple remote MTAs since each MTA involved in the

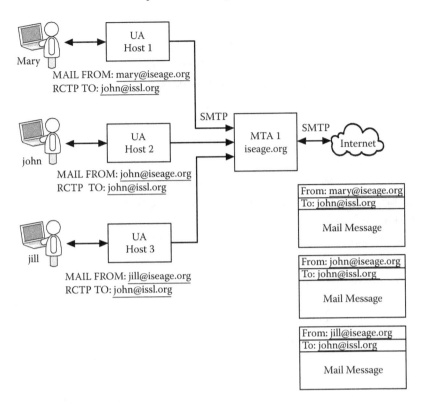

Figure 9.5: Email relay.

source route will need to accept relaying. From a security standpoint there is no real difference between email forwarding and source routing.

A problem with email relaying is that an attacker can use a relay to fake the return address and use the victim's mail server to send spam and malicious emails. There are public domain attack tools that search for an MTA that allows relaying. All an attacker needs to do is to open the connection to the MTA and send a RCPT TO: user@domain, and if the MTA responds with a 250, then it will accept relaying. Most MTAs that allow relaying restrict who can send a relayed message based on the IP address of the machine connected to the MTA server. This is not a perfect solution since IP addresses can be spoofed, and if a machine in the acceptable IP address range has been compromised, then it could be the source of the relayed email.

Another authentication-based attack is username probing. This attack is simple to carry out, but has minimal security implications. As we saw in Figure 9.3, the RCPT TO: command returns an error if the user is not valid. This could be used to find usernames, or at least to verify usernames. If the attacker has no information about the target, using SMTP to guess usernames would be very time-consuming and would be logged. Most of the time email usernames are known, and therefore it would not gain the attacker much additional information by probing for usernames.

9.1.1.4 Traffic-Based Attacks

In addition to authentication-based attacks, traffic-based attacks can be played out against email systems. The most common attack is to flood the email server with large messages that consume the disk storage. As the size of disk storage increases, this attack is becoming less useful. In addition, many email systems place a quota on the size of an inbound mailbox, which causes this type of attack to only impact individual users and not the entire system. There have been some clever flooding attacks where you get an email server to respond to a spoofed return address. An attacker can send email from machine A to machine B with a return address of machine C. Machine B would respond back to machine C. Another common flooding attack is often accidental and happens when a user sends an email using a relay to a large list of users. If we remember from Figure 9.3, the sender can send the command RCPT TO: multiple times. This will cause the relaying MTA to make a copy of the message for each outbound destination. If the email message is large, the user could fill up the outbound message queue. However, the outbound queue usually empties as the MTA makes contact with the destination MTAs.

Another traffic-based attack is sniffing the SMTP traffic. Sniffing traffic from the Internet is difficult, but an attacker could sniff the traffic inside an organization if he or she has gained access to the organization's network. The SMTP protocol is not encrypted, so an attacker would be able to read the email messages. The next section describes a couple of encryption methods for the SMTP traffic.

9.1.1.5 General Countermeasures

In addition to the vulnerabilities and countermeasures described above, there are several additional authentication-based countermeasures that have been proposed to aid in email security. These are the STARTTLS and AUTH commands in the SMTP protocol. STARTTLS is used to negotiate the parameters for the Transport Layer Security protocol [15–18]. This protocol provides an authenticated and encrypted delivery of mail to an MTA. This does not provide end-to-end authentication and encryption of the message. Nor does it provide user-to-user authentication and encryption.

AUTH provides a mechanism for users connecting to an MTA to authenticate themselves for the purpose of sending outbound messages. Both STARTTLS and AUTH are typically used for remote access to the MTA for relaying. For example, a user that takes his laptop on the road and needs to send email as if he is part of the home network would use these protocols to prove to the MTA that it could relay messages. These protocols are not used to secure email messages between two end users, nor do they help in fighting spam. There is an ongoing debate about whether email delivery using SMTP should be an authenticated service as a way to reduce spam. Another idea is to add a charge for email, which would also require authentication. It is this author's belief that email delivery should remain unauthenticated and that email security should be handled by the user agents.

Definitions

Email relay.

Sending email messages with a new return address that matches the return address of the organization's email server. This allows multiple internal MTAs, and clients look like they are using just one MTA.

Email spoofing.

The process of creating an email message where the sending address is not the same as the address of the actual sender.

Message transfer agent (MTA).

The application that handled the reception and delivery of email messages. Its operation is similar to the postal system.

Simple Mail Transfer Protocol (SMTP).

The protocol used to transfer email messages between MTAs and from an email client to an MTA.

User agent (UA).

The name given to the client application that is used to create and read email messages.

9.2 POP and IMAP

As shown in Figure 9.1, the user has more than one way to access her inbound email. Figure 9.6 shows three methods for the user to access her email stored on the MTA. In one method (local user agent), the inbound mail messages are stored

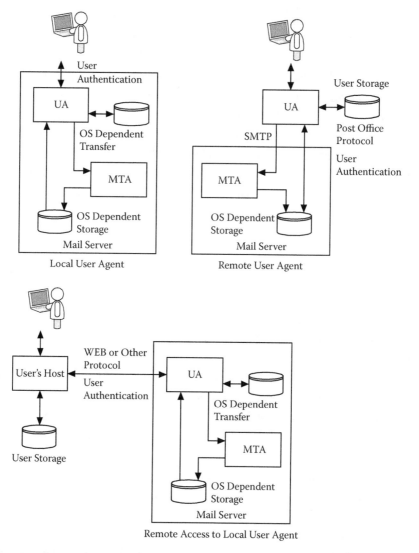

Figure 9.6:   User agent access.

on the same system where the user has an account. The user authenticates herself with the server (typically by logging into the server) and then runs the user agent application, which has direct access to the user's inbound emails. This method does not rely on any networking other than the user may use network protocols to access the server.

In the second method (remote access to local user agent), the user remotely accesses the user agent running on the server. The most common implementation of this method is web-based email. The security implications of this method fall under the discussion of web applications.

In the third method (remote user agent), the user agent is remote from the mail server and the user agent uses a network protocol to access and transfer the email messages to the remote user agent. There are two common protocols used to support access to email by a remote user agent. The first is Post Office Protocol (POP), and the second is Internet Message Access Protocol (IMAP) [19–21]. The basic functionality of each protocol is similar, and the security issues are common.

POP is used to transfer email from a mail server to a computer running a user agent. POP provides the ability to preview email and limited management of remote email. POP also provides user authentication before access to the email is granted. POP is patterned after the real post office where a user has a P.O. box with some type of user authentication. The P.O. box is designed to be intermediate storage of mail until the user retrieves the mail and takes it with her or throws it away while at the post office. The POP protocol works the same way. The user authenticates with the server, and then she can look through the email and decide what should be thrown away and what should be transferred to the user's computer. Like many protocols, POP has gone through several versions, and for the purpose of this text, we will focus on version 3, which is the most current.

Version 3 of POP (often called POP3) uses TCP to connect the client's user agent to the server. The POP3 server listens on port 110 and waits for a client to connect and for the user to authenticate. The POP3 protocol is a command-and-response protocol like SMTP. The POP3 commands and response codes are shown in Table 9.4.

There are two response codes: ERR indicates an error and OK indicates the command was successful. (Note that ERR starts with a − and OK starts with a +.)

Figure 9.7 shows the typical interaction between the client and server using the POP3 protocol. Note that the username and password are sent to the server with no encryption. If the username is incorrect, most POP3 servers will still prompt for a password, thus not letting an attacker know if he or she has guessed a valid username. How is this different than the way SMTP handled the RCPT TO: command? The major difference is that the email address for the user handled by the SMTP server may not be the username on the server, whereas the usernames in the POP3 protocol are valid usernames on the server. This means an attacker could use that username to log in to the server if he or she knew the password.

TABLE 9.4:   Common POP3 Commands and Responses

Command	Action
USER name	User name for authentication
PASS string	Send the password for the user
STAT	Returns the number of messages
LIST [msg]	Returns the size of message or the size of all messages if none is specified
RETR msg	Send full message to client
DELE msg	Delete message from server
NOOP	No operation, returns OK status code
RSET	Reset deletion indicators
QUIT	Quit the session
TOP msg n	Returns the first n lines of message
UIDL msg	Returns a unique id string for the requested message; does not change during the session
Response Codes	Action
–ERR message	Error
+OK message	Command was successful

As shown in Figure 9.7, once the POP3 client has been authenticated, the server responds back with the number of email messages. The client can then retrieve any message and can also delete any message. Note the messages are not deleted until the session ends with the QUIT command. When the client retrieves a message, it uses the message number and is given the number of bytes in the message, and then the message is sent by the server. Also note that the message is terminated with a <cr><lf>.<cr><lf>.

The POP3 protocol is designed to facilitate the transfer of email messages from the server to the client, but if a user has multiple computers where she accesses her email, then there is problem keeping the email in sync, since the email will end up transferred to several different computers. Since POP is not really designed to keep the email on the server, another protocol was created: the Internet Message Access Protocol (IMAP).

There are a couple of differences between IMAP and POP. IMAP supports mailboxes on the server as a way to organize email. IMAP also supports moving messages between the client and server folders, searching the server folders, and managing the server folders. When the user stores her email on the server, she

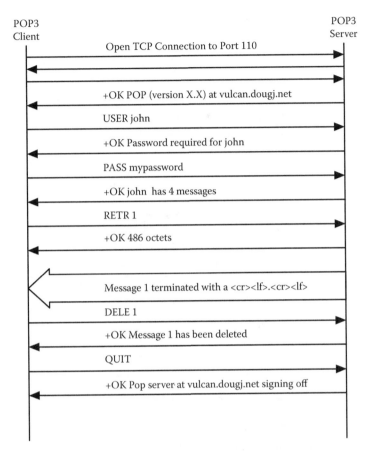

Figure 9.7: POP3 protocol diagram.

can easily move between multiple clients. Figure 9.8 shows how mailboxes are handled in a typical IMAP implementation. There are user mailboxes on the server that can be accessed by any user agent that knows the username and password associated with the mailboxes. The UA can use the IMAP protocol to create, manage, and delete remote mailboxes and to move email between the local and remote mailboxes. The user can create a number of mailboxes to help her organize her mail.

IMAP is a command-and-response protocol. A subset of the IMAP commands is shown in Table 9.5. IMAP is a more complicated protocol and provides better support for multiple remote user agents. From a security standpoint, IMAP and POP3 have the same security concerns, and therefore we will not explore the IMAP protocol in detail.

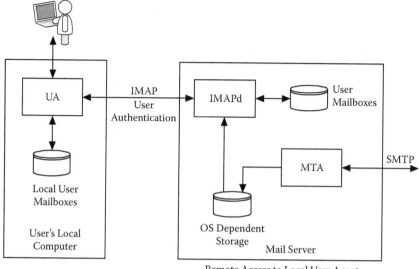

Figure 9.8:   IMAP mailboxes.

9.2.1   Vulnerabilities, Attacks, and Countermeasures

9.2.1.1   Header- and Protocol-Based Attacks

POP and IMAP have not had many header and protocol vulnerabilities over the years. Both protocols are simple and the headers are freeform text.

9.2.1.2   Authentication-Based Attacks

There are numerous network applications that require a user to authenticate over the network with a username and password. This allows an attacker to send usernames and passwords in an attempt to break into the computer. POP will allow a user to try an unlimited number of login attempts. The code to carry out a password-guessing attack against a POP or IMAP would be easy to write, but the probability of the attack being successful is low. There are too many possible password combinations to guess every password, so attackers often rely on a dictionary of words. See Appendix A for more details on the strength of passwords. These types of direct password-guessing attacks can be successful against configuration vulnerabilities, where the default passwords have not been changed. With POP and IMAP, every login attempt is logged along with every email transaction. However, the log file becomes quite large and is often overlooked by system administrators. There are not any good countermeasures for

TABLE 9.5: Common IMAP Commands

Command	Action
CAPABILITY	Returns a list of capabilities the server supports
NOOP	No operation
LOGOUT	Ends the session
AUTHENTICATE type	Indicates the client wants to authenticate using the specified type
LOGIN name password	Log in using username and password
SELECT mailbox	Select the mailbox to be used (inbox is the inbound mail queue)
EXAMINE mailbox	Read-only version of SELECT
CREATE mailbox	Create a new mailbox on the server
DELETE mailbox	Delete the mailbox on the server
RENAME current new	Rename the current mailbox to a new name
CLOSE	Close the mailbox and all mail marked to be deleted will be deleted
EXPUNGE	Delete all messages marked for deletion
SEARCH criteria	Search the mailbox for messages that match the criteria
FETCH message items	Fetch the message items. (Note: The client can request the entire message or parts of the message or information about the message.)

remote user authentication. One method is to limit where a user can authenticate, from using the IP address of the user's computer, for example, only allowing POP or IMAP access from a certain IP address range. This can also be accomplished by not allowing the POP or IMAP protocols to cross the perimeter of the network through the use of firewalls or screening routers. These types of network-wide solutions are discussed in Part IV of the book. We find that most users want access to their email from wherever they are, which makes restricting user access to an IP address range or to the organizational network not practical.

Depending on the level of security desired, some organizations use VPN software on remote clients, which provides an encrypted and authenticated connection into the organization's network. With VPN software the organization can restrict the POP and IMAP protocols to only run inside their network. Another countermeasure is to not allow remote access to POP or IMAP, but allow remote email access through a web client, as shown in Figure 9.6. Web servers have their own authentication system and support encrypted traffic. Some organizations have adopted web-based user agents for all email access.

9.2.1.3   Traffic-Based Attacks

POP and IMAP could be subject to traffic-based attacks, but the damage would be limited. An attacker has little to gain from trying to overwhelm a POP or IMAP server with traffic since a new server is started for every user connection.

A vulnerability that exists in most protocols is that the data is transferred in clear text, and therefore any attacker that can sniff the traffic can read the data. As we described in Chapter 3, the attacker needs to be connected to the network where the traffic is passing to be able to sniff the packets. This vulnerability has different effects, depending on the application. In the case of POP and IMAP, the biggest issue is that the username and password are transferred in clear text, and that an attacker could capture usernames and passwords. The general countermeasure is to use encryption technologies to ensure the data cannot be read. There are secure versions of both POP and IMAP that use public key encryption to exchange a symmetrical key. All traffic is then encrypted, including the username and password exchange. Appendix A provides an overview of encryption methods. While these secure versions do fix the clear text problem, they are not widely used. Most of the newer user agents support secure IMAP and POP that use Transport Layer Security (TLS). TLS was discussed as a countermeasure in Chapter 7.

Definitions

Internet Message Access Protocol (IMAP).

A protocol used by a user agent to transfer email from an MTA to the user computer. IMAP also allows for the creation and maintenance of mailboxes on the MTA.

Post Office Protocol (POP).

The protocol used by a user agent to transfer email from an MTA to the user's computer.

9.3   MIME

In this chapter we have looked at protocols to move email from one server to another and protocols used to transfer email from the server to the user agent. There is another protocol, Multipurpose Internet Mail Extensions (MIME), that

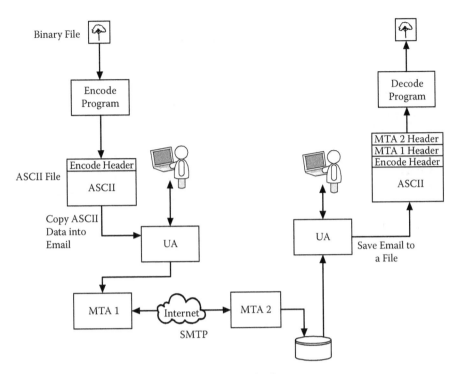

Figure 9.9: Email encode and decode methods.

is used to format the email messages themselves [8–12]. MIME is more of a message format than an actual protocol. From a network security standpoint, MIME is worth discussing since it is used to transport any data type and present it to the user. The MIME protocol has been used to transport viruses, worms, and other malicious code. MIME also enables inserting pictures and web links into email messages, which are used in spam and identity theft. In this section we will briefly discuss the MIME protocol and then look at how the protocol is used to carry out attacks.

SMTP, designed to carry 7-bit ASCII data, worked well in the early days of email. However, even in the early days of email, users wanted to send more than simple text. They created a simple encoding method that converted binary data into ASCII data. A user would first take the binary file and encode it, and then the user would email the file to another user. The receiving user would store the email message as a file and then strip away the headers and pass the message through the decode routine. This is shown in Figure 9.9. The encode and decode functions were separate from the user agent, and several different methods were created to

TABLE 9.6:   MIME Headers

Header	Function
MIME-Version	Indicates a MIME message. The current version is 1.1.
Content-Type	Indicates the type of content contained in the message
Content-Transfer-Encoding	Indicates how the content is encoded
Content-Id	Optional identifier used for multiple messages
Content-Description	Optional description of the object that can be displayed by the user agent
Content-Disposition	Optional description of the method to use to display the object in receiving the user agent

enable users to transfer non-ASCII data. As you can imagine, this was not very user-friendly.

As the sophistication of the user agent programs increased, and with the advent of graphical user interfaces, there was a need to design a protocol that the user agents could use to exchange non-ASCII data. MIME was designed to support arbitrary data formats and allow for new data formats. MIME has a freeform header format, and unlike typical network protocols, there is no exchange of packets. The sending user agent assembles a MIME message and includes that as part of the message. The receiving user agent will interpret the message using the MIME headers to decode each part. The receiving user agent does not need to interact with the sending user agent to decode the messages. Another interesting aspect of MIME is that since the MIME encoded message is in ASCII, non-MIME user agents can receive the message. However, they are not able to display that data in the original format. MIME also supports messages that can be seen with both MIME and non-MIME user agents.

The MIME protocol has three required headers and three optional headers that are included in the message given to the message transfer agent by the user agent. In Figure 9.2 we saw that the message created by the sending user agent contained a MIME header, and that header was read by the receiving user agent. The MIME headers are shown in Table 9.6 and are described in the following paragraphs.

The first header indicates the message is in MIME format and is found once in the message. As shown in Figure 9.10, the other headers can appear multiple times in the message, typically once for each object in the message.

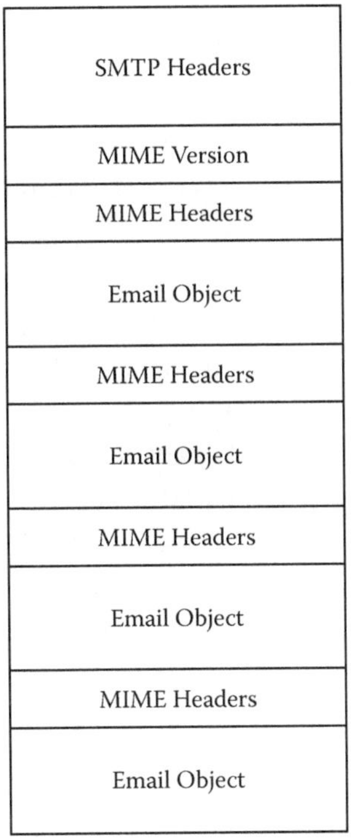

| SMTP Headers |
| MIME Version |
| MIME Headers |
| Email Object |
| MIME Headers |
| Email Object |
| MIME Headers |
| Email Object |
| MIME Headers |
| Email Object |

Figure 9.10: MIME headers.

The following list will look at each of the six headers and will give some examples of each header in use. We will then look at several different attacks that use MIME and how to mitigate them.

MIME-Version: The MIME-Version is used to indicate that the remainder of the message is in MIME format. The syntax is:

MIME-Version: 1.1

Content-Type: The Content-Type header is use to indicate what type of objects are contained in the message. The syntax of the header is:

Content-Type: type/subtype; parameters

The MIME protocol supports several object types, each with one or more subtypes. Table 9.7 shows many of object types supported by the MIME protocol. These types and some of the

TABLE 9.7:   MIME Object Types

Type	Subtype	Description
Text	Plain	Unformatted text
	HTML	Text in HTML format
Multipart	Mixed	Multiple ordered objects
	Parallel	Multiple object, not ordered
	Digest	Multiple ordered RFC 822 objects
	Alternative	Alternate methods of representing the same object
Message	RFC 822	Encapsulated message
	Partial	Part of a larger message
	External—body	Object is a reference to an external message
Image	JPEG	JPEG image
	GIF	GIF image
Video	MPEG	MPEG movie
Audio	Basic	Audio object
Application	Postscript	Adobe Postscript object
	Octet-stream	8-bit binary object

subtypes are described below. It is not necessary to completely enumerate all of the MIME headers for us to understand the security implications and to develop methods to mitigate the vulnerabilities.

Content-Type: Text/Plain: Seven-bit ASCII text that is displayed by the receiving user agent in a format that it chooses. This is used by MIME-capable agents when the user sends a text message. A non-MIME user agent that receives the message will display the MIME headers along with the text message. Text/Hypertext Markup Language (HTML) is used to transfer HTML-formatted documents. This has become commonplace in email messages and allows users to create email text that is formatted. This also allows users to create email messages that look like web sites and can contain hyperlinks to web sites. This is also used by spammers and other attackers to get users to click on a link and either buy something or provide them with personal information.

```
Email Header
MIME-Version: 1.0
UA Header
Content-Type: multipart/mixed;
 boundary="------------ 0906030800000040609050705"
This is a multi-part message in MIME format.
```

```
---------- 0906030800000040609050705
Content-Type: multipart/alternative;
 boundary="------------ 00040703080300090108005"

      -------------- 00040703080300090108005
      Content-Type:text/plain;charset = ISO-8859-1;
      format=flowed
      Content-Transfer-Encoding: 7bit

      ASCII text message
      -------------- 00040703080300090108005

      Content-Type: multipart/related;
       boundary="------------ 0808030900003030603090002"

         -------------- 0808030900003030603090002
         Content-Type: text/html; charset=ISO-8859-1
         Content-Transfer-Encoding: 7bit

         HTML Text
         <img src="cid:part1.09040604.05020804@iastate.edu"
         alt=""><br>
         HTML Text

         -------------- 0808030900003030603090002
         Content-Type: image/gif;
          name="logo.gif"
         Content-Transfer-Encoding: base64
         Content-ID: <part1.09040604.05020804@iastate.edu>
         Content-Disposition: inline;
          filename="logo.gif"

         GIF File in base64
         -------------- 0808030900003030603090002 --
      -------------- 00040703080300090108005   --
```

OR
```
      -------------- 0906030800000040609050705
      Content-Type: image/gif;
       name="logo.gif"
      Content-Transfer-Encoding: base64
      Content-Disposition: inline;
       filename="logo.gif"

      GIF File in base64
      -------------- 0906030800000040609050705 --
```

Figure 9.11: Multipart MIME message.

Content-Type: Multipart: Used to create documents that contain multiple objects. This is used to support attachments in email messages or to include multiple objects within a single email message. Figure 9.11 shows an email message with multiple parts. As we see in Figure 9.11, there are multiple MIME headers for each object type. This content type is used to transport malicious code, and depending on how the receiving user agent is set up, the malicious code may be executed when the email message is opened.

Content-Type: Message: Used if the object is a whole mail message or part of a mail message. The most interesting security aspect of this header is the ability to point to another message stored on a remote site. Again, depending on how the user agent is configured, remote messages can be used to transport malicious code. It can also be used to tell if an email message was opened. This is often referred to as an email bug, and will be discussed in the vulnerability section of this chapter.

The remaining content type headers are self-explanatory and do not represent additional security threats beyond what has already been described. They are methods to attach different file types and have the receiving user agent be able to process them.

Content-Transfer-Encoding: The content transfer encoding header indicates what data format is used to encode the objects contained in the message. The syntax of the header is:

Content-Transfer-Encoding: type

There are several types defined and this header does not represent a vulnerability since the encoding methods are simple translations.

Content-Id: The content id header is used to identify the message in a multiple-part message, and does not create any security threats.

Content-Description: The content description header is used to provide a description of the content. The syntax of the header is:

Content-Description: <description>

Depending on how the user agent presents this to the user, this could be used to mask the real identity of a file. For example, an attacker could provide a description of an attachment that indicates it is a JPEG picture file, but the content type header indicates it is an executable. If the user agent displays the content description to the user, then the user may try to open the file thinking it is picture when in reality the file could contain malicious code.

Content-Disposition: The content disposition header is used to tell the receiving user agent how to display the content. The syntax of the header is:

> Content-Disposition: type

The two types of interest are inline and attachment. The inline type tells the user agent to display the object automatically in the message on the user's display. The attachment type indicates the object should be shown as an attachment to the user. The inline type could be used to help an attacker force the display of pictures or other objects in the output window. This could have two damaging side effects. If the picture or object contained malicious code, it could be used to attack the user agent when the email was opened. The second side effect is in spam emails, where the spammer wishes to embed his spam message as a picture to evade detection. These messages would be displayed and seen by the user.

There have been numerous addendums to the MIME protocol to support many additional file types. It is beyond the scope of this book to examine all aspects of the MIME protocol. From a security viewpoint, the MIME protocol provides an attacker with a method to directly access a naive user in order to get him or her to help with the attack. This makes email an interesting attack method since it can target both the application and the user.

9.3.1 Vulnerabilities, Attacks, and Countermeasures

There are not a large number of vulnerabilities in the MIME protocol. As we have seen, the MIME protocol enables attacks against the user. Many of the countermeasures are common across the categories of attacks. Probably the most effective countermeasure to combat attacks against the user is awareness and training.

9.3.1.1   Header-Based Attacks

Invalid header-based attacks in MIME are handled by the user agent, and often the result is that the email message is not displayed. The biggest header-based vulnerability is that the headers can be used to hide the actual content of the message. As discussed earlier, there is a content description that can be used by the user agent to display the content type. This allows an attacker to create an email that claims to have a picture as an attachment, but really has an executable. Providing proper user education and training can help with this attack, and there are general email countermeasures that can mitigate some of these attacks.

Another method of attack is to use HTML-based email to hide the actual values that are in the mail messages. A mail message can contain a hyperlink to a web page. The text that a user clicks on to access the hyperlink can say anything. So a user can be fooled into clicking on a link and going to someplace other than where he thought he would end up. User education and training is the best way to mitigate this attack.

9.3.1.2   Protocol-Based Attacks

Since the MIME protocol does not involve interaction between the two layers, the protocol-based attacks are different than the protocol attacks we have discussed before. A MIME-based protocol attack uses the MIME protocol to attach malicious files. The user would activate the malicious code either by viewing the email or opening an attachment. This malicious code can attack other programs on the user's computer that are used to view the file. Many user agents have the ability to display the attached file directly, which is convenient for the user but can be a problem for security. There have been worms and viruses that have taken advantage of some user agents' ability to directly view attached data types. One such worm was the Nimda worm, which was launched by simply reading the email message. The worm then copied itself to the hard drive of the user's computer and emailed itself to users in the recipient's address book. Other user agents did not automatically open the attachment, but if the user opened the attachment, the machine became infected.

Typical countermeasures for protocol-based MIME attacks consist of disabling the features that allow direct viewing of attached data. Most user agents have a mode where they will ask before displaying inline content like pictures. There are technologies that will attempt to filter out malicious attachments. Another countermeasure that has become common is to use host-based scanners and fire-walls that can restrict the spread of the malicious code. A host-based firewall can prevent unauthorized programs from accessing the network, which works well against attached malicious code. However, if the user agent is the program that is spreading the malicious code, then the firewall typically will not stop it, since the user agent is an authorized user of the network. Again, since the MIME protocol directly interfaces with the user, it is important to educate the user on how to handle email attachments.

9.3.1.3 Authentication-Based Attacks

MIME does not directly support user authentication, but in a way it can enable spoofed authentication. MIME gives an attacker the ability to create convincing emails that look like they come from established organizations. One additional authentication-based attack is the use of email bugs to track where and when an email is opened. This can be done by inserting a picture into the email document, typically as part of an HTML document. The picture is 1×1 pixels in size and actually is stored on a remote web server. When the user reads the email message, the picture is downloaded from the remote web server. The remote web server logs the access from the user, providing the date and time, the IP address, and other information about the client software. The most common countermeasure is for the user agent to prompt the user before showing images on an email message. However, if the user always clicks yes, then this countermeasure is not effective.

9.3.1.4 Traffic-Based Attacks

MIME does not have any traffic-based vulnerabilities, but it does tend to create larger email messages, and with attachments can create massive email messages. The common countermeasure is to set a limit on the size of an email message that can be received by the MTA. This does not stop someone from sending a large number of smaller messages.

The threat of sniffing has not changed because of the MIME protocol. The coun-termeasures to network sniffing of email can be pushed to the user as described in the next section, or can be pushed on to the network as described later.

Definitions

Email bug.

A method of embedding a link to a web site inside an email message to enable the sender to see if the email was opened.

> **MIME transfer encoding.**
> The encoding method used by MIME to convert the non-ASCII data to ASCII text.
> **Multipurpose Internet Mail Extensions (MIME).**
> A message format used to support nontext content in email messages.

9.4   General Email Countermeasures

What we are looking for in a countermeasure is a way to authenticate the end users and to ensure that email messages are sent in such a way that they are unchanged, unread, and authenticated. There are some end user applications that can provide this kind of secure email.

Several vulnerabilities are caused by unauthenticated delivery of email, including spam email, phishing email, viruses, and other malicious code. There are several network-based technologies that can mitigate many of these attacks.

This section will examine several of these countermeasures and will also discuss methods to trace suspicious email messages or tell if an email is suspect.

9.4.1   Encryption and Authentication

Encryption has been used to prevent accidental or malicious viewing of data and to prevent sniffing of network traffic. Encryption can also be used to provide authentication of one or both communicating parties. Appendix A discusses several aspects of encryption that apply to network security. In the case of email, there are several possible places that encryption can be deployed, as shown in Figure 9.12.

Each of the possible encryption points shown in Figure 9.12 provides a different level of security, and each has its own set of problems. The first encryption point is the traffic between the MTAs. As we discussed earlier in the chapter, there have been proposals to encrypt traffic between the MTAs that would provide authentication of each MTA. This has been proposed as a method to reduce spam since only authorized MTAs can send email. From an implementation standpoint, this has several problems, including finding a way for each MTA to share the encryption keys (see Appendix A for a description of public keys and key distribution). The encryption keys are used as authenticators, and therefore they must be protected on the MTA, and the methods to distribute keys between MTAs must also be secure.

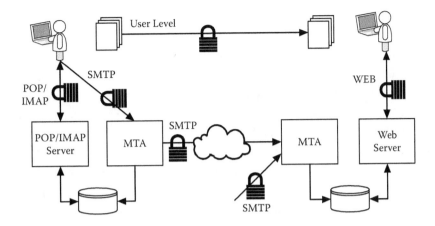

Figure 9.12: Possible encryption and authentication points.

There are several social and political issues that come into play when we require every MTA to be authenticated, including how to handle anonymous email. Another question is who decides which MTAs are trusted and how that process is managed. It is also unclear that such a system could actually keep out spam, since attackers could just take over trusted MTAs. Encrypting traffic between MTAs would stop the sniffing of any traffic between MTAs, which is possible at the egress points of an organization's network, but is very difficult across the Internet.

Another place where SMTP can be encrypted is between the user within a network and the MTA. This biggest benefit would be the authentication of the user in order to support the replaying of email. There is still the issue of key distribution, which can be handled using public keys. As discussed earlier, the most common way to handle this is using the IP address of the user agent.

The next point at which encryption could be deployed is between the MTA and the recipient's computer. As discussed earlier in the section, there are secure versions of POP and IMAP. These versions provide additional authentication using public keys and also protect the username and password from eavesdropping. These methods are quite effective, especially when remote access to the email is required. The methods used for this encryption are the same as those used in link-level encryption, as discussed in Chapters 5 and 6.

When the user accesses his email via a web site, that traffic can also be encrypted using the same methods that are employed by any secure web site. This method uses public keys and is built into the web browsers. This web-based encryption is discussed in the next chapter.

The encryption methods discussed so far have only protected the transmission of email between two devices and only provided authentication of the devices. What is really needed with email is the authentication of the sending and receiving users. In addition, if there is a concern about unauthorized viewing of email messages, then the email should be protected using end-to-end encryption.

One email issue that should be addressed is whether all email needs to be protected. An argument can be made that not all email needs to be protected, and that the identities of the sender and receiver are not critical or can be obtained via the message itself. However, there are cases where the email message might contain confidential information or we need to verify that only the intended recipient was able to read the message. Since the email system consists of multiple applications communicating using multiple protocols, the only logical method to provide end-to-end security and authentication is to rely on the user agents. The most common protocol is Pretty Good Privacy (PGP), which was developed by Philip Zimmerman in the early 1990s [24, 25]. PGP allows a user to create an email message that has been signed and encrypted so that the recipient is confident that the message came from a user that knew the private key of the sender, and the sender is confident that only a user that knows the private key of the receiving user can read the message. Figure 9.13 shows the PGP message structure and how an email message is signed and encrypted for transmission to the recipient. The following discussion assumes knowledge of basic encryption. The reader may wish to review Appendix A.

As shown in Figure 9.13, PGP feeds the user's message into a hash function. The hash value is encrypted using the private key of the sender, which is used to produce the digital signature. The digital signature is added to the message, and the signed message is then compressed and encrypted using symmetric key encryption. The encryption key is generated using a pseudorandom number generator. This one-time session key needs to be transmitted to the recipient in a manner that only the recipient can open. This is accomplished by encrypting the session key using public key encryption. The encryption key is the recipient's public key. The encrypted session key is attached to the encrypted message. The resulting message is converted to ASCII so it can be transmitted via email.

As shown in Figure 9.14, the process is reversed to extract the message. The inbound message is converted from ASCII to its binary form. The encrypted session key is extracted from the message. In addition to the encrypted session key, the message contains information to identify the intended recipient of the message. This allows a person to have multiple identities, each with different

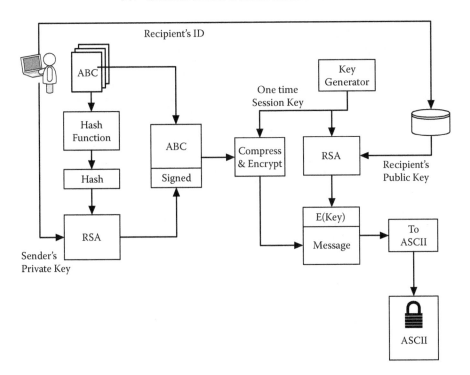

Figure 9.13: PGP message flow.

public–private key pairs. The id from the encrypted key field is used to index the private key. The private key of the recipient is used to decrypt the session key. The session key is used to decrypt the message. The message digital signature is extracted, and contained within the message digital signature field is an id that indicates the user who sent the message. That sender id is used to look up the sender's public key, which is used to decrypt the digital signature and extract the hash value. The message is then passed through the hash function and the two hash values are compared. If they are equal, then the message was successfully received.

What do we know about the sender and recipient after the message is successfully decrypted? We know from the digital signature that the message was created by someone that knows the private key of the sender. We also know that only a person that knows the private key of the recipient can successfully decrypt the message. The strength of this method is based on the level of protection used on the private keys.

PGP has had a moderate level of adoption. The strength of PGP has been well tested, and there have not been any major security issues. Its widespread adoption

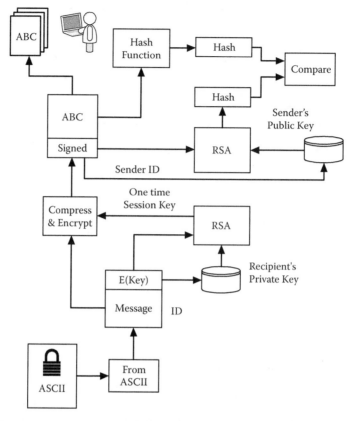

Figure 9.14: PGP message verification.

is hindered by issues with key distribution and key management. The primary issue with key distribution is how to know the owner of a public key and how to obtain someone's public key. There is no widely adopted method to distribute public keys and to make sure those keys represent the actual people. In addition, most people do not think their email is critical enough to warrant this level of security. However, PGP can solve the problems of eavesdropping and can be used to verify the sender and receiver of the email message.

9.4.2   Email Filtering

As we saw during the discussion of the MIME protocol, email can be used to transport malicious payloads and can be used for spam email and phishing attacks. There have been several proposed protocol modifications that have tried to address these issues; however, most have been unworkable. We have seen improvements

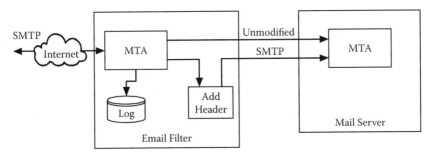

Figure 9.15: Email filtering.

in the user agents in an attempt to make them less susceptible to malicious code. One method that is gaining adoption is the use of email filters. An email filter typically sits in front of the email server and is the first MTA to receive the message. Depending on the filter type, the message can be passed on unmodified, modified to remove malicious payloads, or just deleted. Figure 9.15 shows a typical email filter and how it interacts with the organization's email server [26–37].

The inbound email arrives at the filter and is processed. The filter then forwards the email to the organization's email server, where it is handled like any other email message. Outbound email is forwarded from the organization's email server to the email filter, which will scan for outbound problems.

One type of email filter detects spam and phishing attacks. There are several approaches to handling spam email. The first involves trying to classify the email as spam by analyzing the message based on past message classification. The goal is to train the system to learn what spam email looks like. This type of classification has also been placed in most user agents. This allows the user to create a customized spam filter. These types of filters are not exact and can have false positives, which are when the email is classified as spam when it is not. A network-based spam classification filter will mark the message as spam by putting a line (spam marker) in the header of the email message; this way the user agent can trigger the spam marker and classify the message as spam. The user agent can be set up to mark the message as spam and display it with the nonspam messages, or it can automatically move the message into a spam folder. Since this method is not accurate, most organizations will not automatically delete messages based on the results of a classification filter.

Spammers keep adapting to new defense methods. One new method of bypassing the spam filters is to use the MIME protocol and not transfer any text, but create an email message that is a picture. The picture contains the advertisement the spammers want the user to see. The classification systems cannot tell if the message is spam since they cannot analyze the contents of a picture. Another method often used is to spoof the sending address to make it something you would want to open. The spammers also create subject lines that make you want to open the emails, or use random subject lines to bypass the filters. All of these attacks are supported by the unauthenticated email system and the desire to have a user-friendly user agent.

Another spam filtering method (which also can work with other malicious emails) is using a filtering list. A filtering list can be used to reject email messages from a list of sites using the SMTP protocol. There is a question about what to use as the address for the filtering list. If you use the IP address of the sending MTA, then you will not stop email that has been forwarded through another MTA. You can use the sender's address information (username and domain name), but that can be spoofed. Even with these inherent problems, there are some benefits to email filtering lists. There are three types of email filtering lists.

The first type is called a blacklist and consists of banned email senders. The list can consist of domain names, user@domain, and IP addresses. The biggest problem with a blacklist is maintaining it. Email spammers are constantly changing their domains. There are web sites that maintain lists of banned sites, but this method only offers a small amount of relief.

A whitelist is the opposite of the blacklist and is very restrictive. The list contains the names or IP addresses of authorized email senders. This is useful for a private email system set up between several MTAs within an organization. Whitelists do not work for a public MTA, since the MTA has no way of knowing the users that will be sending mail beforehand.

The third type is called greylisting. Greylisting uses a feature of the SMTP protocol to stop robot-based spammers. A robot-based spammer uses a small application to create and send email messages to an MTA. The robot application does not implement all of the functionality of an MTA. A normal MTA will hold outbound email messages that have experienced a temporary failure when communicating with an MTA. The MTA will try to send the message again after waiting for some period of time and will continue to try for several days. The robot-based spammer will try to send a message, and if the receiving MTA sends a temporary failure message, it will quit and go on to the next destination.

A greylist filtering device will respond to the first email message from a new sender with a temporary failure message (SMTP response code of 451). If the sender sends the message again after a waiting time, then the filtering MTA will allow the message and add the sender to the greylist. The next time the sender

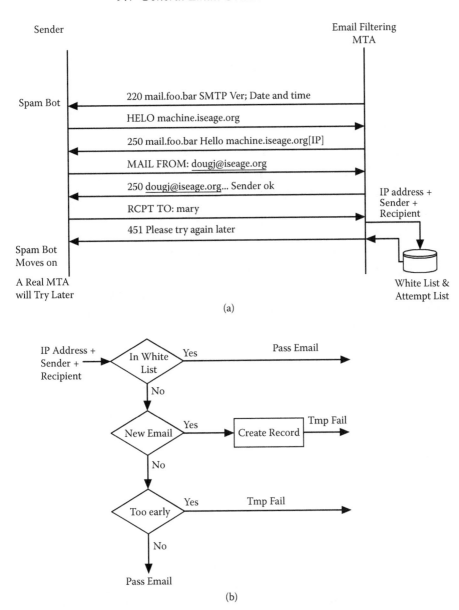

Figure 9.16: (a) Email greylisting. (b) Email greylist flowchart.

sends a message it will be allowed. Figure 9.16 shows how the greylist operates with both a real MTA and a spam robot.

As we see in Figure 9.16, the greylist also works with a whitelist, where the domains in the whitelist do not pass through the greylist process. The greylist looks at the IP, sender's, and recipient's addresses to identify the email message. Greylisting can help reduce spam; however, the system can be defeated if the spammers resend the message after some waiting time or forward their spam through another MTA that is not using greylisting.

9.4.3 Content Filtering

Another method to help provide email security is to use an email content filtering device. This is different than the spam filter in that it will look for specific content that could cause a security problem. These devices do operate as an MTA and will analyze the content of the email messages to determine if they contain malicious payloads. The most common type is an email virus scanner, which scans all email messages for viruses. If a virus is found, the content filter would remove the offending message and allow the cleaned message to continue. It often adds a note in the message to indicate the email has been cleaned and can be configured to send a message back to the sender, informing her that her email contained a virus.

A content filter needs to understand the MIME protocol in order to decode the messages and scan them. In addition, most virus scanners will check both outbound and inbound email messages to prevent malicious payloads from leaving as well as entering the network. Since email is a store-and-forward application, the virus scanner has time to fully decode and check the email messages. These systems use a signature-based method to determine if the content contains a virus. The difficulty is in creating signatures that will detect only malicious code and not stop benign code. Another problem is keeping the signatures up to date with the viruses. There have been cases where several modified versions of the same virus have been released within a 24-hour period in an effort to evade the virus scanners.

Another type of content filter targets outbound content that should not leave a network. Government regulations have forced many organizations to install methods to prevent private data from leaving a network. Healthcare and financial records are protected by government regulations. An outbound email content filter will examine all outbound email messages looking for content that should not leave, such as social security numbers. This can be done through signatures or through exact content matching. Once an email has been tagged as containing private content, the filter can store the message and notify the sender about the violation. Some vendors have produced a system to encrypt the message before it leaves. They send the encrypted message to an off-site MTA that will send notification to the recipient that private content is on this web site. The recipient would then log in to the web and retrieve the email using a secure web transaction. This method is good when we are only concerned about keeping others from reading the private data. If we are concerned about private data leaving the organization through email (either by accident or through a malicious act), then the best method is to quarantine the email.

Content filters have one weakness in that they cannot open or analyze encrypted email like PGP. For outbound content filters this is a problem for malicious data loss, but not a problem if your goal is to keep the email from being read by a third party. For virus scanners there have been cases where the attacker encrypts the virus and then attaches it to an email message. The body of the email explains to the recipient that for security reasons the attachment has been encrypted, and the attacker provides the encryption key in the message. This requires the user to take an additional step to infect the machine. Depending on the type of virus scanner, it may not be able to analyze compressed attachments since the signature would not be found in the data. As with most defense methods, attackers work hard to find ways to work around them.

9.4.4 Email Forensics

Since email has become one of the primary methods of attack against the users of a network, it is useful to understand how to read email messages in order to trace back a message to the sender. It is often not possible to trace the email back to the actual person, but you can trace the email back to the sending MTA [38]. Figure 9.17a to c shows the headers from various email messages. These email headers are from actual email messages; however, the names and IP addresses have been changed. As we discussed earlier, headers are added to the front of the mail message as each MTA processes the message; the exception to this is with spam filters. A spam filter will place information about the spam message in the MIME header section.

Figure 9.17a shows an email header that was sent from a web email system to a user. You can analyze the email headers from either the top or the bottom. Each device that touches the email adds a header. As shown in Figure 9.17a, four devices handled the email message and each placed a header in the message. Starting with the first device that placed header A on the message, we can see that it used the HTTP protocol to receive the message and the message is from Harry6502@spammer.fake and is destined to john@ee.mail.spam. Figure 9.17a also shows a picture that was derived from the headers depicting the path the

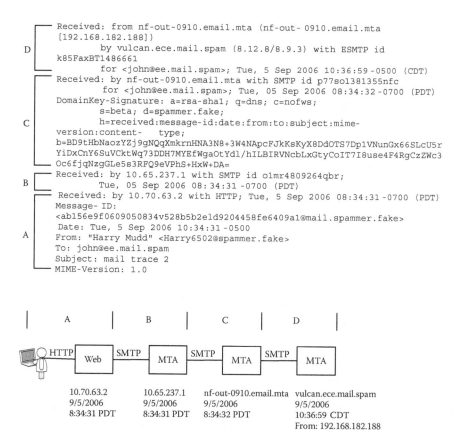

```
      ┌─ Received: from nf-out-0910.email.mta (nf-out- 0910.email.mta
      │   [192.168.182.188])
  D   │        by vulcan.ece.mail.spam (8.12.8/8.9.3) with ESMTP id
      │   k85FaxBT1486661
      └─       for <john@ee.mail.spam>; Tue, 5 Sep 2006 10:36:59 -0500 (CDT)
      ┌─ Received: by nf-out-0910.email.mta with SMTP id p77so1381355nfc
      │        for <john@ee.mail.spam>; Tue, 05 Sep 2006 08:34:32 -0700 (PDT)
      │   DomainKey-Signature: a=rsa-sha1; q=dns; c=nofws;
      │        s=beta; d=spammer.fake;
  C   │        h=received:message-id:date:from:to:subject:mime-
      │   version:content-   type;
      │   b=BD9tHbNaozYZj9gNQqXmkrnHNA3N8+3W4NApcFJkKsKyX8DdOTS7Dp1VNunGx66SLcU5r
      │   YiDxCnY6SuVCktWq73DDH7MYEfWgaOtYd1/hILBIRVNcbLxGtyCoIT7I8use4F4RgCzZWc3
      └─  Oc6fjqNzgGLe5s3RFQ9eVPhS+HxW+DA=
      ┌─ Received: by 10.65.237.1 with SMTP id o1mr4809264qbr;
  B   └─       Tue, 05 Sep 2006 08:34:31 -0700 (PDT)
      ┌─ Received: by 10.70.63.2 with HTTP; Tue, 5 Sep 2006 08:34:31 -0700 (PDT)
      │   Message- ID:
      │   <ab156e9f0609050834v528b5b2e1d9204458fe6409a1@mail.spammer.fake>
      │   Date: Tue, 5 Sep 2006 10:34:31 -0500
  A   │   From: "Harry Mudd" <Harry6502@spammer.fake>
      │   To: john@ee.mail.spam
      │   Subject: mail trace 2
      └─  MIME-Version: 1.0
```

Figure 9.17a: Email headers.

emails took to reach the destination. The email headers also contain a time and date stamp when the message was received by each computer, as well as the machine name, IP address, or both. With this information we can tell where the message was sent from and what time it was sent. We cannot tell anything about the user agent other than it is a web-based user agent. By contacting the network registration authorities you can determine the owner of the IP address. The actual email message did use internal IP addresses for the first two machines, and therefore you cannot determine the location using the IP address. The MTA named "nf-out-0910.email.mta," however, did have a public IP address (in the original email message) and can be traced.

Figure 9.17b shows an email message that originates from a non-web-based user agent and passes through two different organizations with email filters. The transfer marked as A shows an email message being received by vulcan.ece.mail.spam

```
      ┌─ Received: from pop-5.mail.spam (pop-5.mail.spam [172.16.7.12])
      │        by vulcan.ece.mail.spam (8.12.8/8.9.3) with ESMTP id
  F   │  k85FjSBT1508024
      └─        for <john@EE.MAIL.SPAM>; Tue, 5 Sep 2006 10:45:28 -0500 (CDT)
      ┌─ Received: from devirus-2.mail.spam (devirus-2.mail.spam [172.16.7.10])
      │        by pop- 5.mail.spam (8.12.11.20060614/8.12.11) with SMTP id
  E   │  k85Fgt28016542
      └─        for <john@mail.spam>; Tue, 5 Sep 2006 10:42:55 -0500
      ┌─ Received: from (despam-3.mail.spam [172.16.7.5]) by devirus - 2.mail.spam
      │  with smtp
  D   │        id 0df9_ae8af2c2_3cca_11db_969a_001372537fef;
      └─        Tue, 05 Sep 2006 10:38:34 +0000
      ┌─ Received: from magellan.sender.mta (magellan.sender.mta
      │  [192.168.16.211])
      │        by despam- 3.mail.spam (8.12.11.20060614/8.12.4) with ESMTP id
  C   │  k85FgttT020053
      └─        for <john@mail.spam>; Tue, 5 Sep 2006 10:42:55 -0500
      ┌─ Received: from vulcan.ece.mail.spam (vulcan.ece.mail.spam [172.20.5.6])
      │        by magellan.sender.mta (8.13.6/8.13.6) with ESMTP id
      │  k85Fgemo030599
      │        for <dwj@sender.mta>; Tue, 5 Sep 2006 10:42:40 -0500 (CDT)
  B   │        (envelope-from john@mail.spam)
      ┌─ Received: from [172.21.4.7] (babylon4.ece.mail.spam [172.21.4.7])
      │        by vulcan.ece.mail.spam (8.12.8/8.9.3) with ESMTP id
      │  k85Fj6BT1501144
      └─        for <dwj@sender.mta>; Tue, 5 Sep 2006 10:45:06 -0500 (CDT)
         Message-ID: <44FD9AEC.4040103@mail.spam>
         Date: Tue, 05 Sep 2006 10:42:36 -0500
      ┌─ From: Harry Mudd <Harry@mail.spam>
      │  Organization: ISU Information Assurance Center
      │  User-Agent: Mozilla Thunderbird 1.0.7 (Windows/20050923)
      │  X-Accept-Language: en-us, en
  A   │  MIME-Version: 1.0
      │  To: Dave Johnson <dwj@sender.mta>
      │  Subject: test 4
      │  Content-Type: text/plain; charset=ISO-8859-1; format=flowed
      └─ Content-Transfer-Encoding: 7bit
      ┌─ X-Filter-MailScanner- Information: Please contact the ISP for more
      │  information
      │  X-Filter-MailScanner: Found to be clean
      │  X-Filter-MailScanner-SpamCheck: not spam, SpamAssassin (score=-2.6,
      │        requ ired 6, autolearn=not spam, BAYES_00 - 2.60, SPF_PASS -0.00)
      │  X-Filter-MailScanner-From: john@mail.spam
      │  X-PMX-Version: 5.2.0.264296, Antispam-Engine: 2.4.0.264935, Antispam-
Spam  │  Data: 2006.9.5.82442
Filters│ X-Perlmx-Spam: Gauge=IIIIIII, Probability=7%, Report='__C230066_P5 0,
      │   __CP_URI_IN_BODY 0, __CT 0, __CTE 0, __CT_TEXT_PLAIN 0, __HAS_MSGID 0,
      └─  __MIME_TEXT_ONLY 0, __MIME_VERSION 0, __SANE_MSGID 0, __USER_AGENT 0'
```

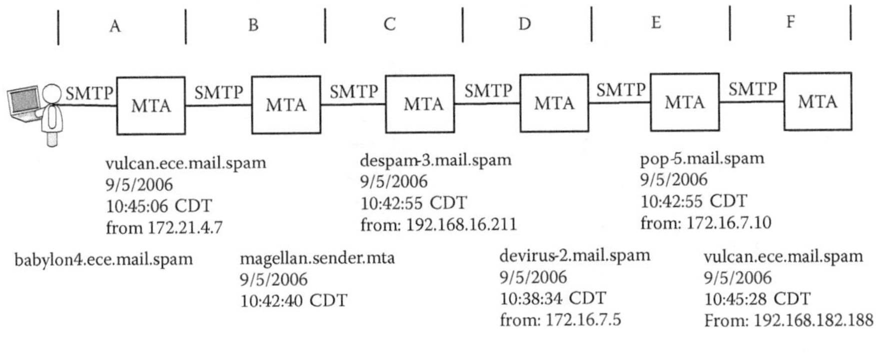

| A | B | C | D | E | F |

```
[user] SMTP [MTA] SMTP [MTA] SMTP [MTA] SMTP [MTA] SMTP [MTA] SMTP [MTA]
```

vulcan.ece.mail.spam   despam-3.mail.spam   pop-5.mail.spam
9/5/2006   9/5/2006   9/5/2006
10:45:06 CDT   10:42:55 CDT   10:42:55 CDT
from 172.21.4.7   from: 192.168.16.211 from: 172.16.7.10

babylon4.ece.mail.spam   magellan.sender.mta   devirus-2.mail.spam   vulcan.ece.mail.spam
                         9/5/2006   9/5/2006   9/5/2006
                         10:42:40 CDT   10:38:34 CDT   10:45:28 CDT
                                               from: 172.16.7.5   From: 192.168.182.188

Figure 9.17b: Email headers.

```
          (Removed local headers)
       ┌─ Received: from ns09.egujarat.net (202-149-46- 162.static.exatt.net
  D    │  [202.149.46.162] (may be forged))
       │         by despam- 2.iastate.edu (8.12.11.20060614/8.12.4) with ESMTP id
       │  k89KIRCr017274
       └─         for <dougj@iastate.edu>; Sat, 9 Sep 2006 15:18:28 -0500
       ┌─ Received: from ns09.egujarat.net (localhost.localdomain [127.0.0.1])
  C    │         by ns09.egujarat.net (8.13.5/8.13.5) with ESMTP id
       │  k89H5sYI007263
       └─         for <dougj@iastate.edu>; Sat, 9 Sep 2006 22:37:19 +0530
       ┌─ Received: (from administrator@localhost)
  B    │         by ns09.egujarat.net (8.13.5/8.13.5/Submit) id k89Gxf4q006335;
       └─         Sat, 9 Sep 2006 22:29:41 +0530
       ┌─ Date: Sat, 9 Sep 2006 22:29:41 +0530
       │  Message-Id: <200609091659.k89Gxf4q006335@ns09.egujarat.net>
  A    │  To: dougj@iastate.edu
       │  Subject: Password change required!
       │  From: "eBay Inc." <admin@eBay.com>
       └─ Content-Type: text/html
```

Spam   ┌─ X-egujarat-MailScanner- Information: Please contact the ISP for more
Filter 2│ information
        │ X-egujarat-MailScanner: Found to be clean
        └─ X-MailScanner-From: administrator@ns09.egujarat.net

Spam   ┌─ X-PMX-Version: 5.2.0.264296, Antispam- Engine: 2.4.0.264935, Antispam-
Filter 1│ Data: 2006.9.9.124943
        └─ X-Perlmx- Spam: Gauge=XXXXXXXXXIIIIIIIII, Probability=99%,

```
        <p><img src= "http://pics.ebaystatic.com/aw/pics/navbar/eBayLogoTM.gif"
        width="150" height="70"></p>
        <BR>
```
Logo   Dear sir,


```
                        We recently have determined that different computers
        have logged onto your eBay  account, and multiple
        password failures were present before the logons. We strongly advice
        CHANGE YOUR PASSWORD. <BR>
                          <BR>
                        If this is not completed by <STRONG>September 15,
        2006</STRONG>, we will be forced to suspend your
        account indefinitely, as it may have been used for fraudulent purposes.
        Thank you for your cooperation. <BR>
                          <BR>
```
Phishing
Site   `<A`
```
        href="http://linux.net zero.idv.tw/~ming/.change/index.php?MfcISAPIComma
        nd=ChangeFPP"
```
```
        target=_blank>Click here to Change Your Password</A></TD>
```

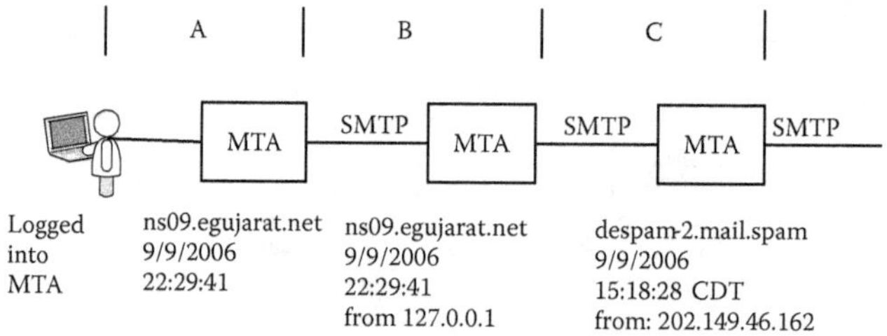

	A		B		C	

Logged into MTA

ns09.egujarat.net
9/9/2006
22:29:41

ns09.egujarat.net
9/9/2006
22:29:41
from 127.0.0.1

despam-2.mail.spam
9/9/2006
15:18:28 CDT
from: 202.149.46.162

Figure 9.17c: Phishing email.

from a machine called babylon4.ece.mail.spam that is destined for the user dwj@ sender.mta. Notice that the user agent that created the email message left information in the header. We know the user agent was Thunderbird running on a Windows machine, and we know the name of an organization that was configured in the user agent.

The transfer marked as B shows the message arriving at the destination. The message is then sent to despam-3.mail.spam and is destined for a different user. The email was forwarded so the user dwj sent his email to the user john on the machine mail.spam. The mail then follows a path through a spam filter and a virus filter, finally arriving at the machine vulcan.ece.mail.spam. Even though this email came back to the sending machine, you can see how email messages can be traced.

The spam filters added headers in the MIME header section. A user agent can be configured to take action based on the values found in these fields. Notice that the email was sent through two different spam and virus scanners. The first four lines (each starting with X-Filter) were added by one of the spam filters, and it determined the email was not spam and had no viruses. The lines starting with X-PMX and X-Perlmx are from a different spam filter, and it also determined the message did not contain spam. In some cases the antispam filter will also add text in front of the subject line to help the user tell if a message is spam.

The last email message, shown in Figure 9.17c, is an actual spam message with the sending addresses in tact. The recipient's addresses have been changed. This message also shows using MIME to create an email message to trick the user into going to a web site and entering her account information. This is known as phishing.

As we see in Figure 9.17c, in header A the sender's domain (ebay.com) does not match the name of the first MTA (ns09.egujarat.net). Headers B and C indicate that the sender of the email was logged into the machine that created the message. The IP address of ns09.egujarat.net was 221.128.130.1, which is not the IP address of the machine connecting to despam-2, as shown in header D. This indicates the machine name was spoofed by the sender. The message came from an IP that belongs to an ISP. Also notice that two spam filter headers have been added. Spam filter header 1 was added by the recipient's network, and spam filter header 2 was added by the spammer.

Figure 9.17c also shows how an image is copied from another web site to show up in the email. In this case, a logo from eBay is included in the email. The email also contains a link to a web site that will carry out the phishing attack. Parts of the message body have been removed to save space.

There are commercial tools that help trace back an email message. These tools just automate what can be done by hand.

Definitions

Email blacklist.

A method of filtering email where the filter maintains a list of bad email servers, called a blacklist.

Email content filter.

A method of filtering email where the filter examines the contents of the email and determines if the email should be filtered, altered, or quarantined.

Email filter.

A device that examines email messages and determines if the email should be delivered or modified based on a set of rules.

Email forensics.

A process of analyzing email headers to determine the actual sender of the email messages.

Email greylist.

A method of filtering email where all unknown incoming email messages are temporally rejected until they retry. This is designed to stop programs that send email messages without the use of an MTA.

Email phishing.

Email messages that are designed to trick the reader into providing information to the attacker.

Email whitelist.

A method of filtering email where the filter maintains a list of good email servers that it will only accept email from, called a whitelist.

PGP email.

A method to encrypt and sign email messages between users.

Homework Problems and Lab Experiments

Homework Problems

1. Assume a user is sending a message containing only the word "hello" to the email server dougj.net.

    a. Show the protocol exchange required to send the word "hello" to dougj@dougj.net from john@issl.org. Include the TCP open and close exchange.

    b. Estimate the total number of bytes (TCP payload) required to send this message. Assume each message is sent as one TCP packet.

    c. What is the total number of bytes transmitted on the network, including all packets?

    d. What is the total overhead (total number of bytes sent on the wire versus the total size of the payload)?

    e. What is the total overhead (total number of bytes sent on the wire versus the total size of the user message)?

2. Research the 1988 Internet worm and how it propagated.

3. MTAs are unauthenticated. What effect would requiring user authentication to send email have on the email system?

4. Why are POP and IMAP protocols authenticated services and the SMTP service unauthenticated?

5. Research the various methods that have been proposed to reduce spam email and comment on why they have not been effective.

6. Research methods spammers use to bypass spam filters and comment on how effective they have been.

7. Research email virus scanners and compare them to how host-based virus scanners work.

8. Research the methods attackers are using to bypass virus scanners to get users to run malicious code. Theorize some mitigation methods.

9. There are several different encryption methods that have been proposed for email, as was shown in Figure 9.12. They can be divided into three types: SMTP encryption, POP/IMAP encryption, and user-to-user encryption. Comment on the pros and cons of each one. If you had to pick just one to provide email security, which would it be and why?

10. Email was originally designed to be used to send simple text messages. MIME has enabled the transfer of complex data types. Comment on the security versus usability of having MIME-enabled email.

11. Research and find web sites that monitor the spam bots.

12. What type of information in headers can be used to trace an email message back to the sender? Comment on how useful the traceback would be in finding someone that is using email for illegal purposes.

13. Examine the headers of spam email you have received in the past few days. Build a table showing how many messages came from each country (if you can tell).

Lab Experiments

1. Use TELNET to connect to the email server in the test lab. Send an email message to your user account pretending to be anyone. You will need to enter the SMTP commands by hand.

2. Use TELNET to connect to the POP3 server on the same computer you used in experiment 1. Retrieve the email message you sent yourself in experiment 1 using the POP3 commands.

3. Find an email traceback website on the Internet. Take several email messages you have received and look at the results of the traceback.

4. Use tcpdump or wireshark to capture the sending of an email message between two machines in the test lab. Try to capture SMTP, POP, and IMAP.

Programming Problems

1. Download the file spam.tar from ftp://www.dougj.net. This file contains the core code to interact with an MTA using SMTP. There is a description of the program in spam.tar located on the web site. Perform the following:

   a. Modify the program to send email to your account on the email server in the test lab from a nonexistent user. Use the parameter (-s user@host) to pass in the fake source address and the parameter (-u user) to pass in the username of the target.

   b. Log in to the email server and view your email.

   c. Modify the program to accept a file as a parameter (-f filename) and send the file as email.

   d. Create an HTML file with the MIME headers and send it yourself using the modified spam program. Log in to the server to read the email.

2. Use the code you downloaded for Chapter 5 and modified in Chapter 6. Add code to perform the following:

  a. Decode and print SMTP payload. Print the payload in ASCII.

  b. Decode and print POP payload. Print the payload in ASCII.

  c. Decode and print IMAP payload. Print the payload in ASCII.

  d. Add to the set of counters a counter for the number of SMTP, POP, and IMAP packets. Add code to print the values of these counters to the subroutine program_ending().

References

[1] Leiner, B. M., et al. 1999. A brief history of the Internet. Arxiv preprint cs.NI/9901011.

[2] Segal, B. 1995. A short history of Internet protocols at CERN. http://www.cern.ch/ben/TCPHIST.html, accessed August 23, 2008.

[3] Mowery, D. C., and T. Simcoe. 2002. Is the Internet a US invention? An economic and technological history of computer networking. *Research Policy* 31:1369–87.

[4] Leiner, B. M., et al. 1997. The past and future history. *Communications of the ACM* 40:103.

[5] Hafiz, M. 2005. Security patterns and evolution of MTA architecture. In *Conference on Object Oriented Programming Systems Languages and Applications*, San Diego, CA: 142–43.

[6] Giencke, P. 1995. The future of email or when will grandma be on the net? In *Electro/95 International. Professional Program Proceedings*, Boston, MA: 61–67.

[7] Knowles, B., and N. Christenson. 2000. Design and implementation of highly scalable e-mail systems. Paper presented at Proceedings of the LISA Conference, New Orleans, December.

[8] Freed, N., and N. Borenstein. 1996. *Multipurpose Internet mail extensions (MIME) part one: Format of Internet message bodies*. RFC 2045.

[9] Freed, N., and N. Borenstein. 1996. *Multipurpose Internet mail extensions (MIME) part two: Media types*. RFC 2046.

[10] Moore, K. 1996. *MIME (multipurpose Internet mail extensions) part three: Message header extensions for non-ASCII text*. RFC 2047.

[11] Freed, N., J. Klensin, and J. Postel. 1996. *Multipurpose Internet mail extensions (mime) part four: Registration procedures*. RFC 2048.

[12] Freed, N., and N. Borenstein. 1996. *Multipurpose Internet mail extensions (MIME) part five: Conformance criteria and examples*. RFC 2049.

[13] Postel, J. B. 1982. *SMTP-simple mail transfer protocol*. RFC 821. http://www.ietf.org/rfc/rfc0821.txt, accessed August 23, 2008.

[14] Leiba, B., et al. 2005. SMTP path analysis. Paper presented at Proceedings of the Second Conference on E-mail and Anti-Spam (CEAS). Stanford, CA.

[15] Secure, S. 2002. Network working group p. Hoffman request for comments: 3207 Internet mail consortium obsoletes: 2487 February category: Standards track.

[16] Hoffman, P. 1999. *SMTP service extension for secure SMTP over TLS*. RFC 2487.

[17] Hoffman, P. 2002. *SMTP service extension for secure SMTP over transport layer security*. RFC 3207.

[18] Manabe, D., S. Kimura, and Y. Ebihara. 2006. *A compression method designed for SMTP over TLS*, 803. Lecture Notes in Computer Science 3961.

[19] Gray, T. 1993. Comparing two approaches to remote mailbox access: IMAP vs. POP, 1–4. http://www.imap.org/imap.vs.pop.brief.html, accessed August 23, 2008.

[20] Newman, C. 1999. *Using TLS with IMAP, POP3 and ACAP*. RFC 2595.

[21] Crispin, M. 1996. *Internet message access protocol—version 4rev1*. RFC 2060. Sebastopol, CA.

[22] Garfinkel, S. 1995. *PGP: Pretty good privacy*. O'Reilly.

[23] Garfinkel, S. L., et al. 2005. How to make secure email easier to use. In *Proceedings of the SIGCHI Conference on Human Factors in Computing Systems*, Portland, OR: 701–10.

[24] Zhou, D., et al. 1999. Formal development of secure email. Paper presented at Proceedings of the 32nd Annual Hawaii International Conference on System Sciences. Maui, HI.

[25] Borisov, N., I. Goldberg, and E. Brewer. 2004. Off-the-record communication, or, why not to use PGP. In *Proceedings of the 2004 ACM Workshop on Privacy in the Electronic Society*, Washington, DC: 77–84.

[26] Hidalgo, J. M. G. 2002. Evaluating cost-sensitive unsolicited bulk email categorization. In *Proceedings of the 2002 ACM Symposium on Applied Computing*, Madrid, Spain, 615–20.

[27] Michelakis, E., et al. 2004. Filtron: A learning-based anti-spam filter. Paper presented at Proceedings of the First Conference on Email and Anti-Spam (CEAS). Mountain View, CA.

[28] Bass, T., and G. Watt. 1997. A simple framework for filtering queued SMTP mail (cyberwar countermeasures). In *MILCOM 97 Proceedings*, Monterey, CA: 3.

[29] Cerf, V. G. 2005. Spam, spim, and spit. *Communications of the ACM* 48:39–43.

[30] Jung, J., and E. Sit. 2004. An empirical study of spam traffic and the use of DNS black lists. In *Proceedings of the 4th ACM SIGCOMM Conference on Internet Measurement*, Taormina, Sicily, Italy. 370–75.

[31] Golbeck, J., and J. Hendler. 2004. Reputation network analysis for email filtering. Paper presented at Conference on Email and Anti-Spam (CEAS). Mountain View, CA.

[32] Kartaltepe, E. J., and S. Xu. 2006. Towards blocking outgoing malicious impostor emails. In *Proceedings of the 2006 International Symposium on World of Wireless, Mobile and Multimedia Networks*, Buffalo, NY: 657–61.

[33] Gansterer, W. N., A. G. K. Janecek, and P. Lechner. 2007. A reliable component-based architecture for e-mail filtering. In *Proceedings of the Second International Conference on Availability, Reliability and Security*, 43–52.

[34] Twining, R. D., et al. 2004. Email prioritization: Reducing delays on legiti-mate mail caused by junk mail. In *Proceedings of Usenix Annual Technical Conference*, Boston, MA: 45–58.

[35] Levine, J. R. 2005. Experiences with greylisting. Paper presented at Con-ference on Email and Anti-Spam. Stanford University, Stanford, CA.

[36] Wiehes, A. 2005. Comparing anti spam methods. Masters of Science in Information Security, Department of Computer Science and Media Tech-nology, Gjøvik University College.

[37] Miszalska, I., W. Zabierowski, and A. Napieralski. 2007. Selected methods of spam filtering in email. In *CADSM'07. 9th International Conference: The Experience of Designing and Applications*, Chapel Hill, NC: 507–13.

[38] de Vel, O., et al. 2001. Mining e-mail content for author identification forensics. *ACM SIGMOD Record* 30:55–64. Santa Barbara, CA.

Chapter 10

Web Security

The World Wide Web (WWW) is more than a collection of protocols [1–7]. The web consists of a large number of servers that are each identified by a host name. Each server contains documents that can be accessed using the document's address. The web has had the largest impact on the Internet and has driven many of the newest technological changes. Primarily because of the web we now have Internet access almost everywhere. The web has taken the Internet from a network used by researchers and academicians to a network that is used by the masses.

Because of the large number of servers and the large number of users, the web has also become a primary target of hackers. Before we begin looking at the network protocols, we need to understand the basic structure of the web and the applications that support it. Figure 10.1 shows how a document is addressed within the World Wide Web.

As we see in Figure 10.1, the user provides an address to a document using the host name of the server and the location of the document within the server. This address is called the Uniform Reference Locator (URL). The URL uniquely identifies a document within the web. Documents can contain links to other documents called hyperlinks. These hyperlinks are also URLs. A web designer uses hyperlinks to create a path or series of paths that provide a way for the user to navigate through the documents stored on the web server. The web was not designed to have a central index to keep track of the location of documents, which is the reason for the popularity of search engines. A search engine visits web sites and examines the documents and catalogs their contents. The search engines follow the hyperlinks to gather additional content. The information that is gathered is searched to provide answers to the user's query. The search engines are web sites that produce a web document with hyperlinks to the documents that match the user's query.

Figure 10.2 shows how one hyperlink can provide the location of a series of documents. The user can access a search engine to get the location of the first web site, or the user may know what site he or she wishes to visit. Figure 10.2 shows the user accessing the document D1, which contains links to other sites, on the server S1 using the URL HTTP://S1/D1. The user goes to another site by

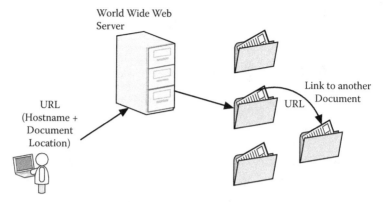

Figure 10.1: Document addressing in the World Wide Web.

just clicking on the hyperlink. In addition, a site may contain content that comes from yet another site, which is accessed when the user views the site. So, for example, document D2 on server S2 may contain a picture stored on server S3. This highly distributed nature of the web provides access to vast amounts of data. The distributed nature also provides many ways for attackers to compromise the data or the servers.

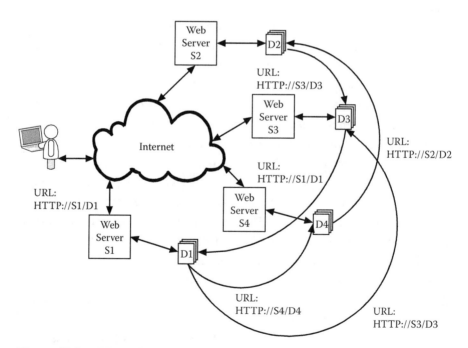

Figure 10.2: Hyperlinked documents in the World Wide Web.

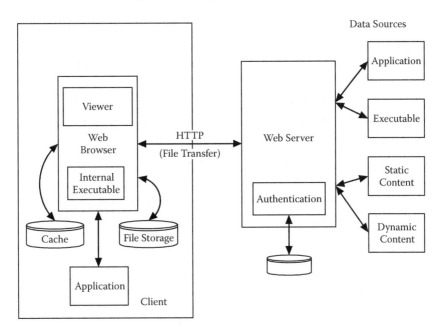

Figure 10.3:   Web client/server.

The web was first designed for text-based data and provided access to library materials. As computers became more powerful and graphical user interfaces became more common, the content available on the web changed. The modern web involves a graphical client and a web server, as shown in Figure 10.3.

As we see in Figure 10.3, the client used to access the web is called the browser, and it consists of several parts. It has a viewer that interprets the data received from the server and displays it for the user. The user can also download documents and store them on the user's computer. In addition, it has a cache to store images and other documents received from the servers. The browser also has the ability to run applications to help the user interpret the data; for example, it can launch a media player to play a song. The browser can also run programs provided by the server, which allows for animations and complex interaction with the server. The browser uses a file transfer protocol called Hypertext Transfer Protocol (HTTP) to move data to and from the web server.

The web server sends files identified by a unique URL, requested by the browser, using the HTTP protocol. The requested documents can come from several sources, as shown in Figure 10.3. The most common are documents that are simple text files, whose content is static. Dynamic documents are produced by a program running on the server that interprets the URL and creates a document from gathered or stored data that is sent back to the browser. For example, the document produced by a search engine as the result of a user's query is dynamically created from the search results. In addition to static and dynamic documents, the browser may request data from an application that is running on the server or from a program initiated by the server. The server also can provide user authentication to restrict access to certain documents.

We will first examine the HTTP protocol and look at its security vulnerabilities, then look at the document format. Since both the client and server can execute code, we will examine the server-side and client-side executables, and finally we will discuss several general network-based countermeasures used for web security.

10.1   Hypertext Transfer Protocol (HTTP)

The HTTP protocol is a command-and-response protocol with ASCII-based commands [8–11]. The structure is more complex than what we have seen with the email protocols. The basic message structure for the commands and responses is shown in Figure 10.4.

10.1.1   Command Message

As shown in Figure 10.4, the command message starts with a request line that has a request type, a URL, and the HTTP version. The request is:

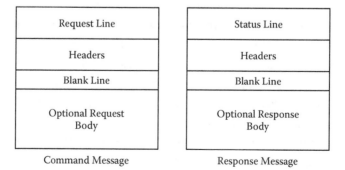

Figure 10.4:   HTTP command and response message structure.

Format	request type<sp>URL<sp>HTTP/version
Example	GET http://www.iseage.org HTTP/1.1

GET is a request type used to request a document specified by the URL (http://www.iseage.org) and the protocol version is HTTP/1.1. The format of a URL is:

method://host[:port][/path]

The method indicates the file transfer protocol that is used to obtain the document. The default is HTTP. Browsers may support other file transfer types such as File Transfer Protocol (FTP). The optional port number is the server port used for the connection. The default for HTTP is port 80. The optional path is the location of the document on the server. If no path is given, the server will return a site-specific default document. The HTTP protocol supports several request types, as shown in Table 10.1. As we have seen with other protocols, many of the request types are often disabled for security reasons (as indicated in Table 10.1).

TABLE 10.1: HTTP Request Types

Type	Action
GET	Retrieve a document specified by the URL.
HEAD	Retrieve the headers from the document specified by the URL (response does not contain the body).
POST	Provide data to the server.
PUT	Provide new or replacement document specified by the URL (disabled).
PATCH	Provide differences to document specified by the URL in order to change the document (disabled).
COPY	Copy the document specified by the URL to the file specified in the header (disabled).
MOVE	Move the document specified by the URL to the file specified in the header (disabled).
DELETE	Delete the document specified by the URL (disabled).
LINK	Create a link to the document specified in the URL. The name of the link is specified in the header (disabled).
UNLINK	Remove the link specified in the URL (disabled).
OPTION	Ask the server what options are available.

TABLE 10.2: Response Code Format

Code	Response Status
1XX	Information messages
2XX	Successful requests
3XX	Redirect the client to another document specified as a URL
4XX	Client-side errors
5XX	Server-side errors

10.1.2   Response Message

Just as the commands are in ASCII, response messages are also in ASCII. The response message starts with a status line that consists of the HTTP version, a three-digit ASCII number, or response code, and a status phrase as shown below:

Format	HTTP/version<sp>status code<sp>status phrase
Example	HTTP/1.1 404 File not found

The first digit of the response code (404 in the above example) indicates whether the command worked or failed, the second digit specifies what type of code (typically 0), and the third digit is used to indicate specific codes. The response code syntax is shown in Table 10.2, and Table 10.3 shows several common response codes.

10.1.3   HTTP Headers

The next part of the HTTP request and response messages is the headers. As shown in Figure 10.5, the header format for request and response messages is the same. It should be noted that the headers can be optional, especially in the request message.

The HTTP header consists of one or more lines of text, each starting with a header name, followed by a colon, a space, and the header values as shown below:

Header Name:<sp>Header Value

The general header contains information about the request or response. The common general headers are shown in Table 10.4.

The request header is used in the request message. This header provides the server information about the client's configuration and indicates the preferences

TABLE 10.3: Common Response Codes

Code	Phrase	Meaning
100	Continue	First part of the request has been received. The client can continue.
200	OK	Successful request
204	No content	The body contains no content.
302	Moved permanently	The document specified by the URL is no longer on the server.
304	Moved temporarily	The document specified by the URL has temporarily moved.
400	Bad request	The request contained a syntax error.
401	Unauthorized	The authentication failed for the requested document.
403	Forbidden	The service requested is not allowed.
404	Not found	The document requested is not found.
405	Method not allowed	The method requested in the URL is not allowed.
500	Internal server error	The server failed.
501	Not implemented	The requested action cannot be preformed by the server.
503	Service unavailable	The request cannot be accomplished right now; try again later.

the client has about the format of the documents. From a security standpoint, this header can provide the server with information about the browser and the user. The common request headers are shown in Table 10.5.

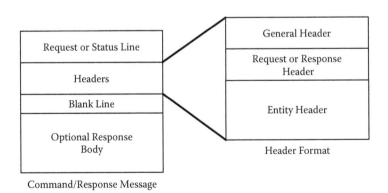

Figure 10.5: HTTP message header format.

TABLE 10.4:   Common General Headers

Header	Function
Cache-control	Used to specify information about the client-side cache
Connection	Indicates whether the connection should be closed
Date	Provides the current date
MIME-version	Indicated the MIME version being used
Connection	Use to determine connection type
Keep-alive	Used to manage keep-alive connection

The response header reports back information about the server and about the requested document, as shown in Table 10.6.

The entity header contains information about the data contained in the body of the message, such as the type of encoding and the length of the data. The common entity headers are shown in Table 10.7.

An example exchange between a web browser and a web server is shown in the next several figures. Figure 10.6 shows the web page that was retrieved by the browser, and Figure 10.7 shows a summary of the packets used to load the web page.

Figure 10.8 shows the request message, and Figure 10.9 shows the response message. Figure 10.10 shows the request for the first image, and Figure 10.11 shows the response. Figures 10.12 and 10.13 show the packet exchange to retrieve the file favicon.ico, which is the small picture shown next to the URL in the browser window. This web site did not have the favicon.ico file, so the web server returned an error.

TABLE 10.5:   Common Request Headers

Header	Function
Accept	Indicates which data formats the browser can accept
Accept-charset	Indicates the character set(s) the browser can accept
Accept-encoding	Indicates what encoding methods the browser can process
Accept-language	Indicates what language the browser can accept
From	Provides the e-mail of the user on the browser
Host	Provides the host and ephemeral port of the browser
Referrer	Provides the URL of the linked document
User-agent	Provides information about the browser software

TABLE 10.6:   Response Header

Header	Function
Accept-range	Indicates the server accepts the range requested by the browser
Retry-after	Indicates the date when the server will be available
Server	Provides the server application name and version

TABLE 10.7:   Common Entity Headers

Header	Function
Allow	Provides a list of methods allowed for the URL
Content-encoding	Indicates the encoding method for the document
Content-language	Indicates the language of the document
Content-length	Indicates the length of the document
Content-location	Real name of the document requested
Content-type	Indicates the media type of the document
Etag	Provides a tag for the document
Last-modified	The date the document was last modified

If you can see this, it means that the installation of the Apache web server software on this system was successful. You may now add content to this directory and replace this page.

Seeing this instead of the website you expected?

This page is here because the site administrator has changed the configuration of this web server. Please **contact the person reponsible for maintaining this server with questions.** The Apache Software Foundation, which wrote the web server software this site administrator is using, has nothing to do with maintaining this site and cannot help resolve configuration issues.

The Apache documentation has been included with this distribution.

You are free to use the image below on an Apache-powered web server. Thanks for using Apache!

Figure 10.6:   Web page image.

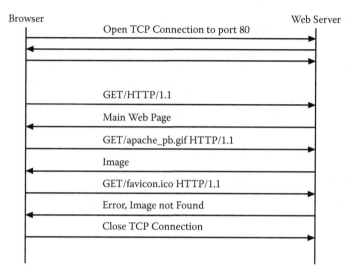

Figure 10.7:   HTTP protocol exchange.

Request Line

```
GET/HTTP/1.1
```

General Header

```
Keep-Alive: 300
Connection: keep-alive
```

Request Header

```
Host: spock.ee.iastate.edu
User-Agent: Mozilla/5.0 (Windows; U; Windows NT 5.1; en-US; rv:1.8.0.7)
     Gecko/20060909 Firefox/1.5.0.7
Accept: text/xml, application/xml, application/xhtml + xml, text/html;
     q = 0.9, text/plain; q = 0.8, image/png, */*; q = 0.5
Accept-Language: en-us, en; q = 0.5
Accept-Encoding: gzip, deflate
Accept-Charset: ISO-8859-1, utf-8; q = 0.7, * ; q = 0.7
```

No Entity Header
Blank Line
No Body

Figure 10.8:   HTTP request message.

Status Line

```
HTTP/1.1 200 OK
```

General Header

```
Date: Sat, 28 Oct 2006 16:01:55 GMT
Keep-Alive: timeout = 15, max = 100
Connection: Keep-Alive
```

Response Header

```
Server: Apache/1.3.33 (Unix)
Accept-Ranges: bytes
```

Entity Header

```
Content-Location: index.html.en
Last-Modified: Fri, 04 May 2001 00:00:38 GMT
ETag: "428fd8-5b0-3af1f126;452e43f5"
Content-Length: 1456
Content-Type: text/html
Content-Language: en
```

Blank Line

```
HTML Document (1456 bytes long)
```

Figure 10.9: HTTP response message.

Request Line

```
GET/apache_pb.gif HTTP/1.1
```

General Header

```
Keep-Alive: 300
Connection: keep-alive
```

Request Header

```
Host: spock.ee.iastate.edu
User-Agent: Mozilla/5.0 (Windows; U; Windows NT 5.1; en-US; rv:1.8.0.7)
    Gecko/20060909 Firefox/1.5.0.7
Accept: image/png, */*; q = 0.5
Accept-Language: en-us, en; q = 0.5
Accept-Encoding: gzip, deflate
Accept-Charset: ISO-8859-1, utf-8; q = 0.7, * ; q = 0.7
Referer: http://spock.ee.iastate.edu/
```

No Entity Header
Blank Line
No Body

Figure 10.10: HTTP request message.

Status Line

```
HTTP/1.1 200 OK
```

General Header

```
Date: Sat, 28 Oct 2006 16:01:55 GMT
Keep-Alive: timeout = 15, max = 99
Connection: Keep-Alive
```

Response Header

```
Server: Apache/1.3.33 (Unix)
Accept-Ranges: bytes
```

Entity Header

```
Last-Modified: Wed, 03 Jul 1996 06:18:15 GMT
ETag: "428fd1-916-31da10a7"
Content-Length: 2326
Content-Type: image/gif
```

Blank Line

```
GIF image (2326 bytes long)
```

Figure 10.11:   HTTP response message.

Request Line

```
GET/favicon.ico HTTP/1.1
```

General Header

```
Keep-Alive: 300
Connection: keep-alive
```

Request Header

```
Host: spock.ee.iastate.edu
User-Agent: Mozilla/5.0 (Windows; U; Windows NT 5.1; en-US; rv:1.8.0.7)
     Gecko/20060909 Firefox/1.5.0.7
Accept: image/png, */*; q = 0.5
Accept-Language: en-us, en; q = 0.5
Accept-Encoding: gzip, deflate
Accept-Charset: ISO-8859-1, utf-8; q = 0.7, *; q = 0.7
```

No Entity Header
Blank Line
No Body

Figure 10.12:   HTTP request message.

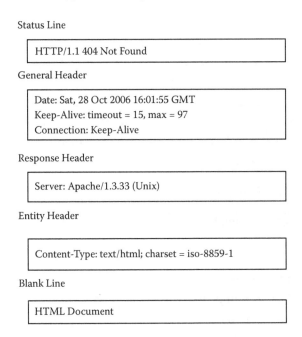

Status Line

> HTTP/1.1 404 Not Found

General Header

> Date: Sat, 28 Oct 2006 16:01:55 GMT
> Keep-Alive: timeout = 15, max = 97
> Connection: Keep-Alive

Response Header

> Server: Apache/1.3.33 (Unix)

Entity Header

> Content-Type: text/html; charset = iso-8859-1

Blank Line

> HTML Document

Figure 10.13: HTTP response message.

10.1.4 Vulnerabilities, Attacks, and Countermeasures

Even though the HTTP protocol is straightforward, there are several vulnerabilities. If we refer back to the four categories of vulnerabilities and attacks discussed in Part I, we will see that authentication-based and traffic-based attacks are most common.

10.1.4.1 Header-Based Attacks

Header-based attacks are not very common since the headers are simple and any command or response that is invalid is ignored. The HTTP protocol does present some interesting problems since both the client (the browser) and the server use freeform headers that can contain several options that control the way the data is interpreted. The early versions of web servers and browsers were subject to buffer overflow attacks. There have been several attacks that were able to exploit the fixed-size buffer by sending commands that were too long. Today the bigger problem is with client- and server-side executables, which will be discussed later. As we saw in Figure 10.3, the web server can be a front end for another program by passing data directly from the browser to another application. This allows an attacker to use the HTTP protocol to transport attacks to another application.

Another header attack uses the HTTP protocol to fetch files that are not part of any set of hyperlinked documents. An attacker can search a web site for files that are sometimes left on a server by default by including a file name in the URL. These files often contain no useful information for the attacker, but sometimes the files might contain authentication information or other critical data. A common configuration error is to leave the web password file inside the document tree. If an attacker can find the file, he or she would be able to use public domain attack software to discover valid usernames and passwords.

10.1.4.2   Protocol-Based Attacks

The HTTP protocol is simple and there are very few protocol-based attacks.

10.1.4.3   Authentication-Based Attacks

Authentication-based attacks are the most common type of HTTP attacks. There are several authentication methods used in a web server, and many are implemented by the application and not directly supported by the HTTP protocol. The authentication data is sent as payload in the HTTP packets. The HTTP protocol supports authentication to control access to files stored on the web server. A web server contains documents that are stored in files that can be organized into a series of directories and subdirectories. Figure 10.14 shows a typical organizational structure for a web site where the document root contains documents and directories.

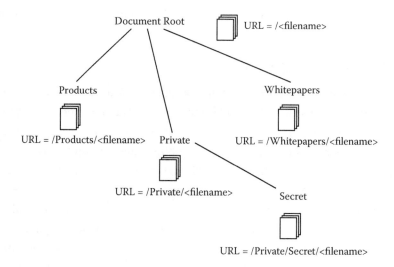

Figure 10.14:   Typical web site directory structure.

Documents in the document root are addressed using a "/" followed by the file name, and documents in the subdirectories are addressed using a "/" followed by the subdirectory name(s) followed by a "/" and the file name. For example, files in the subdirectory "Products" are referred to with the URL Host://Products/<filename>.

HTTP-based authentication is designed to control access to a directory based on a username and password. In addition, access to documents in a directory can be based on the IP address of the browser. IP-based authentication was discussed in Chapter 6. For example, in Figure 10.14 the directory "Private" can be set up to require a username and password before any documents in that subdirectory can be accessed. All subdirectories of the directory "Private" are also protected by the same authentication. This is done by setting up the web server to support authentication and by placing an authentication file into the directory "Private." When the browser requests a file contained in the directory for the first time, or any subdirectory of the protected directory, the server asks the browser for authentication. For example, if a user tried to access the URL Host://Private/Secret/<filename>, he or she would be asked to provide authentication. Figure 10.15 shows the partial HTTP headers used when the browser requests a document from a protected directory.

Figure 10.15 shows a request for a document with the URL /~dougj/private/doc.html in the first request header. The server responds with a 401 response header,

Request Header

```
GET/~dougj/private/doc.html HTTP/1.1
Host: spock.ee.iastate.edu
```

Response Header

```
HTTP/1.1 401 Authorization Required
Date: Tue, 14 Nov 2006 22:37:47 GMT
Server: Apache/1.3.33 (Unix)
WWW-Authenticate: Basic realm = "Enter Password"
```

Request Header

```
GET/~dougj/private/doc.html HTTP/1.1
Host: spock.ee.iastate.edu
Authorization: Basic bG9yaWVuOmZpcnN0b25l
```

Figure 10.15:   Authentication protocol exchange.

which indicates the server requires authentication. The server also sends the type of authentication and an authentication message called the realm. The realm is used to help the browser keep track of different authenticators used on the same web site. For example, another directory might have a different username and password to gain access. In this example the message is "Enter Password." The browser is responsible for prompting the user for a username and password. Once the user has entered the username and password, the browser will send another request to the server with the authenticator. The authenticator is the username and password separated by a ":" and is encoded in base64. The authenticator is included in every request to the same realm.

From a network security standpoint, the HTTP authenticator is not very secure since the username and password are sent in clear text. In addition, the passwords can be guessed and are subject to the same problem as any network-based login mechanism. The solution to the password problem is educating the user to chose secure passwords. The solution to traffic sniffing is discussed in the next section.

Another authentication-based attack is spoofing. This is where a user is tricked into going to a web site he or she believes belongs to a certain organization when in reality the site is fake. Since it is very easy to capture everything from a web site, it is easy to set up a fake web site that looks just like the real site. (There are several programs designed to download all content from a web site.) The spoofed web site can cause the user to unknowingly reveal data like passwords, account information, and personal information. Email messages that contain hyperlinks are often used as one method to get users to go to the spoofed web site. This attack requires user education to mitigate since there is no host authentication for most web sites. Encryption can help provide host authentication; however, most people do not pay much attention to whether they are connected to an encrypted web. Plus, if you normally transact business with a secure site and are tricked into going to an unencrypted spoofed site, the browser will not warn you.

10.1.4.4   Traffic-Based Attacks

A web server is vulnerable to several traffic-based attacks. Attackers can overwhelm a web server by making a large number of requests. A web server is limited in the number of simultaneous connections it will allow. Sometimes just normal traffic can cause a web server to reach its limit and start rejecting connections. This can happen when a site becomes very popular in a short period of time. There are also attack tools that will cause the same effect. It is very simple to open up multiple connections and keep them alive for the server limit. This will

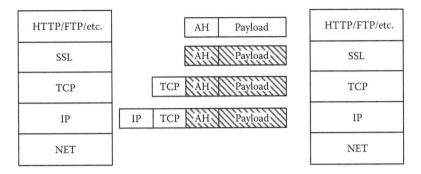

Figure 10.16: HTTPS architecture.

effectively shut down the web site. There is no good method to prevent this from happening since more often than not the goal of a web site is to attract traffic, not restrict it. Another side effect of this type of attack is to cause the router(s) close to the web server to overload with traffic and become the bottleneck. The result can be an almost complete shutdown of Internet access.

Another major problem with the HTTP protocol is that it is a clear text protocol, and therefore is subject to packet sniffing. In some cases this may be more of a privacy issue than a security issue. For example, it would be possible to tell which web site someone visited and which pages he viewed by sniffing the traffic. However, even if the web traffic is encrypted, a sniffer could still tell which IP addresses were visited. There are also cases where the web traffic is sensitive. For example, access to a bank account in clear text could reveal financial data. The primary mitigation method for network sniffing is to use encryption of the data. The primary method for encrypting a connection to a web site is HTTPS, which uses Secure Sockets Layer (SSL). SSL is used by multiple applications to provide an encrypted channel. Figure 10.16 illustrates the HTTPS architecture.

HTTPS uses port 443 and is typically transparent to the user. A web browser will indicate when the connection is encrypted through an icon (often a padlock) displayed on the screen. The browser has the public key of the web server or the public key of a signature authority that has signed a public key of a web server. In this chapter we will briefly discuss public key handling as it applies to the World Wide Web. We discussed the SSL protocol exchange in Chapter 7.

See Appendix A for information about public key encryption and how it uses certificates as a method to both authenticate and distribute the public keys.

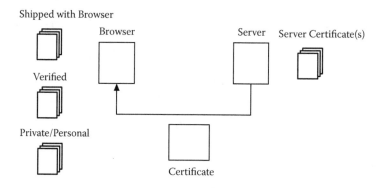

Figure 10.17:   WWW certificates.

Figure 10.17 shows a web server with one or more public key certificates and a browser with multiple public key certificates.

The server presents a public key certificate to the browser to authenticate the server and to start the negotiation of a session encryption key. The server's public key certificate can be signed by a signature authority. The signature authority is used to verify the authenticity of the public key certificate. The browser examines the certificate provided by the server for the signature authority. The browser then checks its current certificates to see if it has a certificate that matches the signature authority certificate. If there is a match, the browser will use the public key of the signature authority to verify the authenticity of the received certificate. How does the browser get the first certificate, and how does it know it is valid? Companies that operate as signature authorities pay browser companies to include their certificates with the browser distribution. As shown in Figure 10.18, the certificate chain of authority is typically traced back to one of the certificates provided with the browser.

As the user visits various secure web sites, she will pick up new certificates. The user can also pick up new signature authority certificates that provide authority other certificates. A server can also provide the browser with a certificate that has not been signed by a certificate authority, or by a certificate authority known to the browser. In this case, the browser will prompt the user to see if she will accept the certificate. The user can either reject the certificate, accept it for the session, or accept it permanently.

Figure 10.18 shows that the certificate received by the browser was signed by the verified certificate. That certificate is verified by a certificate that was supplied with the browser. The received certificate is verified by taking the public

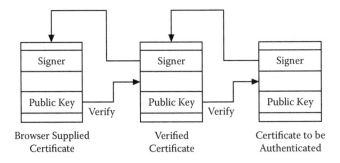

Figure 10.18: Certificate chain of authority.

key from a verified certificate and using that key to decrypt the digital signature of the certificate. Since the digital signature was created using the private key of the signature authority, we can assume the certificate was created by the signature authority. What we get from the certificate is a valid public key that has been mapped back to the server. We can use that public key to encrypt a message that only the web server should be able to decipher, since only the web server should know the private key that is associated with the public key. So in reality, the signature authority does not validate the web server; it validates that the public key in the certificate belongs to the web server. If the web server has its private key compromised, then someone could spoof a secure web site since the certificates are public knowledge. Once the browser has the public key of the web server, it can negotiate a one-time session key and use that to encrypt all traffic between the browser and the server.

Definitions

HTTPS.
An encrypted version of the HTTP protocol that uses Secure Sockets Layer (SSL).

Hyperlink.
A URL that is embedded inside a web document.

Hypertext Transfer Protocol (HTTP).
The protocol used by the World Wide Web to transfer data to and from the web servers.

Uniform Resource Locator (URL).
The address of a document in the World Wide Web.

10.2   Hypertext Markup Language (HTML)

As we discussed earlier in this chapter, the World Wide Web consists of transferring files from servers to browsers to be processed. The primary language used to display content is called Hypertext Markup Language (HTML) [12–17]. HTML documents are interpreted by the browser, and their commands dictate how the document contents are to be displayed. Since documents are processed by browsers, a server can create documents that could pose a security risk. It is not the goal of this book to examine the HTML protocol in detail; however, there are certain aspects of the protocol that can cause security problems. Figure 10.19 shows the general format of an HTML document, which consists of two parts: head and body. The head contains information used by the browser, and the body contains information to be displayed on the page. The entire HTML document consists of tags that are used to instruct the browser how to display the contents. As shown in Figure 10.19, each HTML tag has a starting marker and an ending marker.

Table 10.8 shows several of the HTML tags that can cause security problems. From a security standpoint, the three HTML commands of greatest concern are <a URL>, which allows hyperlinks; <img>, which displays images; and <APPLET>, which downloads executable code. Each of these HTML tags is briefly described next. Their security threats will be discussed in more detail in the section on HTML vulnerabilities.

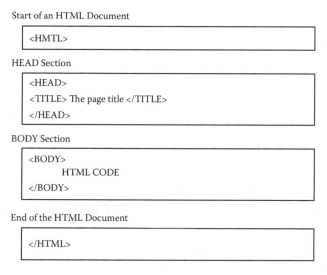

Figure 10.19:   HTML format.

TABLE 10.8:   Common HTML Tags

Tag	Function
<HMTL>	Tells the browser where the HTML document starts and ends
<HEAD>	Indicates the start of the head section
<TITLE>	Text to be displayed in the title bar of the browser
<BODY>	Indicates the start of the body of the document
<a URL>	Hyperlink
<img>	Embedded image to be displayed
<APPLET>	Client-side executable
<! Comment>	Used to add comments to the document

The hyperlink tag <a URL> is used to display a hyperlink on the screen. The tag has two parts: the hyperlink itself, which is a URL that points to a new document, and the text that is displayed on the screen. For example, the HTML tag shown below is a link to the document index.html on the server www.iseage.org. The browser will display the text string "Click Here" as the hyperlink.

```
<a href=http://www.iseage.org/index.html>Click Here </a>
```

The image tag is used to display an image on the screen. The tag specifies the location of the image, which can be local to the server or can reside on a different server. Unlike the hyperlink tag, which requires user action, the image tag causes the image to be downloaded and displayed by the browser. In addition to the image location, the tag also has text that will be displayed if the image cannot be loaded. The format of the image tag is shown below. The first example shows an image loaded from the local server, and the second example shows an image being loaded from the web server www.iseage.org.

```
<img src=image.gif alt="image" />
<img src="http://www.iseage.org/image.gif" alt="remote image" />
```

The APPLET tag is used to download a Java applet to the browser. The Java applet is an executable program that is run by the browser and can have parameters that are passed to the program. Applets are treated like an image in that they are displayed on the screen at a certain location and a given size as defined by the HTML code. Just like the image tag, the applets can be automatically downloaded without user intervention if the user has enabled Java applets in the browser settings. The format of the applet tag is shown below and shows the browser calling an applet named TheApplet and passing the string "Hello Doug" as a parameter. The PARAM tag is optional and is only used if the applet needs parameters. The HTML tag <P>Hello Doug</P> is displayed if the applet cannot be executed.

```
<APPLET CODE="TheApplet.code" WIDTH=200 HEIGHT=100>
<PARAM NAME=TEXT VALUE="Hello Doug" >
<P>Hello Doug</P>
</APPLET>
```

Figure 10.20 shows the HTML code to produce the web page shown in Figure 10.6. A few things to notice about the document are the comments, the hyperlink, and the embedded image.

```
<!DOCTYPE html PUBLIC "-//W3C//DTD XHTML 1.0 Transitional//EN"
   "http://www.w3.org/TR/xhtml1/DTD/xhtml1-transitional.dtd">
<html xmlns = "http://www.w3.org/1999/xhtml">
<head>
<title>Test Page for Apache Installation</title>
</head>
<!-- Background white, links blue (unvisited), navy (visited), red (active)-->
 <body bgcolor = "#FFFFFF" text = "#000000" link = "#0000FF" vlink = "#000080"
alink = "#FF0000">
 <p>If you can see this, it means that the installation of the
<a href = "http://www.apache.org/foundation/preFAQ.html">Apache web server</a>
software on this system was successful. You may now add content to this directory and
replace this page.</p>

<hr width = "50%" size = "8" />
<h2 align = "center">Seeing this instead of the website you expected?</h2>

<p>This page is here because the site administrator has changed the configuration of this
web server. Please <strong>contact the person responsible for maintaining this server with
questions.</strong> The Apache Software Foundation, which wrote the web server software
this site administrator is  using, has nothing to do with maintaining this site and cannot help
resolve configuration issues.</p>

<hr width = "50%" size = "8" />
 <p>The Apache <a href = "manual/">documentation</a> has been included with this
distribution.</p>

<p>You are free to use the image below on an Apache-powered web server. Thanks for
using Apache!</p>

<div align = "center"><img src = "apache_pb.gif" alt = "" /></div>
</body>
</html>
```

Figure 10.20:   Example HTML document.

10.2.1 Vulnerabilities, Attacks, and Countermeasures

10.2.1.1 Header-Based Attacks

HTML documents have a complex freeform header format. Most of the attacks against the HTML headers involve three tags: image, applet, and hyperlink. The hyperlink tag vulnerability is due to the ability to set the link information displayed on the screen to anything with no correlation to the URL. This can be used to redirect people to spoofed web sites. We often see this in HTML email, where the hyperlink text may indicate the URL is a bank, but in reality it is someplace else. This same thing can happen in a web site where a hyperlink can mislead the user and cause him to go someplace he was not expecting. Hyperlinks do not just point to other websites or other HTML documents, they can also point to other types of documents that either can contain malicious code or are themselves malicious. For example, a hyperlink may indicate the document is a certain type (HTML, text, etc.) when in fact it maybe an executable. Even though the browser asks what to do with an executable file type, the user only needs to click yes and the file will be executed. This problem will also be discussed in the section on client-side executables.

The image tag allows a web site to include images that might be stored on another web site. While this may not represent a clear security vulnerability, it can lead to privacy concerns. A web server can log the site that contained the link to the image as well as when the image was accessed. This information can enable the web server to track where a user has visited. This is called a "web bug" or a "clear gif." The image is often a 1-pixel-wide clear image that is obtained from another site. There are other methods used to track web and network activities that will be discussed in the chapter on peer-to-peer and anonymous networking.

The applet tag lets the web server download code to your browser that is run locally. The applet can also return data to the web server. There were several vulnerabilities when Java applets were first implemented that primarily dealt with the applets' ability to read files and data that should not have been accessed. This allowed attackers to write malicious code that could extract data from the computer running the browser. Today the browsers have limited what data Java applets can access. However, many users and organizations simply disable applets from untrusted sources.

The only real countermeasure for HTML header-based attacks is user education. As with most attacks that target the user through social engineering, the only way to stop them is to create a better-educated user. The biggest problem with HTML attacks is the ease with which a web site can be spoofed and the speed with which the social engineering methods can change. We need to teach users how to handle these attacks in general, as opposed to focusing on specific examples.

10.2.1.2   Protocol-Based Attacks

HTML is not a protocol in the sense of needing a message exchange to function. In some sense we can classify many of the header-based attacks as protocol based since we are using the HTML protocol. One protocol-based attack is when the HTML code designer embeds information within the HTML document, either in the form of comments or as fixed values to be passed to a server-side executable. Since the HTML code is in clear text when processed by the browser (even if it was transferred via an encrypted channel), anyone that can display the page pointed to by the URL can read the source code. There have been cases where attackers have modified web pages and loaded them locally and used the web pages to send bogus information to the web server. The most famous cases were where attackers used modified web pages that had the price of merchandise embedded in the HMTL document. By changing the price in the HTML document, the attackers were able to purchase products at a greatly reduced price.

10.2.1.3   Authentication-Based Attacks

HTML does not directly support authentication, and therefore there are no user authentication-based vulnerabilities. The only authentication issue is host-to-user authentication since most web sites are not authenticated. This makes web site spoofing possible. The certificate-based authentication discussed earlier can help with web server authentication, but since many web sites are not encrypted, this will not solve the problem.

10.2.1.4   Traffic-Based Attacks

The only traffic-based vulnerability is traffic sniffing, which was discussed earlier along with possible countermeasures.

Definitions

HTML APPLET tag.
An instruction in HTML that allows for the insertion of a Java applet in the document.
HTML img tag.
An instruction in HTML that allows for the insertion of an image in the document.

HTML URL tag.
An instruction in HTML that allows for the insertion of a URL in the document.
Hypertext Markup Language (HTML).
A specification for the format of the documents used in the World Wide Web.
Web bug/clear gif.
A small image embedded in a web page that is used to tell when the web page is viewed.

10.3   Server-Side Security

As was shown in Figure 10.3, a web server can obtain data from executable programs. A URL can point to a program that is run on the server. Therefore, an HTML document can cause code to be executed on the server [18–27]. The most common method is using what is called the Common Gateway Interface (CGI), which is not a programming language, but a standard that defines how a program interfaces with the web server. CGI programs can be self-contained with no parameters or can be passed parameters via the URL or the HTTP POST command. The output of a CGI program is HTML code. The CGI program can also interface with other applications running on the server or on other servers. Figure 10.21 shows how a CGI program interacts with the browser, the web server, and other applications.

As we see in Figure 10.21, the browser will send the URL that is a call to a CGI script. The call can contain parameters that are passed via the URL or through the POST command. Examples of both methods are shown below. If the URL is part of a HTML document, then the server-side script will be invoked without the knowledge of the user.

http://www.iseage.org/cgi- bin/program.pl?name=Doug;state=IA

The example above shows the script program.pl being invoked with two parameters (name and state), each with a value (Doug and IA). A question mark separates the path to the executable from the parameter field, and semicolons are used to separate the parameters. This method works well when the parameters are fixed for the HTML document. However, if the user needs to enter parameters, then the FORM tag is often used in the HTML document, as shown next.

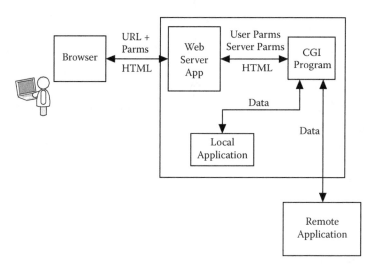

Figure 10.21:   CGI interaction.

```
<FORM ACTION="/cgibin/program.pl">
Your Name: <INPUT NAME=name><BR>
Your State: <INPUT NAME=state><BR>
<INPUT TYPE=SUBMIT>
</FORM>
```

These HTML commands will produce two text input boxes labeled "Your Name:" and "Your State:" and a "Submit Query" button. When the user presses the submit query button, the values entered into the text boxes will be placed into a URL and submitted to the web server. In addition, you can use the POST method to send the data to a CGI program.

In addition to the parameters passed to the CGI script from the user, several parameters are passed to the script from the web server. Table 10.9 shows several of these parameters that are made available to the CGI script.

Once the CGI script is invoked with the parameters, the script can run with no additional interaction or it can spawn off another program. The CGI script can also communicate to a remote application like a database server. The interaction between the CGI script and other applications is not covered in the CGI specification. This interaction with other applications allows data to be passed from the browser to an application that may not be normally accessible to the browser or to anyone via the network. For example, you could create a CGI script that would display the contents of a text file to the screen by calling a program on

TABLE 10.9: CGI Parameters

Name	Function
Query_string	The string passed to the script through the URL
Remote_address	IP address of the browser
Remote_host	Host name of the browser
Server_name	Host name of the server
Server_software	Web server software
HTTP_user_agent	Browser software
HTTP_referrer	IP address of the machine that contained the link
HTTP_accept	List of document types accepted by the browser

the server. Even if the CGI script is embedded within the HMTL document with fixed parameters, an attacker could figure out where the CGI script is located and could pass its own parameters to the script, asking for the contents of any file stored on the computer.

The last step in the process for the CGI script is to send the text back to the browser in HTML. The data the CGI script gets from other applications can be in HTML or raw text, in which case the CGI script needs to convert the data to HTML.

10.3.1 Vulnerabilities, Attacks, and Countermeasures

10.3.1.1 Header-Based Attacks

Since CGI scripts accept parameters from the network, buffer overflows are a common problem. This is compounded by the fact that CGI scripts often provide network access to applications that were not designed for network access. For example, an application may be designed to read data from the keyboard and will make an assumption that the input will be limited by the OS to a fixed size. When the CGI script invokes the application, it will pass the data it receives from the network to the application. This will bypass the size restriction that is enforced by the operating system and can cause a buffer overflow in the application. The CGI script can be subject to buffer overflow attacks since they are often written in languages that do not enforce buffer protection. Another vulnerability exposed when using a CGI script to access an application is that there may not be strong type checking of the parameters by the application, and the CGI script could pass invalid parameters to the application. This happens when CGI scripts are used to access an application such as a database that may have its own application front end that checks parameters. The CGI script might bypass the front end and directly access the application.

Another common vulnerability is when an attacker uses the CGI script to access files or programs that were not intended to be accessed. This happens when there is a mistake in the CGI script and the parameters are not restricted.

When using CGI scripts, the header problems are not just with the CGI script, but also with the application, which makes mitigation very complex. CGI scripts should validate all input data and take extra care when providing access to files or other applications.

10.3.1.2   Protocol-Based Attacks

Since CGI is not really a network protocol, there are no protocol-based vulnerabilities.

10.3.1.3   Authentication-Based Attacks

The primary authentication vulnerability is not with the CGI script itself, but with the CGI script providing access to the authentication system of another application. CGI scripts can provide network access to the authentication methods of applications that were not designed to accept network-based authentication. In addition, poorly written CGI scripts may pass the user authentication as a parameter in the URL. This would make it easier for an attacker to automate password guessing. These attacks are mitigated through good design of the CGI scripts and proper use of application authentication.

Another type of authentication vulnerability is that there is no way for a client to authenticate the web server or to know if server-side executables are being used. There is very little threat to the actual browser from server-side executables, but they can be used to collect data on the user. However, CGI scripts do not provide any more of a privacy threat than any other web activity since most of the data automatically collected by a CGI script is also collected by the web server. The only additional privacy threat is if the CGI script asks for information from a user that the user should not give out, like social security numbers, etc.

10.3.1.4   Traffic-Based Attacks

There are not additional traffic-based attacks from the use of CGI scripts.

Definitions
Common Gateway Interface (CGI).
A method that defines the inputs to a server-side executable passed via the URL.

Server-side executable.

A program that runs on a web server in response to an action by a user of the web server.

10.4 Client-Side Security

In addition to HTML documents, the browsers can handle other document types, including images, word processing files, and executables [28–38]. Figure 10.22 shows the various ways a document can be handled by a browser.

As shown in Figure 10.22, the browser often needs to use a plugin, which is an executable program that enables the browser to handle various document types. Plugins are often written by third parties, many of which are individuals, rather than companies, making the software available to others. The plugins can be classified based on the type of document they handle. Executable plugins handle code that is executed on the browsers like Java applets. Document plugins handle other document types, like PDF files, and viewing plugins handle the display of other document types, like images, audio, or real-time graphics. Sometimes the document needs to be viewed by an external application like a word processor.

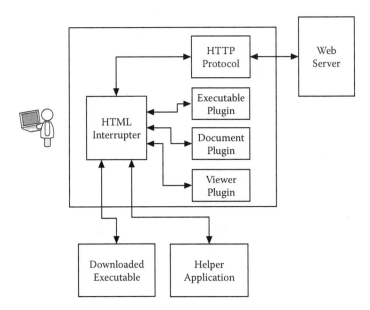

Figure 10.22:   Client-side executables.

In addition to viewing various documents, the browser itself can execute code sent to it by the server. In all of the cases shown in the figure, the web server is providing documents and possibly executable code that is handled by the browser with the help of other programs. Some documents are handled automatically by the browser and are executed as part of the HTML document. The most common example of client-side executables handled as part of the HTML document is a Java applet.

Most client-side executables are downloaded and handed off to another application as the result of the user clicking on a hyperlink. In these cases, if the document is handled by a plugin, the browser will not prompt the user and will just process the document. If the document is to be opened by a helper application or is to be executed by the operating system, the browser will ask the user if he or she is sure about downloading the file. The user typically has three choices: download the document to a file, open or execute the document, or cancel the operation.

Another issue with client-side security is the use of cookies. Cookies are small data elements stored on the browser's computer by the web server. They contain data placed there by the server that can be read back by the server. Cookies are useful since HTTP is stateless, which means as you browse a site, it may involve multiple connections. Since each HTTP connection is independent, a web server has no way of connecting the user to his or her past activities. A web site that wishes to keep track of users can place a cookie on the browser's computer. The cookie often contains a user identifier that indicates who the user is. As you traverse the web site, the cookies may be used to track what you have done, either by rewriting the cookie or by maintaining a database on the web site that is indexed by the user id. Cookies represent more of a privacy issue than a security issue. One way cookies are used is to track users as they visit web sites. If a web site places an advertisement on the site, that advertisement can come from an advertisement clearinghouse, and if the user clicks on the advertisement, cookies can track which advertisements the user clicks on. The security of cookies has been debated for years, and in the early days of cookies, any web server could read any cookie placed by other web sites. Today cookies are protected so that only the web server that placed them can read them, though this is host name and IP based, so it is not completely secure. Another issue with cookies is when public computers are used to access the Internet. The cookies and other browser history will be updated. Another user can come by later and tell what sites other users have visited. This issue will be discussed in more detail in the chapter on peer-to-peer and anonymous Internet.

10.4.1   Vulnerabilities, Attacks, and Countermeasures

10.4.1.1   Header- and Protocol-Based Attacks

There are no header- or protocol-based vulnerabilities since there is no header or protocol beyond what has been discussed.

10.4.1.2   Authentication-Based Attacks

Most client-side executables are not authenticated, which can lead to malicious code. We need to discuss each of the three types of documents separately to understand the security vulnerabilities. Referring back to Figure 10.22, we can see that malicious documents can be handled by the plugin, a helper application, or can be run on the browser's computer.

Plugin attacks can be the hardest to detect and mitigate since they are handled automatically and the user sometimes does not even know that the plugin has been invoked. In the case of document and viewer plugins there are not many vulnerabilities, but if there are, they can be difficult to mitigate, since the plugin is written by a third party. The Java executable plugin, for example, had several security vulnerabilities when it was first designed. Most involved its ability to access the computer's files and to send data to other computers on the Internet. Today Java has been locked down so that is has limited access to files and to where it can communicate. Browsers can be set to allow executable plugins to run on a per-site basis, not at all, only if the user approves, or all the time. It is common to either disable or prompt the user when a Java applet is to be activated. There are some web sites that will not function unless Java applets are allowed.

The vulnerabilities associated with helper applications are the concern of the helper application. There have been macro viruses that have attacked word processors, and the web can be a method to propagate the virus; however, email seems to be the preferred method of propagating helper application attacks.

Executable files that are downloaded through the web are the largest client-side threat. The web provides an easy method to download executable files and can contain malicious code like Trojan horses, spyware, and key loggers. The malicious code may be embedded in other applications that actually perform the functions that they are reported to do. While vulnerabilities exploited by these executables are not network based, the network enables the code to be downloaded and the web facilitates the download. Sometimes email is used to draw people to the web site that contains the malicious code. By using email to entice someone to a web site and then using social engineering to convince him to download and execute a program, the attacker can bypass email virus scanners.

The best mitigation for these attacks is user education and good client-side security techniques like local virus scanners and personal firewalls. It is difficult to deploy network-based mitigation techniques against client-side attacks since the data transfer can be encrypted and the number of possible attack methods is large.

10.4.1.3   Traffic-Based Attacks

There are not very many traffic-based vulnerabilities associated with client-side executables, other than the sniffing vulnerability, which is less of an issue on client-side downloads. There are cases when the client-side executable can generate a large amount of traffic, which can cause network problems. For example, there are plugins and web sites that provide real-time stock market information or real-time weather data. There is a large amount of traffic that can be generated by the server to the client-side plugin. User education and company policies may help mitigate the traffic volume problem. Another method is to block access to certain web sites that provide excess data. This is discussed in the next section as a general web countermeasure.

Definitions

Browser plugin.
An application that is added to a Web browser. The applications are designed to handle non-HTML data.
Cookies.
Files place on the computer running the browser by a web server. The files are used by a web server to help track the user's activity on the web site.
Helper application.
An application that is called by the browser to handle data that is not handled by the browser or a browser plugin.
Java applet.
A Java executable that is downloaded from a web server and run by the browser using the Java plugin.

10.5   General Web Countermeasures

There are two active network components to the World Wide Web: web server and browser. Each has a different set of requirements for network-based counter-measures. The server needs to be protected from attacks that can target both the

web server application and the actual server. The general network-based countermeasures for the web server are the same types of countermeasures used to
protect the network from an attack and will be discussed in a later chapter.

The client side has to protect the user from attacks that are often initiated by
the actions of the user. As we have seen in this chapter, the user can be directed
to spoofed web sites, can be tricked into downloading malicious code, and can
be enticed into going to web sites that are inappropriate. One method to help
protect the user is to use web filtering to prevent the user from going to locations
that can cause harm, or to prevent the user from transferring files that she should
not [39–46]. Many of these filters are installed to prevent the user from going to
inappropriate web sites. This is not really a security issue; however, web filters
can keep users from sites that could cause security breaches from malicious code.
There are two categories of web filters: the URL filter and a content filter. Both
categories can be placed on a single device.

10.5.1 URL Filtering

One of the early methods of client-side web protection is the URL filter, which
controls which URL a user is allowed to visit. The URL filter decision is based
on the final destination or URL that is requested. There are three primary methods of URL filtering—client side, proxy, and network—and each method can
implement a blacklist of restricted sites or a whitelist of the only sites that can
be visited. As with any blacklist-based filter, the biggest issue is keeping the
list current. This is very difficult and labor intensive. If the list is to remain current, the list provider will need to constantly search the Internet for URLs that
match the filtering criteria. Typically the list provider groups URLs in the filter
list into categories. The end user can then chose which categories to block. The
database of URLs often only contains the hash values of the URLs and not the
actual URL. This is done to speed up searching and reduce the storage requirements. It is also done to protect the intellectual property (the URL list) of the list
provider.

The client-side filter is typically implemented as a software wedge that is
inserted into the network protocol stack and monitors all of the web traffic. Figure
10.23 shows a possible location of the software wedge.

Placing the filter in the protocol stack makes it difficult for a user to disable.
The exact location in the protocol stack is dependent on the filter implementation.
As shown in the figure, the filter either has a local database of sites or has a remote
database that is queried before the connection is allowed.

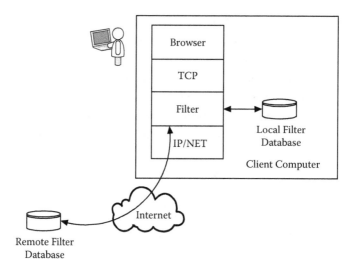

Figure 10.23: Client-side URL filter.

A proxy-based filter uses a web proxy that is a server that handles incoming web requests from the browsers and will retrieve the document from the Internet or a local cache. Web proxies were designed to reduce network traffic and speed up requests since they cache the answers to requests. In order to use a web proxy, the browser needs to be told that it should ask the proxy for the URL. Figure 10.24 shows the interactions among the browser, proxy server, and remote web site. The filter database can be housed in the proxy server or can be remote, just as with the client-side filter.

As we see in Figure 10.24, the browser sends an HTTP request to the proxy that contains the URL of the document. The IP address used is the IP address

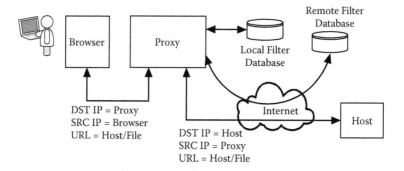

Figure 10.24: Web proxy filter.

of the proxy server. This is different from a normal HTTP request, where the IP address would be the IP address of the destination host that has the document. The proxy then sends an HTTP request to the final host, and the response is cached and returned to the browser. If the URL violates the filter rule, then the proxy can return a web page indicating the user has requested a URL that is not allowed. As we will see in the chapter on anonymous Internet, the proxy can also be used to help hide the clients since every client using the proxy will have the same return address as far as the web server is concerned.

A network-based URL filter sits at the egress point of the network and examines the traffic across the network. Unlike the client- or proxy-based approach, there is no need to change the clients. The network-based approach can be implemented as a network device like a router and is sometimes part of the firewall. In this case the device needs to have an IP address and will also route packets. The network-based filter can also be implemented as a transparent device. A transparent device does not actually route traffic; it sniffs the traffic on the network and determines if the connection should be terminated. There are two types of transparent network filters: inline and passive. The inline device has two network connections and passes all traffic from one port to another port while listening to the traffic. The passive device sniffs the traffic using a promiscuous mode interface. Figure 10.25 shows the three different network-based filters.

Each of the three methods can use a local database or a remote database. Another difference between the network-based filter and the client- or proxy-based filter is the method used to stop the connection. In the proxy- or client-based filter it is easy to stop the connection and return a blocking message. The client-side filter can return the block as network traffic (a block message as part of an HTML document) or as a message through the operating system. As discussed above, the proxy can return an HTML document that contains the blocking message. In the case of the network-based filter, the source computer has already made a network connection with the destination, and the URL is carried as network traffic. There are two primary methods used depending on the desired outcome. If the connection is only to be terminated, then the device can send a packet to the source and destination computers telling each side to terminate the connection. The network filter spoofs the IP addresses of the browser and the server to make each side think the other side requested the connection termination.

The other method is to steal the connection from the server and send an HTTP redirect message back to the browser. This is done by sending a connection terminate packet to the server pretending to be the client, and by sending an HTTP redirect to the browser pretending to be the server. The browser is then

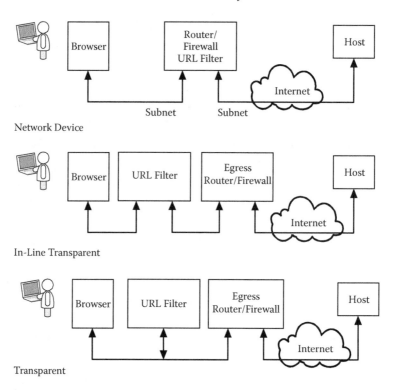

Figure 10.25: Network-based URL filter.

redirected to a web page that tells it what it did wrong. Figure 10.26 shows the two methods and the values of the IP addresses that are spoofed by the network filter.

There are proxies designed to bypass network-based filters by using SSL to encrypt the traffic between the browser and the proxy. This can be handled by blocking the IP address of the proxy. There are other methods to bypass filters and to remain anonymous on the Internet that will be discussed in Chapter 9.

10.5.2   Content Filtering

Content filtering takes the idea of URL filtering one step further and tries to examine the HTTP payload. The implementation of a content filter is no different than that of a URL filter, except they are often network devices and not client-side applications. Some URL filters also implement content filtering. There are two primary types of content filters, inbound and outbound. The only difference between the two is what type of content they are looking for.

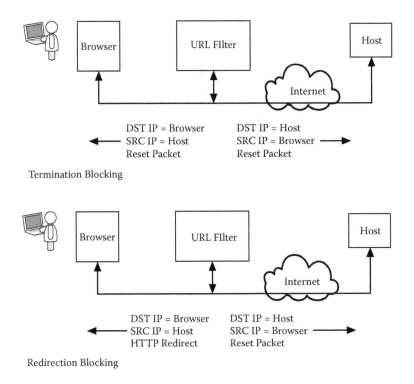

Figure 10.26: Network connection blocking.

An inbound content filter is primarily concerned with web-based attacks against the browser. There are some inbound web content filters that also focus on protecting web servers from invalid data. These devices work like virus scanners in that they look through the payload and try to determine if the payload contains malicious code. This is more difficult with the web since the traffic is close to real time. With email a virus scanner can hold the messages and then release them if there are no problems. An inbound content filter works best with a proxy server so it can store and then forward content, as shown in Figure 10.27.

Figure 10.27 shows the browser making a request for a document through the proxy. The proxy downloads the document and examines it for malicious code. If the document is clean, it is passed to the browser. If the document is not clean, the proxy either sends an empty document or sends a redirect to indicate there was a problem with the document. However, if the URL uses another method to transfer the file (like the File Transfer Protocol [FTP]), then a web filter will not stop the malicious code.

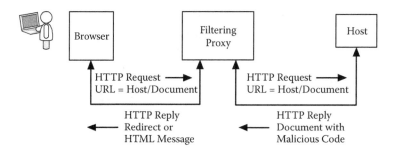

Figure 10.27:   Proxy-based content filter.

An outbound content filter will examine the HTTP content for information that should not leave an organization. While this is not a direct security threat, it can be a privacy issue. An outbound content filter will often use a blacklist of content to be stopped. The filter can also use expressions to filter out content. For example, social security numbers could be matched by looking for three numbers and a dash followed by two numbers and a dash followed by four numbers. Of course, the problem with this method is how to create expressions that will stop all social security numbers and allow non–social security numbers to pass. An outbound filter is implemented the same way as a proxy.

There are several problems with content filters that make them difficult to use. First, is the issue of marking a good document as bad (called a false positive). Other content can also be a problem. At one time there was a URL filter on the market that also tried to block based on images. It examined the image and tried to determine if there were enough flesh tones to call the image pornography. This did not work very well since it was hard to determine what flesh tones are and if the flesh tones belonged to people. Another attempt at URL filtering was to filter on words or phrases in the document, like *breast*. This led to problems of banning sites talking about Thanksgiving and turkey breasts.

Another problem is missing bad documents (called false negative). There is often a trade-off between false negatives and false positives. If the filter rules are broad, they may miss very few bad documents but may stop a large number of good documents. If the rules are restrictive, then a large number of bad documents may get through.

Another problem with content filters is encrypted content. The filter is unable to open encrypted content and will not be able to determine if it should be stopped. In addition, they often have problems with compressed content.

In general, URL and content filters have a place in network security and do offer some benefits. They should also be coupled with user education and company policies. As we have seen, technology alone cannot stop a user from doing things that can cause security problems.

Homework Problems and Lab Experiments

Homework Problems

1. Show the HTTP commands to do the following:

    a. Get the web page "/index.html"

    b. Get the web page "/files/index.html"

    c. Call the CGI "/cgi-bin/print-me" with "hello there" as a parameter

2. Show the HTML code to do the following:

    a. Display a hyperlink to a local PDF file called figure.pdf.

    b. Display a hyperlink to www.dougj.net.

    c. Display a GIF image called picture.gif.

    d. Display a GIF image from a remote web site (www.dougj.net/picture.gif).

3. Show the code for a CGI UNIX shell script that prints who is logged in to the computer. Comment on whether this script should be made available to the public.

4. Research the growth of the World Wide Web, including the number of pages and the number web sites.

5. Research software that captures an entire web site and comment on how this software could be used for good and bad.

6. Research software that scans a web server for vulnerabilities.

7. Research the HTML format and software that creates HTML.

8. Research Structure Query Language (SQL) injection attacks along with other server-side injection attacks. Comment on how these attacks could be mitigated.

9. Research the various common server-side scripting languages.

10. Research client-side attacks and compare them against the taxonomy.

11. Research the Request for Comments (RFCs) associated with the HTTP protocol and the HTTPS protocol.

12. Research several URL filtering companies and determine the size of their URL filtering list and the number of filtering categories. Also determine if they are proxy based, client based, or a passive network device.

Lab Experiments

1. Use TELNET to connect to the web server in the test lab. Issue the command to get the main web page.

2. Use tcpdump or wireshark to capture a web session between a machine in the lab and a web server. Click on several links on the web server. Look at the network capture and comment on the number of connections needed and the amount and type of data transfers. Examine the headers used. Examine the source of the main page and relate it to the network capture.

3. Use tcpdump or wireshark to capture a web session between a machine in the lab and a web server. Click on the link to the password protected and enter the password. Look at the network capture. Find and decode the password.

4. Use tcpdump or wireshark to capture a web session between a machine in the lab and a web server. Then capture a secure web session between a machine in the lab and a secure web server. Comment on what you see and the differences between the two captures.

5. Examine the contents of a browser's certificates and cookies. Comment on what information can be obtained and how it could be used for good and for bad.

6. Examine the log file of the web server in the test lab. Comment on how these files could be used to help secure the web server.

Programming Problems

1. Download the file spam.tar from ftp://www.dougj.net. Using this program as a framework, perform the following:

   a. Modify the program to ask for the header using the HTTP HEAD command. Use the parameter (-h host) to pass in the host address of the web server and the parameter (-f filename) to pass in the filename of the target file.

   b. Use the program to search for files on the web server. Test the program by checking for index.htm.

   c. Comment on how this program could be used to attack a web site.

2. Use the code you downloaded for Chapter 5 and modified in Chapters 6 and 9. Add code to perform the following:

   a. Decode and print HTTP payload. Print the payload in ASCII.

   b. Add to the set of counters a counter for the number of HTTP packets. Add code to print the values of this counter to the subroutine program_ending().

3. Write a CGI script that prints the parameters it was passed.

References

[1] Catledge, L. D., and J. E. Pitkow. 1995. Characterizing browsing strategies in the world-wide web. *Computer Networks and ISDN Systems* 27:1065–73.

[2] Lawrence, S., and C. L. Giles. 1998. Searching the World Wide Web. *Science* 280:98.

[3] Albert, R., H. Jeong, and A. L. Barabasi. 1999. The diameter of the World Wide Web. Arxiv preprint cond-mat/9907038.

[4] Vass, J., et al. 1998. The World Wide Web. *IEEE Potentials* 17:33–37.

[5] Murtaza, S. S., and H. Choong Seon. 2005. A conceptual architecture for the uniform identification of objects. Paper presented at Fourth Annual ACIS International Conference on Computer and Information Science. Jeju Island, South Korea: 100–104.

[6] Schatz, B. R., and J. B. Hardin. 1994. NCSA mosaic and the World Wide Web: Global hypermedia protocols for the internet. *Science* 265: 895–901.

[7] Berners-Lee, T., et al. 1992. World-wide web: The information universe. *Internet Research* 2:52–58.

[8] Berners-Lee, T. Hypertext transfer protocol. 1996. Work in progress of the HTTP working group of the IETF.< URL: ftp://nic.merit.edu/documents/internet-drafts/draft-fielding-http-spec-00.txt.

[9] Fielding, R., et al. 1999. *Hypertext transfer protocol—http/1.1*. RFC 2616.

[10] Fielding, R., et al. 1997. *Hypertext transfer protocol—http/1.1*. RFC 2068.

[11] Touch, J., J. Heidemann, and K. Obraczka. 1998. Analysis of HTTP performance. ISI Research Report ISI/RR-98-463, USC/Information Sciences Institute. http://www.Isi.edu/touch/pubs/http-perf96.

[12] Raggett, D., A. Le Hors, and I. Jacobs. 1999. HTML 4.01 specification. Paper presented at W3C Recommendation REC-html401-19991224, World Wide Web Consortium (W3C). Cambridge, MA.

[13] Berners-Lee, T., J. Hendler, and O. Lassila. 2001. The semantic web. *Scientific American* 284:28–37.

[14] Lemay, L. 1994. *Teach yourself web publishing with HTML in a week.* Indianapolis: Sam's Publishing.

[15] Niederst, J. 2003. *Learning web design: A beginner's guide to HTML, graphics, and beyond.* O'Reilly Media.

[16] Hendler, J. 2003. Communication: Enhanced: Science and the semantic web. *Science* 299:520–21.

[17] Pfaffenberger, B., and B. Karow. 2000. *HTML 4 bible*. New York: Wiley.

[18] Kirda, E., et al. 2006. Noxes: A client-side solution for mitigating cross-site scripting attacks. In *Proceedings of the 2006 ACM Symposium on Applied Computing*, Dijon, France: 330–37.

[19] Jiang, S., S. Smith, and K. Minami. 2001. Securing web servers against insider attack. In *Proceedings of the 17th Annual Computer Security Applications Conference (ACSAC 2001)*, New Orleans: 265–76.

[20] Thiemann, P. 2005. An embedded domain-specific language for type-safe server-side web scripting. *ACM Transactions on Internet Technology (TOIT)* 5:1–46.

[21] Xie, Y., and A. Aiken. 2006. Static detection of security vulnerabilities in scripting languages. In *Proceedings of the 15th USENIX Security Symposium*, Vancouver, B.C., Canada: 179–92.

[22] Minamide, Y. 2005. Static approximation of dynamically generated web pages. In *Proceedings of the 14th International Conference on World Wide Web*, Chiba, Japan: 432–41.

[23] Jim, T., N. Swamy, and M. Hicks. 2007. Defeating script injection attacks with browser-enforced embedded policies. In *Proceedings of the 16th International Conference on World Wide Web*, Banff, Alberta, Canada: 601–10.

[24] Yu, D., et al. 2007. Javascript instrumentation for browser security. In *Proceedings of the 34th Annual ACM SIGPLAN-SIGACT Symposium on Principles of Programming Languages*, Nice, France: 237–49.

[25] Erlingsson, U., B. Livshits, and Y. Xie. 2007. End-to-end web application security. Paper presented at Proceedings of the Workshop on Hot Topics in Operating Systems (HotOS XI). San Diego, CA.

[26] Huseby, S. H. 2005. Common security problems in the code of dynamic web applications. Paper presented at Web Application Security Consortium. http://www.webappsec.org/projects/articles/062105.TX?

[27] Kumar, A., R. Chandran, and V. Vasudevan. 2006. Web application security: The next battleground. In *Enhancing Computer Security with Smart Technology*. Boca Raton, FL: CRC Press, 41–72.

[28] Marchesini, J., S. W. Smith, and M. Zhao. 2005. Keyjacking: The surprising insecurity of client-side SSL. *Computers and Security* 24:109–23.

[29] Jovanovic, N., C. Kruegel, and E. Kirda. 2006. Pixy: A static analysis tool for detecting web application vulnerabilities. Paper presented at IEEE Symposium on Security and Privacy. Oakland, CA.

[30] Jackson, C., et al. 2006. Protecting browser state from web privacy attacks. In *Proceedings of the 15th International Conference on World Wide Web*, 737–44.

[31] Kirda, E., and C. Kruegel. 2005. Protecting users against phishing attacks with antiphish. Paper presented at Proceedings of 29th COMPSAC. Edinburgh, Scotland.

[32] Raffetseder, T., E. Kirda, and C. Kruegel. 2007. Building anti-phishing browser plug-ins: An experience report. Paper presented at Proceedings of the Third International Workshop on Software Engineering for Secure Systems. Minneapolis, MN.

[33] Jakobsson, M., and S. Stamm. 2006. Invasive browser sniffing and countermeasures. In *Proceedings of the 15th International Conference on World Wide Web*, 523–32.

[34] Reynaud-Plantey, D. 2005. New threats of Java viruses. *Journal in Computer Virology* 1:32–43.

[35] Fu, S., and C. Z. Xu. 2006. Mobile code and security. In *Handbook of information security*. Hoboken, NJ: John Wiley & Sons, V. III, Chapter 144.

[36] Tilevich, E., Y. Smaragdakis, and M. Handte. 2005. Appletizing: Running legacy Java code remotely from a web browser. Paper presented at IEEE International Conference on Software Maintenance (ICSM). Budapest, Hungary.

[37] Adelsbach, A., S. Gajek, and J. Schwenk. 2005. Visual spoofing of SSL protected web sites and effective countermeasures. Paper presented at Information Security Practice and Experience Conference. Singapore.

[38] Herzog, A., and N. Shahmehri. 2005. An evaluation of Java application containers according to security requirements. In *Proceedings of the 14th IEEE International Workshops on Enabling Technologies: Infrastructure for Collaborative Enterprise (WETICE'05)*, Linköping, Sweden. 178–83.

[39] Kendall, K. E., and J. E. Kendall. 2002. *Systems analysis and design*. Upper Saddle River, NJ: Prentice-Hall.

[40] Bergmark, D. 2002. Collection synthesis. In *Proceedings of the 2nd ACM/IEEE-CS Joint Conference on Digital Libraries*, 253–62.

[41] Kim, J., K. Chung, and K. Choi. 2007. Spam filtering with dynamically updated URL statistics. *IEEE Security and Privacy*, 33–39.

[42] Lee, P. Y., S. C. Hui, and A. C. M. Fong. 2002. Neural networks for web content filtering. *IEEE Intelligent Systems* 17:48–57.

[43] Hammami, M., Y. Chahir, and L. Chen. 2003. Webguard: Web based adult content detection and filtering system. In *Proceedings of IEEE/WIC International Conference on Web Intelligence (WI 2003)*, Beijing, China: 574–78.

[44] Lee, P. Y., S. C. Hui, and A. C. M. Fong. 2003. A structural and content-based analysis for web filtering. *Internet Research: Electronic Networking Applications and Policy* 13:27–37.

[45] Zittrain, J., and B. Edelman. 2003. Internet filtering in China. *IEEE Internet Computing*, 70–77.

[46] Sugiyama, K., K. Hatano, and M. Yoshikawa. 2004. Adaptive web search based on user profile constructed without any effort from users. In *Proceedings of the 13th International Conference on World Wide Web*, New York, NY: 675–84.

Chapter 11

Remote Access Security

Remote access to computing resources has been a requirement of computer users since the earliest days of computing. The first computer communication systems were designed to support remote access to large mainframe computers using simple terminal devices to connect remote users using the telephone network or dedicated wires. The next phase of remote access was using personal computers as dumb terminals over the same dedicated lines or telephones lines. This led to the proliferation of terminal programs like Kermit, ProComm, Qmodem, etc. [1–3]. As desktop computers started to support networking, the requirements for remote access shifted from simple terminal access across dedicated connections to remote access from one computer to another over the Internet. This led the way to the development of several Internet protocols that supported remote terminal access from one computer to another. The first protocol developed in 1969 was called Teletype Network (TELNET). The TELNET protocol allows a computer running the TELNET client to connect to a computer running the TELNET server. Another protocol that was designed to support remote user access is called rlogin, and like TELNET, it allowed a user at one computer to connect to another computer. Unlike TELNET, rlogin was designed for UNIX-based computers and was designed for an environment where everyone was trusted. In addition to TELNET and rlogin, other protocols have been developed over the years to support remote access. Another protocol of interest is X-Windows, which allows a user on a computer running the X-Windows server to connect to a remote computer. The user's computer will display graphical content, and the user can use a mouse as an interface to the remote computer. The security vulnerabilities are the same for many of these protocols.

In addition to the need for remote terminal access there has been a need to transfer data files between computers. Several methods were developed in the early days of networking, and a couple of protocols emerged to become commonly used. The File Transfer Protocol (FTP) was one of the first to support file transfers between computers on the Internet, and like TELNET, it was designed for dissimilar computers. Another protocol that is part of the rlogin suite of commands is called Remote Copy Protocol (RCP). RCP was designed to copy files between trusted computers running UNIX.

A new generation of file transfer protocols has emerged in the last decade that are designed for a large network of computers all sharing data with one another. The protocols are often designed to evade conventional security devices. These new networks are called peer-to-peer (P2P) networks.

In this chapter we will examine remote access protocols like TELNET, rlogin, and X-Windows. We will also examine the several file transfer protocols, including peer-to-peer protocols. After understanding these protocols and their vulnerabilities, we will look at general countermeasures and several secure protocols that are deployed today to provide secure remote access.

11.1   Terminal-Based Remote Access (TELNET, rlogin, and X-Windows)

11.1.1   TELNET

The TELNET protocol defines how a remote computer running the TELNET client can communicate with a computer running the TELNET server [4–13]. TELNET was designed so that applications on the server would not have to be modified to interact with the client TELNET application. In order to allow computers that use different character sets to communicate with each other, TELNET defines a Network Virtual Terminal (NVT) character set. Figure 11.1 shows the basic concept behind the TELNET server and its interaction with the applications.

In Figure 11.1 the TELNET server accepts connections on port 23 and connects the remote TELNET client to the applications on the server through a pseudoterminal driver. Typically the first application provides authentication and challenges the user for his or her username and password. Figure 11.1 shows the authentication application interacting with the TELNET client through the pseudoterminal and with the password file on the server. The authentication application can use any method to verify the identity of the user as long as the data is transmitted via the TELNET protocol. If the authentication fails, the authentication application will terminate the connection with the client. It is up to the authentication application to determine what constitutes an authentication failure. One example of an authentication failure is three failed login attempts.

The applications running on the server interact with the pseudoterminal driver as if a terminal was directly connected to the server. This way there are no

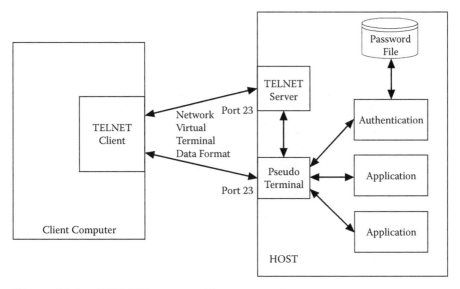

Figure 11.1: TELNET server architecture.

modifications needed in the server applications. The TELNET protocol is designed for terminal-based applications and is not suited for graphical-based systems like Microsoft Windows. There is a TELNET client that runs on MS Windows that can be used to connect to a terminal-based computer, often a UNIX system.

Figure 11.2 shows how the TELNET client and server applications interact to allow a user to connect to a remote computer.

As shown in Figure 11.2, the TELNET client application connects to the TELNET server application on port 23. The characters typed by the client are converted to NVT (which is 7-bit ASCII) and sent to the server, where they are converted to the native character set of the server and passed to the application. In order for the user to get the impression he or she is directly connected to the server application, TELNET typically sends each character typed as a separate packet using the Transmission Control Protocol (TCP) PUSH packet discussed in Chapter 7. Typically the TELNET client relies on the server side to echo every character typed by the user, which also creates the need to transfer each character as soon as possible and not wait for the TCP stream buffer to fill. In addition to transferring the user's data across the TELNET connection, TELNET uses the same connection to pass control information that is used during the initial connection, and is also used to pass special characters from the client to the server. The TELNET commands are

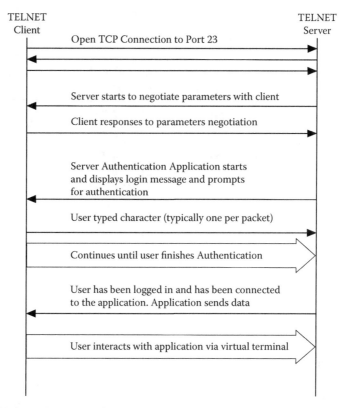

TELNET
Client

TELNET
Server

Open TCP Connection to Port 23

Server starts to negotiate parameters with client

Client responses to parameters negotiation

Server Authentication Application starts
and displays login message and prompts
for authentication

User typed character (typically one per packet)

Continues until user finishes Authentication

User has been logged in and has been connected
to the application. Application sends data

User interacts with application via virtual terminal

Figure 11.2: TELNET client-server interaction.

also characters, but they have the upper bit set to a 1. Table 11.1 shows some of the TELNET commands and options.

The commands BRK, IOP, and EC are used during normal data flow to handle the differences between the client's and server's interpretation of the characters. For example, the EC command allows a client that uses the control-h character as a backspace to interact with a server that uses the delete character as a backspace. When the user presses the control-h key, the TELNET client will send an EC command, which will be interrupted by the server and translated into the delete character.

In addition to the data flow commands, TELNET also uses a simple command response protocol to negotiate the initial parameters using the negotiation commands shown in the Table 11.1. By default, TELNET clients do not start the negotiation of the parameters and just establish a connection without sending any data. The TELNET server starts the parameter negotiation as shown in Table 11.2.

TABLE 11.1: TELNET Commands

Value	Abbreviation	Command
		TELNET Commands
240	SE	End of subnegotiation
241	NOP	No operation
242	DM	Data mark (stream sync character)
243	BRK	Break
244	IOP	Interrupt process
247	EC	Erase character
250	SB	Begin subnegotiation
251	WILL	Negotiation command (sender wants to enable the option)
252	WON'T	Negotiation command (sender does not want to enable the option)
253	DO	Negotiation command (sender would like the other side to enable the option)
254	DON'T	Negotiation command (sender would not like the other side to enable the option)
255	IAC	Interpret following characters as a command
		TELNET Options
ID	**RFC**	**Name**
0	856	Binary transmission
1	857	Echo
5	859	Status
24	930	Terminal type

As we see in Table 11.2, the TELNET server requests several parameters be enabled, and the client responds with what it is willing to do. Once the negotiation is complete, the TELNET server connects to the authentication application, and that application responds to the client with an authentication message. We see a single packet per character sent by the client during the authentication, and the server echos the characters back to the client. Notice that the server can respond back with multiple characters per packet when it has a longer message. Also note that the password is not echoed back to the client by the authentication application.

TABLE 11.2:   TELNET Data Flow

Direction	Data	Comments
C ← S	0xff 0xfd 0x01	IAC, do echo (request client echoes)
	0xff 0xfd 0x22	IAC, do linemode (request client sends a line at a time)
	0xff 0xfb 0x05	IAC, will status (server wishes to send status info)
C → S	0xff 0xfb 0x01	IAC, will echo (client will echo characters)
	0xff 0xfc 0x22	IAC, won't linemode (client will not do linemode)
	0xff 0xfe 0x05	IAC, don't status (client does not want server to send status information)
C ← S	0xff 0xfe 0x01	IAC, don't echo (tell client not to echo)
	0xff 0xfb 0x01	IAC, will echo (tell client-server will echo)
C → S	0xff 0xfc 0x01	IAC, won't echo (tell server client will not echo)
	0xff 0xfd 0x01	IAC, do echo (tell server it is OK to echo)
C ← S	\r\n login:	Send authentication application prompt
C → S	j	First character of username
C ← S	j	Echo of the character
		Repeat until enter key is pressed
C → S	\r\n	Send carriage return + linefeed
C ← S	\r\n	Echo carriage return + linefeed
C ← S	Password:	Send authentication application prompt
C → S	p	First character of password (server will not echo)
		Repeat until enter key is pressed
C → S	\r\n	Send carriage return + linefeed
C ← S	\r\n	Echo carriage return + linefeed
C ← S		User is now connected and server application will send message

11.1.2   rlogin

TELNET was originally designed to connect dissimilar client and server computers and does not directly support any user or host authentication. TELNET simply connects the client and server applications together, and it is up to the server to authenticate the user. In 1983 a new terminal program called rlogin was included

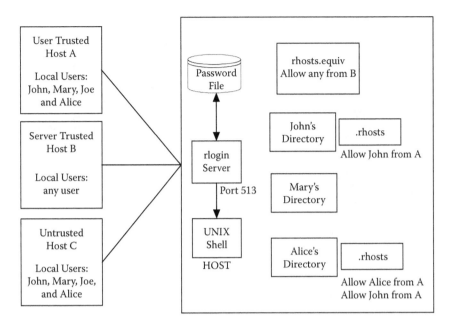

Figure 11.3: rlogin architecture.

with the release of BSD4.2 UNIX [14–20]. rlogin was designed to allow trusted UNIX machines to connect with other trusted UNIX machines with little or no user authentication. Unlike TELNET, the rlogin protocol supports authentication. The user authentication is based on the client machine IP address, the username of the client user, and the username of the server user. If these three parameters are considered trusted, then the client user is logged into the server computer without a password. If any of the parameters are untrusted, then a password is required and a prompt is displayed asking for the password. Figure 11.3 shows the architecture of the rlogin process and configuration files required for rlogin to function.

Figure 11.3 shows an rlogin server listening on port 513 waiting for a client to connect. When a client connects, it sends the local username, the remote username, and the terminal type to the server. The rlogin server consults the hosts.equiv file and the .rhosts file for the local user to determine if the remote user on the remote computer should be trusted. The hosts.equiv file can grant unauthenticated access on a systemwide scale. If the hosts.equiv file does not grant access, then the .rhosts file located in the local user's directory is checked, and if the remote user is trusted, then he or she is connected to the UNIX shell. Figure 11.4 shows a flowchart of the process used by the rlogin server to determine trust of the remote user.

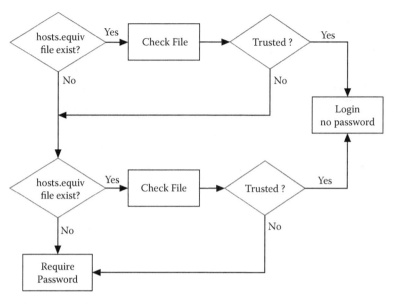

Figure 11.4:   rlogin server trust flowchart.

An example of the trust mechanism is shown in Figure 11.3. The rlogin server is listening on port 513 for rlogin client connections. Of the three remote computers (A, B, C), machines A and C each have four users (John, Mary, Joe, and Alice). The hosts.equiv file is set up to allow any user from host B to log in to the server as any of the valid users on the server without authentication (a trusted user). The server has three users (John, Mary, and Alice). John and Alice each have an .rhosts file configured. The rlogin server relies on the authentication of the user's local computer to support trusted authentication to the server. In other words, the rlogin client sends the username of the user on the client as part of the protocol, and the server trusts the client is providing the username of a locally authenticated user. Table 11.3 shows the possible combinations of remote client users, remote hosts, and server users, and what the resulting trust relationship is.

If the user on a trusted client machine is trusted to log in as a user on the server, then the server will not require a password. When the user types in the rlogin command, he or she will receive a command prompt from the server. If the user on a client machine is not trusted, then the user will be prompted for a password.

As we saw in the example above, the user does not need to type any user information into the rlogin command. The rlogin client, as part of the initial message, sends the client user, the server user, and the terminal type. The terminal type is sent so the server applications know what type of terminal is running on

TABLE 11.3: rlogin Trust Example

Client Host	Client-Side User	Server-Side User	Result
	John	John	Trusted
		Mary	Not trusted
		Alice	Trusted
	Mary	John	Not trusted
		Mary	Not trusted
A		Alice	Not trusted
	Joe	John	Not trusted
		Mary	Not trusted
		Alice	Not trusted
	Alice	John	Not trusted
		Mary	Not trusted
		Alice	Trusted
B	Any user	Any user	Trusted
	John	John	Not trusted
		Mary	Not trusted
		Alice	Not trusted
	Mary	John	Not trusted
		Mary	Not trusted
C		Alice	Not trusted
	Joe	John	Not trusted
		Mary	Not trusted
		Alice	Not trusted
	Alice	John	Not trusted
		Mary	Not trusted
		Alice	Not trusted

the client. The initial protocol exchange is shown in Figure 11.5, and Table 11.4 shows the data flow for both a trusted and untrusted user.

The prompting for a password and the response are handled as part of the data flow, and not part of the initial protocol exchange. Also, the password exchange takes place in clear text.

Once the user is connected via rlogin, all characters typed by the client are sent to the server without modification, and all characters sent by the server are received by the client unaltered. Unlike TELNET, rlogin does not translate characters.

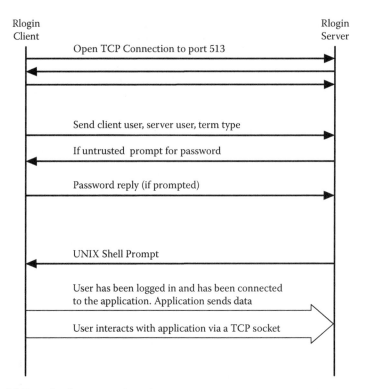

Figure 11.5: rlogin protocol exchange.

11.1.3 X-Windows

TELNET and rlogin allowed a remote user to connect to a computer as a remote terminal. This limits the types of applications a remote user can operate to command line or simple graphics applications. Both the TELNET and rlogin protocols send the terminal type to the remote server, so that the remote applications could manipulate the remote terminal. This makes it difficult to create graphical applications since the terminals vary in capabilities.

To fix this problem, a protocol called X-Windows was developed in 1984 that supported graphical applications [21–26]. The idea behind X-Windows was to define a standard set of graphical commands that can be used by an application to control a graphical display and to accept input from a keyboard and mouse. The X-Windows protocol allows application writers to create graphical user interfaces that are terminal independent. X-Windows defines a minimum set of terminal characteristics that allow for higher-quality graphical user interfaces. Figure 11.6 shows how X-Windows-based applications interface with the remote terminal.

TABLE 11.4: rlogin Data Flow

Direction	Data	Comments
C → S	john 0x00	Client-side username
	john 0x00	Server-side username
	xterm\34800 0x00	Terminal type and speed
		If authentication is required (user is untrusted)
C ← S	Password:	Prompt for password
C → S	p	First character of password (server will not echo)
		Repeat until enter key is pressed
C → S	\r	Send carriage return
C ← S	\r\n	Echo carriage return + linefeed
		If authentication worked or user was trusted
C ← S	Data from server	User is now connected and server will display the UNIX shell prompt

As shown in Figure 11.6, the terminal that provides the graphical display and mouse input is the server, and the application is the client that connects to the display. In a remote X-Windows environment the client computer often connects to the remote computer using TELNET or some other remote access protocol.

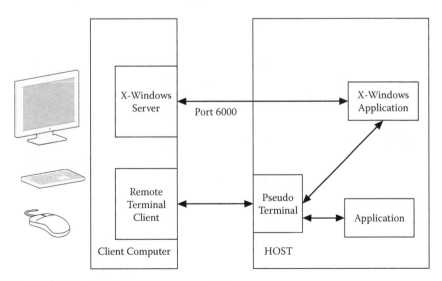

Figure 11.6: X-Windows remote architecture.

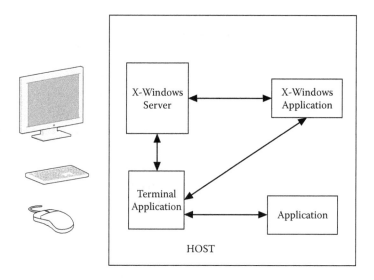

Figure 11.7:   X-Windows local architecture.

Once the user has been authenticated, he or she can run an X-Windows application. That application opens a connection back to the client computer's X-Windows server. The client's X-Windows server takes graphic commands from the application and displays them on the screen, and takes input from the user via the keyboard and mouse and sends that information back to the application using the X-Windows protocol. For the purpose of this book, we will not examine the X-Windows protocol, but from a security standpoint it is important to know that it is a clear text protocol with limited host authentication.

The X-Windows terminal was originally designed as a stand-alone one, but today it is an application that can run on either the local computer or a remote computer. Figure 11.7 shows an X-Windows server local to the same host as the application.

The X-Windows protocol does not have many security vulnerabilities, and therefore we will not examine the protocol in detail. It is an open protocol with several commercial and public domain servers. Most public domain UNIX systems support X-Windows as the primary graphical user interface.

11.1.4   Vulnerabilities, Attacks, and Countermeasures

Even though the TELNET and rlogin protocols are straightforward, there are several vulnerabilities that involve authentication. X-Windows also has authentication vulnerabilities, but is more complex since the server runs on the user's computer.

11.1.4.1 Header-Based Attacks

TELNET and rlogin do not have any headers, and therefore are not subject to header-based attacks. The X-Windows protocol does have headers and has a fairly complex encoding scheme. X-Windows is vulnerable to buffer overflow attacks. Buffer overflows can affect both the client application and the X-Windows server. Several buffer overflow vulnerabilities have been discovered in different X-Windows servers over the years.

11.1.4.2 Protocol-Based Attacks

The protocol used by TELNET and rlogin is simple and, after the initial connection, is nothing more than a direct connection from the client to the server over the TCP stream service.

TELNET does allow a user running the TELNET client access to any TCP-based application. A user could enter commands directly to an application and could create commands that violate an application layer protocol. This is not a vulnerability of the TELNET protocol and is more of a feature of the TELNET client. As we have seen in the earlier chapters of this book, we can use the TELNET client to test applications by directly connecting to them and issuing application layer commands. For this reason, we often find the TELNET client on many computers even though the use of TELNET is discouraged and is not enabled on most servers.

The X-Windows protocol is event driven and has not had many identified vulnerabilities. The X-Windows server is under control of the X-Windows application, and therefore is vulnerable to rogue applications. There is nothing built into the X-Windows protocol to help verify the integrity of the application sending commands to the server. This could also be considered a host-to-host authentication problem.

11.1.4.3 Authentication-Based Attacks

The TELNET protocol does not directly support user authentication, so it is not subject to authentication attacks. However, the TELNET server does allow a remote user to connect to the server computer and then enter a username and password. Thus, TELNET does provide remote access to the authentication mechanism of a server computer, just like Post Office Protocol version 3 (POP3) and Internet Message Access Protocol (IMAP) allow access to a computer's authentication mechanism. This remote access can be used for password guessing. Since TELNET does not support authentication, it is up to the remote computer's authentication mechanism to protect itself from attackers. One method used is to close the TCP connection after several failed user authentication attempts on the server. This causes the TELNET client to quit and close the TCP connection. This forces an attacker to reopen the connection to continue to try passwords. The server computer's authentication mechanism will often log the failure attempts, thus providing the computer's administrator a chance to take action. Often the administrator will block the remote IP address from making new connections. In reality, TELNET is not very useful for an attacker that has to guess passwords. The best way to mitigate TELNET authentication attacks is to use something other than simple username passwords for authentication. One method is to use what is referred to as two-factor authentication. This is where the user wishing access uses two methods, like a username password and a smartcard. Since two-factor authentication is the responsibility of the application or host, it is beyond the scope of this text.

As we saw, rlogin does support authentication, and therefore is subject to authentication-based attacks. A rlogin server uses IP addresses and usernames to prove the identity of the remote user. If the remote user is untrusted, then rlogin will request a password. If a remote user is trusted, then an attacker can use rlogin to gain access from a compromised trusted host to another host in the network. An rlogin server is also vulnerable to spoofing attacks since the client provides the identity of the client-side user as part of the protocol exchange. This would allow a rogue client to place any username in the protocol message, thus pretending to be an authenticated user on the client. Figure 11.8 shows how an attacker can use rlogin to step from one computer to another.

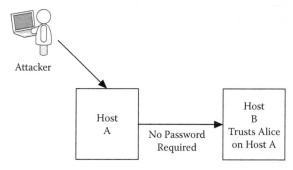

Figure 11.8: rlogin stepping attack.

As we see in Figure 11.8, the attacker gains access to host A as Alice, and since Alice on host A is trusted by host B, the attacker can gain access to host B as Alice. The attacker does not need to be authenticated as Alice on host A if it can spoof the username Alice in the rlogin protocol exchange. The best way to mitigate this is not to allow trusted hosts or users. This will require a password each time rlogin is used.

Like TELNET, rlogin will also ask for a password and is subject to password guessing attacks. This is not used very often as a method of attack since it can take too long and system administrators will be notified after several wrong guesses. The best way to mitigate these attacks is to not use the protocol or couple it with additional authentication. Since rlogin has authentication as part of the protocol, it is harder to use two-factor authentication.

The X-Windows server uses the IP address of the client to authenticate access to the server. It is possible to allow unauthenticated access to an X-Windows server. There is no user-based authentication. This means that if the trusted machine running the client code is compromised, the attacker on that machine would have access through X-Windows to the hosts running the X-Windows server.

11.1.4.4 Traffic-Based Attacks

Since TELNET, rlogin, and X-Windows are clear text protocols, they are subject to sniffing attacks. An attacker that can capture the traffic would be able to capture the username and password inside the session. An attacker would also be able to capture all of the keystrokes and responses between the client and server. This could compromise other applications and allow the attacker to obtain additional usernames and passwords that the user typed during the session. The best way to mitigate sniffing vulnerabilities is through encryption. There are a couple of methods used to provide encryption for remote access protocols. The most common is to use a protocol called Secure Shell (SSH), which replaces rlogin and provides an encrypted connection. Since SSH can protect more than just remote terminal connections, we will discuss it as part of the section on general countermeasures. There is an encrypted version of TELNET that is not used very often. It is based on a shared secret key. Since SSH is the predominant method of encrypted remote access, we will focus on that protocol as a solution.

TELNET and rlogin protocols are not susceptible to traffic flooding attacks. However, they can generate a large number of packets when the remote computer is responsible for echoing each character back to the client. Often this results in two packets for every character typed by the user. The client side is limited by the speed at which a user can type, and therefore these protocols typically do not create a large traffic load on the network. The X-Windows protocol can produce a greater load on the network and the computing resources of the X-Windows server. Therefore, it is more susceptible to traffic-based attacks.

Definitions

Network Virtual Terminal character set.

A character set that all implementations of an application agree upon to encode their data. Typically it is 7-bit ASCII.

Stepping stone.

An attacker enters one device and from there enters another device, and continues until it reaches the target. This is done to either hide the true location of the attacker or take advantage of a trust relationship.

Trusted host.

A host that is allowed access typically based on its IP address as an identifier.

11.2   File Transfer Protocols

The need to transfer files between computers existed long before networks. The advent of networks has enabled easy transfer of files between computers. We have seen that Hypertext Transfer Protocol (HTTP) is basically a file transfer protocol used by the web browsers and servers. In this section we will explore file transfer protocols and examine their security implications.

11.2.1   File Transfer Protocol (FTP)

FTP is a common protocol used to transfer files between computers [27–32]. FTP supports user authentication and provides limited data translation between dissimilar computers. FTP also provides a common command structure to support directory and file management (create directories, list files, remove directories, etc.). The common command structure allows a user to interact with a remote computer without knowing the commands for every computer he or she wishes to transfer files between. FTP uses a simple set of ASCII commands to support the interaction between computers.

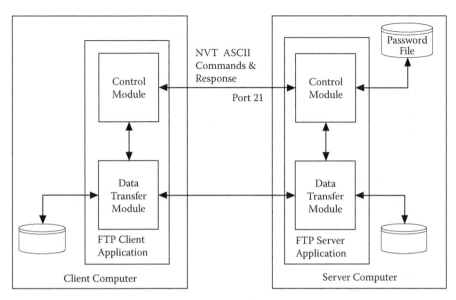

Figure 11.9: FTP client-server architecture.

To facilitate the interaction between the FTP client and the FTP server, the FTP protocol uses two TCP connections. When the FTP client connects to the server using the command port (port 21), the user is prompted for a username and password. The command–connection remains open during the session and is used to send commands and responses between the client and server. The command protocol is a command response protocol and is described below. If there is any data that needs to be transferred, the client and server will open a data connection. Depending on the configuration, the server may initiate the data connection to the client, or the client may initiate the data connection to the server. A new data connection is opened for each data transfer. Figure 11.9 shows the FTP client-server architecture and the command and data modules within the FTP client and server applications. As shown in Figure 11.9, the client and server command modules interact using the NVT ASCII that is also used by TELNET. Note that you can use a TELNET client to interact with the command module, but you will not be able to transfer any data.

As mentioned earlier, the command protocol is a simple ASCII-based command-and-response protocol that is very similar to the Simple Mail Transfer Protocol (SMTP) in that every command has a three-digit response code. Table 11.5 shows common FTP commands.

Each response code consists of a three-digit ASCII number and a text field. The first digit of the response code indicates if the command worked or failed,

TABLE 11.5: FTP Commands

Command	Action
	Authentication
USER username	Send the username to the server
PASS password	Send the user password to the server
QUIT	Finish session
	File Management
CWD directory_name	Change directory on the server
CDUP	Change to the parent directory on the server
DELE filename	Delete the file from the server
LIST directory_name	List the files on the server
MKD directory_name	Make a new directory on the server
PWD	Print the current directory on the server
RMD directory_name	Delete a directory from the server
RNFR old_file_name	Name of file on the server to be renamed
RNTO new_file_name	Name of file on the server to rename the file to
	Data Format
TYPE (A, I)	Set data transfer type, A = ASCII, I = image
	Data Port
PORT 6-digit identifier	Client sends the port number for the server to connect to for the data transfer
PASV	Server sends the port number for the client to connect to for the data transfer
	File Transfer
RETR filename(s)	Transfer the file(s) from the server to the client using the data connection
STOR filename(s)	Transfer the file(s) from the client to the server using the data connection
	Miscellaneous
HELP	Server will return information

the second digit specifies what type of code, and the third digit is used to indicate specific codes. The response code syntax is shown in Table 11.6. Table 11.7 shows the common FTP response codes.

The client and server data transfer modules use a separate connection for each data transfer. There are two methods of data transfer based on whether the client

TABLE 11.6: FTP Response Codes

Code	Response Status
1XX	Positive preliminary reply—Indicates the server will respond with another response code before the client can continue
2XX	Positive completion reply—Indicates the command was successful and a new command can be issued
3XX	Positive intermediate reply—Indicates the command was successful, but the action is held up pending receipt of another command from the client
4XX	Transient negative completion reply—Indicates the command was not accepted; however, the error is temporary
5XX	Permanent negative completion reply—Indicates the command was not accepted

Code	Response Type
X0X	Syntax error or unimplemented commands
X1X	Information—Reply to a request for information
X2X	Connections—Reply to a request for connection
X3X	Authentication—Reply to authentication commands
X4X	Unspecified
X5X	File system—Reply to file system-based requests

TABLE 11.7: Common FTP Response Codes

Code	Responses
150	Data connection will open
200	Command acknowledgment
220	Service ready
225	Data connection open
226	Closing data connection
230	User logged in
331	User needs password
425	Cannot open data connection
500	Syntax error
530	User login failure

or the server opens the connection. Typically we think of the server waiting for a connection from the client, which is called passive mode. The most common method used by FTP is to have the client data transfer module listen for the data connection from the server. In order for the server to know the port number, the client is waiting for the connection on the client uses the PORT command to send the IP address and port number. The server data transfer module connects to the client data transfer module and performs the data transfer specified by the client command. Either method of data transfer does add some complexity when an organization tries to use a firewall to block connections. Often the firewall blocking rules are based on port numbers. The firewall can overcome the dynamic port number assignment by trying to associate connections to open FTP command connections. If the firewall knows there is an open FTP command connection, then it can allow other connections between the FTP client and server. Figure 11.10 shows both the user interaction during an FTP session and the resulting command and data protocol interaction of the FTP session.

In Figure 11.10 the user starts by running the FTP client and connecting to the server. The data entered by the user is in bold text. The server responds with an ASCII response code (220) and a text message. The client displays the message it receives from the server. The client prompts the user for the username, and once the username has been entered, the client sends the USER command with the username typed by the user as the parameter. Note that unlike in TELNET, the username is contained in one packet. The FTP server responds with 331, indicating a password is required. The server responds with this code even if the username is not a valid user. This prevents using FTP as a method to guess valid usernames. The client prompts the user for a password and does not echo the typed password back to the user. The entered password is sent to the server using the PASS command with the user-provided password as a parameter, and the server responds with a 230 if the user was logged in successfully and returns a 530 if the authentication failed. Once the client is connected and authenticated with the server, the user can send commands to the server.

In Figure 11.10 the user requests a directory listing, which requires the client and server to open a data connection. This is shown by the client sending the port command. The first four parameters of the port command are the IP address of the client as a comma-separated list. The last two parameters are used to compute the port number the client is listening on for the server connection. In the figure these two values are 19 and 137, which are converted to a port number by multiplying 19 by 256 and adding 137. This corresponds to port number 5001. The client

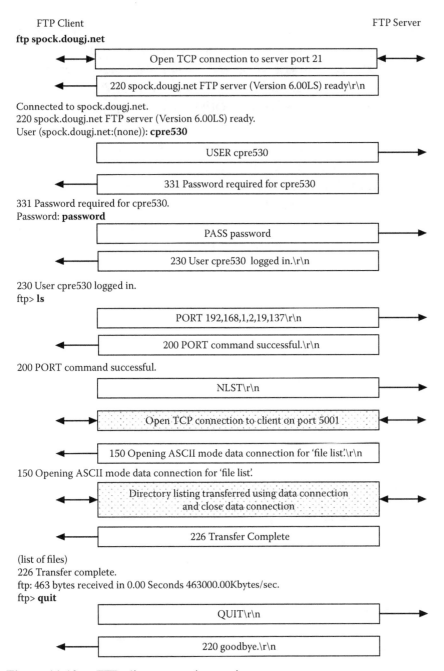

Figure 11.10: FTP client-server interaction.

then sends the NLST command, and the server opens a connection to the client and sends the data. The server also sends a response code of 150 back to the client, indicating the data connection has been opened. Once the data has been transferred, the server closes the connection and sends a response code of 226, which indicates the transfer is completed. Another data transfer starts with the client sending the port command followed by the request. The client can close the command connection by sending a QUIT command, and the server responds with a 220.

As we saw in Figure 11.10, the server requires a username and password before the client is allowed to interact with the server. In some cases it is useful to have unauthenticated file transfers. Typically an unauthenticated file transfer is limited to transfers from the server to the client. FTP is a common protocol to distribute software and other large files. In order to support unauthenticated file transfers, FTP supports what is called anonymous FTP. To use anonymous FTP, the client enters "anonymous" as the username and typically his or her email address as the password. Most servers do not check the password to see if it is a valid email address. The user can then have access to all of the files stored on the FTP site. In Figure 11.10 the only change in the protocol exchange for an anonymous file FTP session would be the username and password. The response code sent by the server after the USER command would still be 331. Table 11.8 shows a sample session with an anonymous FTP server.

Anonymous FTP is also used by web browsers when the URL is of the form ftp://machine.net/file. The only difference between user-authenticated FTP and anonymous FTP is the server configuration. Figure 11.11 shows the typical

TABLE 11.8:   Anonymous FTP Access

$ ftp spock.dougj.net

```
Connected to spock.dougj.net.
220 spock.dougj.net FTP server ready.
User (spock.dougj.net:(none)):
```

anonymous
```
331 Guest login ok, type your name as password.
Password:
230 Guest login ok, access
restrictions apply.
ftp
```

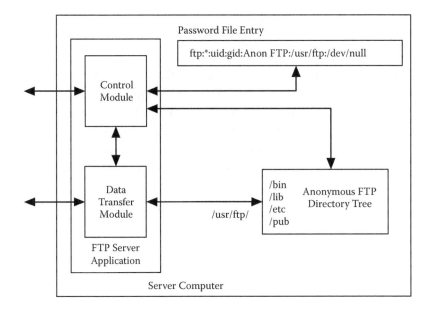

Figure 11.11: Anonymous FTP server configuration.

anonymous FTP server configuration. In this figure we see the password file has an entry for the user FTP, but there is no password for the user, nor is there any shell program. This account is disabled for all other authentication-based applications (TELNET, POP, IMAP, etc.). The home directory in this example is /usr/ftp, and this becomes the root of the directory path for the anonymous user that connects to the FTP server. This restricts the anonymous user to only the directories that are subdirectories of /usr/ftp. Since anonymous FTP uses the same FTP server, all of the commands are enabled, including the commands that allow the remote user to upload, delete, and rename files. The remote user also has access to the commands to manipulate the directories.

It should be noted that there are programs available that search the Internet for anonymous FTP sites that have writable directories. The attackers use these anonymous FTP sites to store copyrighted music, software, movies, and other illegal materials. To prevent the anonymous user from adding or changing files, the server should be configured so that all of the directories are read only.

11.2.2 Trivial FTP

There are times when we need a simple file transfer protocol that can be used to transfer files without the overhead of the TCP layer [33–38]. This is often seen in

TABLE 11.9:   TFTP Packet Types

Name (opcode)	Parameters	Function
RRQ (1)	Filename (var), 0x00 Mode (var), 0x00	Read request; mode is either netascii or octet.
WRQ (2)	Filename (var), 0x00 Mode (var), 0x00	Write request; mode is either netascii or octet.
DATA (3)	Block number (2 bytes) Data (0–512 bytes)	Block number starts at 1; all blocks except the last must be 512 bytes long. A block that is less than 512 bytes is used to indicate the last block, and the file transfer is done.
ACK (4)	Block number (2 bytes)	Used to acknowledge the data block
ERROR (5)	Error number (2 bytes) Error data (var), 0x00	Used to indicate an error; the error data is text data.

diskless workstations or network devices. Trivial File Transfer Protocol (TFTP) was designed to use the User Datagram Protocol (UDP) transport layer and to operate without authentication. For the purpose of this book, we will not go into the details of this protocol other than to explore the packet format and security implications of an unauthenticated file transfer protocol. Since TFTP uses UDP, there is no guarantee of reliable and ordered data transfer. The protocol is simple and only has five packet types, as shown in Table 11.9.

The TFTP protocol is configured like anonymous FTP in that it can be confined to only allow access to part of the server's file system. Just like with anonymous FTP, care should be taken to make the directories read only. Most organizations do not need to run a TFTP server, or if they do, they only need one server.

11.2.3   RCP

Another method of file transfer, called Remote Copy Protocol (RCP), is part of the rlogin set of protocols and uses the same trust method as described in the section on rlogin. The primary difference is that RCP does not support authentication, and if the user is not trusted, then the copy will not take place.

> The syntax of the command is:
> rcp machine.user:source_file machine.user:destination_file

If the user and machine are trusted based on the rules described in the section on rlogin, then the copy will take place; otherwise, it will fail. There is very little reason to use RCP since it forces the use of unauthenticated access.

11.2.4   Vulnerabilities, Attacks, and Countermeasures

This section reviewed three file transfer protocols. These protocols have several common security vulnerabilities, and each has vulnerabilities that are unique to the protocol. Each protocol will be compared to the taxonomy.

11.2.4.1   Header-Based Attacks

Only FTP and RCP are subject to header-based attacks. TFTP has a simple header structure, and if the header is invalid, the protocol will produce an error. FTP and RCP also have simple header formats, and there have not been many attacks against the header structure. There have been some attacks where the file name or directory name is too long for the FTP server to handle, which has either forced the server to hang or has forced a buffer overflow. For the most part, these vulnerabilities have been patched.

11.2.4.2   Protocol-Based Attacks

TFTP has a simple protocol and is not subject to protocol-based attacks. If there is something wrong, the TFTP client or server will time out and abort the transfer. RCP also does not have much of a protocol and just uses the TCP stream socket to transfer a file once the authentication has been established. The FTP protocol has the most vulnerabilities. This is due mostly to the complexity of the multiple data connections and how they relate to the command connection. The protocol-based attacks against FTP have primarily focused on using the data connection to bypass perimeter defenses like firewalls. Most firewalls are capable of handling the dynamic nature of the data connection by correlating the data connection requests to a current command connection.

One interesting protocol attack is to redirect the FTP server to another computer using the port command. This can be done using TELNET to connect to an FTP server, or with exploit code. The biggest trick is to get something on the FTP server you can then send to the target. Following is an example using an anonymous

FTP server that has a file (m1) that contains the email commands to interact with an SMTP server. The port command is used to direct the FTP server to connect with the computer at 192.168.1.40 on port 25, which is the email port. The FTP commands direct the FTP server to connect to the email server and send the file m1. This attack is limited in what it can do, but you could write a script that forces an FTP server to make a large number of connections to any IP address and try a denial of service, or just try to get the FTP server blacklisted. This could also be used to probe systems inside a firewall. When you try to open a connection to a port with no service running, you get an error. This method of probing is very time-consuming and not very efficient.

```
$ telnet klingon.dougj.net 21
220 klingon.doug.net FTP server ready.
user anonymous
331 Guest login ok, type your name as password.
pass doug
230 Guest login ok, access restrictions apply.
port 192,168,1,40,0,25
200 PORT command successful.
retr m1
150 Opening ASCII mode data connection for 'm1' (84 bytes).
226 Transfer complete.
quit
```

```
HELO cia.gov
MAIL FROM: badperson@cia.gov
RCPT TO: user
DATA
(any mail message)
```

11.2.4.3   Authentication-Based Attacks

The largest vulnerability associated with file transfer applications is authentication. As we saw earlier in this section, FTP uses the server authentication and prompts the user for a username and password. This provides an attacker a way to guess passwords. However, as discussed in the section on remote access, it is not a viable method to guess a large number of usernames and passwords. Anonymous

FTP can provide additional authentication problems since any user can connect to the FTP server. If there are directories that are writable, an attacker could place files on the anonymous FTP and share them with other users. As mentioned before, there are programs that scan the Internet and look for FTP servers that support anonymous access and then check for writable directories. In Figure 11.10 we can see that all the attacker needs to do is send "USER anonymous" and "PASS john@cia.gov" and see if the code 230 is returned. This will find an anonymous FTP server, and then all the attacker needs to do is send a file to the FTP server and see if the server returns an error. Since many system administrators do not closely monitor the anonymous FTP log files, these sites can often go undetected.

Another authentication problem with FTP is that the newer clients designed to run on personal computers have the option to store the username and password so that the user does not have to remember them to connect to the FTP server. This can lead to problems if a personal computer is a mobile device, is compromised, or is in an unsecured location. For example, if someone can access the computer with your FTP passwords, he or she could gain access to the FTP site. Depending on how the passwords are stored, he or she may be able to read the passwords and then use them to gain access to the server.

There are also FTP servers that can be configured to listen on any port and can be run by users. A normal FTP server needs to be executed by the privileged user since it uses a lower-numbered port and the operating system protects those ports. These user-configured FTP servers are often used to share illegal materials. There are even servers that will track the amount of data that is uploaded to the FTP sever and then allow you to download data based on the amount uploaded. This way the operator of the FTP server is asking people to contribute to the site before getting any benefit from it.

We also saw that TFTP and RCP are nonauthenticated services. RCP uses trust based on username and IP addresses. Both of these protocols should only be used when absolutely necessary, and there is a secure replacement for the RCP protocol that will be discussed in the next section.

11.2.4.4 Traffic-Based Attacks

Since all of the file transfer protocols we discussed are clear text protocols, they are subject to sniffing attacks. An attacker that can capture the traffic would also capture the username and password inside the session. An attacker can also capture all of the keystrokes and responses between the client and server. This could compromise other applications and could allow the attacker to obtain additional usernames and passwords that the user typed during the session. The best way to mitigate sniffing vulnerabilities is through encryption. We will review several encryption methods in the next section.

FTP can be susceptible to traffic flooding attacks. This is sometimes seen in anonymous FTP sites where attackers have placed a large amount of information that is made available to the public. If a large number of people try to download very large files at the same time, the FTP server can become overwhelmed. Large file transfers can add a lot of traffic to the network and can cause reduced network bandwidth, especially through a lower-bandwidth ISP connection.

Definitions

Anonymous FTP.
An FTP server that accepts the username "anonymous" and requires no password.

User-configured FTP server.
An FTP server installed by a user that typically uses a different port number and is often used to share copyrighted material.

11.3 Peer-to-Peer Networks

The basic idea behind peer-to-peer networks is to allow users to search for files and to share files with other users without authentication. Unlike the World Wide Web, where data is stored on web sites and users can download information from the web site, peer-to-peer networks allow users to connect to each other and transfer data directly from user to user. The users of peer-to-peer networks typically do not know each other, nor do they have any relationship outside the peer-to-peer network. These networks are designed to facilitate the searching and transfer of files. Many of the peer-to-peer protocols are designed to evade detection by network filters. There are two basic types of peer-to-peer networks—centralized and decentralized (often called ad hoc)—as shown in Figure 11.12 [39–49].

The centralized peer-to-peer network uses a central server that contains an index of files that are offered by the users of the network. The files are stored on the users' computers and not on the central server. Users send a list of files they have to share to the central index server. Users query the central index server to find a file that matches their search criteria. Files are transferred from one user

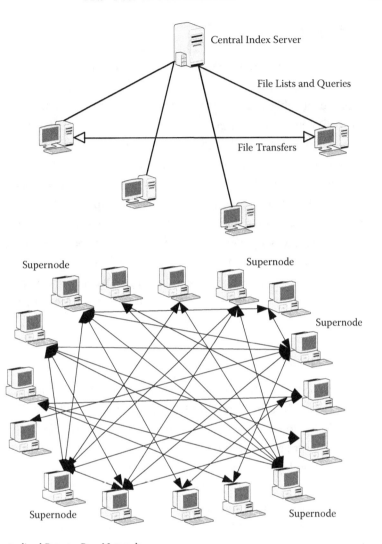

Decentralized Peer-to-Peer Network

Figure 11.12:   Peer-to-peer networks.

to another user. In addition, users can connect directly to each other and search
for files without the central index server. The central index server simply makes
searching easier. The central index server model can have more than one index
server interconnected in its own peer-to-peer network. This is done to speed up
searches and distribute the workload between several servers. This also provides
redundancy, so that if one server node quits, the other nodes can still function and
the network is still usable.

With an ad hoc peer-to-peer network, every computer that is part of the network has its own list of files that are shared, and each computer is connected to a small number of other computers (neighbors). Each neighbor is connected to a small number of computers, and so on. When a user wishes to search for a file, a request is sent to each neighbor, and each neighbor sends the request to the next neighbor, and so on. When a computer gets the search request, it searches its shared files, and if there is a match, it will send a message back to the requester telling him or her that it has the file(s) and some basic information about the files.

The ad hoc network can have different types of nodes, often called leaf nodes and super nodes. A leaf node is often a user's computer, and the super nodes are designed to have a large number of leaf nodes connected to them. This way the distance between any two users (number of peer-to-peer nodes between two computers) is reduced, thus making the network faster.

In this section we will look at three different protocols used to support peer-to-peer networks. We will also look at the vulnerabilities in peer-to-peer networks and methods used to block peer-to-peer networks.

11.3.1 Centralized Peer to Peer

There are two popular centralized peer-to-peer protocols. The first is called Napster and was one of the first centralized peer-to-peer networks [50–58]. The second centralized peer-to-peer network is called KaZaA [59–70]. KaZaA runs a protocol called Fasttrack. Both Napster and KaZaA were designed to share music between users and were established as free music sharing systems. Both Napster and KaZaA have converted to a pay-per-song model, and the Napster protocol is not widely used. There are several applications that still use the Fasttrack protocol to share files without paying for them. Both protocols are very similar to each other. The primary difference is that in the Napster protocol the central index server keeps a record of every file transfer, and in the Fasttrack protocol the central index server does not. The Napster protocol is shown in Figure 11.13.

Napster uses TCP between the client and the central index server. In the figure we see the packet format is simple, consisting of a 2-byte-long field, which is the length of the packet. The type field is 2 bytes long and contains a number that indicates the packet type. The content of the data depends on the type of packet. The client logs in to the server and notifies the server which files it has to share. The client can then issue search requests and the server will return the results. The results contain information about the files that matched the search

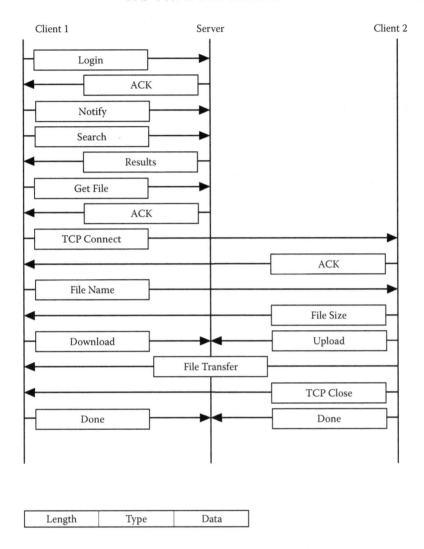

Figure 11.13: Napster protocol.

along with the location (IP address) where the file can be found. When a client wishes to retrieve a file it issues a get packet to the index server and the index server responds with an ACK packet. The client then connects to the peer client that has the file. The two clients exchange packets to determine which file should be transferred. The file transfer then takes place using the TCP connection that was established between the two peer clients. Both clients notify the central index server that a file transfer has been started. The peer clients notify the central index server when the file transfer is complete. Napster can also handle the case where

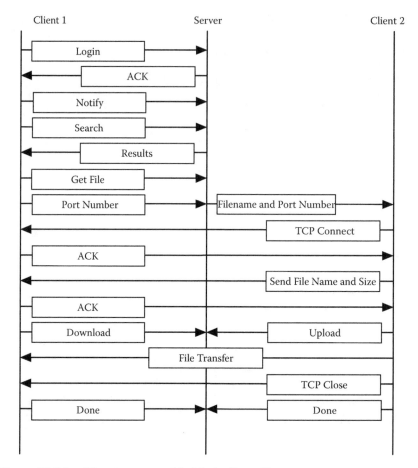

Figure 11.14:   Napster protocol behind a firewall.

one client is behind a firewall that blocks incoming connections. Figure 11.14 shows the Napster protocol with a firewall.

Figure 11.14 shows the protocol assuming client 2 is behind a firewall, which means client 1 cannot connect to it. Client 2 tells the server when it connects to the server if it is behind a firewall. Client 1 tells the server which port number it will use to wait for a connection. The server tells client 2 which port number to use to connect to client 1, and when client 2 connects, it tells client 1 which file it is sending. The remainder of the protocol works the same way as shown in Figure 11.13.

Napster was the first music sharing peer-to-peer network to lose a lawsuit brought by the record companies. This was due in part to the fact that the central index server keeps track of what files are transferred. Napster could not claim it just provided a protocol. Several other companies that produced peer-to-peer software have also been forced to change how they operate due to the recording industry suits. The Fasttrack protocol is still widely used today to share copyrighted material. The Fasttrack protocol is best known by the application KaZaA, which has changed its business model to charge for content.

11.3.2 KaZaA

KaZaA is a centralized index server peer-to-peer network based on the Fasttrack protocol. KaZaA has a shared folder that is uses to store files that are downloaded from other users. By default, this shared folder is located in the KaZaA program directory. KaZaA also provides the ability for the user to set up additional sharing folders that are used to share files with other KaZaA users. When a user starts KaZaA, he or she is connected to a super node and KaZaA offers or advertises the files it has to share. Figure 11.15 shows the Fasttrack protocol.

To advertise a file the user must put the files into either the download folder or one of the additional sharing folders that KaZaA uses. Any files within these shared folders are advertised and can be downloaded by other users of the KaZaA network. The advertisement consists of a set of identifiers that are used to tie the file back to the users. These identifiers include the IP address of the client offering the files, the name of the file, the file size, and the content hash. In addition, there are file descriptors that provide information like the artist name, album name, and user text. This information is used in the search process. The user text field is used to provide a description of the files and is part of the KaZaA system. The content hash is a mathematical function that is used to identify files that are the same. This allows the user to search for the file if the original file download fails.

To find a file, the user submits a query to the super node. The super node looks in its database for the file that matches the search parameters. If one or more of the users connected to the super node has the file that matches the request, then the super node returns the IP addresses and the file descriptions of all matches. Super nodes can send queries between each other. Users can also connect directly with each other, so if you find a file on a user's machine, you can then query it to see what other files are offered for sharing. The file transfer takes place between the two clients using the HTTP protocol.

Unlike Napster, in the Fasttrack protocol the index server does not record which files are transferred between clients.

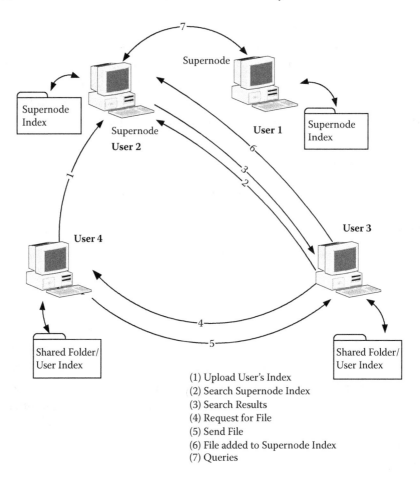

Figure 11.15: Fasttrack protocol.

11.3.3 Decentralized Peer to Peer

The first widely used decentralized peer-to-peer protocol is called Gnutella and is still in use today [71–78]. There are several applications that have been designed to use the Gnutella protocol that run on most major operating systems. Unlike centralized peer-to-peer protocols, Gnutella applications need to discover their neighbors and all searches flow through the applications that are part of the Gnutella network. Another decentralized peer-to-peer network is called BitTorrent [71–83]. BitTorrent is designed to allow the shared file to be split among multiple clients. This is done to speed up the download of large files like movies and CD-ROM images. We will not examine the BitTorrent protocol as part of this book. The vulnerabilities that exist with BitTorrent are the same as those of other peer-to-peer protocols. The mitigation methods are also the same.

11.3.3.1 Limewire, Bearshare, and Gnutella

Limewire, Bearshare, and Gnutella are all ad hoc peer-to-peer networks. Gnutella is the protocol used by applications like Limewire. These applications have a shared folder that is used to store files that are downloaded from other users. When a user starts a Gnutella-based program, she is connected to a Gnutella network.

To advertise a file the user must put the file into either the download folder or one of the additional sharing folders that she sets up. Any files within these shared folders are advertised and can be downloaded by other users of the Gnutella network. The advertisement consists of a set of identifiers that are used to tie the file back to the user. These identifiers include the IP address of the client offering the files, the name of the file, the file size, and the content hash. In addition, there are file descriptors that provide information like the artist name, album name, and user text. This information is used in the search process. The user text field is used to provide a description of the file and is part of the Gnutella system. This field is not part of the original data stored on a CD and is added by users who put files into the Gnutella shared folders. The content hash is a mathematical function that is used to identify files that are the same. This allows the user to search for the file if the original file download fails. Figure 11.16 shows a typical Gnutella network.

Figure 11.16 shows several nodes connected to neighbor nodes using the Gnutella protocol. An issue with ad hoc peer-to-peer networks is how to create and maintain the network. Gnutella uses a protocol based on sending out "ping" packets and then waiting for responses (called a pong). The protocol is shown in Figure 11.16.

The packet format is simple (as shown in Figure 11.6). The payload indicates what type of packet it is, the time-to-live (TTL) field indicates the lifetime of the packet, and the hop count indicates how far the packet has traveled. Just like in an IP protocol, the TTL is decremented by each client that forwards the packet. The hop count starts out at zero and is incremented by each client that forwards the packet. Figure 11.16 shows the client sending out a ping packet with an ID of 4 to its neighbor nodes. When the ping packet is received by a neighbor, the neighbor forwards the ping packet on to its neighbors and also responds back to the originator with a pong packet. The ping packet will continue to be forwarded from neighbor to neighbor until the TTL equals zero. Each neighbor that gets a unique ping packet (the ID field is used to tell if the neighbor has seen the same

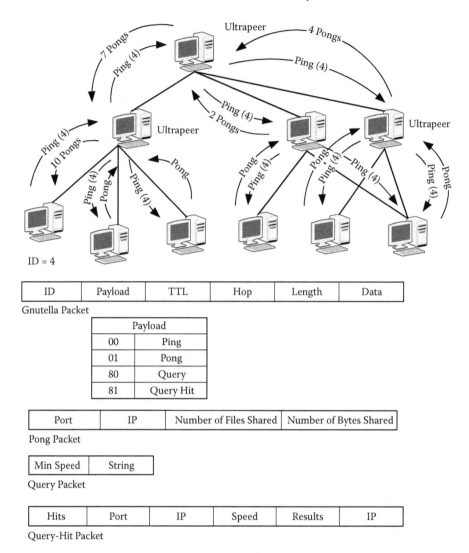

ID	Payload	TTL	Hop	Length	Data

Gnutella Packet

Payload	
00	Ping
01	Pong
80	Query
81	Query Hit

Port	IP	Number of Files Shared	Number of Bytes Shared

Pong Packet

Min Speed	String

Query Packet

Hits	Port	IP	Speed	Results	IP

Query-Hit Packet

Figure 11.16: Typical Gnutella network.

ping packet more than once) sends a pong back to the originator. The pong packet is returned following the same path as the ping packet. This creates a large amount of traffic between neighbors. The pong packet contains the port number of the responding application, the IP address of the application, the total number of files shared, and the total number of kilobytes of shared data. As we see in the figure, the single ping packet generated multiple ping packets and ten pong packets were sent back in response to the single ping.

Figure 11.16 also shows the query and query-hit packets. A client wishing to find a file sends out a query packet to its neighbors. The neighbors pass the packet on to their neighbors, and this continues until the maximum number of hops is reached. Each application that gets a query searches through its shared files to determine if there is a match. If there is a match, the application responds using the query-hit packet. The response is routed back through the Gnutella network until it reaches the original sender. The client that sent the query can then chose which result to use to get the file. The file transfer takes place between the client with the file and the client wanting the file. The clients use the HTTP protocol to transfer the file.

11.3.4 Vulnerabilities, Attacks, and Countermeasures

There are numerous vulnerabilities associated with peer-to-peer networks. In addition to those vulnerabilities associated with the taxonomy there are legal issues with sharing copyrighted materials. Several copyright holders have started programs to identify and prosecute people who share copyrighted material using peer-to-peer networks. The network-based peer-to-peer vulnerabilities and attacks are described in the next sections.

11.3.4.1 Header- and Protocol-Based Attacks

The headers in the peer-to-peer networks are simple, and any header-based vulnerabilities would be limited to disabling the communication of the client. The centralized protocols could be subject to header-based attacks against the central index server that could disable the index server. Likewise, any protocol-based attacks would be limited to clients or the index server. An attacker has very little to gain from a header- or protocol-based attack since these applications run as a user and do not provide access to the system.

11.3.4.2 Authentication-Based Attacks

Peer-to-peer networks are designed to be anonymous, and therefore the concept of authentication does not apply. This leads to several security problems, primarily focused around the validity of the content. In all of the peer-to-peer protocols we have examined, the files to be shared are reported by the clients with the files. Since anyone can join a peer-to-peer network, there is no checking as to the validity or intentions of the person offering the files for sharing. This leads to attackers sharing files that contain viruses or other malicious code. These files are often named to match a desired file. Corrupted files are also put out in the network so when a client downloads the file, it is not valid. This sometimes happens with copyrighted material in an effort to slow down file sharing.

A common misconception about peer-to-peer networks is that they are only used to share music. In fact, they share all files within the directories the user specifies to be shared. A user could share the contents of his entire hard drive. This can lead to accidental sharing of files that the user did not intend to be shared.

Another problem with peer-to-peer networks is the perceived feeling of privacy when in fact the users of peer-to-peer networks can be traced and some of their activity can be monitored. Even though the peer-to-peer network does not require authentication, the IP address of the user with the files to be shared needs to be known in order to transfer files from the user. Someone could do a search and, based on the results, transfer a file and determine the IP address of the computer that has the file. Also, when users issue a search, the search query goes through either a central index server or the neighbors in a decentralized network. It would be possible to capture the search strings, but not possible (unless you are part of the file transfer) to determine if a file was transferred as the result of a search. However, the search data could be used tell what someone is looking for, which could be embarrassing to the user.

11.3.4.3   Traffic-Based Attacks

Peer-to-peer networks can generate large amounts of traffic either because they encourage large file transfers or because the protocol itself generates a large number of packets. The decentralized protocols like Gnutella route traffic through the clients, which means that even if a client is not transferring files there can still be a large amount of traffic. Any devices that have large files offered for sharing can also create traffic problems. Super nodes and index servers can also generate a larger amount of traffic without transferring files.

Sniffing of the traffic is possible in most peer-to-peer networks. This is not much of a problem since the applications are not authenticated. Some peer-to-peer networks use encryption, but this is used to help prevent any countermeasures from examining the data.

11.3.4.4   Peer-to-Peer Countermeasures

Many of the peer-to-peer protocols have been designed to avoid detection and evade normal countermeasures. Network-based peer-to-peer countermeasures need to examine the TCP payload to determine if the TCP connection is being used to transport peer-to-peer traffic. There are two types of devices on the market designed to detect and mitigate the effects of peer-to-peer networks: an inline device and a passive device. Both types need to examine the payload and take action based on the packet exchange. The action can be to block, log, or in some cases reduce the bandwidth of the offending traffic.

An inline device will operate at the physical network layer, and therefore does not need to be configured like a router. There are routers that can also provide peer-to-peer detection and mitigation. A passive device sniffs the traffic and uses the TCP reset packet to terminate the connection, as described in Chapter 7. The advantage of the passive device is that there is no latency. Another aspect of the countermeasure is to limit the bandwidth of the peer-to-peer protocols. This is best done with the inline device and involves manipulating the TCP window size. Bandwidth reduction only mitigates the traffic-based vulnerabilities of peer-to-peer protocols, since the protocol is still allowed to function.

Definitions

Central index server (super node).

The server that supports a centralized P2P network.

Centralized P2P network.

A P2P network where each user connects with a central server. The central server keeps an index of the files each user is sharing. Users send search requests to the server and tell the requester which user has the file.

Decentralized P2P network.

A P2P network where each user connects to several neighbors to create a large network of interconnected users. Searches are propagated from computer to computer through the network. The identity of the computer with the file is returned to the requester. The requester can then get the file directly from the source.

Peer-to-peer (P2P) network.

An application that allows a group of users to connect with each other for the purpose of searching for files and exchanging files.

Ultrapeer.

A computer in the Gnutella P2P network that supports a large number of clients. This speeds up the searches.

11.4   General Countermeasures

As we saw in the discussion concerning vulnerabilities with both remote access protocols and file transfer protocols, the two biggest issues were authentication and clear text data transfer. In this section we will examine several protocols that can help mitigate these issues.

11.4.1   Encrypted Remote Access

When we look at the two most common issues (authentication and clear text), an obvious solution comes to mind, which is to encrypt the traffic and use encryption keys to help verify authenticity of the hosts. There are several methods to provide encrypted traffic, including encryption at the lower layers. For example, wireless networks support encrypted traffic. The most complex issue with network encryption is key distribution and key authentication. Appendix A provides an overview of data encryption and key distribution.

There are several methods commonly used to provide data encryption of remote access protocols. These methods can be grouped into two categories: application-based encryption and tunnel-based encryption. Application-based encryption is where the application protocol includes the encryption functionality. For example, this would include secure TELNET. Tunnel-based encryption uses a software wedge (and sometimes hardware to support the tunnel) to create an encrypted tunnel where the application can function without alteration. Transport Layer Security/Secure Sockets Layer (TLS/SSL) is an example of tunnel-based encryption at the transport layer, and virtual private networks (VPNs) are an example of tunnel-based encryption at the IP layer. Figure 11.17 shows the difference between the two methods.

Both methods provide encrypted traffic across the network. The tunnel-based method can handle multiple application types. It is also possible to combine the two methods. For example, an application with built-in encryption can connect to a tunnel-based layer as long as it understands the protocol.

All of the protocols have several common features that are outlined in Figure 11.18. Protocols start out with a protocol identification and key negotiation phase. This is followed by an optional user authentication phase where the application may require the user to authenticate his or her identity. This is followed by the data transfer phase and then session termination phase. There are some protocols that might change the keys during the data transfer phase. Typically the key negotiation phase consists of two parts, where the two sides

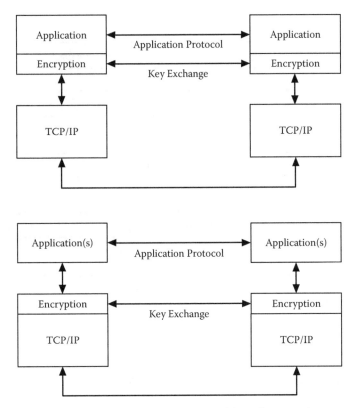

Figure 11.17: Application-based versus tunnel-based encryption.

use a shared secret to negotiate a one-time session key that is used for the data transfer.

In the next couple of sections we will examine a few protocols that are in common use today. These protocols are either replacements or enhancements for the remote access protocols described in this chapter.

11.4.2 SSH

Secure Shell (SSH) is an open source protocol that supports machine authentication and encrypted traffic [84–90]. With clients and servers available for most operating systems, SSH has become a de facto standard for secure remote access. SSH is modeled after the rlogin remote access protocol in that it does very little translation of data. Any data translation is left up to the client and server. SSH can also support tunneling of other protocols, including X-Windows. In this section we will examine how SSH functions and look at a few vulnerabilities that exist.

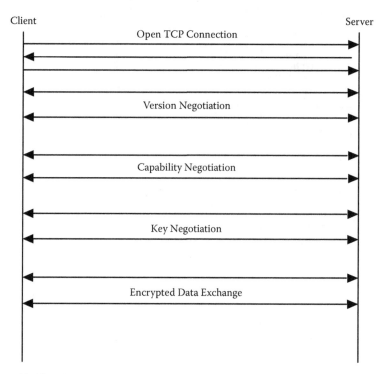

Figure 11.18:   Encrypted remote access protocols.

SSH is designed to use both public and symmetric key encryption (see Appendix A for a description of encryption methods). The public key encryption is used to authenticate the SSH server, and the symmetric key is used to encrypt the data transfer. Figure 11.19 shows the protocol exchange for an SSH session. Note that the exact packet format and data payload value are not shown or discussed. This exploration is left up to the reader as a set of lab experiments included at the end of this chapter.

In Figure 11.19 the server starts by announcing its version, and the client responds. Then the server and client exchange capabilities and preferences. The client and server negotiate a session key based on the key exchange preferences. The session key is used to encrypt the traffic exchange between the client and server. Once the client and server have negotiated a session key, the user can be authenticated. The application authentication is handled outside the SSH protocol and is treated as data by SSH.

SSH supports server machine authentication by using the server's public key as an identifier. When a client makes contact with a server, it checks to see if

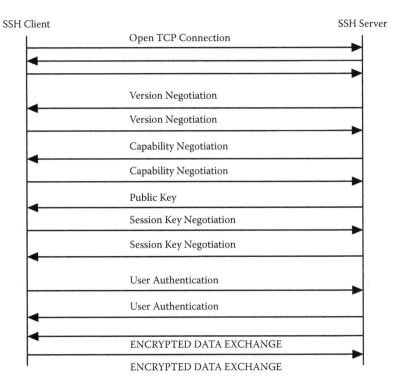

Figure 11.19:   SSH protocol exchange.

the server's public key is known to the client. If it is the first time the client is connecting to the server, the user will be prompted to verify the server public key. Once the server public key has been verified, the next time the client connects to that server the advertised public key will be compared to the public key stored on the client, and if they match, the client finishes the key exchange. If the transmitted server public key does not match the server public key stored on the client, then the client does not connect. This can lead to a problem if the server public key changes. The server public key can change if the server is upgraded or the server suffers a system crash and must be rebuilt. The user then needs to clear the old server public key so the client software thinks that it is talking to the server for the first time and stores the new key for the server.

The biggest weakness in SSH is a man-in-the-middle attack. This type of attack is complex to carry out since it requires convincing the client that the attacker is the server. This can be done with DNS or ARP poisoning. However, if the client has connected with the server before the attack, the attacker's public key

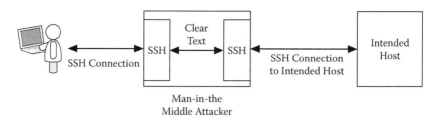

Figure 11.20: SSH man-in-the-middle attack.

would not match the stored public key of the server and the connection would be rejected. If the attacker manages to fool the client user, then the attacker just needs to open an SSH connection with the intended server and pass all traffic from the user to the intended server. As the traffic passes through the attacker, it would be in clear text. Figure 11.20 illustrates a successful man-in-the-middle attack.

11.4.3　Remote Desktop

Remote Desktop (RDP) is a protocol and application used by Microsoft to enable clients to connect to Microsoft Windows–based servers [91–93]. This can be thought of as X-Windows for Microsoft. For the purpose of this book, we are not going to examine the protocol in detail, nor will we look at the features supported by the applications. Unlike X-Windows, Remote Desktop supports encryption and user authentication. The original versions of Remote Desktop use the encryption that is part of the RDP protocol, which is modeled after the T.120 set of protocols. The RDP protocol uses a symmetric key encryption algorithm (RC4) for the one-time session key. The one-time session key is exchanged after the client and server exchange public keys. This exchange is very similar to the method used by SSH. The RDP protocol supports three RC4 key sizes that correspond to three different security levels:

High-level security: Uses a 128-bit key to encrypt the data in both directions.

Medium-level security: Uses a 56-bit key (or 40-bit, depending on the Operating System (O.S.) version of the client) to encrypt the data in both directions.

Low-level security: Uses a 56-bit (or 40-bit) key to encrypt the data from the client to the server.

Remote Desktop is vulnerable to session key decoding if the security level is low or medium. Even with high-level security it might be possible to guess the key. In order to guess the session key, the attacker needs to be able to capture the network traffic in an open wireless environment. The low-level security is really only used to protect the password, since all data from the server to the client is in clear text.

Newer versions of Remote Desktop can use TLS to provide data encryption. This provides a more secure connection between the client and the server. Remote Desktop is vulnerable to a man-in-the-middle attack, just like SSH, and as with the man-in-the-middle attacks against SSH, it takes several things to happen at once for the man-in-the-middle attacks on RDP to be successful.

11.4.4 Secure File Transfer (SFTP, FTPS, HTTPS)

There are several protocols that have been designed to replace FTP for encrypted file transfer. These protocols are designed to protect the authentication exchange and the data transfer from eavesdropping. Most of these protocols build on either SSH or SSL encryption protocols. In this section we will briefly examine the most common secure file protocols by looking at what underlying secure data transfer protocol they use and how they differ from each other.

SSH File Transfer Protocol (SFTP) is an FTP-like client and server in that it supports the same types of commands and functions that are supported by FTP. SFTP uses the SSH protocol to encrypt both the command channel and the data channel. SFTP is not simply FTP operating over an SSH tunnel, but a new protocol that is based on the SSH protocol. SFTP requires both a client and server that understand the protocol. SFTP has clients and servers available for most operating systems. The SFTP protocol is vulnerable to a man-in-the-middle attack, but this attack would be even more difficult to carry out than an SSH man-in-the-middle attack since the protocol is much more complex. A man-in-the-middle attack on SFTP would work best to obtain usernames and passwords.

File Transfer Protocol/SSC (FTPS) is a secure version of the FTP protocol that uses the SSL/TLS secure transport layer protocols. FTPS is an enhancement to the standard FTP protocol and, using the secure features, is something that can be negotiated during the initial connection phase using the AUTH TLS command. The FTPS server waits on port 21 like the standard FTP server and can operate like a standard FTP server. SSL and TLS were described earlier in the book, and therefore we will not reexamine them now.

HTTP over SSL (HTTPS) is another method used for secure file transfer. This happens through a secure web site when you click on a link that contains a file. The file is transferred over the secure connection. The reader is directed to Chapter 10 on the web to understand how HTTPS works and its vulnerabilities.

Homework Problems and Lab Experiments

Homework Problems

1. Research the RFCs associated with TELNET and comment on the changes in the protocol over the years.

2. Research the RFCs associated with the security extensions of TELNET.

3. Comment on the security of running a TELNET server on a host.

4. Comment on the security of running or using the TELNET client.

5. Show the packet exchange for a user to log in to a TELNET server using the username "bob" and the password "alice." Compute the overhead involved during the exchange (total number of bytes in the packets versus the actual payload).

6. Show the packet exchange for a user to log in to an rlogin server using the username "bob" and the password "alice." Compute the overhead involved during the exchange (total number of bytes in the packets versus the actual payload).

7. Research the RFCs associated with the FTP protocol.

8. Research the Secure Copy Protocols (SCPs).

9. Research different peer-to-peer applications. Develop a table showing the different protocols used versus the actual application names. Provide comments on each protocol type as to how hard it would be to detect the protocol.

10. Research the legal battles between the copyright holders and the various companies and groups that create peer-to-peer software.

11. Research several P2P filtering products and determine how they operate. Compare P2P filtering products with bandwidth shaping products.

12. Research the SSH protocol and the attacks against it. Comment on the likelihood of the various attacks being successful.

13. Research the RFCs associated with the two versions of secure FTP (FTPS, SFTP). Comment on the differences between the two protocols. Why do you think there are two protocols?

Lab Experiments

1. Use TELNET to connect to various applications (web, FTP, email, rlogin, etc.). Comment on how attackers could use what they find by using TELNET to connect to each application.

2. Use tcpdump or wireshark to capture a TELNET session between two machines in the lab. Issue several commands to generate traffic.

    a. Look at the network capture and find the username and password.

    b. Look for the command and the results of the commands in the network traffic.

    c. Comment on what you see.

3. Use tcpdump or wireshark to capture an rlogin session between two machines in the lab. Issue several commands to generate traffic.

    a. Look at the network capture and find the username and password.

    b. Look for the command and the results of the commands in the network traffic.

    c. Comment on what you see.

4. Use tcpdump or wireshark to capture an FTP session between two machines in the lab. Issue several commands to generate traffic.

    a. Look at the network capture and find the username and password.

    b. Look for the command and the results of the commands in the network traffic.

    c. Comment on what you see.

5. Use tcpdump or wireshark to capture an X-Windows session between two machines in the lab. Issue several commands to generate traffic.

   a. Look for the command and the results of the commands in the network traffic.

   b. Comment on what you see.

6. Use tcpdump or wireshark to capture a SSH session between two machines in the lab. Issue several commands to generate traffic.

   a. Look at the network capture and find the clear text parts of the session.

   b. Comment on the protocol exchange and the overhead involved in both initial connection and the data transfer.

7. Use tcpdump or wireshark to capture a Remote Desktop session between two machines in the lab. Issue several commands to generate traffic.

   a. Look at the network capture and find the clear text parts of the session.

   b. Comment on the protocol exchange and the overhead involved in both initial connection and the data transfer.

8. Use tcpdump or wireshark to capture peer-to-peer traffic in the test lab.

   a. Look at the network capture and find the clear text parts of the session.

   b. Comment on the protocol exchange and the overhead involved in both initial connection and the data transfer.

Programming Problems

1. Use the code you downloaded for Chapter 5 and modified in Chapters 6, 9, and 10. Add code to perform the following:

   a. Add a flag to the program (-p) that will disable printing of all header information and will only look for usernames and passwords in the FTP and TELNET protocols.

   b. Modify the program to print usernames and passwords it finds along with the IP address of the machines.

   c. Use the program to search for usernames and passwords on the network.

   d. Comment on how this program could be used and how it could be placed on a network.

   e. Comment on any possible countermeasures for this program.

2. Use the code you downloaded for Chapter 5 and modified in Chapters 6, 9, and 10, and in programming problem 1. Add code to perform the following:

   a. Decode and print TELNET and FTP payload. Print the payload in ASCII.

   b. Add to the set of counters a counter for the number of TELNET packets and the number of FTP packets. Add code to print the values of these counters to the subroutine program_ending().

   c. Add to the set of counters a counter for the number of SSH packets and the number of X-Windows packets. Add code to print the values of these counters to the subroutine program_ending().

3. Use the code you downloaded for Chapter 5 and modified in Chapters 6, 9, and 10, and in programming problems 1 and 2. Add code to perform the following:

   a. Add a flag to the program (-s) that will disable printing of all header information and will only look for ASCII characters in the payload of all packets and will print the characters.

   b. Add to the set of counters a counter for the number of ASCII bytes found in the traffic. Add code to print the values of this counter to the subroutine program_ending(). This counter should be updated and printed independent of the value of the flag (-s).

   c. Add to the set of counters a counter for the number of total bytes found in the traffic. Add code to print the values of this counter to the subroutine program_ending(). This counter should be updated and printed independent of the value of the flag (-s).

References

[1] Page, J. 1986. Kermit: A file-transfer protocol. *Accounting Review* 61: 368–69.

[2] Walters, W. 1987. Implementing a campus-wide computer-based curriculum. In *Proceedings of the 15th Annual ACM SIGUCCS Conference on User Services*, Kansas City, MO: 465–68.

[3] Banks, M. A. 2000. *The modem reference*. Medford, NJ: Cyberage Books.

[4] Khare, R. 1998. Telnet: The mother of all (application) protocols. *IEEE Internet Computing* 2:88–91.

[5] Borman, D. 1994. *Telnet environment option interoperability issues.* RFC 1571.

[6] Altman, J., and T. Ts'o. 2000. *Telnet authentication option.* RFC 2941.

[7] Murphy, Jr., T., P. Rieth, and J. Stevens. 2000. *5250 Telnet enhancements.* RFC 2877.

[8] Hedrick, C. L. 1988. *Telnet remote flow control option.* RFC 1080.

[9] Postel, J., and J. K. Reynolds. 1983. *Telnet protocol specification.* RFC 0854.

[10] Leiner, B., et al. 1985. The DARPA Internet protocol suite. *IEEE Communications Magazine* 23:29–34.

[11] Tam, C. M. 1999. Use of the Internet to enhance construction communication: Total information transfer system. *International Journal of Project Management* 17:107–11.

[12] Day, J. 1980. Terminal protocols. *IEEE Transactions on Communications* 28:585–93.

[13] Cohen, D., and J. B. Postel. 1979. On protocol multiplexing. In *Proceedings of the Sixth Symposium on Data Communications*, Pacific Grove, CA: 75–81.

[14] Kantor, B. 1991. *BSD rlogin.* RFC 1282.

[15] Kantor, B. 1991. *BSD rlogin.* RFC 1258.

[16] Bahneman, L. 1994. The term protocol. *Linux Journal* 1994(8es).

[17] Stevens, W. R. 1994. *TCP/IP illustrated.* Reading, MA: Addison-Wesley Professional.

[18] Rogers, L. R. 1998. *Rlogin (1): The untold story.* NASA.

[19] Uppal, S. 1989. Performance analysis of a LAN based remote terminal protocol. In *Proceedings of the 14th Conference on Local Computer Networks*, Minneapolis, MN: 85–97.

[20] Stevens, W. R. 1995. *TCP/IP illustrated*. Vol. I, 223–27. Upper Saddle River, NJ: Addision Wesley Publishing Company.

[21] Scheifler, R. W., and J. Gettys. 1986. The X window system. *ACM Transactions on Graphics (TOG)* 5:79–109.

[22] Richardson, T., et al. 1994. Teleporting in an X window system environment. *IEEE Personal Communications Magazine* 1:6–12.

[23] Quercia, V., and T. O'Reilly. 1993. *X window system user's guide*. Sebastopol, CA: O'Reilly.

[24] Nye, A. 1995. *X protocol reference manual*. Sebastopol, CA: O'Reilly.

[25] McCormack, J., and P. Asente. 1988. An overview of the X toolkit. In *Proceedings of the 1st Annual ACM SIGGRAPH Symposium on User Interface Software*, 46–55.

[26] Scheifler, R. W., et al. 1990. *X-window system: The complete reference to XLIB, X protocol, ICCCM, XLFD: X version 11, release*.

[27] Postel, J., and J. Reynolds. 1985. *File transfer protocol (FTP)*. STD 9, RFC 959.

[28] Horowitz, M., and S. Lunt. 1997. *FTP security extensions*. RFC 2228.

[29] Bellovin, S. 1994. *Firewall-friendly FTP*. RFC 1579.

[30] Bhushan, A. K. 1973. *FTP comments and response to RFC 430*. RFC 0463.

[31] Bhushan, A., et al. 1971. *The file transfer protocol*. RFC 0172.

[32] Neigus, N. 1973. *File transfer protocol*. RFC 0542.

[33] Sollins, K. 1992. *The TFTP protocol* (revision 2). RFC 1350.

[34] Emberson, A. 1997. *TFTP multicast option*. RFC 2090.

[35] Malkin, G., and A. Harkin. 1998. *TFTP option extension*. RFC 2347.

[36] Aslam, T., I. Krsul, and E. Spafford. 1996. Use of a taxonomy of security faults. Paper presented at the 19th National Information Systems Security Conference Proceedings, Baltimore.

[37] Stevens, W. R., and T. Narten. 1990. Unix network programming. *ACM SIGCOMM Computer Communication Review* 20:8–9.

[38] Stevens, W. R. 1994. *TCP/IP illustrated*. Vol. 1. *The protocols*, chap. 15. Reading, MA: Addison Wesley.

[39] Golle, P., K. Leyton-Brown, and I. Mironov. 2001. Incentives for sharing in peer-to-peer networks. *Electronic Commerce* 14:264–67.

[40] Tran, D. A., K. A. Hua, and T. T. Do. 2004. A peer-to-peer architecture for media streaming. *IEEE Journal on Selected Areas in Communications* 22:121–33.

[41] Androutsellis-Theotokis, S., and D. Spinellis. 2004. A survey of peer-to-peer content distribution technologies. *ACM Computing Surveys (CSUR)* 36:335–71.

[42] Androutsellis-Theotokis, S. 2002. A survey of peer-to-peer file sharing technologies. Athens University of Economics and Business.

[43] Ramaswamy, L., and L. Liu. 2003. Free riding: A new challenge to peer-to-peer file sharing systems. Paper presented at Proceedings of the Hawaii International Conference on Systems Science. Big Island, HI.

[44] Lui, S. M., and S. H. Kwok. 2002. Interoperability of peer-to-peer file sharing protocols. *ACM SIGecom Exchanges* 3:25–33.

[45] Gummadi, P. K., S. Saroiu, and S. D. Gribble. 2002. A measurement study of Napster and Gnutella as examples of peer-to-peer file sharing systems. *ACM SIGCOMM Computer Communication Review* 32:82.

[46] Daswani, N., H. Garcia-Molina, and B. Yang. 2003. Open problems in data-sharing peer-to-peer systems. In *Proceedings of the 9th International Conference on Database Theory*, Sienna, Italy: 1–15.

[47] Christin, N., A. S. Weigend, and J. Chuang. 2005. Content availability, pollution and poisoning in file sharing peer-to-peer networks. In *Proceedings of the 6th ACM Conference on Electronic Commerce*, San Diego, CA: 68–77.

[48] Yang, B., and H. Garcia-Molina. 2002. Improving search in peer-to-peer networks. In *Proceedings of the 22nd International Conference on Distributed Computing Systems*, Vienna, Austria: 5–14.

[49] Kant, K. 2003. An analytic model for peer to peer file sharing networks. In *IEEE International Conference on Communications (ICC'03)*, Anchorage, AK: 3.

[50] Saroiu, S., K. P. Gummadi, and S. D. Gribble. 2003. Measuring and analyzing the characteristics of Napster and Gnutella hosts. *Multimedia Systems* 9:170–84.

[51] Scarlata, V., B. N. Levine, and C. Shields. 2001. Responder anonymity and anonymous peer-to-peer file sharing. In *Ninth International Conference on Network Protocols*, Riverside, CA: 272–80.

[52] Aberer, K., and M. Hauswirth. 2002. An overview on peer-to-peer information systems. Paper presented at Workshop on Distributed Data and Structures (WDAS-2002). Paris, France.

[53] Moro, G., A. M. Ouksel, and C. Sartori. 2002. Agents and peer-to-peer computing: A promising combination of paradigms. In *Proceedings of the 1st International Workshop of Agents and Peer-to-Peer Computing (AP2PC2002)*, Bologna, Italy. 1–14.

[54] Howe, A. J. 2000. Napster and Gnutella: A comparison of two popular peer-to-peer protocols. Department of Computer Science, University of Victoria, British Columbia, Canada.

[55] Braione, P. 2002. A semantical and implementative comparison of file sharing peer-to-peer applications. In *Proceedings of the Second International Conference on Peer-to-Peer Computing (P2P 2002)*, Linköping, Sweden: 165–66.

[56] Fellows, G. 2004. Peer-to-peer networking issues—An overview. *Digital Investigation* 1:3–6.

[57] Tzanetakis, G., J. Gao, and P. Steenkiste. 2004. A scalable peer-to-peer system for music information retrieval. *Computer Music Journal* 28:24–33.

[58] Lam, C. K. M., and B. C. Y. Tan. 2001. The Internet is changing the music industry. *Communications of the ACM* 44:62–68.

[59] Leibowitz, N., M. Ripeanu, and A. Wierzbicki. 2003. Deconstructing the KaZaA network. In *Proceedings of the Third IEEE Workshop on Internet Applications (WIAPP 2003)*, San Jose, CA: 112–20.

[60] Liang, J., R. Kumar, and K. W. Ross. 2005. The KaZaA overlay: A measurement study. *Computer Networks Journal* 49(6).

[61] Good, N. S., and A. Krekelberg. 2003. Usability and privacy: A study of KaZaA P2P file-sharing. In *Proceedings of the SIGCHI Conference on Human Factors in Computing Systems*, Fort Lauderdale, FL: 137–44.

[62] Bleul, H., and E. P. Rathgeb. 2005. A simple, efficient and flexible approach to measure multi-protocol peer-to-peer traffic. Paper presented at IEEE International Conference on Networking (ICN'05). Reunion Island.

[63] Lowth, C. 2003. Securing your network against KaZaA. *Linux Journal* 2003(114).

[64] Shin, S., J. Jung, and H. Balakrishnan. 2006. Malware prevalence in the KaZaA file-sharing network. In *Proceedings of the 6th ACM SIGCOMM on Internet Measurement*, Rio De Janeiro, Brazil: 333–38.

[65] Sen, S., and J. Wang. 2004. Analyzing peer-to-peer traffic across large networks. *IEEE/ACM Transactions on Networking (TON)* 12:219–32.

[66] Balakrishnan, H., et al. 2003. Looking up data in P2P systems. *Communications of the ACM* 46:43–48.

[67] Liang, J., et al. 2005. Pollution in P2P file sharing systems. In *Proceedings of the 24th Annual Joint Conference of the IEEE Computer and Communications Societies (INFOCOM 2005)*, Miami, FL: 2.

[68] Karagiannis, T., A. Broido, and M. Faloutsos. 2004. Transport layer identification of P2P traffic. In *Proceedings of the 4th ACM SIGCOMM Conference on Internet Measurement*, Taormina, Italy: 121–34.

[69] Spognardi, A., A. Lucarelli, and R. Di Pietro. 2005. A methodology for P2P file-sharing traffic detection. In *Second International Workshop on Hot Topics in Peer-to-Peer Systems (HOT-P2P 2005)*, San Diego, CA: 52–61.

[70] Liang, J., N. Naoumov, and K. W. Ross. 2006. The index poisoning attack in P2P file-sharing systems. Paper presented at Infocom 2006. Barcelona, Spain.

[71] Ripeanu, M. 2001. Peer-to-peer architecture case study: Gnutella network. In *Proceedings of International Conference on Peer-to-Peer Computing*, Linköping, Sweden: 101.

[72] Zeinalipour-Yazti, D. 2002. Exploiting the security weaknesses of the Gnutella protocol. http://www.cs.ucr.edu/ncsyiazti/courses/cs260-2/project/gnutella.pdf, accessed August 23, 2008.

[73] Saroiu, S., P. K. Gummadi, and S. D. Gribble. 2002. A measurement study of peer-to-peer file sharing systems. Paper presented at Proceedings of Multimedia Computing and Networking. San Jose, CA.

[74] Kwok, S. H., and K. Y. Chan. 2004. An enhanced Gnutella P2P protocol: A search perspective. In *18th International Conference on Advanced Information Networking and Applications (AINA 2004)*, Fukuoha, Japan: 1.

[75] Aggarwal, V., et al. 2004. Methodology for estimating network distances of Gnutella neighbors. Paper presented at GI Informatik—Workshop on P2P Systems. Ulm, Germany.

[76] Karagiannis, T., et al. 2004. Is P2P dying or just hiding? Paper presented at IEEE Globecom. Dallas, TX.

[77] Klingberg, T., and R. Manfredi. 2002. *The Gnutella protocol specification v0. 6*. Technical specification.

[78] Matei, R., A. Iamnitchi, and P. Foster. 2002. Mapping the Gnutella network. *IEEE Internet Computing* 6:50–57.

[79] Pouwelse, J. A., et al. 2004. *A measurement study of the BitTorrent peer-to-peer file-sharing system.* Technical Report PDS-2004-007, Delft University of Technology Parallel and Distributed Systems Report Series.

[80] Pouwelse, J. A., et al. 2005. The BitTorrent P2P file-sharing system: Measurements and analysis. Paper presented at International Workshop on Peer-to-Peer Systems (IPTPS). Ithaca, NY.

[81] Yang, W., and N. Abu-Ghazaleh. 2005. GPS: A general peer-to-peer simulator and its use for modeling BitTorrent. In *Proceedings of the International Symposium on Modeling, Analysis, and Simulation of Computer and Telecommunication Systems (MASCOTS)*, Atlanta, GA: 425–32.

[82] Bharambe, A. R., C. Herley, and V. N. Padmanabhan. 2006. Analyzing and improving a BitTorrent network's performance mechanisms. Paper presented at Proceedings of IEEE INFOCOM. Barcelona.

[83] Guo, L., et al. 2005. Measurements, analysis, and modeling of BitTorrent-like systems. In *Internet Measurement Conference*, Berkeley, CA: 19–21.

[84] Davis, B. C., and T. Ylonen. 1997. Working group report on Internet/intranet security. In *Proceedings of the Sixth IEEE Workshop on Enabling Technologies: Infrastructure for Collaborative Enterprises*, Cambridge, MA: 305–8.

[85] Barrett, D. J., R. E. Silverman, and R. G. Byrnes. 2005. *SSH, the secure shell: The definitive guide.* Sebastopol, CA: O'Reilly Media.

[86] Miltchev, S., S. Ioannidis, and A. D. Keromytis. 2002. A study of the relative costs of network security protocols. In *Proceedings of the USENIX Annual Technical Conference, Freenix Track*, Monterey, CA: 41–48.

[87] Poll, E., and A. Schubert. 2007. Verifying an implementation of SSH. Paper presented at Workshop on Issues in the Theory of Security (WITS'07). Braga, Portugal.

[88] Song, D. X., D. Wagner, and X. Tian. 2001. Timing analysis of keystrokes and timing attacks on SSH. In *Proceedings of the 10th Conference on USENIX Security Symposium*, Vol. 10, Washington, DC: 25

[89] Jurjens, J. 2005. Understanding security goals provided by crypto-protocol implementations. In *Proceedings of the 21st IEEE International Conference on Software Maintenance (ICSM '05)*, Budapest, Hungary: 643–46.

[90] Vaudenay, S. 2005. A *classical introduction to cryptography: Applications for communications security*. New York, NY: Springer.

[91] Longzheng, C., Y. Shengsheng, and Z. Jing-li. 2004. Research and implementation of remote desktop protocol service over SSL VPN. In *Proceedings of the IEEE International Conference on Services Computing (SCC 2004)*, Shanghai, China: 502–5.

[92] Tsai, P. L., C. L. Lei, and W. Y. Wang. 2004. A remote control scheme for ubiquitous personal computing. In *2004 IEEE International Conference on Networking, Sensing and Control*, Taipei, Taiwan: 2.

[93] Miller, K., and M. Pegah. 2007. Virtualization: Virtually at the desktop. In *Proceedings of the 35th Annual ACM SIGUCCS Conference on User Services*, Portland, OR: 255–60.

Part IV

Network-Based Mitigation

426

In Part IV we will examine several network-based devices that are used to mitigate or detect attacks contained in network traffic. We will not go into detail as to how these devices operate, but instead provide an overview of the common types of devices and their functions. Network-based mitigation methods are only part of an overall security defense system. As their name implies, these devices work best against network-based attacks.

Chapter 12

Common Network Security Devices

In Chapter 12 we will examine three different types of devices. The first, a firewall, is designed to only allow good traffic into a network. The next type, intrusion detection, is designed to examine the network traffic to determine if the traffic is an attack. The last type, data loss prevention, is designed to stop sensitive or private data from leaving a network. All three of these devices are designed to be deployed on the network at or near the connection to the Internet and may be integrated with other network devices like routers.

12.1   Network Firewalls

A network firewall is designed to examine each packet and decide if the packet should be allowed into the network or should be blocked [1–13]. There are several different types of network firewalls based on the layer at which they operate. By this we mean the layer at which the firewall appears to the network (e.g., router or application) and not the layer header information that is used to determine if the packet is blocked. Network firewalls are common in devices like wireless routers. Figure 12.1 shows the general concept behind a network firewall.

Figure 12.1 shows a network firewall with two network interfaces. Every packet that arrives on the inbound interface is compared against a set of rules by the rule engine. If the inbound packet matches the allowed criteria in the rule set, the packet is passed to the internal network. It should be noted that there are many different configurations of firewalls beyond the types discussed here; however, the basic concepts are the same. The rule engine uses the protocol headers and, in some cases, the payload to make the filtering decision.

There are two general types of rules that are used by the rule engine (stateless and stateful). A stateless rule is applied to each packet independent of any other packet. Typically items like port numbers and IP addresses are used in stateless

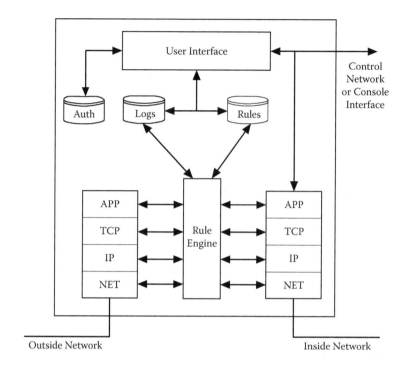

Figure 12.1: Network firewall.

rules. For example, a rule to block all UDP ports but port 53 (DNS) would be a stateless rule. A stateful rule uses multiple packets to determine if the packet should be blocked or allowed. For example, a rule that blocks all incoming DNS packets on port 53 unless there is a pending outbound DNS request pending is a stateful rule. Stateful rules are more complex to implement and configure, but do provide more control over which packets enter the network. Most firewalls implement a combination of both types of rules.

Figure 12.1 also shows a user interface that provides access to the firewall configuration mechanism. The configuration mechanism is accessed through either the inside network, a separate network interface, or a directly connected console. The network-based user interface is often web based and provides a method to update the rules and access log files produced by the firewall. Access to the firewall configuration mechanism through the user interface is often password protected. Most organizations configure their firewalls to be managed from the inside interface. A common mistake users make is to allow their firewall to be managed from the outside interface. Often this occurs with a wireless router. Some organizations

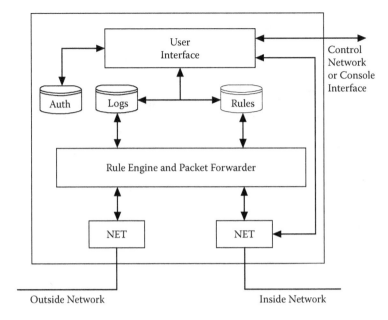

Figure 12.2:   Transparent firewall.

will install a separate network that is used to manage all network and security devices. The separate network is typically separated from the Internet by a NAT or firewall.

In this section we will examine four different types of network firewalls. Each of these types are available in the public domain and can be installed on a standard personal computer with two network cards. These firewalls are also available from many different security and network vendors. Figure 12.2 shows a firewall that operates at the physical network layer and is often referred to as a transparent firewall.

A transparent firewall is one that does not appear on the network as a router, NAT, or application. Figure 12.2 shows a firewall with two network interfaces configured to sniff traffic. As far as the network and the devices on the network are concerned, a transparent firewall does not exist on the network. The transparent firewall rules engine examines all parts of the packet to determine if the packet should be allowed based on the rules. If the packet is allowed, it is forwarded to the other interface. Typically a transparent firewall rule set consists of blocking rules and the default case to the forward traffic. The advantage of a transparent firewall is that there is no need to change the network configuration to deploy the firewall. Transparent firewalls could be deployed throughout an organization to help restrict

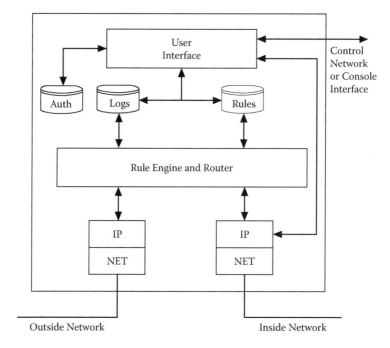

Figure 12.3:   Filtering router.

access to internal resources from internal users. A transparent firewall typically implements stateless rules and simple stateful rules because it cannot slow down the traffic flow and does not have much time to process the packets. Another method to implement a transparent firewall is to use one network interface. This type of transparent firewall works on Transmission Control Protocol (TCP) traffic by using TCP reset packets to block unwanted application protocols.

The next type of firewall is often called a filtering or screening router and is shown in Figure 12.3. A filtering router works like a normal router, except it uses a rule engine to determine if the traffic should be filtered. Typically a filtering router allows traffic to pass, and the rule set consists primarily of blocking rules. The rule set is typically stateless since routers are already a traffic bottleneck. Most routers have rule engines that allow them to filter traffic based on protocol type, IP addresses, and port numbers. We discussed this concept earlier in the book when we talked about blocking Internet Control Messaging Protocol (ICMP) echo request traffic as a mitigation technique. A filtering router is often implemented in the router connected to the Internet.

The third type of firewall is embedded into a NAT. The internal configuration is the same as a filtering router, except the rule engine and router are replaced

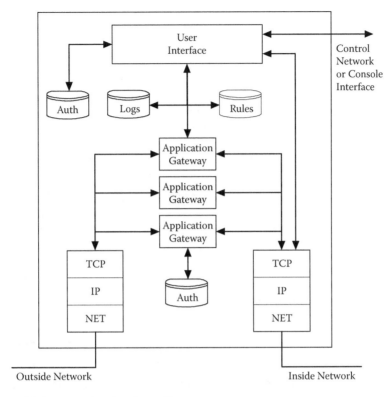

Figure 12.4:   Application firewall.

with a rule engine and NAT. As we already discussed, a NAT by default stops all incoming traffic unless there is a tunnel. This makes a fairly effective firewall. The difference between a pure NAT and a combination firewall NAT is that the firewall NAT will use the rule engine to further restrict traffic. A standard NAT uses the IP address and port numbers to determine how to handle the traffic.

The last type of firewall is called an application firewall. Figure 12.4 shows a typical application firewall. An application firewall uses application gateways that allow a user to connect with the gateway running on the firewall, and then uses the application gateway to connect to the internal application. The application gateways may require the user to provide authentication before using the application gateway. The authentication process on the firewall is separate from the authentication process on the final application. An application firewall is very restrictive and is not transparent to the user. A typical application firewall supports tunneling like a NAT in combination with simple firewall rules.

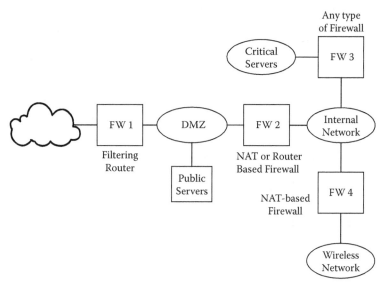

Figure 12.5:   Firewall deployment.

One other issue with a firewall is placement within the network. We mentioned earlier that a firewall is typically placed between the organization and the Internet. Figure 12.5 shows several common places to deploy a firewall. It should be noted there are many different topologies that can be used to deploy firewalls, depending on the organization's access and security requirements.

As we see in Figure 12.5, firewall FW1 is a filtering router that is part of the router that connects the organization to the Internet. Behind the filtering router is a network called the DMZ. This network contains servers that are accessed by users in the Internet, like the public web server and email server. The idea behind a DMZ is that users get full access to the network from the Internet, and that the servers placed in the DMZ are under attack. The DMZ is separated from the organization's internal network through another firewall (FW2). This firewall is typically a NAT or router-based firewall. This firewall has more restrictive rules than firewall FW1. Often the only rules in firewall FW2 are to allow inbound traffic from the public servers on a limited number of ports.

Most organizations will implement a DMZ. The figure shows two additional firewalls placed inside the organization. Firewall FW3 is placed to protect critical servers within the organization. Any type of firewall works to protect the internal servers and depends on the type of access that is required for users to access the servers. Firewall FW4 is used to protect the internal network from the wireless network and is implemented as part of the wireless router.

Definitions

Application-based firewall.

A firewall that implements application gateways and often requires user authentication to access the gateway.

DMZ.

A network between two firewalls where public servers are placed.

Filtering router.

A router that uses a rule engine to determine which packets should be routed and which packets should be dropped.

Firewall rule engine.

A process that examines each packet and compares the contents of the packet to a set of rules to determine if the packet should be passed on or dropped.

NAT-based firewall.

A NAT that uses a rule engine to determine which packets to allow or drop.

Stateful rule set.

A set of firewall rules that are applied to each packet based on previous packets.

Stateless rule set.

A set of firewall rules that are applied to each packet independently of any other packet.

Transparent firewall.

A firewall that is transparent to other devices on the network. It operates by sniffing the traffic on the network and passing acceptable traffic on to the other interface.

12.2 Network-Based Intrusion Detection and Prevention

Network-based intrusion detection (IDS) is based on the concept of watching the network for traffic patterns that might indicate an attack. A network-based IDS logs traffic that matches entries in the rule set that indicates an attack. An intrusion prevention device is like an IDS, except it can block traffic that matches an attack rule [14–35]. Just like firewalls, there are several public domain intrusion detection/prevention programs that can be installed on a standard PC platform. Several network security vendors also sell intrusion detection and prevention devices. Figure 12.6 shows a typical intrusion detection/prevention device.

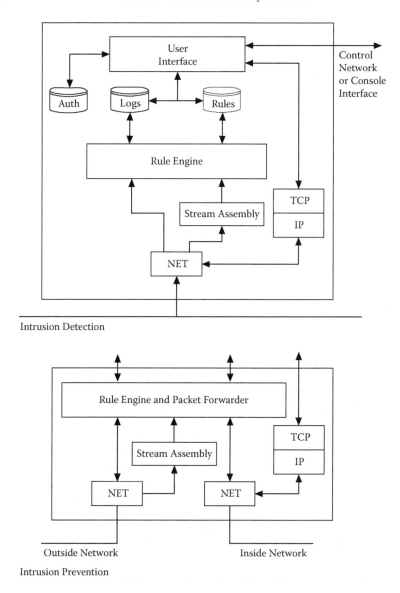

Figure 12.6: Network-based intrusion detection/prevention device.

As we see in Figure 12.6, an intrusion detection device has one network interface that sniffs traffic, which is processed by a rule engine. Since some of the attacks are contained in the TCP payload, the IDS also needs to assemble the TCP stream, which may be contained in multiple packets. The rule engine compares each packet or packet stream to the set of rules to determine if there is an attack.

The rules are divided into two types (signature based and anomaly based). Signature-based uses a set of rules that match data patterns in the packets. For example, a certain string of characters may represent a web-based attack. The rule would consist of the attack string and the port number (80). When the rule engine sees the string in a packet stream destined for port 80, it flags that traffic as a possible attack. With an anomaly-based rule set the rule engine looks for traffic that is not normal for that network. For example, an excess of a certain type of traffic could indicate an attack. The most common type of IDS is signature based, with a few anomaly-based rules.

The primary difference between an IDS and an intrusion prevention system (IPS) is that an IPS typically has two network interfaces and is often configured like a transparent firewall. The IPS uses the rule engine to block traffic that matches the rule set.

There are two issues that make the use of intrusion detection/prevention devices complicated. The first is how well they detect an attack. The rule set of an intrusion detection/prevention device can be complex and will not always correctly identify an attack. There are three possible outcomes from a rule engine. The first is that the rule engine correctly identifies the packet or packet stream as an attack or as normal traffic.

The second outcome is that the rule engine identifies the traffic as an attack when is it not. This is called a false positive. False positives can cause problems by filling up the log files and causing resources (people, time, etc.) to be spent on chasing nonattacks. For intrusion prevention devices false positives can cause the device to block good traffic. This is one reason many organizations do not widely deploy intrusion prevention devices, and if they do, they only enable blocking on a subset of the rules. Another type of false positive is when the device detects an attack, but the attack does not work on any of the devices within the organization. For example, the IDS might detect an attack against the TELNET protocol, but if the organization does not run any TELNET servers, the attack will not affect any devices. This type of false positive fills up the log files.

The third outcome is when the device does not detect an attack. This is called a false negative. False negatives cause obvious problems since the attack traffic goes unnoticed. Manufacturers of intrusion detection and prevention devices work to reduce the number of false positives and the number of false negatives; however, there is a trade-off between the two. Often when you decrease one, you increase the other.

The second issue is the placement of the intrusion detection/prevention device. Referring to Figure 12.7, an IDS/IPS could be deployed in several places. The

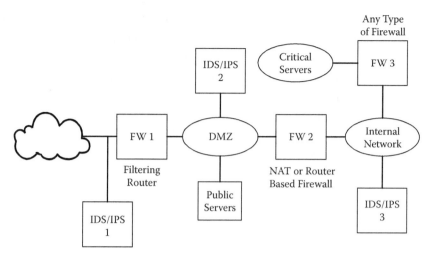

Figure 12.7:   IDS/IPS deployment.

first place is between the router and the Internet. Placing an IDS here will show there are a large number of attacks coming from the Internet. Since many of the attacks will not pass through the firewalls, the device logs attacks that do not need to be logged. The only reason to place an intrusion detection device here is to get a sense of the level of attack traffic targeting the organization to see if there are any trends.

Another place to deploy an intrusion detection device would be in the DMZ. This allows you to monitor attacks against the devices inside the DMZ as well as attacks against the internal network. You might also deploy an intrusion prevention device between the internal DMZ firewall and the internal network to stop any attacks that might get by the firewall. The final place to put an intrusion detection device is inside the internal network. This is to detect any attacks that get through the firewall and could be used to detect some internal attacks. An organization might also deploy an intrusion detection device near the critical servers.

Intrusion detection and prevention devices can be useful tools to detect attacks. However, many organizations soon realize these devices can generate a large amount of logs, and unless someone is dedicated to monitoring the devices, their data might be ignored. Another use for intrusion detection is to provide data after an attack. After an attack has been detected on a host, the IDS logs can be examined to see if any network attacks occurred that could have caused the attacks. This information could be used to help reconfigure the defenses to stop the attack in the future or figure out why the defenses failed.

> **Definitions**
>
> **False negative.**
> Marking traffic as good when it really contains an attack.
> **False positive.**
> Marking traffic as an attack when it is not.
> **Intrusion detection.**
> A device used to detect a network-based attack.
> **Intrusion prevention.**
> A device used to detect and block network-based attacks.

12.3 Network-Based Data Loss Prevention

All of the devices we have looked at in this chapter have focused on detecting and stopping attacks from entering the network. A new and growing market is for devices designed to keep confidential and private data (e.g., credit card numbers, social security numbers, and medical records) from leaving an organization. This new market is called data loss prevention (DLP). Figure 12.8 shows a typical configuration of a DLP device.

As we see in the figure, the device looks like an intrusion detection/prevention device. The primary differences are in the rule engine and the addition of proxy servers. The rule engine analyzes the payload of the TCP stream to determine if the content violates the data privacy policy.

There are several methods used to determine if the data is confidential or private. The data can be classified in two types (structured and unstructured). Structured data consists of data elements that can be matched from a list or follow a structured format like credit card numbers. Unstructured data are typically documents that contain private information like memos, letters, or other internal documents. Structured data can be detected using several different methods. Exact matches are where the DLP device has a list of private data elements and compares the network traffic against the list. It should be noted that most of the DLP devices store the hashes of the data elements and compute the hashes of the network traffic and compare the two hashes. Another method to classify structured data is by using regular expressions. Social security numbers often fit into this category since they can be represented in many different forms (e.g., with dashes, without dashes).

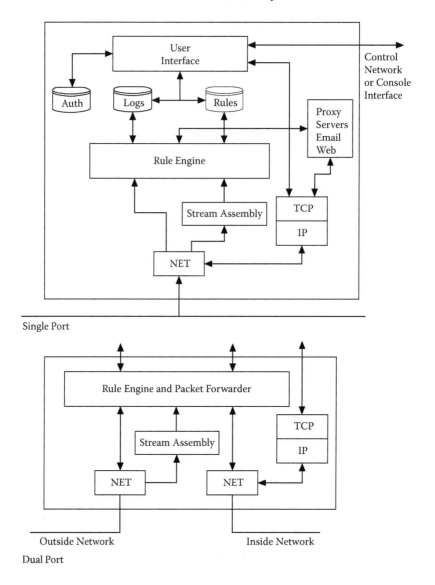

Figure 12.8: Network-based data loss prevention.

A method to handle unstructured documents is called fingerprinting. This method requires that the original documents are analyzed and fingerprints are created. A fingerprint is a hash of part of the document. The network traffic is fingerprinted, and the network fingerprints are compared against the list of fingerprints that were created from the original documents. Another method to handle unstructured documents is called lexical analysis. This method analyzes the traffic to see if a document matches a set of rules. For example, a medical record might contain medical terms and an id number and something that looks like a patient name. A combination of these items would cause the document to be classified as private.

There are several ways a DLP device handles private data once it detects it. There are some devices that are designed to capture all traffic on the network so an organization can show if there were any violations. These devices typically do not try to stop violations. Another type of device will try to stop violations. This can be difficult since the analysis can take a large amount of time. Many of these devices block violating traffic that is routed through a proxy. The two most common types of proxies are email and web. The email proxy just looks like an MTA. Once the DLP device has detected a violation, it can block it, or in the case of email, it might forward the message to the destination using encryption. This is common for data like social security numbers and credit card numbers. The DLP device may also hold the violating email message until an administrator releases it or deletes it.

Definitions

Data loss prevention (DLP).
A device designed to detect confidential or private data that is leaving a network. The DLP device may also block the violating traffic.

Homework Problems and Lab Experiments

Homework Problems

1. Research different commercial firewalls and public domain firewalls. Determine if there are any differences between the various firewalls. Why would someone use a commercial firewall?

2. Research different commercial IDS/IPS and public domain IDS/IPS. Determine if there are any differences between the various products. Why would someone use a commercial IDS/IPS?

3. Research the Snort IDS rules.

4. Make a case for using an IDS and where you would place the IDS within an organization.

5. Make a case for using an IPS and where you would place the IPS within an organization.

6. Research different methods proposed to create an anomaly-based IDS.

7. Research different data loss prevention (DLP) products. Build a table showing the differences between the various DLP products.

Lab Experiments

1. Use the firewall in the test lab. Try setting up rules to block or allow traffic.

2. Use the Snort IDS in the test lab. Look at the reports to see what types of attacks have been detected. If you have an IDS outside a firewall and one inside a firewall, compare the logs from the two.

References

[1] Lucas, M., A. Singh, and C. Cantrell. 2006. Firewall policies and VPN configurations. Rockland, MA: Syngress Media.

[2] Rowan, T. 2007. Application firewalls: Filling the void. *Network Security* 2007:4–7.

[3] Gouda, M. G., and A. X. Liu. 2007. Structured firewall design. *Computer Networks* 51:1106–20.

[4] Loh, Y. S., et al. 2006. Design and implementation of an XML firewall. In *2006 International Conference on Computational Intelligence and Security*, Guangzhou, China: 2.

[5] Jia, Z., S. Liu, and G. Wang. 2006. Research and design of NIDS based on Linux firewall. In *2006 1st International Symposium on Pervasive Computing and Applications*, Xinjiang, China: 556–60.

[6] Gawish, E. K., et al. 2006. Design and FPGA-implementation of a flexible text search-based spam-stopping firewall. Paper presented at Proceedings of the Twenty-Third National Radio Science Conference, Menout, Egypt. (NRSC 2006).

[7] Goldman, J. E. 2006. Firewall architectures. In *Handbook of information security*, Vol. III, Chapter 170.

[8] Goldman, J. E. 2006. Firewall Basics. In *Handbook of information security*, Vol. III, Chapter 169.

[9] Byrne, P. 2006. Application firewalls in a defense-in-depth design. *Network Security* 2006:9–11.

[10] Hamed, H., and E. Al-Shaer. 2006. Dynamic rule-ordering optimization for high-speed firewall filtering. In *Proceedings of the 2006 ACM Symposium on Information, Computer and Communications Security*, Taipei, Taiwan: 332–42.

[11] Zhou, C., Z. Dai, and L. Jiang. 2007. Research and implementation of complex firewall based on netfilter. *Jisuanji Celiang yu Kongzhi/Computer Measurement and Control* 15:790–91.

[12] Zhang, C. C., M. Winslett, and C. A. Gunter. 2007. On the safety and efficiency of firewall policy deployment. In *IEEE Symposium on Security and Privacy*, Oakland, CA: 33–50.

[13] Firewall, B. I. M. 2006. Product roundup. *Infosecurity Today* 3:12.

[14] Biermann, E., E. Cloete, and L. M. Venter. 2001. A comparison of intrusion detection systems. *Computers and Security* 20:676–83.

[15] Hegazy, I. M., et al. 2005. Evaluating how well agent-based IDS perform. *IEEE Potentials* 24:27–30.

[16] Bace, R., and P. Mell. 2001. *NIST special publication on intrusion detection systems.*

[17] Antonatos, S., et al. 2004. Performance analysis of content matching intrusion detection systems. In *Proceedings of the 2004 International Symposium on Applications and the Internet*, Tokyo, Japan: 208–15.

[18] Jansen, W. A. 2002. Intrusion detection with mobile agents. *Computer Communications* 25:1392–401.

[19] Cavusoglu, H., B. Mishra, and S. Raghunathan. 2005. The value of intrusion detection systems in information technology security architecture. *Information Systems Research* 16:28–46.

[20] Markatos, E. P., et al. 2002. Exclusion-based signature matching for intrusion detection. In *Proceedings of the IASTED International Conference on Communications and Computer Networks (CCN)*, Cambridge, MA: 146–52.

[21] Undercoffer, J., A. Joshi, and J. Pinkston. 2003. Modeling computer attacks: An ontology for intrusion detection. Paper presented at 6th International Symposium on Recent Advances in Intrusion Detection. Pittsburg, PA.

[22] Mell, P., D. Marks, and M. McLarnon. 2000. A denial-of-service resistant intrusion detection architecture. *Computer Networks* 34:641–58.

[23] Pillai, M. M., J. H. P. Eloff, and H. S. Venter. 2004. An approach to implement a network intrusion detection system using genetic algorithms. In *Proceedings of the 2004 Annual Research Conference of the South African Institute of Computer Scientists and Information Technologists on IT Research in Developing Countries*, Maputo, Mozambigue: 221.

[24] Charitakis, I., K. Anagnostakis, and E. Markatos. 2003. An active traffic splitter architecture for intrusion detection. In *11th IEEE/ACM International Symposium on Modeling, Analysis and Simulation of Computer Telecommunications Systems (MASCOTS 2003)*, Orlando, FL: 238–41.

[25] Axelsson, S. 1999. The base-rate fallacy and its implications for the difficulty of intrusion detection. In *Proceedings of the 6th ACM Conference on Computer and Communications Security*, Singapore: 1–7.

[26] Alpcan, T., and T. Basar. 2003. A game theoretic approach to decision and analysis in network intrusion detection. In *Proceedings of the 42nd IEEE Conference on Decision and Control*, Maui, HI: 3.

[27] Sequeira, D. 2003. Intrusion prevention systems: Security's silver bullet? *Business Communications Reviews* 33:36–41.

[28] Rash, M., and A. Orebaugh. 2005. *Intrusion prevention and active response: Deploying network and host IPs*. Syngress. Rockland, MA: Media.

[29] Mattsson, U. 2004. A practical implementation of a real-time intrusion prevention system for commercial enterprise databases. *Data Mining V: Data Mining, Text Mining and Their Business Applications*, 263–72.

[30] Zhang, X., C. Li, and W. Zheng. 2004. Intrusion prevention system design. In *Fourth International Conference on Computer and Information Technology (CIT '04)*, Wuhan, China: 386–90.

[31] Wilander, J., and M. Kamkar. 2002. A comparison of publicly available tools for static intrusion prevention. In *Proceedings of the 7th Nordic Workshop on Secure IT Systems*, Karlstad, Sweden: 68–84.

[32] Janakiraman, R. W., and M. Q. Zhang. 2003. Indra: A peer-to-peer approach to network intrusion detection and prevention. In *Proceedings of the Twelfth IEEE International Workshop on Enabling Technologies: Infrastructure for Collaborative Enterprises (WET ICE 2003)*, Linz, Austria: 226–31.

[33] Ierace, N., C. Urrutia, and R. Bassett. 2005. Intrusion prevention systems. *Ubiquity* 6:2.

[34] Fuchsberger, A. 2005. Intrusion detection systems and intrusion prevention systems. *Information Security Technical Report* 10:134–39.

[35] Schultz, E. 2004. Intrusion prevention. *Computers and Security* 23:265–66.

Appendix A

Cryptology

In this appendix we will examine the basic concepts behind three basic crypto-graphic methods often used in network security: hash functions, symmetric key encryption, and asymmetric key encryption [1–11]. A hash function is used to convert data into a fixed-length representation of the original data. Encryption is used to convert data into a format that can only be read by someone with secret knowledge. The goal of this appendix is to provide basic information the reader needs to understand the functions of the three concepts, and not the inner workings of the algorithms.

A.1   Hash Functions

A hash function is a one-way function that takes arbitrary length input and converts it to a fixed-length data element. The function is called a many-to-one function, which means there are many different input data sets that produce the same output value. A hash function is designed so that knowing the output cannot give you input. The size of the hash function output determines the number of possible hash values. The typical hash size is 16 bytes, which yields 2^{128} possible hash values (approximately 3.4×10^{38} values).

Hash functions have several uses in the context of network security. Hash functions are a common method for converting passwords into values that are stored in password files. Figure A.1 shows using the hash function to create and check passwords. The hash function is used to create the password that is stored in the password file. When the system needs to authenticate a user, the user provides his or her username (which is used to index the hash function in the password file) and the password. The user password is hashed and the value is compared with the value stored in the password file. Using the hash function allows the system to store the password value in a format that is not easily decoded. Typical methods of decoding the password entry require the use of a software program that takes password combinations and runs them through the hash function and compares the two hashes.

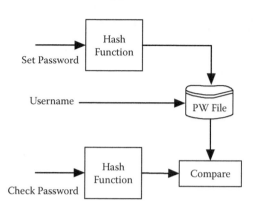

Figure A.1:   Using a hash functions for passwords.

Another use of the hash function is to show that data has not been modified, which is called a signature. Hash signatures are also used to uniquely identify a file when issuing a search for files. One issue with hash signatures is how to guarantee the hash signature has not been changed, and that the signature corresponds to the original file. One way is to publish the hash value along with the file. This method is typically used with files that are obtained from web sites. Open-source applications use this method to help ensure the software is valid. Another method to ensure the hash value has not been changed and belongs to a file is to encrypt it. This is called a digital signature and will be discussed in the section on asymmetric encryption.

A.2   Symmetric Key Encryption

Symmetric key encryption is a method where the secret key is known by everyone that needs to encrypt and decrypt the data. As shown in Figure A.2, the encryption and decryption algorithms are the same. When you apply the key to the original data, it is converted to cipher text. The cipher text is converted back to the original data by using the same key that was used to encrypt the data. There are numerous algorithms that provide symmetric key encryption. The differences between the various algorithms are the key size and the computation time of the algorithm.

There are several security-related issues that need to be considered with the use of symmetric key encryption. The first is key distribution. As we saw in Figure A.2, the sender and receiver of the message need to know the encryption

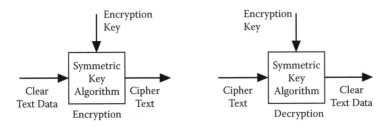

Figure A.2: Symmetric key encryption.

key. The symmetric key is called a shared secret. The strength of any system that uses symmetric key encryption is dependent on the methods used to share and protect the shared secret key. A common use of symmetric key encryption is to encrypt data between two applications. A new secret key is generated for each connection between the applications and is passed between applications using asymmetric key encryption.

Since we sometimes use encryption to prove the identity of an application, device, or person, we need to look at what it means to be able to encrypt and decrypt a message. In symmetric key encryption an encrypted message can only be decrypted by someone who knows the shared secret. Figure A.3 shows an example of using symmetric key encryption to help authenticate users. We see

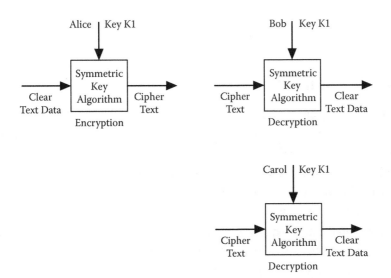

Figure A.3: Multiple key encryption.

that Alice encrypts a message using key K1 and sends that message. If Bob and Carol each know key K1, they can decrypt the message. The question is: What does this prove? Alice knows that only people that know K1 can open the message, and therefore must trust that Bob and Carol keep the key secure. Bob and Carol know that someone who knows key K1 created the message, which could be any of the three users. This shows the fundamental problem with symmetric key encryption. In order to ensure security between any pair of people, we need a separate key for each possible communication. In the example shown in Figure A.3 we would need three keys. This becomes very difficult to manage as the number of users increases. Asymmetric key encryption fixes this problem.

The next issue is the possibility of breaking the encryption. Basically, encryption is a mathematical function that uses the key to manipulate the data. The goal is to make the key large enough that it takes too long to try every possible combination. Unlike passwords, where the key size is short and restricted to printable characters, keys used in typical symmetric key systems are large and are not restricted to certain characters. Typical key sizes for symmetric key systems range from 128 bits (3.4×10^{38} possible keys) to 1,024 bits (1.7×10^{308} possible keys). This makes trying every possible combination almost impossible. Attackers often try to attack the key generation methods or the key distribution system instead of guessing all possible keys. There are methods to attack the encryption algorithms given enough data. These attacks are beyond the scope of this book.

A.3 Asymmetric Encryption

Asymmetric key encryption, often called public key encryption, uses two keys that are mathematically related. Figure A.4 shows the operation of asymmetric encryption. The figure shows two algorithms, one for encryption and one for decryption. One of the matched keys can be used to encrypt the data, and the other key is used to decrypt the data. The idea is to use one of the matched keys as a public key that is meant to be known by everyone. The other matched key is a private key that is to be kept secret. Figure A.5 shows how the public and private keys can be used to encrypt data between multiple applications. If Alice encrypts the data using her private key, then anyone that knows Alice's public key can read the message. In the figure, both Bob and Carol could decrypt the message, and they know that someone who knows Alice's private key created the message.

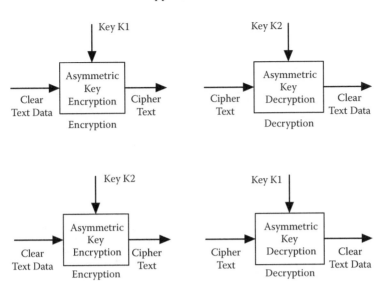

Figure A.4: Asymmetric key encryption.

If Alice wants to send an encrypted message to only Bob, she would encrypt the message using Bob's public key. Only someone that knows Bob's private key could open the message. One very important aspect of asymmetric key encryption is the security of the private key. The private key is often protected by encrypting it with symmetric key encryption. That way, in order for someone to use his private key he would need to know the password.

There are several ways that the asymmetric encryption method can be used. One way is to create a digital signature, as shown in Figure A.6. A digital signature is the hash of the data that has been encrypted using the private key of the sender. This encrypted hash is then sent with the original file. The receiver of the message uses the public key of the sender to open the encrypted hash, and then compares that value with the hash of the received data. If the two are equal, then the receiver knows the data was sent by someone who knows the private key of the sender. A question that comes to mind is: Why not just encrypt the message with the private key instead of encrypting the hash? One reason is that asymmetric encryption is much slower than symmetric key encryption. Another reason is that the goal may be to show that the data has not been changed. Once you decrypt the data, it could be modified. The digital signature can always be used to show the data has not been modified.

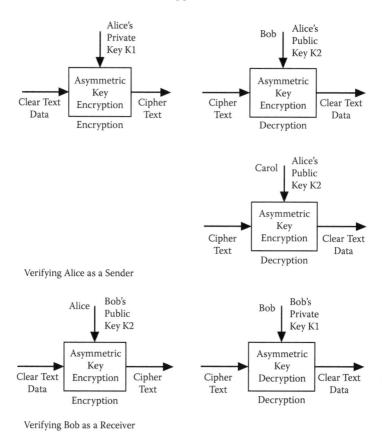

Figure A.5:   Using asymmetric key encryption.

Another use of asymmetric encryption is to exchange symmetric keys. Figure A.7 shows an example where symmetric keys are exchanged as part of the message using asymmetrical key encryption. The digital signature is created using Alice's private key and combined with the message. The message is then encrypted using a symmetric key that was randomly generated. The random key is encrypted using the public key of the receiver (Bob). The encrypted key is combined with the encrypted message. When Bob gets the message, he decrypts the symmetric key using his private key and then uses the symmetric key to decrypt the message. The digital signature would then be used to ensure the data was unaltered and was sent by the sender (Alice). In this example, Alice knows that only someone who knows Bob's private key could open the message, and Bob knows that only someone that knows Alice's private key could have sent the message.

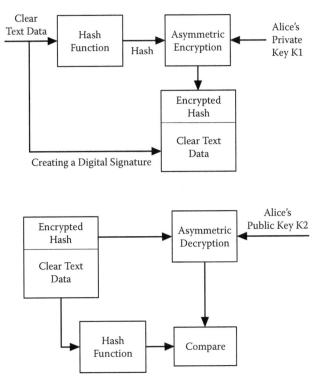

Figure A.6: Digital signature.

Figure A.8 shows how a symmetric key can be exchanged to use to encrypt network traffic. In this case, Alice picks a symmetric key (called a session key) and encrypts it using Bob's public key and sends it to Bob. Bob and Alice can now send data that is encrypted with the shared session key. The session key ensures that only someone who knows Bob's private key can read the network traffic. If Bob wants to make sure it is Alice, he can request that Alice send a message encrypted with her private key.

Definitions
Digital signature.
An encrypted hash of data that can be used to tell if the data has been altered and who sent the data.
Private key.
One half of a key pair that is kept secret by its owner.
Public key.
The other half of the public–private key pair that is known by others.

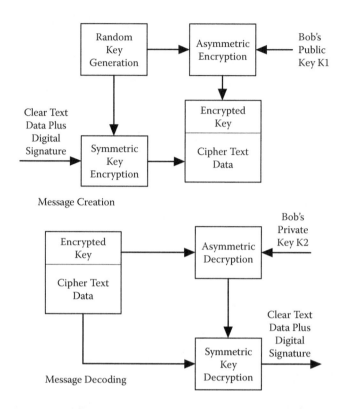

Figure A.7:   Message-based symmetric key distribution.

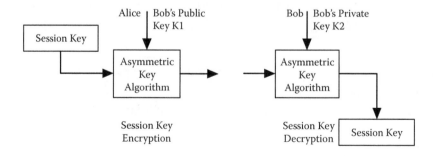

Figure A.8:   Network-based symmetric key exchange.

Homework Problems

1. Research the various symmetric key cryptographic algorithms. Build a table comparing the algorithms based on key size.

2. For each of the algorithms in problem 1, assume you can try a key once every microsecond, and, once every nanosecond, compute the time it would take to try every key. How fast would you have to try the keys to break the encryption in a month?

3. Research any weaknesses in commonly used cryptographic algorithms.

4. Research public key infrastructure (PKI) and comment on why there is not a single PKI system.

5. Research tools designed to break password encryption and network encryption (e.g., wireless encryption).

6. Using a web browser, look at the certificates used by the browser and determine the vendors that produced them.

References

[1] Stallings, W. 2006. *Cryptography and network security: Principles and practice*. Englewood Cliffs, NJ: Prentice Hall.

[2] Ferguson, N., and B. Schneier. 2003. *Practical cryptography*. New York: John Wiley & Sons.

[3] Enge, A. 1999. *Elliptic curves and their applications to cryptography: An introduction*. Norwell, MA: Kluwer Academic.

[4] Mollin, R. A. 2001. *An introduction to cryptography*. Boca Raton, FL: CRC Press.

[5] Cohen, H., G. Frey, and R. Avanzi. 2006. *Handbook of elliptic and hyperelliptic curve cryptography*. Boca Raton, FL: CRC Press.

[6] Dent, A. W., and C. J. Mitchell. 2005. *User's guide to cryptography and standards.* Boston: Artech House.

[7] Wayner, P. 2002. *Disappearing cryptography: Information hiding: Steganography and watermarking.* San Francisco, CA: Morgan Kaufmann.

[8] Oppliger, R. 2005. *Contemporary cryptography.* Boston: Artech House.

[9] van Tilborg, H. 2005. *Encyclopedia of cryptography and security.* New York, NY: Springer.

[10] Mollin, R. A. 2003. *RSA and public-key cryptography.* London: Chapman & Hall/CRC.

[11] Boneh, D. 2003. Advances in cryptology-crypto 2003. Paper presented at Proceedings of the 23rd Annual International Cryptology Conference, Santa Barbara, CA, August 17–21.

Appendix B

Laboratory Configuration

This appendix describes a small test laboratory that aids in the understanding of the concepts described throughout the book. The laboratory described is modeled after the laboratory used by the author to teach this topic. The laboratory supports about 100 students. The students access the laboratory remotely, which reduces the space required and the amount of overall computers. The laboratory could be modified to support students sitting in front of the equipment by adding additional computers. The next three sections describe the hardware configuration of the laboratory, the software configuration for the computers in the laboratory, and the issues with remote access. The final section of the appendix provides additional supporting materials that can be used to help with the use of the laboratory. The web site www.dougj.net has additional descriptions of the laboratory configuration and software requirements. The web site also contains scripts and configuration instructions to help set up and run the laboratory.

B.1 Hardware Configuration

The hardware configuration for the laboratory is shown in Figure B.1. This configuration supports the laboratory experiments and programming problems described in the book and will handle 50 to 100 students accessing the laboratory remotely. The hardware requirements of the laboratory are minimal. Figure B.1 shows the laboratory connected to the Internet using a router. It is helpful to have the laboratory on its own subnet; this makes it easier to talk about address ranges, helps keep unwanted traffic from entering the laboratory, and keeps users inside the laboratory from sniffing traffic that is not part of the laboratory. The router can be a commercial router or can be created using a UNIX-based PC with two network cards. Figure B.1 also shows an optional firewall or NAT between the laboratory and the outside network. The firewall/NAT can be combined with the PC-based router. If you want students to remotely access the laboratory, then you do not want to use a NAT. Tunneling through the NAT can be complex. The firewall is

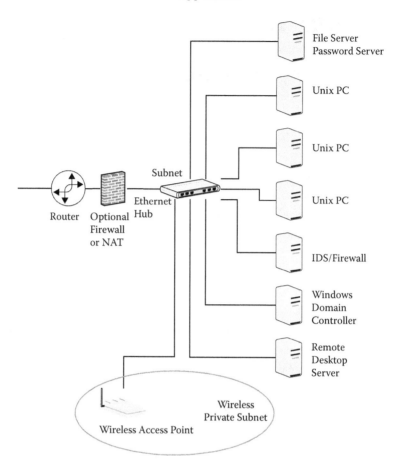

Figure B.1: Laboratory hardware configuration.

used to restrict outbound traffic that comes from network scans or other traffic that should stay off the main network. The computers in the lab are connected with an Ethernet hub. This allows the computer to sniff all of the traffic generated in the network. You can also install a wireless access point to create a second subnet. It is best to make the wireless subnet a private network by configuring the wireless router as a NAT. By then configuring the computers with wireless Ethernet in addition to the wired Ethernet, you can cause traffic to be generated on either network by picking the appropriate subnet.

The UNIX PCs in the lab can be basic computers. The disk requirements are minimal since all of the user file storage is located on the file server. The processor and memory requirements are based on the number of users per machine. The packet sniffer labs consume the most resources. The author created his lab using computers that the department replaced during a lab upgrade. The file server needs to have enough disk space to handle the number of students. The packet sniffer labs require a large amount of disk space to store the packet captures. Assume 2 gigabytes per user. The windows domain controller can also be a standard PC. The remote desktop computer is the most powerful computer in the lab, and depending on the number of students, you may need to set up a load-balancing server. The author uses two PCs with 2 GB of memory each to the remote desktop computer.

B.2   Software Configuration

The software configuration for the laboratory consists of primarily UNIX-based computers. The author uses FreeBSD. However, any version of UNIX will work. The web site has detailed information about software configurations for the various computers in the laboratory along with supporting programs that are used to create logins and support the packet sniffer programming assignments. The computers need to have the C programming environment installed. The IDS computer runs the Snort public domain IDS. You need to install a web server, an email server (sendmail, IMAP, and POP3), a TELNET server, and a File Transfer Protocol (FTP) server on at least one of the computers. (The same computer does not need to have all of the servers.) You could also install a Domain Name Service (DNS) server and put the addresses of the private wireless network in the server. This would allow students to look at DNS configuration files and sniff DNS traffic. The students do not have login access to the UNIX file server or to the domain controller.

B.3   Remote Access Issues

The author has implemented his version of the laboratory for remote access only. This allows the laboratory to be housed in a small room. The computers used are connected using a KVM so that only two monitors and keyboards are needed. Students use SSH and remote desktop to connect to the laboratory computers. There are some access issues that the author has encountered, so his lab supports both SSH and TELNET access. There have been cases when students have been unable to use SSH and have had to rely on TELNET. A student can use a Windows machine to access the laboratory without installing any additional software if he or she relies on TELNET and FTP. You can also install the X-Windows environment on the UNIX-based machines so students can use a graphical interface. This requires additional software on the computers the students use to access the laboratory.

B.4 Supporting Material

There are additional supporting materials on the web site. The following tables show the packet formats for TCP/IP and ARP. These tables are helpful for the sniffing programming assignments.

TCP/IP Packet Format (Carried in an Ethernet Packet)

Byte	Field	Comment	
1–6	DA	Ethernet destination address	Ethernet header
7–12	SA	Ethernet source address	Ethernet header
13–14	Type	Type field 0x800—IP 0x806 ARP	Ethernet header
15	Ver/IHL	Ver = 4 IHL = no. of 4-byte words in the header	IP
16	Type	Type of service (typically 0)	IP
17–18	T-len	Total length of packet in bytes, including IP header	IP
19–20	ID	Unique ID for packet	IP
21	Flags	3 bits 0 – DF – MF DF = 0 May fragment MF = 0 last fragment	IP
21–22	Offset	Fragment offset in 64-bit blocks	IP
23	TTL	Time to live no. of hops the packet can live	IP
24	Protocol	Upper-level protocol carried in data	IP
25–26	Checksum	Checksum of the header	IP
27–30	SA	IP source address	IP
31–34	DA	IP destination address	IP
35–36	S-port	Source port	TCP
37–38	D-port	Destination port	TCP
39–42	Seq num	Sequence number	TCP
43–46	ACK	Acknowledgment number	TCP

(Cont.)

TCP/IP Packet Format (Carried in an Ethernet Packet) (*Cont.*)

Byte	Field	Comment	
47	len	4 bits; size of the TCP header in 4-byte words	TCP
47–48	Reserved	6 bits not used	TCP
48	Flags	TCP flags U A P R S F U = Urgent, A = ACK, P = PSH, R = Reset, S = SYN, F = FIN	TCP
49–50	Window	TCP window (flow control)	TCP
51–52	Checksum	Checksum for header and data	TCP
53–54	Urgent	Urgent pointer	TCP
55–?	DATA	TCP data	Data
?	FCS	4-byte CRC code	Ethernet header

Common TCP Port Numbers

21	FTP
23	TELNET
25	SMTP
53	DNS
69	TFTP
161	SNMP

ARP Request Packet Format

Byte	Field	Comment	
1–6	DA	Broadcast address (FF:FF:FF:FF:FF:FF)	Ethernet header
7–12	SA	Ethernet source address	Ethernet header
13–14	Type	Type field 0x806 ARP	Ethernet header
15–16	HW type	1 = Ethernet	ARP
17–18	Protocol	Protocol type 0x800	ARP
19	HA length	Hardware address length (6 for Ethernet)	ARP
20	PA length	Length of protocol address (4 for IP)	ARP
21–22	Operation	Operation 1 = ARP request	ARP
23–28	Send HA	Sender hardware address	ARP
29–32	Send PA	Sender protocol address	ARP
33–38	Target HA	Target hardware address 0:0:0:0:0:0	ARP
39–42	Target PA	Target protocol address	ARP
43–60	PAD	Pad bytes	Ethernet
61–64	FCS	Frame check sequence	Ethernet header

ARP Reply Packet Format

Byte	Field	Comment	
1–6	DA	Ethernet destination address	Ethernet header
7–12	SA	Ethernet source address	Ethernet header
13–14	Type	Type field 0x806 ARP	Ethernet header
15–16	HW type	1 = Ethernet	ARP
17–18	Protocol	Protocol type 0x800	ARP
19	HA length	Hardware address length (6 for Ethernet)	ARP
20	PA length	Length of protocol address (4 for IP)	ARP
21–22	Operation	Operation 2 = ARP reply	ARP
23–28	Send HA	Sender hardware address	ARP
29–32	Send PA	Sender protocol address	ARP
33–38	Target HA	Target hardware address	ARP
39–42	Target PA	Target protocol address	ARP
43–60	PAD	Pad bytes	Ethernet
61–64	FCS	Frame check sequence	Ethernet header

Appendix C

Homework Solutions

This appendix contains solutions to selected problems in the book.

Chapter 1

Homework problem 4: Four protocol layers means there are 80 total bytes of header. This leaves 1,420 bytes of payload for each packet. To get the total number of packets transmitted, divide the total payload size by 1,420 and round up. To get the total number of bytes transmitted, take the remainder of the total payload size divided by 1,420 and add 80. This gives you the size of the last packet. Take 1,500 times the number of full packets transmitted and add that to the size of the last packet.

User Payload	Packets	Bytes
1,000	1	1,080
10,000	8	10,640
100,000	71	105,680
1,000,000	705	1,056,400

Homework problem 5:

User Payload	Overhead Bytes	Percent Overhead
1,000	80	8%
10,000	640	6.4%
100,000	5,680	5.7%
1,000,000	56,400	5.6%

Chapter 2

Homework problem 7: The problem with two identical IP addresses is getting the packet to the right computer. The packet will be routed to a network defined by the IP address. If both computers are in the same network, then the hardware address the final router has in its table for the destination IP address will determine which computer gets the packet. What often occurs is that you may connect to one computer one time and connect to the other computer the next time. Often the two computers with the same IP address will detect each other and report an error. If the two computers are not in the same network, then the computer on the network defined by the destination IP address will get the packet.

Homework problem 8: If two computers have the same Ethernet address on the same network, neither will be able to function on the network. Both computers receive the same packet and both computers in turn will respond to the sender. This causes the sending computer to receive multiple responses to the same packet, which causes the protocol to fail. Two computers with the same Ethernet addresses on different networks will not cause any problem, since Ethernet addresses are only used locally.

Lab experiment 2: The vendor code can be used by an administrator to track down a computer on the network. The Ethernet vendor code can narrow down the search. This is useful when two computers end up with the same IP address and the administrator needs to track them down.

Chapter 3

Homework problem 2: There is a list of well-known and assigned port numbers located at www.iana.org/assignments/port-numbers. IANA defines the well-known ports as numbered between 0 and 1,024. The file contains about 10,000 TCP and UDP port numbers.

Homework problem 3: No, these are just the registered port numbers. Applications can use any port they want to.

Homework problem 4: The client application connects, and when the client and server applications try to communicate, they will not be able to since the application protocols are not the same. Some client applications (e.g., TELNET) connect to any server application and allow the user to send data to the application. This can be used to help debug or test server applications.

Homework problem 6: No, an application can use other port numbers than what was assigned. Many server applications can be configured to use other port numbers, and many client applications can be told to connect to a user-defined port number.

Homework problem 9: One reason to spoof a hardware address is to connect to an ISP that expects a predefined hardware address. Most wireless routers, for example, allow the user to change the hardware address. This is called MAC address cloning.

Homework problem 12: No, the Internet is designed to route each packet independently. Routers can be configured to route packets based on network load as well as destination address. There may also be a failure in the current path, and the routers can reroute packets around the failure.

Chapter 4

Homework problem 4: The CVE database can be used to help determine if a computer system has a vulnerability. The database is used as part of an intrusion detection system (IDS) to help the user classify the potential attacks that are seen by the IDS to determine if the attacks can possibly be successful. The database can be used for attacking. First, the attacker determines the version numbers of the operating system and the applications. He or she can then search the database of attacks to determine which attacks can be used against the system.

Homework problem 5: No, not all vulnerabilities can be exploited. The vulnerability may be too complex to exploit, or if the vulnerability is exploited, the damage may be minor. In some cases the fix will alter the operation of the application, and that will need to be weighed against the damage caused by a successful exploit.

Homework problem 6: No, some vulnerabilities are inherent in the design of the application or in the protocol.

Chapter 5

Homework problem 2: The length of the frame is returned by the Ethernet hardware. The code that takes the Ethernet packets will put the packets together to create the packets used by the network layer. The header of the network has a length field to indicate the length of the network layer packet.

Homework problem 3: Technically Ethernet addresses do not need to be globally unique. Ethernet addresses only need to be unique in a network. However, since there is no way to guarantee that two Ethernet cards with the same address are not installed in the same network, they are made to be globally unique.

Homework problem 7: Broadcast packets force every device to read and process the packet they received. This causes unnecessary processing time. In addition, some broadcast packets require that every device respond. This causes excess traffic on the network.

Homework problem 12: The biggest deterrent to using WEP or WPA is key distribution. In a public network it is assumed that users come and go. There needs to be a method to pass the key out to the user. Once you start passing out keys, they are no longer a secret.

Chapter 6

Homework problem 2: The ARP request needs to be a broadcast packet since the requester has no knowledge of who will respond. The response is only useful to the requester, so to help reduce the number of broadcast packets, the response is sent only to the requester.

Homework problem 3: In case the hardware address to IP address mapping changes, the ARP cache needs to automatically expire. This is most common in an environment where IP addresses are dynamically assigned and therefore change.

Homework problem 5:

Host 1

Destination	Next Hop	Interface
129.186.5.0	129.186.5.30	
Default	129.186.5.254	

Router 1

Destination	Next Hop	Interface
129.186.5.0	129.186.5.254	En0
129.186.100.0	129.186.100.254	En1
129.186.4.0	129.186.100.253	En1
Default	129.186.100.252	En1

Host 2

Destination	Next Hop	Interface
129.186.100.0	129.186.100.40	
129.186.5.0	129.186.100.254	
129.186.4.0	129.186.100.253	
Default	129.186.100.252	

Router 2

Destination	Next Hop	Interface
129.186.100.0	129.186.100.252	En0
129.186.5.0	129.186.100.254	En0
129.184.4.0	129.186.100.253	En0
Default	10.0.0.5	En1

Host 3

Destination	Next Hop	Interface
129.186.4.0	129.186.4.133	
Default	129.186.4.254	

Router 3

Destination	Next Hop	Interface
129.186.100.0	129.186.100.253	En0
129.186.4.0	129.186.4.254	En1
129.186.5.0	129.186.100.254	En0
Default	129.186.100.252	En0

Homework problem 10: Printers and other devices that are referenced by IP address are often set up as static. Web, email, and other public servers are also often given static IP addresses.

Homework problem 12:

	Request			Reply		
	Net 1	Net 2	Net 3	Net 1	Net 2	Net 3
TCP layer						
Source port	5240	NAT	NAT	80	80	80
Destination port	80	80	80	5240	NAT	NAT
IP layer						
SRC IP address	H1	129.186.4.100	129.186.4.100	H3	H3	H3
Dest IP address	H3	H3	H3	H1	129.186.4.100	129.186.4.100

Chapter 7

Homework problem 2: The TCP sequence and acknowledgment numbers are used to count the number of bytes.

Homework problem 3: The TCP and IP layers each add 40 bytes of header to the payload and Ethernet adds 18 bytes. This assumes no options in either TCP or IP headers.

a. 45 bytes

b. 85 bytes

c. 103 bytes

d. 95% of the packet is overhead

Homework problem 5: Assuming that there are no options in the TCP or IP headers, the best size would be 1,500 – 80, or 1,420 bytes.

Chapter 8

Homework problem 1: Local sockets are used to enable processes on a computer to talk to each other. One example is to provide logging of system events. The logging program would act like a server, and any program wishing to log an event would send a message to the logging program using local sockets. Local sockets are designed to look like TCP sockets to simplify the programming. A client is able to communicate using either the local socket or the TCP socket without changing any of the code other than which socket is opened.

Homework problem 4: Yes, there is a limit to the number of open sockets that is allowed. The limit can come from two places. The application can limit the number of connections, thus limiting the number of sockets. The TCP layer has a limit on the number of sockets based on resource limitations. The most common constrained resource is memory.

Chapter 9

Homework problem 1: The protocol exchange is shown in the following table. This assumes 98 bytes for the TCP, IP, and Ethernet headers. The payload consists of the text string and a <cr>. Your solution may vary based on the values of the text strings.

Overhead for part d is 1,764/1,990 = 88.6%.
Overhead for part e is 1,984/1,990 = 99.7%.

Homework problem 4: POP and IMAP are designed to retrieve email from a user mailbox that is considered to be private and is often stored in the user's

Direction	Packet Type	Payload Size	Packet Size
To server	TCP SYN	0	98
To client	TCP SYN+ACK	0	98
To server	TCP ACK	0	98
To client	220 dougj.net + Greeting text	40 (assumption)	138
To server	HELO issl.org	14	112
To client	250 dougj.net Hello issl.org	29	127
To server	MAIL FROM: john@issl.org	25	123
To client	250 john@issl.org Sender OK	28	126
To server	RCPT TO: dougj	15	113
To client	250 dougj Recipient OK	23	121
To server	DATA	5	103
To client	354 Enter Mail	15	113
To server	HELLO	6	104
To server	.	2	100
To client	250 ID Message accepted	24	122
To server	TCP FIN	0	98
To client	TCP FIN+ACK	0	98
To server	TCP ACK	0	98
Totals		226	1,990

directory. Sending email messages does not need authentication since anyone can send email into the email system to be delivered to a user's mailbox.

Homework problem 9: Pros and cons of each type:

SMTP encryption: This could be used to require users to be authenticated before sending email, which could reduce spam. The problem is key distribution. Using public keys will not fix the spam problem and will only mitigate sniffing attacks. Sniffing attacks are better mitigated using other methods.

POP/IMAP encryption: Can be used to stop sniffing, and therefore protect the usernames and passwords. This encryption could also enhance user authentication with additional certificates. The downside is the complexity in key distribution.

User-to-user encryption: This will prevent unauthorized people from reading the email. This can authenticate both the sender and receiver. Key distribution can be complex.

User-to-user encryption would be the best for most secure email.

Homework problem 12: The headers contain the IP addresses and sometimes the host names of each MTA that handled the email. Depending on how the email was sent, there might be information about the email client that sent the message. The usefulness of email tracing is questionable. You can trace the email back to an MTA that was the first to get the email; you might be able to trace back to the IP address of the machine that contacted the MTA. That machine may have changed IP addresses and may have been comprised with a spambot. In general, it is difficult to trace email back to an individual without good log information from the computers used to send the mail.

Chapter 10

Homework problem 1:

a. GET /index.html HTTP/1.1

b. GET /files/index.html HTTP1.1

c. GET /cgi-bin/print-me/?hello%20there

Homework problem 2:

a. <a href=http://www.dougj.net> Click here for dougj.net </a>

b. <a href=figure.pdf> Click here for PDF Figure </a>

c. <img src=picture.gif alt="picture"/>

d. <img src=http://www.dougj.net/picture.gif alt="picture"/>

Homework problem 3:

```
#! /bin/sh
echo Content-type: text/plain
echo

/bin/who
```

Chapter 11

Homework problem 3: The TELNET server is not considered to be secure and should not be used. The only times it is used is for legacy equipment or internal communications. Typically organizations will block the TELNET protocol at the firewall.

Homework problem 4: The TELNET client presents no security risk and is often used to test other protocols and servers.

Homework problem 5: The protocol exchange is shown below. This assumes 98 bytes for the TCP, IP, and Ethernet headers. The payload consists of the text string and a <cr>. Your solution may vary based on the values of the text strings.

Direction	Packet Type	Payload Size	Packet Size
To server	TCP SYN	0	98
To client	TCP SYN+ACK	0	98
To server	TCP ACK	0	98
To client	Greeting text + Username	40 (assumption)	138
To server	Bob (sent as four packets)	4	396 (98*4 + 4)
To client	Bob (bob echoed, 4 packets)	4	396
To client	Password	10	108
To server	Alice (sent as 6 packets)	6	594 (98*6 + 6)
To client	Text to indicate login	40 (assumption)	138
Totals		24	2,046

Overhead is 2,022/2,046 = 98.8%.

Chapter 12

Homework problem 4: An IDS can show you if your systems are being attacked and can alert you if a critical service is being attacked. The best place to put the IDS is in the DMZ, with the rules tuned to match the devices in the organization being protected. An internal IDS can also be useful to see if any attacks are getting through the firewall.

Homework problem 5: An IPS would be best placed inside the organization and set to block certain attacks against the key services. Placing it in the DMZ can work, but you would need to be careful about what attacks you block.

Appendix A

Homework problem 4: A single PKI system has social and political issues that keep it from being adopted. Most people want multiple identities based on what they are trying to do. For example, buying food only requires that your identity is linked to money (you have enough money to pay). Who you are does not matter. There is also the issue of government-sponsored IDS versus local- or business-sponsored IDS.

Index

A

Abrupt termination, 12, 223, 227, 238
Access point authentication, 116, 118, 123
Acknowledgment number, 226–228, 233,253,458
Ad hoc wireless network, 123
Address based authentication attacks, 237
Address resolution protocol (ARP)
    ARP cache, 147, 153, 159, 180, 210
    ARP cache poisoning, 156, 173
    ARP protocol, 102, 105, 153, 194
    ARP spoofing, 132, 156, 180
Address spoofing, 45, 46
    Email address, 280
    Hardware address, 87, 88, 91
    IP address, 174–176
American National Standards Institute
        (ANSI), 25, 26
Anomaly, 435,440
Anonymous, 355
    Email, 301
    FTP, 388–394
    Peer-to-peer, 403, 419
Antenna, 107, 108, 114, 115
Anti-phishing, 364
Anti-spam, 313, 318–320
Apache, 329–333, 335, 342
Applet, 340–344, 349–352, 364
Application address, 31–35, 42, 50, 75
Application based encryption, 406, 407
Application firewall, 431, 433
Application layer, 17, 18, 23, 259–268
ARPANET, 4, 22, 27
Associate request 119–122
Associate response 119–122
Asymmetric encryption, 446, 448–452
ATM, 17
Attack code, 64–66, 68, 75, 267, 278
Authentication-based attacks, 73, 76

Authentication-based vulnerability, 73, 77
Authenticator, 336
Authorities
    Address, 33
    Registration, 34, 310
    Signature, 338

B

Backbone network, 90, 178
Bandwidth shaping, 412
Base 64, 336
Beacon, 109, 110
Bearshare, 401
Bind, 264, 265
Bittorrent, 400, 401, 422
Blacklist, 196, 208, 306, 314, 353, 358
Blaster worm, 66
BOOTP, 181–189
Bots, 316
Broadcast address, 100, 104, 105, 139, 172
Broadcast domain, 105
Broadcast packet, 75, 141, 189
Browser plugin, 352
Buffer overflow, 266–268, 278, 333, 347, 379, 391

C

Carrier sense multiple access with collision
        avoidance (CSMA/CA), 109–111,
        116, 123
Carrier sense multiple access with collision
        detection (CSMA/CD), 94, 95, 101,
        105, 110
Central index server, 394–397, 403–405
Certificate, 73, 252, 337–339, 344, 360, 453
Checksum, 9, 153, 156, 229
Classless interdomain routing (CIDR),
        142–145, 180, 193, 216
Clear gif, 343, 345

9 781584 885436